INUYASHA

VOL. 14
Action Edition

Story and Art by
RUMIKO TAKAHASHI

English Adaptation/Gerard Jones
Translation/Mari Morimoto
Touch-Up Art & Lettering/Bill Schuch
Cover Design/Hidemi Sahara
Graphics & Design/Sean Lee
Editor/Julie Davis

Managing Editor/Annette Roman
Editorial Director/Elizabeth Kawasaki
Editor in Chief/Alvin Lu
Sr. Director of Acquisitions/Rika Inouye
Senior VP of Marketing/Liza Coppola
Exec. VP of Sales & Marketing/John Easum
Publisher/Hyoe Narita

Printed in Canada.

Published by VIZ Media, LLC
P.O. Box 77010
San Francisco, CA 94107

Action Edition
10 9 8 7 6 5
First printing, June 2003
Fifth printing, April 2006

RATED T+ FOR OLDER TEEN

PARENTAL ADVISORY
INUYASHA is rated T+ for Older Teen. This book contains violence. It is recommended for ages 16 and up.

INUYASHA

VOL. 14

Action Edition

STORY AND ART BY
RUMIKO TAKAHASHI

CONTENTS

THE STORY THUS FAR

Long ago, in the "Warring States" era of Japan's Muromachi period (Sengoku-jidai, approximately 1467-1568 CE), a legendary doglike half-demon called "Inu-Yasha" attempted to steal the Shikon Jewel, or "Jewel of Four Souls," from a village, but was stopped by the enchanted arrow of the village priestess, Kikyo. Inu-Yasha fell into a deep sleep, pinned to a tree by Kikyo's arrow, while the mortally wounded Kikyo took the Shikon Jewel with her into the fires of her funeral pyre. Years passed.

Fast forward to the present day. Kagome, a Japanese high school girl, is pulled into a well one day by a mysterious centipede monster, and finds herself transported into the past, only to come face to face with the trapped Inu-Yasha. She frees him, and Inu-Yasha easily defeats the centipede monster.

The residents of the village, now fifty years older, readily accept Kagome as the reincarnation of their deceased priestess Kikyo, a claim supported by the fact that the Shikon Jewel emerges from a cut on Kagome's body. Unfortunately, the jewel's rediscovery means that the village is soon under attack by a variety of demons in search of this treasure. Then, the jewel is accidentally shattered into many shards, each of which may have the fearsome power of the entire jewel.

Although Inu-Yasha says he hates Kagome because of her resemblance to Kikyo, the woman who "killed" him, he is forced to team up with her when Kaede, the village leader, binds him to Kagome with a powerful spell. Now the two grudging companions must fight to reclaim and reassemble the shattered shards of the Shikon Jewel before they fall into the wrong hands.

THIS VOLUME The secret of the "Scar of the Wind," and a demonic rival for Kagome's affections.

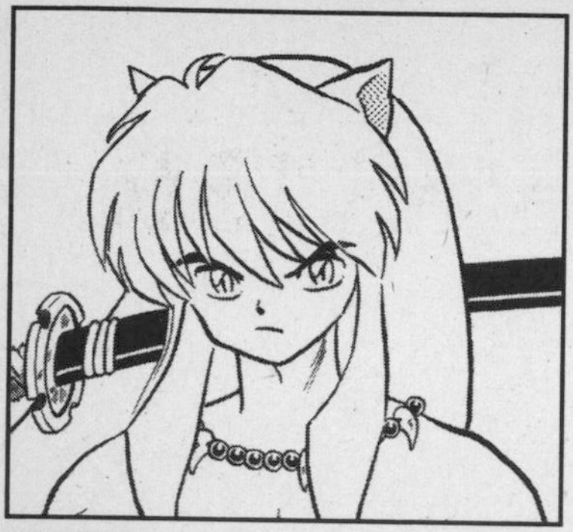

INU-YASHA

A half-human, half-demon hybrid, Inu-Yasha has doglike ears, a thick mane of white hair, and demonic strength. Hoping to increase his demonic powers, he once stole the Shikon Jewel from a village, but was cast into a fifty-year sleep by the arrow of the village priestess, Kikyo, who died as a result of the battle. Now, he assists Kagome in her search for the shards of the Jewel, mostly because he has no choice in the matter—a charmed necklace allows Kagome to restrain him with a single word.

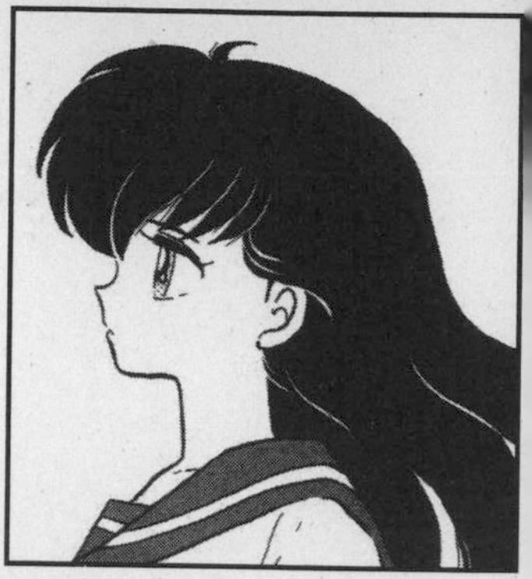

KAGOME

A Japanese schoolgirl from the modern day who is also the reincarnation of Kikyo, the priestess who imprisoned Inu-Yasha for fifty years with her enchanted arrow. As Kikyo's reincarnation, Kagome has the power to see the Shikon Jewel shards, even ones hidden within a demon's body.

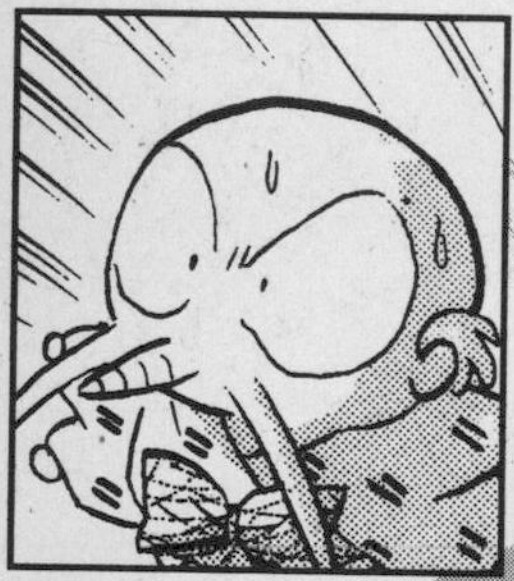

MYOGA

Servant to Inu-Yasha, this flea-demon often offers sage advice, but he is also the first to flee when a situation turns dangerous. His powers are unknown, but his flealike blood-sucking seems to have the ability to weaken certain spells.

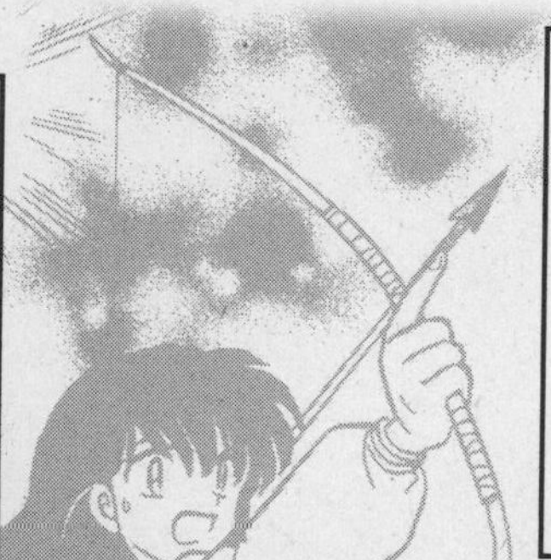

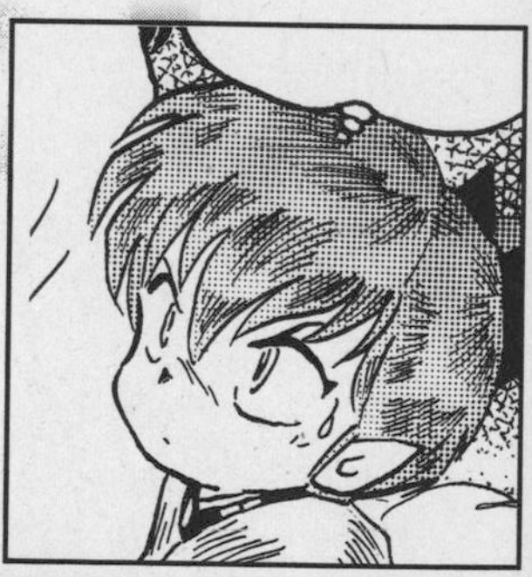

SHIPPO

A young fox-demon, orphaned by two other demons whose powers had been boosted by the Shikon Jewel, the mischievous Shippo enjoys goading Inu-Yasha and playing tricks with his shape-changing abilities.

SCROLL ONE

THE TRUE MASTER

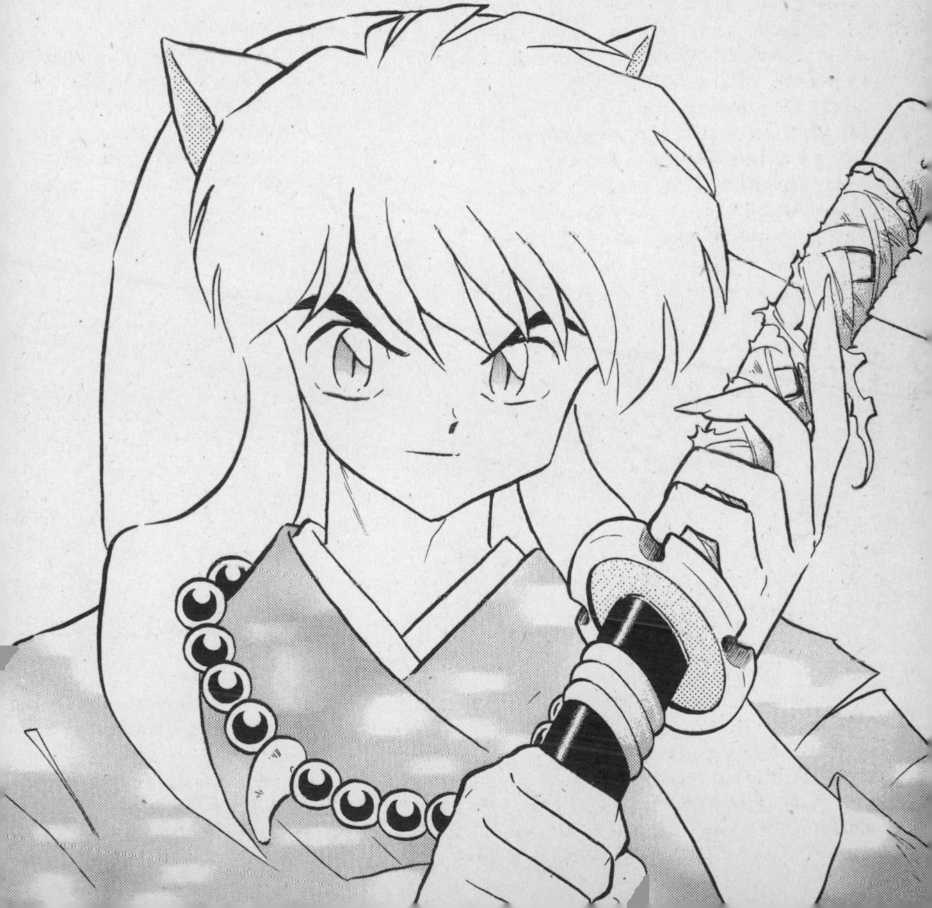

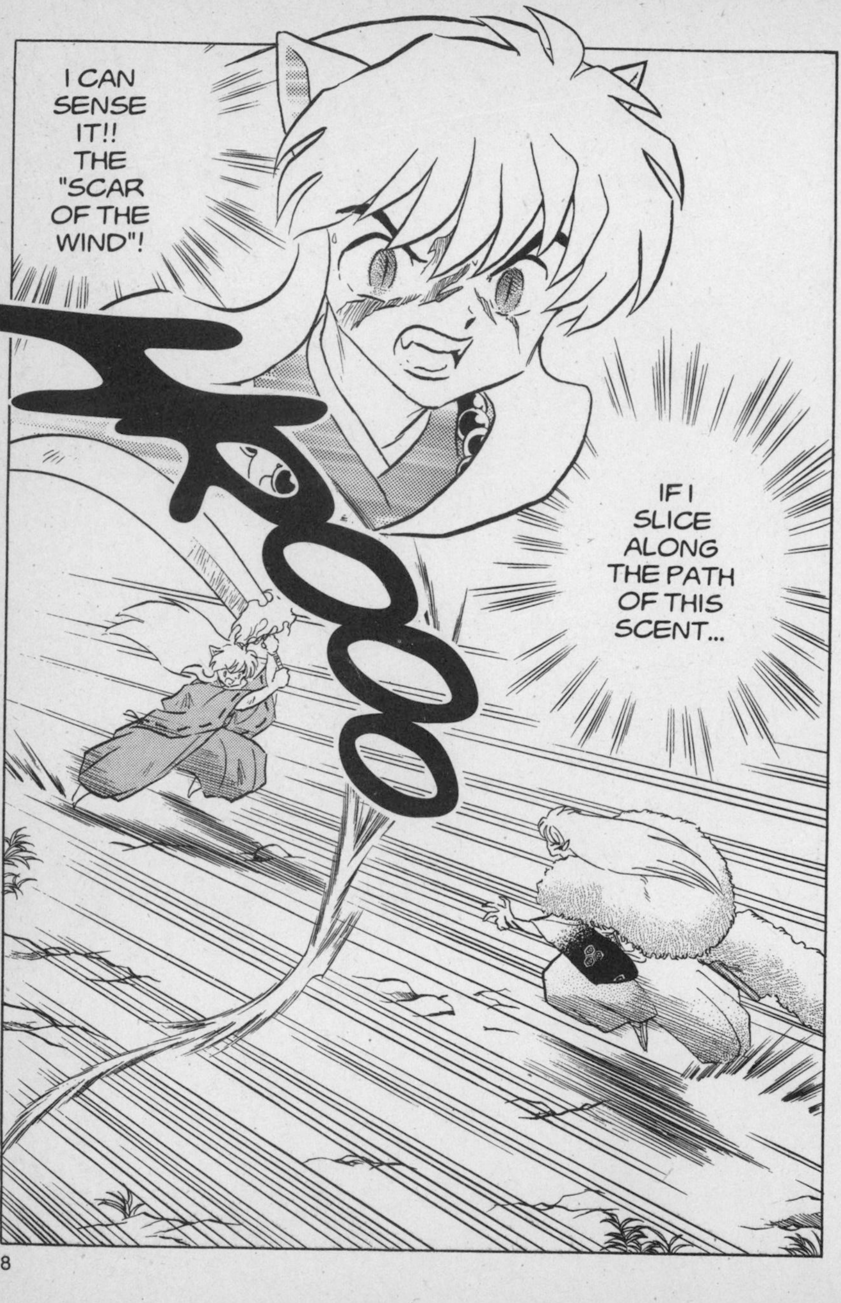
I CAN SENSE IT!! THE "SCAR OF THE WIND"!
IF I SLICE ALONG THE PATH OF THIS SCENT...

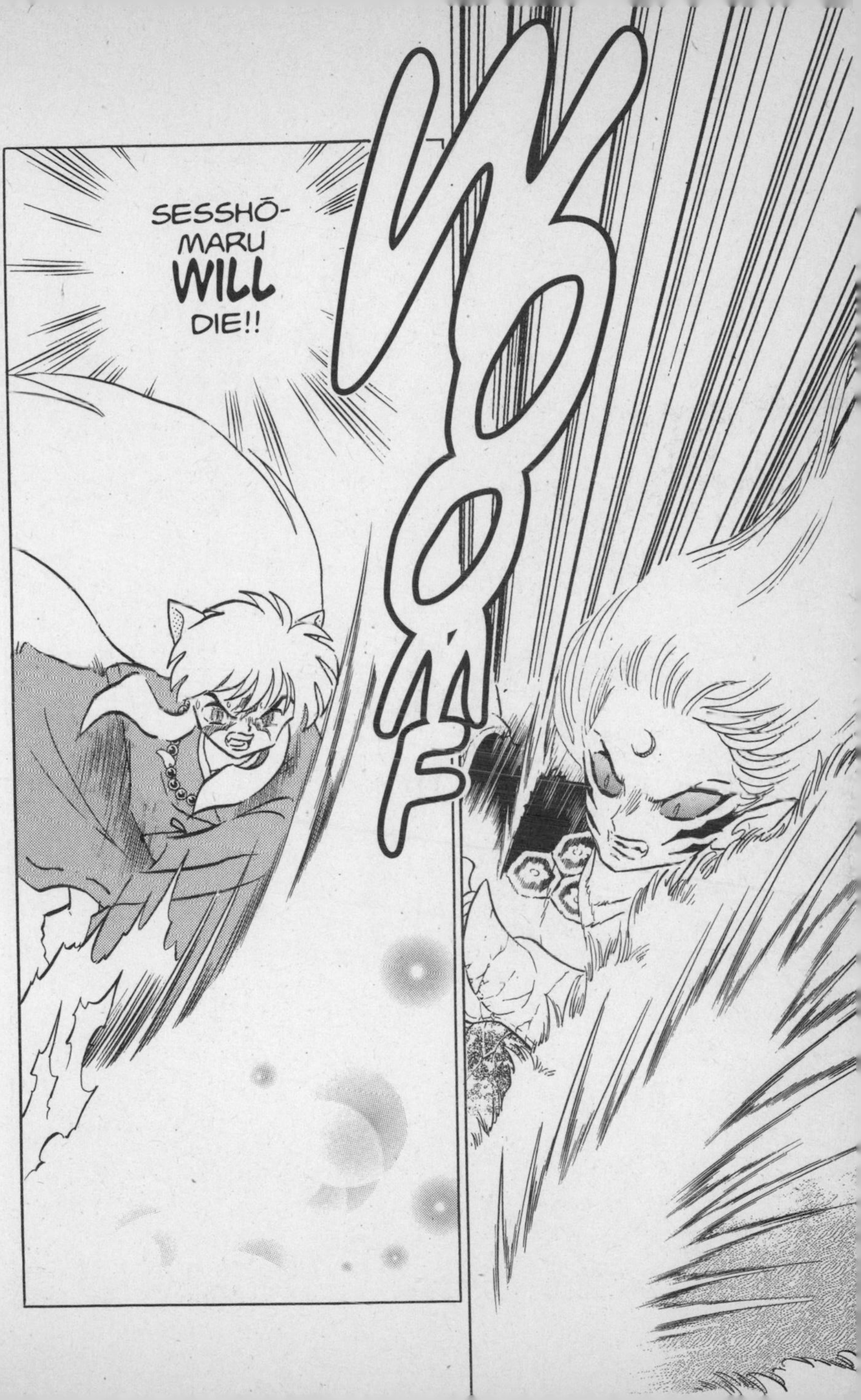
SESSHŌ-MARU WILL DIE!!

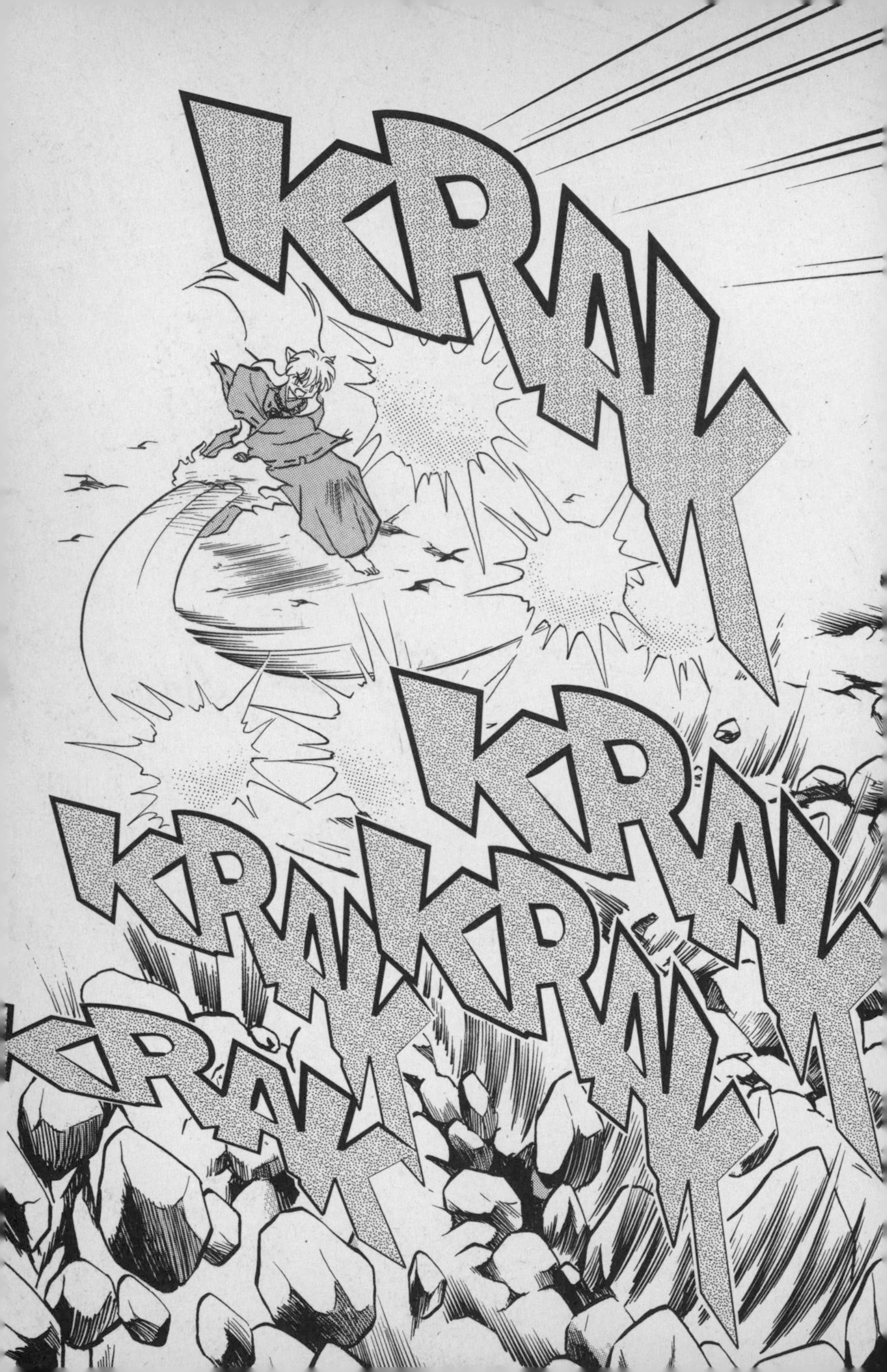
KRAK
KRAK
KRAK
KRAK
KRAK

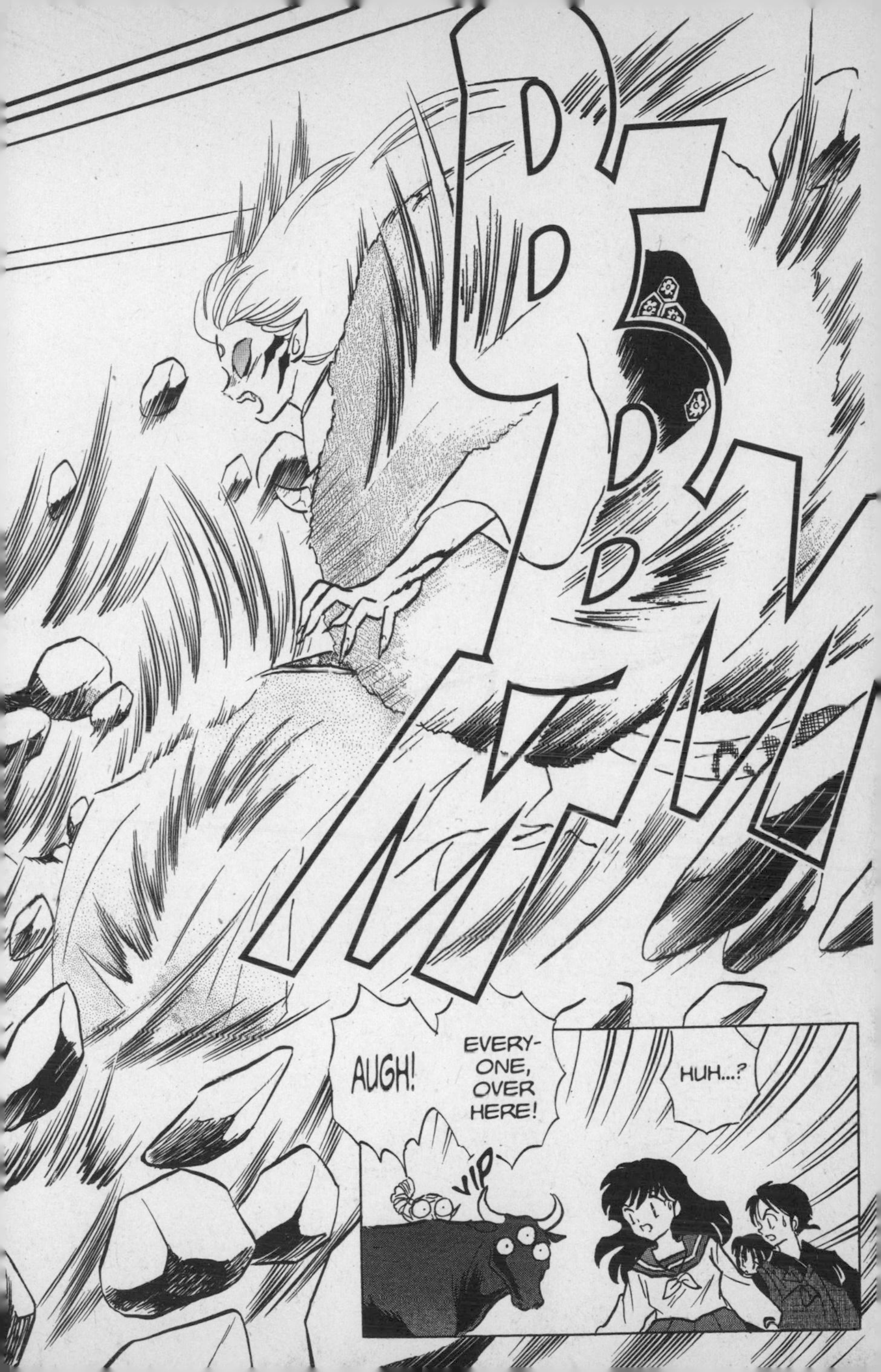
AUGH!
EVERY-ONE, OVER HERE!
HUH...?
YIP

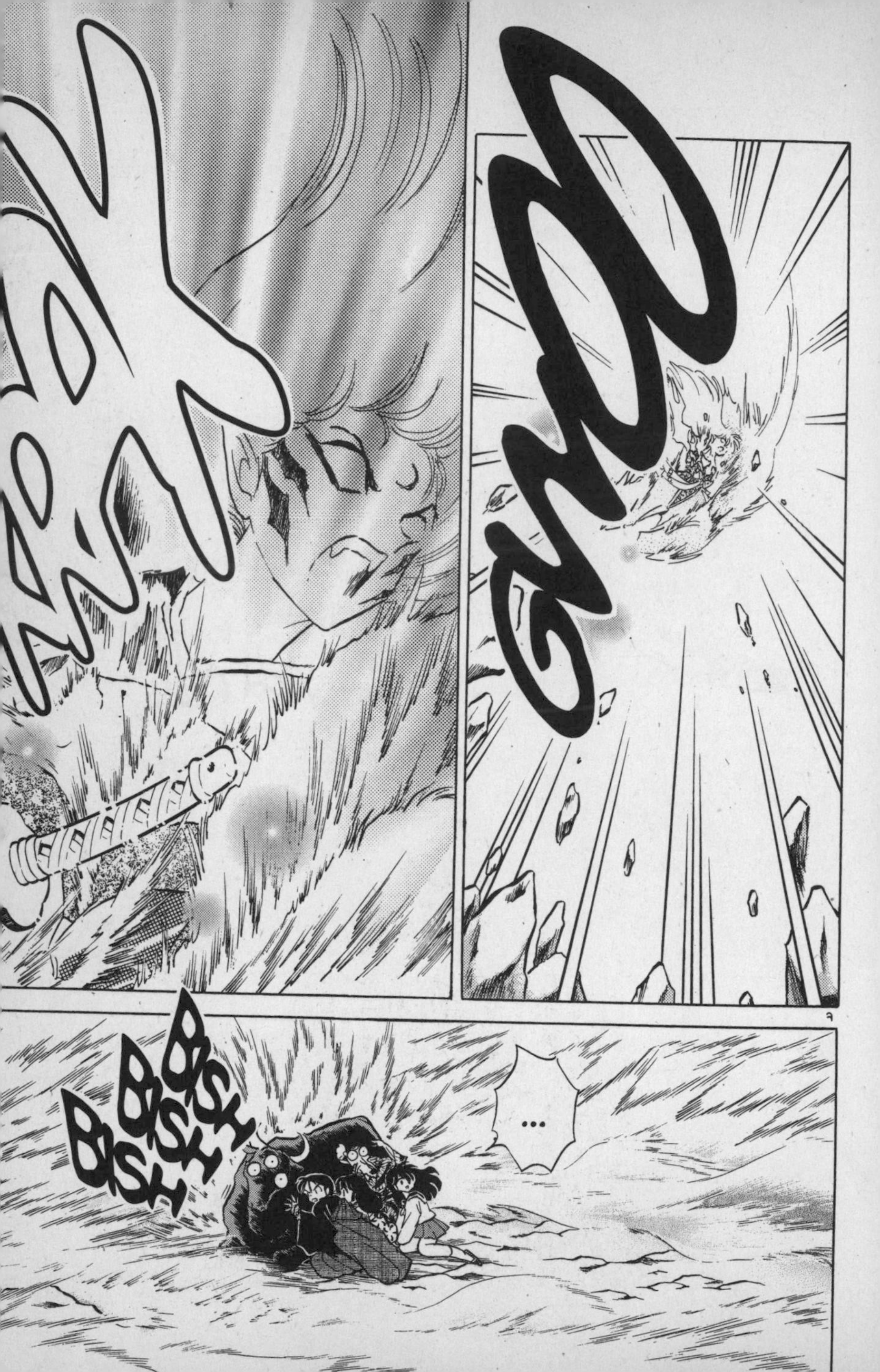
BISH
BISH
BISH
...

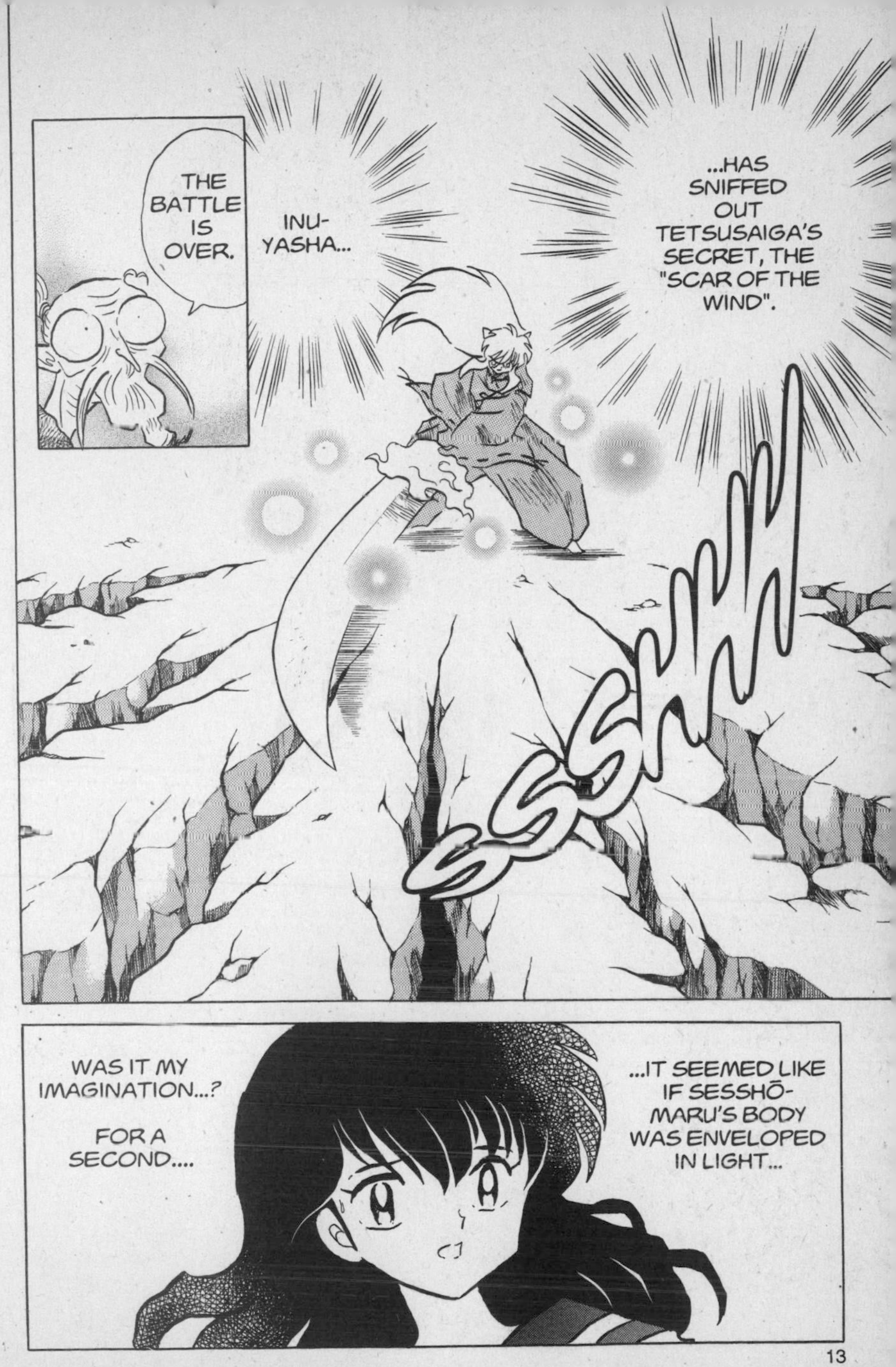

THE BATTLE IS OVER.
INU-YASHA...
...HAS SNIFFED OUT TETSUSAIGA'S SECRET, THE "SCAR OF THE WIND".
WAS IT MY IMAGINATION...?
FOR A SECOND....
...IT SEEMED LIKE IF SESSHŌMARU'S BODY WAS ENVELOPED IN LIGHT...

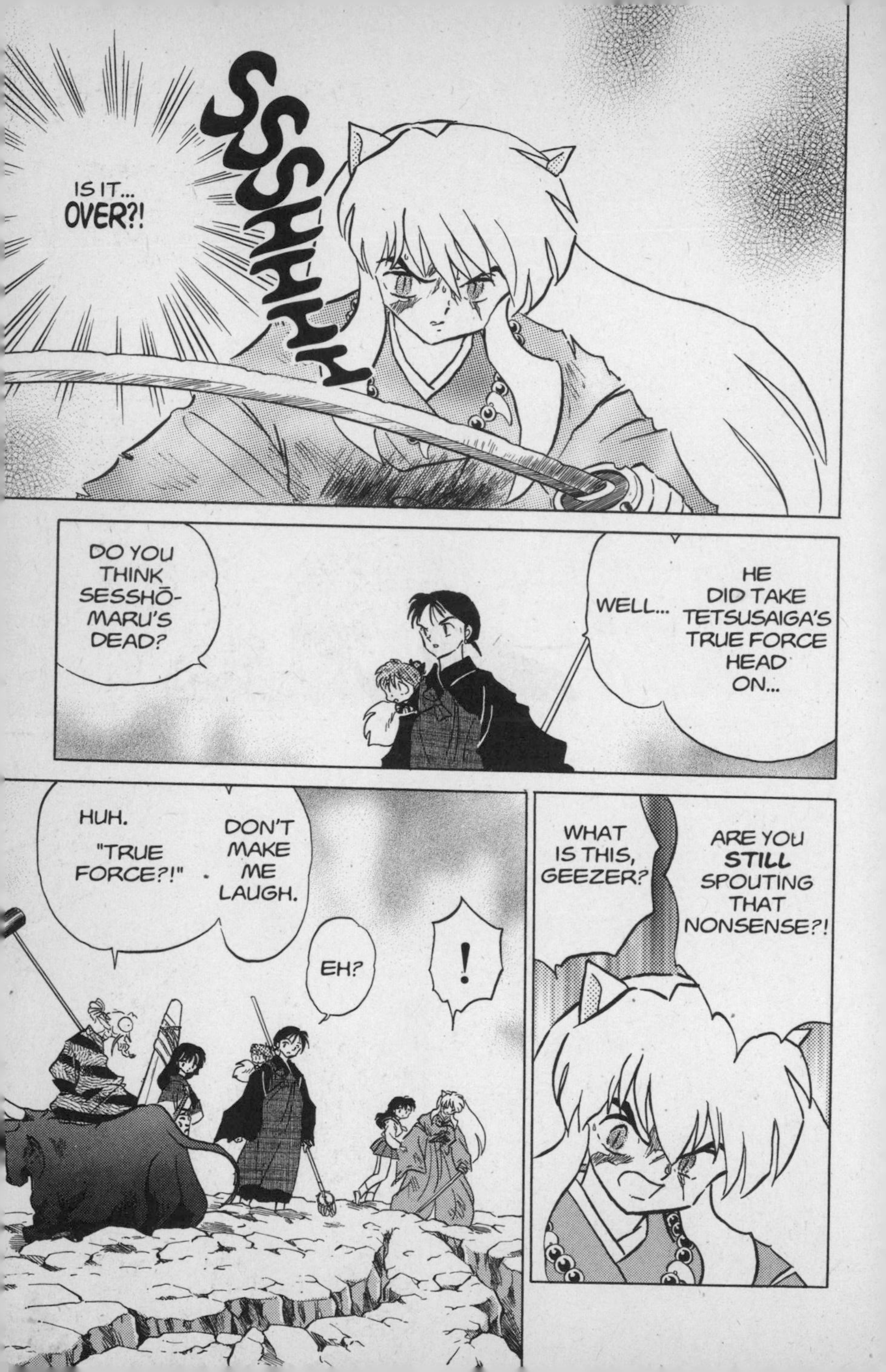
SSSHHHHH
IS IT... OVER?!
DO YOU THINK SESSHŌ-MARU'S DEAD?
WELL...
HE DID TAKE TETSUSAIGA'S TRUE FORCE HEAD ON...
HUH. "TRUE FORCE?!"
DON'T MAKE ME LAUGH.
EH?
!
WHAT IS THIS, GEEZER?
ARE YOU **STILL** SPOUTING THAT NONSENSE?!

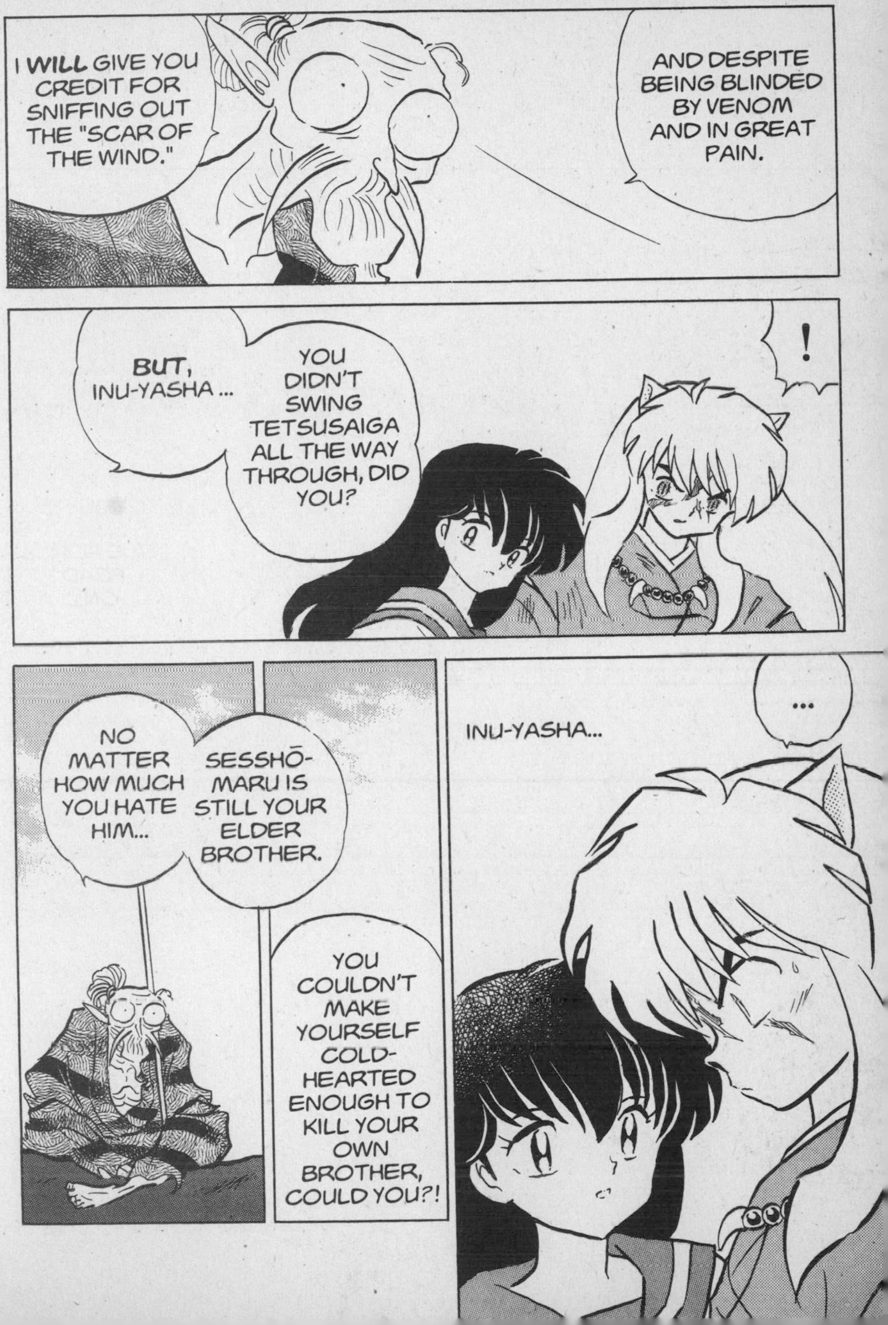
I WILL GIVE YOU CREDIT FOR SNIFFING OUT THE "SCAR OF THE WIND."
AND DESPITE BEING BLINDED BY VENOM AND IN GREAT PAIN.
BUT, INU-YASHA ...
YOU DIDN'T SWING TETSUSAIGA ALL THE WAY THROUGH, DID YOU?
!
NO MATTER HOW MUCH YOU HATE HIM...
SESSHŌ-MARU IS STILL YOUR ELDER BROTHER.
YOU COULDN'T MAKE YOURSELF COLD-HEARTED ENOUGH TO KILL YOUR OWN BROTHER, COULD YOU?!
INU-YASHA...
...

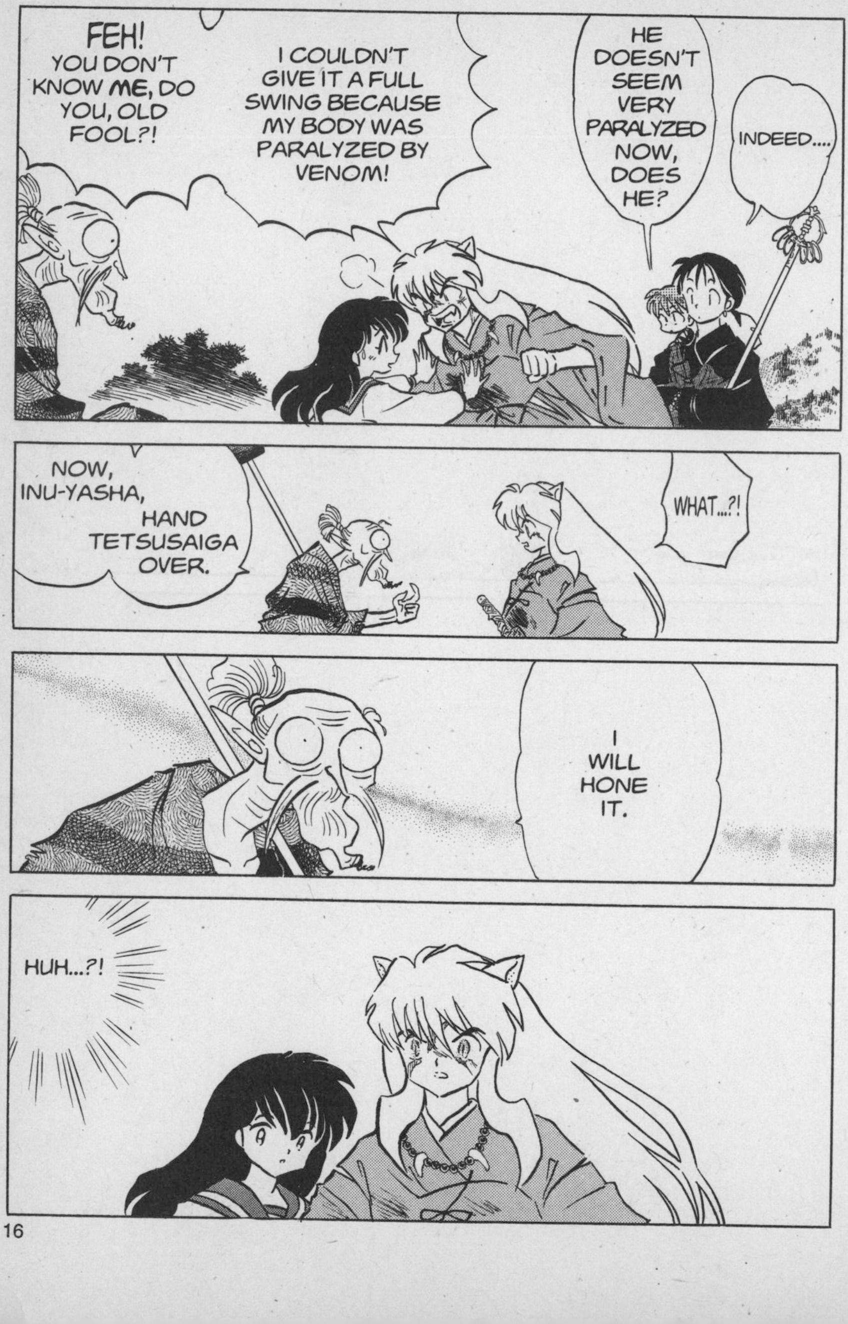

FEH! YOU DON'T KNOW ME, DO YOU, OLD FOOL?!
I COULDN'T GIVE IT A FULL SWING BECAUSE MY BODY WAS PARALYZED BY VENOM!
HE DOESN'T SEEM VERY PARALYZED NOW, DOES HE?
INDEED....
NOW, INU-YASHA, HAND TETSUSAIGA OVER.
WHAT...?!
I WILL HONE IT.
HUH...?!

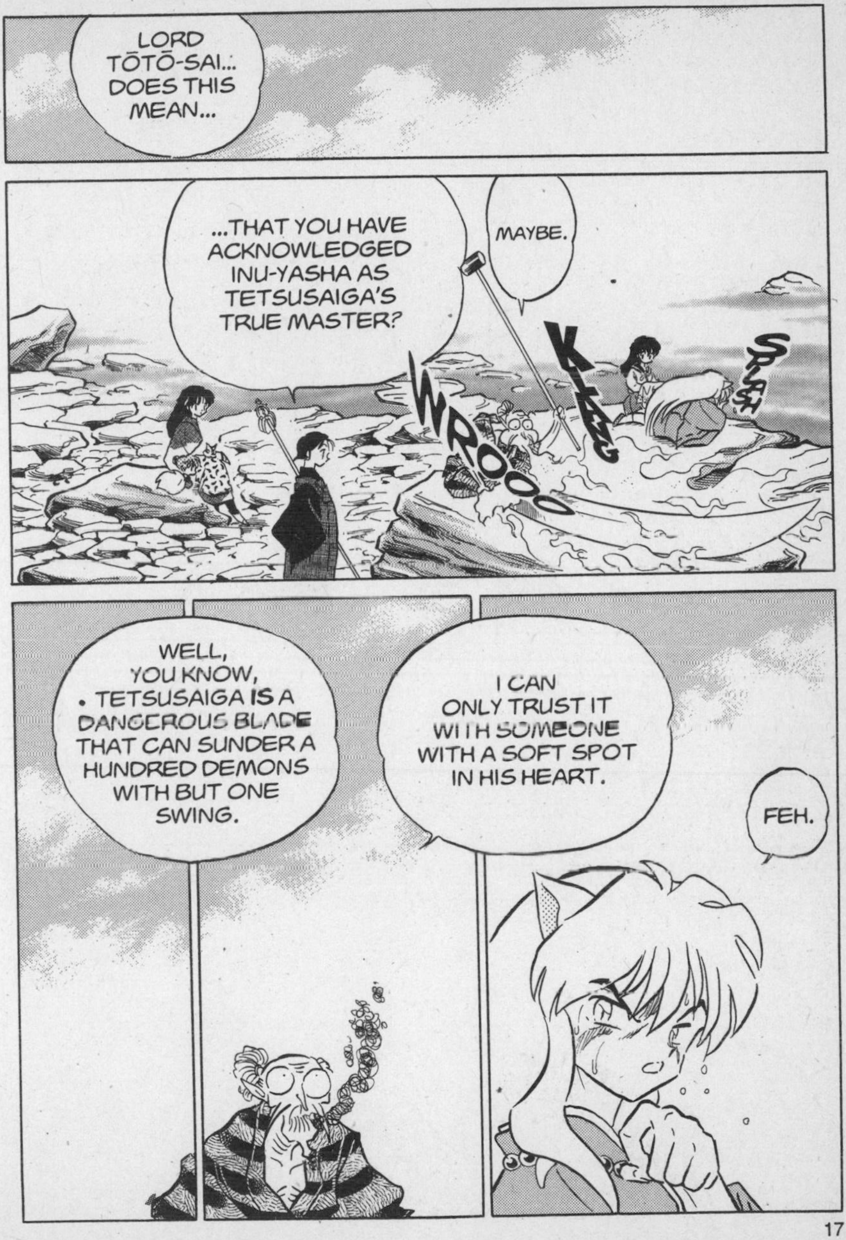
LORD TŌTŌ-SAI... DOES THIS MEAN...
...THAT YOU HAVE ACKNOWLEDGED INU-YASHA AS TETSUSAIGA'S TRUE MASTER?
MAYBE.
WROOOO
KLANG
SPLASH
WELL, YOU KNOW, TETSUSAIGA IS A DANGEROUS BLADE THAT CAN SUNDER A HUNDRED DEMONS WITH BUT ONE SWING.
I CAN ONLY TRUST IT WITH SOMEONE WITH A SOFT SPOT IN HIS HEART.
FEH.

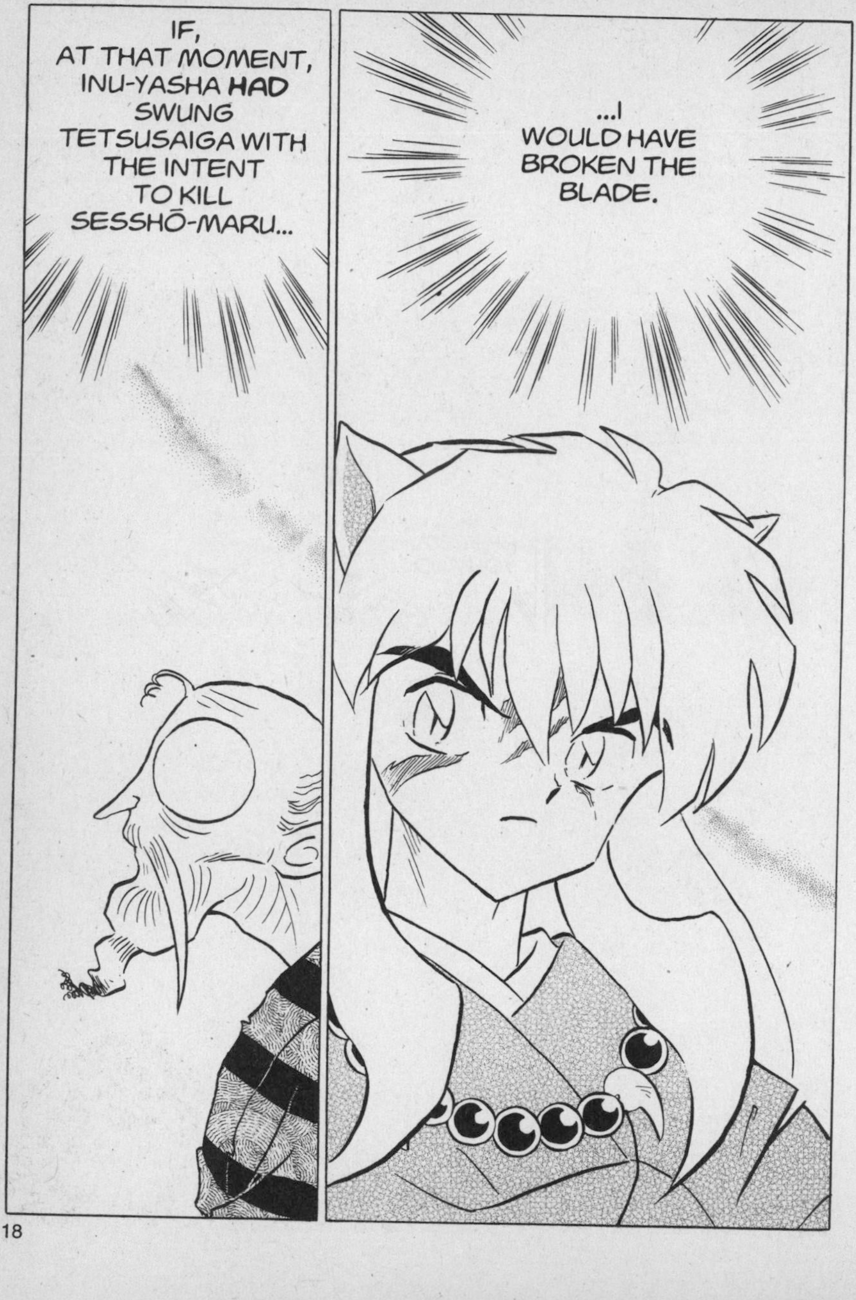
IF, AT THAT MOMENT, INU-YASHA **HAD** SWUNG TETSUSAIGA WITH THE INTENT TO KILL SESSHŌ-MARU...
...I WOULD HAVE BROKEN THE BLADE.

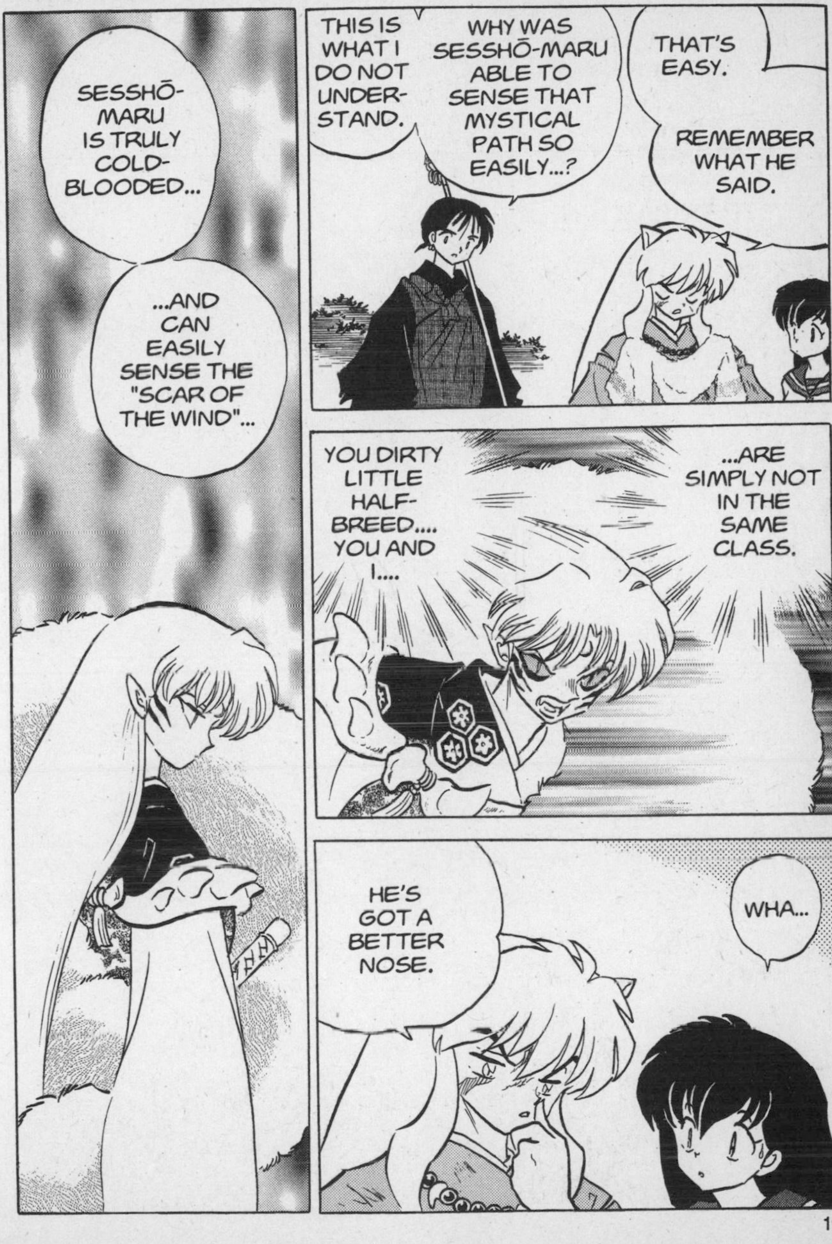
SESSHŌ-MARU IS TRULY COLD-BLOODED...
...AND CAN EASILY SENSE THE "SCAR OF THE WIND"...
THIS IS WHAT I DO NOT UNDER-STAND.
WHY WAS SESSHŌ-MARU ABLE TO SENSE THAT MYSTICAL PATH SO EASILY...?
THAT'S EASY.
REMEMBER WHAT HE SAID.
YOU DIRTY LITTLE HALF-BREED.... YOU AND I....
...ARE SIMPLY NOT IN THE SAME CLASS.
HE'S GOT A BETTER NOSE.
WHA...

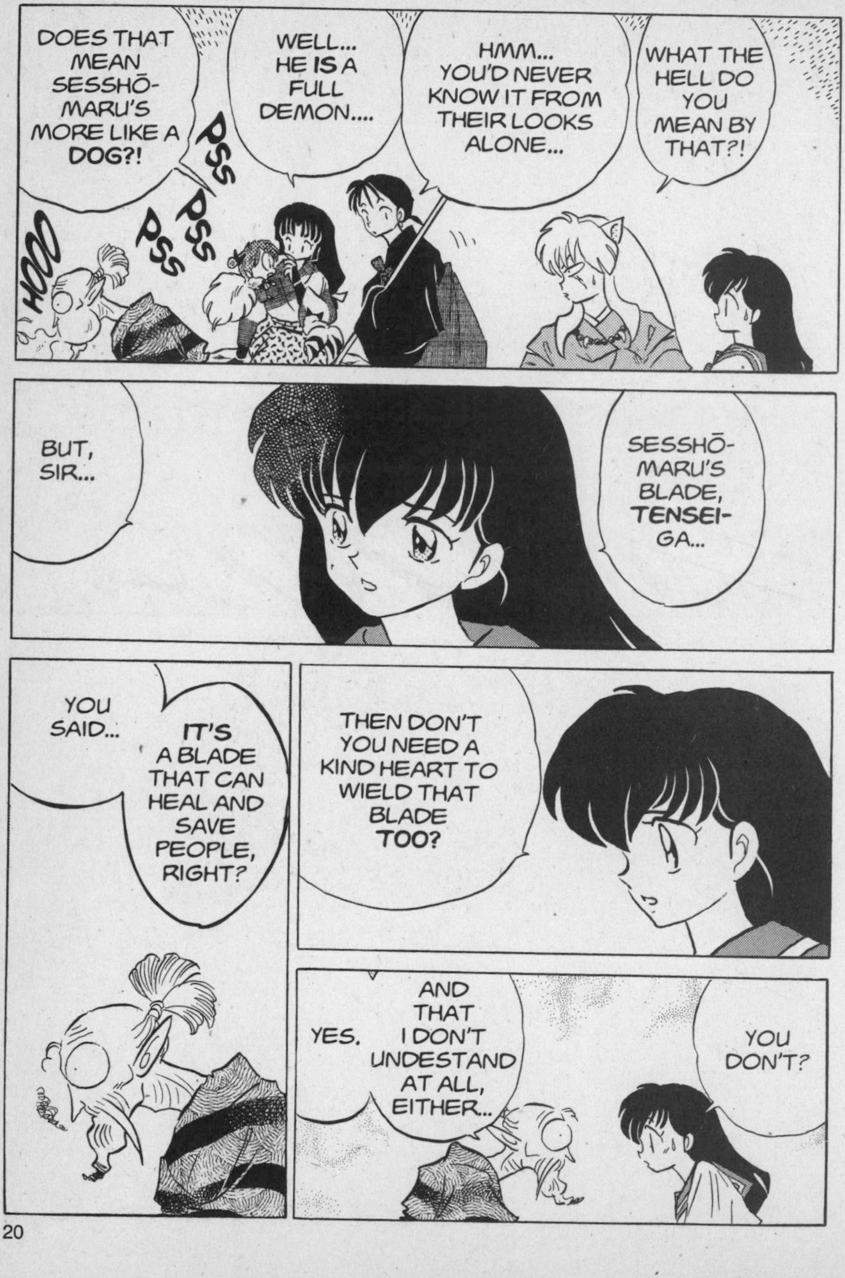
HOOO
DOES THAT MEAN SESSHŌ-MARU'S MORE LIKE A DOG?!
PSS PSS PSS
WELL... HE IS A FULL DEMON....
HMM... YOU'D NEVER KNOW IT FROM THEIR LOOKS ALONE...
WHAT THE HELL DO YOU MEAN BY THAT?!
BUT, SIR...
SESSHŌ-MARU'S BLADE, TENSEI-GA...
YOU SAID...
IT'S A BLADE THAT CAN HEAL AND SAVE PEOPLE, RIGHT?
THEN DON'T YOU NEED A KIND HEART TO WIELD THAT BLADE TOO?
YES.
AND THAT I DON'T UNDESTAND AT ALL, EITHER...
YOU DON'T?

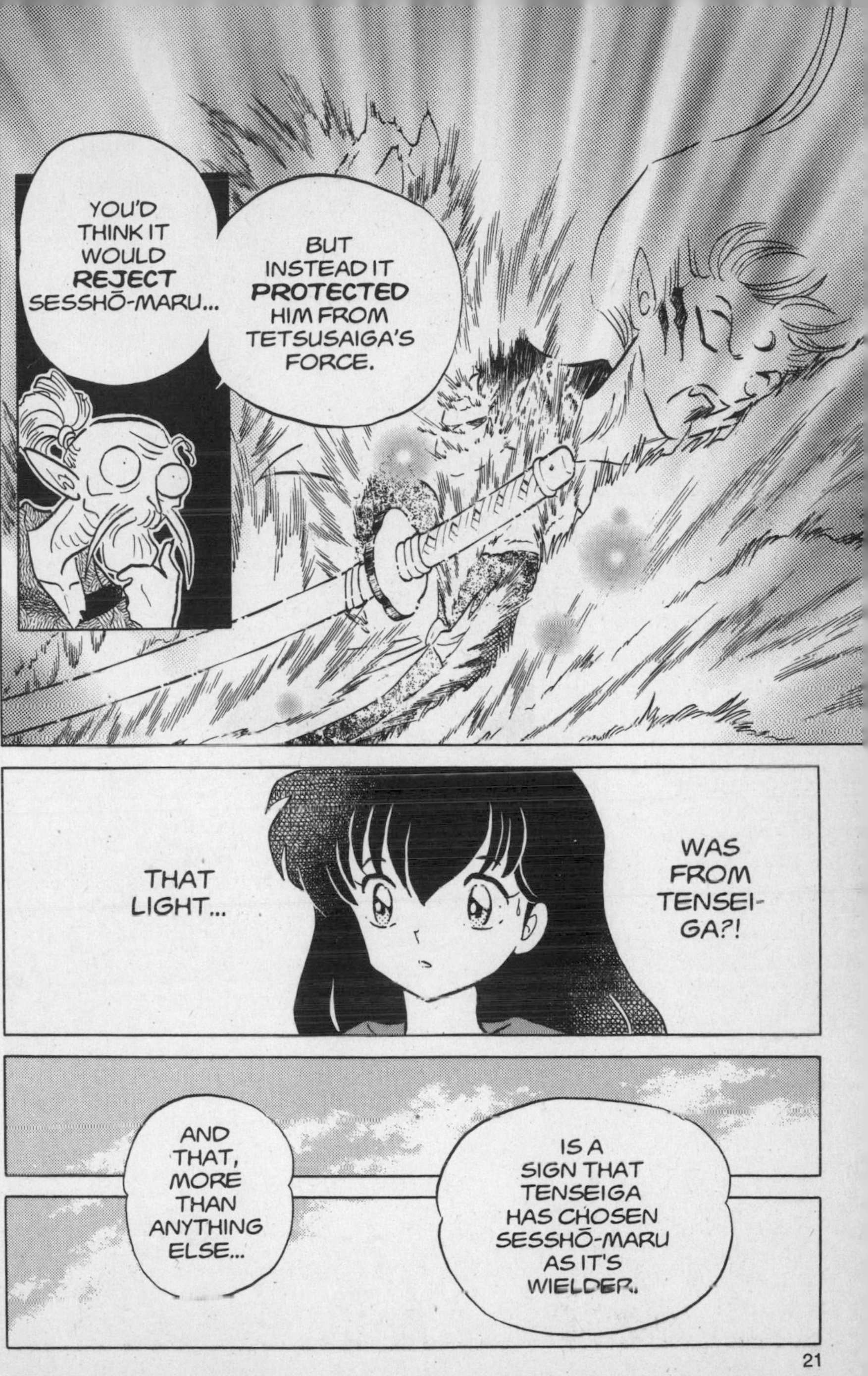
YOU'D THINK IT WOULD **REJECT** SESSHŌ-MARU...
BUT INSTEAD IT **PROTECTED** HIM FROM TETSUSAIGA'S FORCE.
THAT LIGHT...
WAS FROM TENSEI-GA?!
AND THAT, MORE THAN ANYTHING ELSE...
IS A SIGN THAT TENSEIGA HAS CHOSEN SESSHŌ-MARU AS IT'S WIELDER.

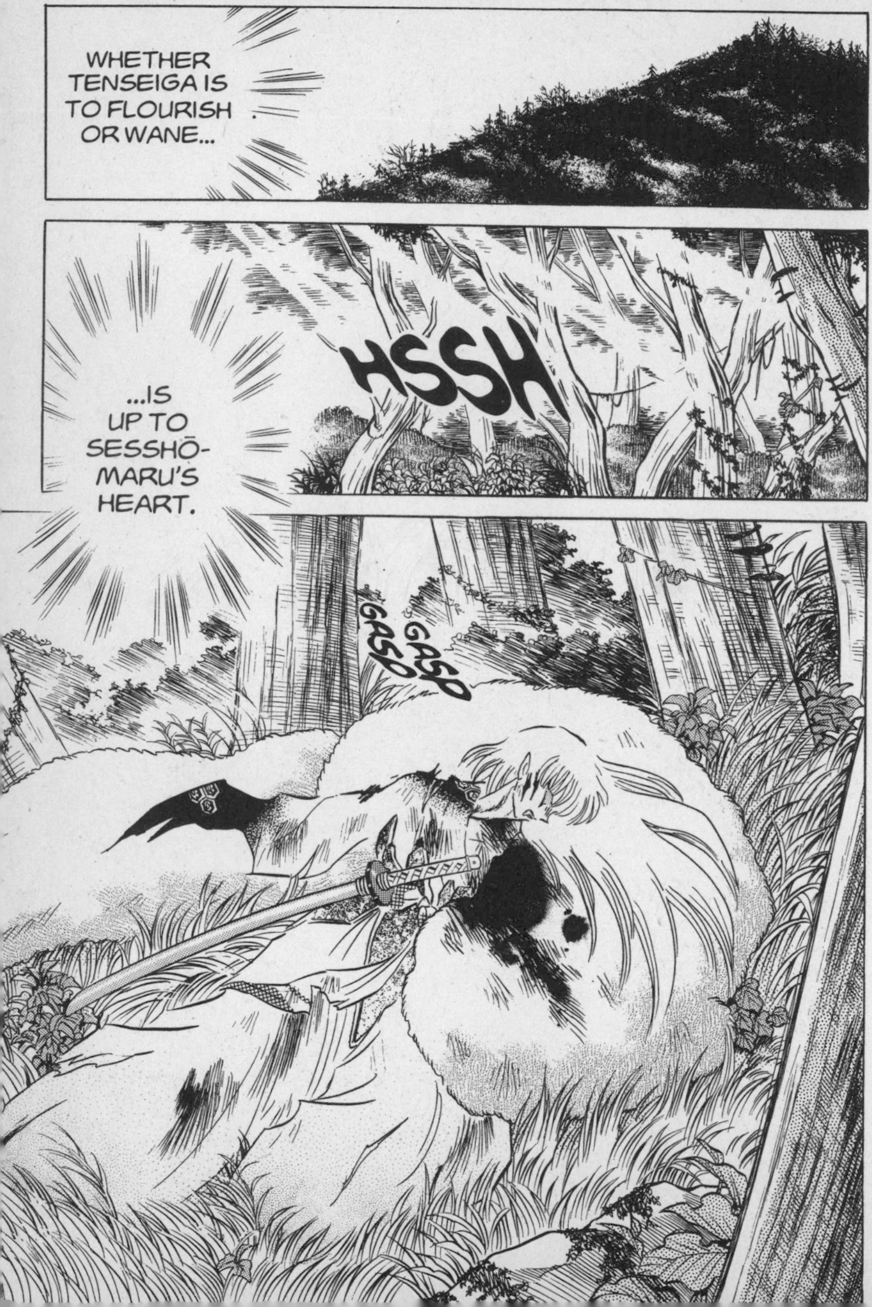
WHETHER TENSEIGA IS TO FLOURISH OR WANE...
...IS UP TO SESSHŌ-MARU'S HEART.
HSSH
GASP GASP

CAN'T MOVE....

SHFF

THE SCENT OF A HUMAN...

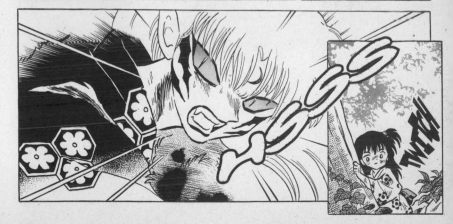

HSSSS

TWITCH

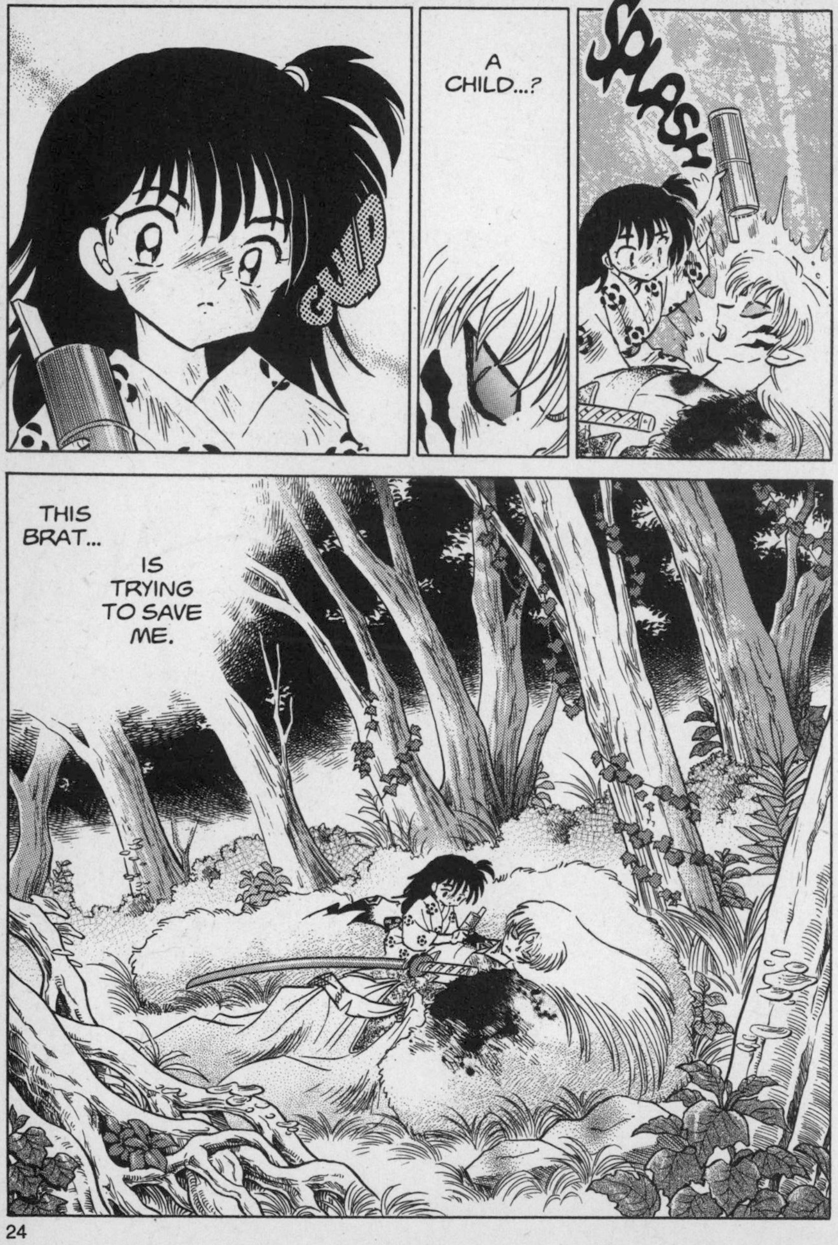
GULP
A CHILD...?
SPLASH
THIS BRAT...
IS TRYING TO SAVE ME.

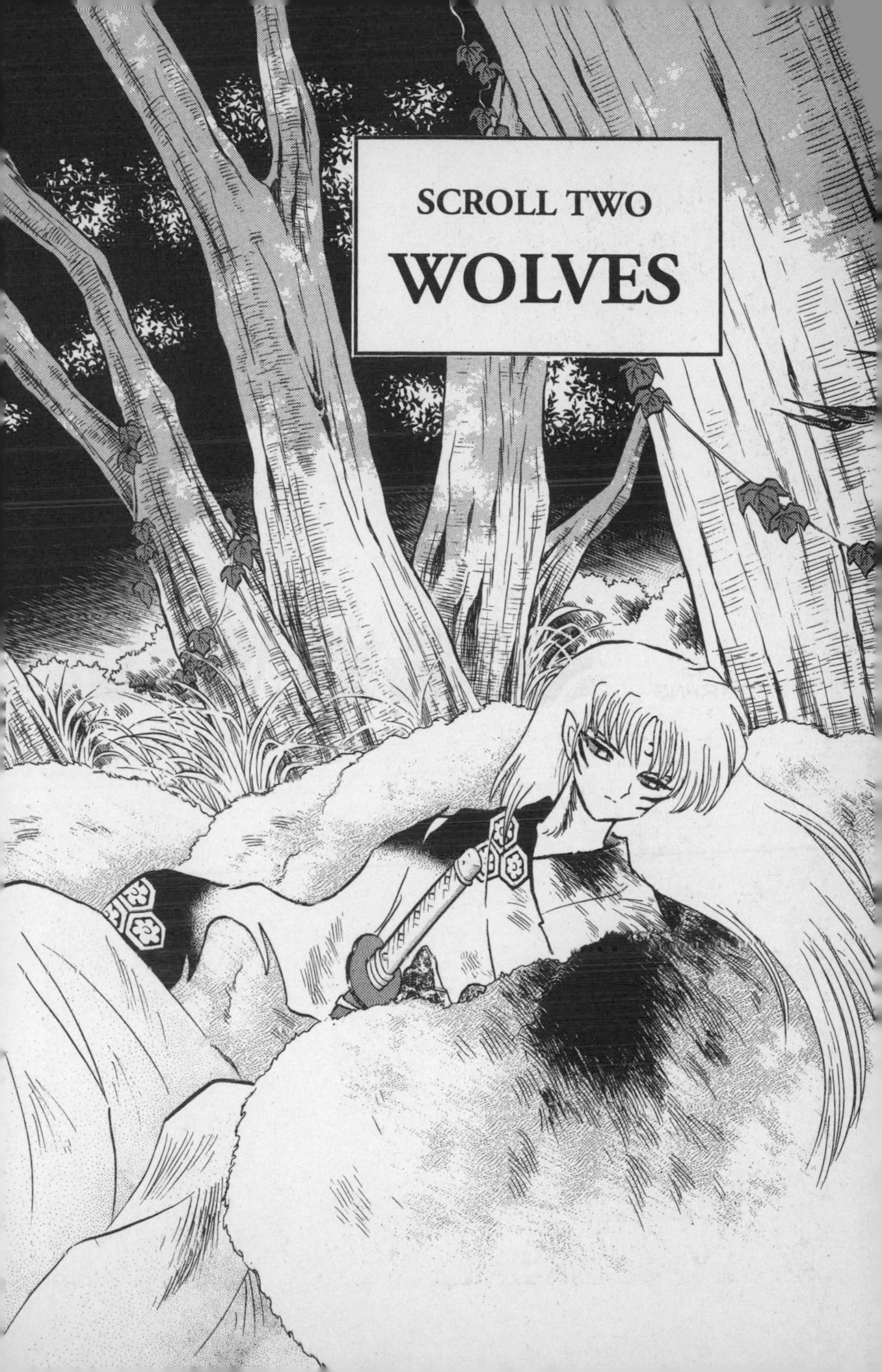
SCROLL TWO
WOLVES

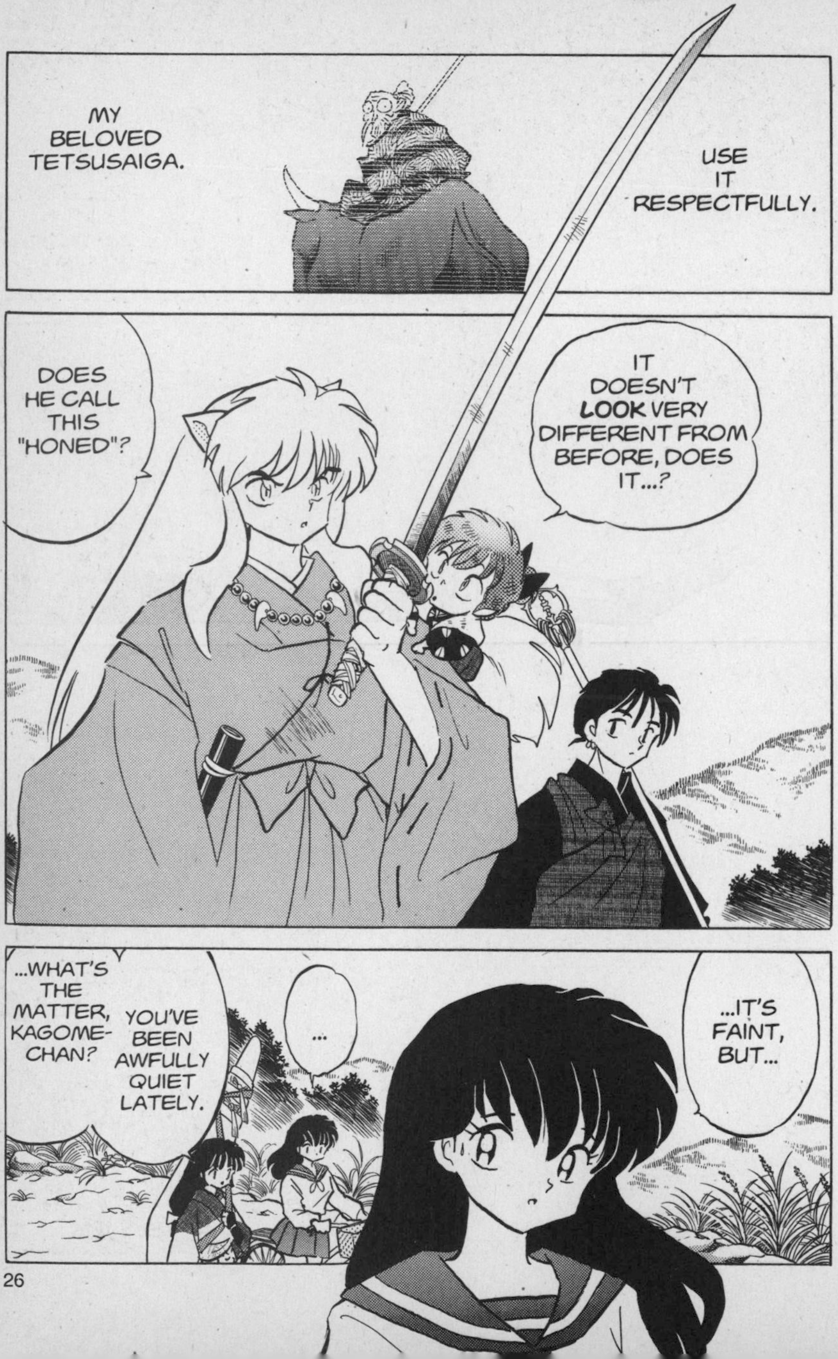
MY BELOVED TETSUSAIGA.
USE IT RESPECTFULLY.
DOES HE CALL THIS "HONED"?
IT DOESN'T **LOOK** VERY DIFFERENT FROM BEFORE, DOES IT...?
...WHAT'S THE MATTER, KAGOME-CHAN?
YOU'VE BEEN AWFULLY QUIET LATELY.
...
...IT'S FAINT, BUT...

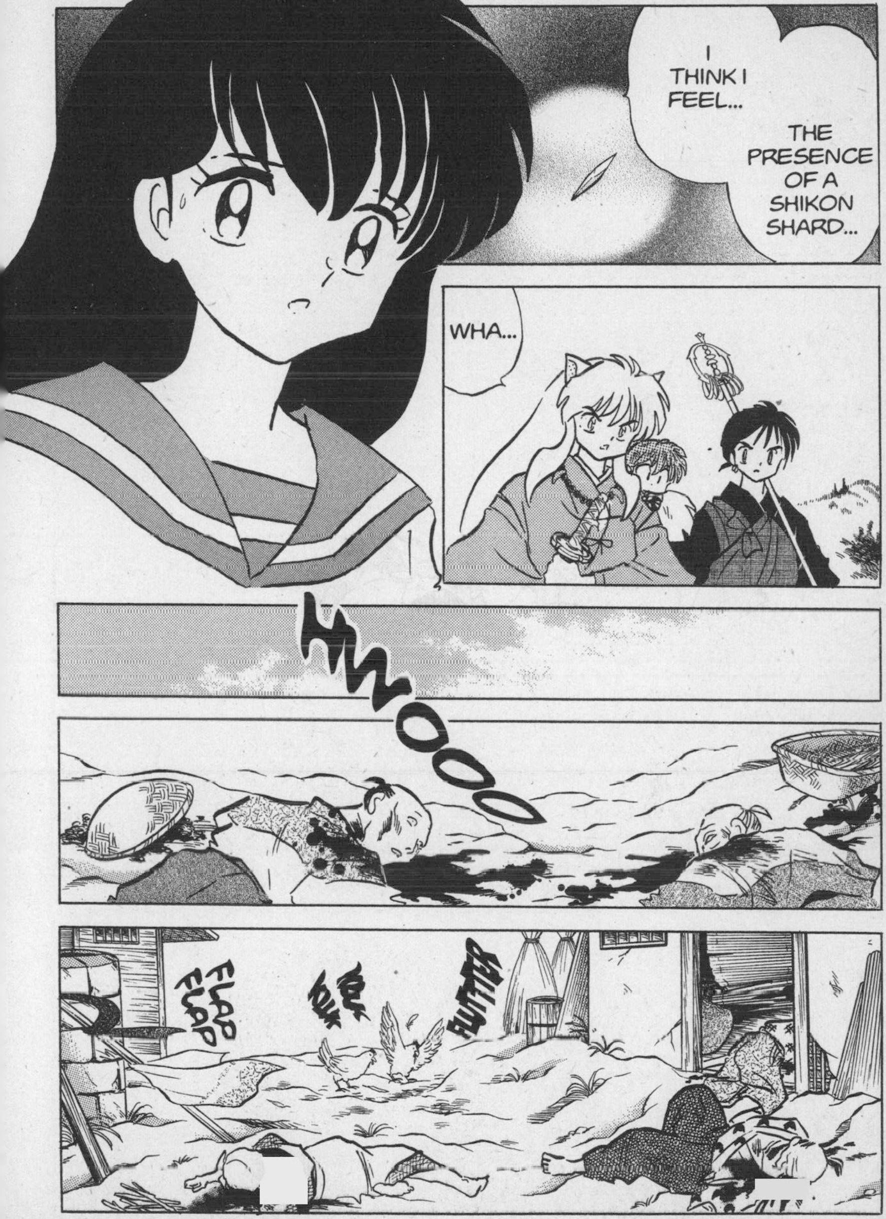
I THINK I FEEL...
THE PRESENCE OF A SHIKON SHARD...
WHA...
HWOOOO
FLAP FLAP
BOK BOK
FLUTTER

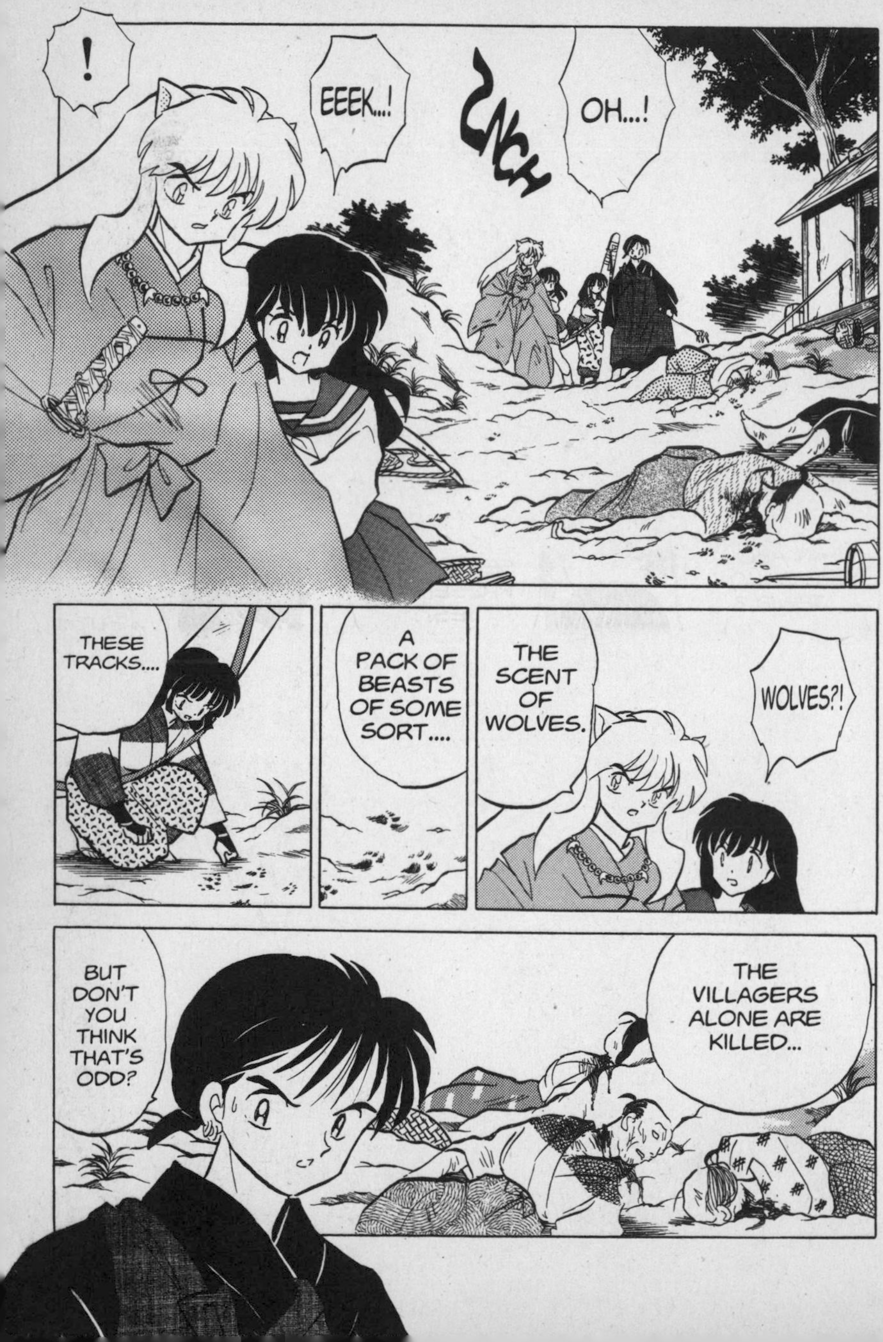
!
EEEK...!
CLINCH
OH...!
THESE TRACKS....
A PACK OF BEASTS OF SOME SORT....
THE SCENT OF WOLVES.
WOLVES?!
BUT DON'T YOU THINK THAT'S ODD?
THE VILLAGERS ALONE ARE KILLED...

...WHILE THE BIRDS AND HORSES THAT WOULD BE THEIR *USUAL* PREY ARE PRACTICALLY UNTOUCHED.

KLUK

I'D SAY THIS IS NOT THE WORK OF ORDINARY WOLVES.

WHINNNY

BRRRR

KAGOME, WHAT ABOUT THE SHIKON JEWEL?

THIS IS NEAR WHERE YOU SENSED ITS PRESENCE, YES?!

Y-YES.

BUT...

IT'S...

...NOT HERE ANYMORE.

IT'S AS IF...

...IT JUST...

RAN AWAY...

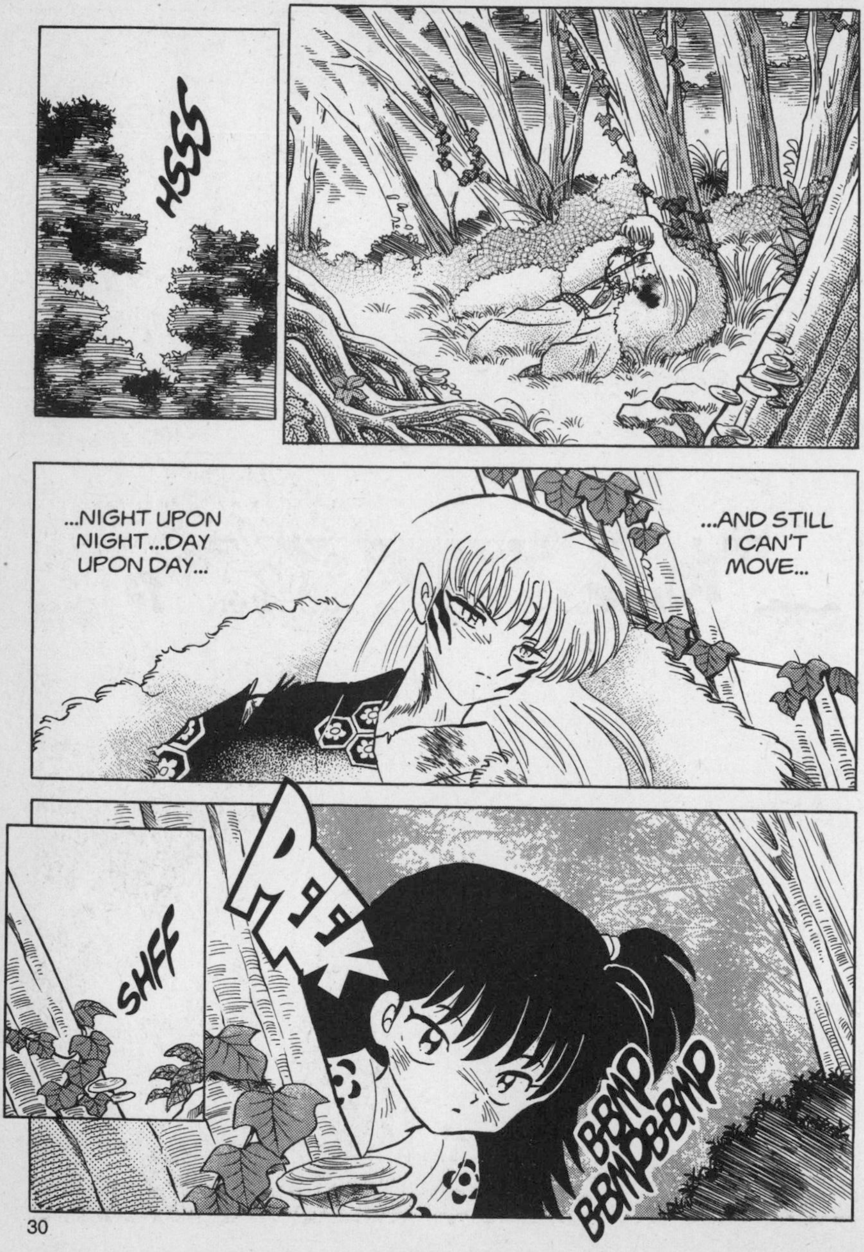
HSSS
...NIGHT UPON NIGHT...DAY UPON DAY...
...AND STILL I CAN'T MOVE...
SHFF
PEEK
B-BMP B-BMP
B-BMP B-BMP

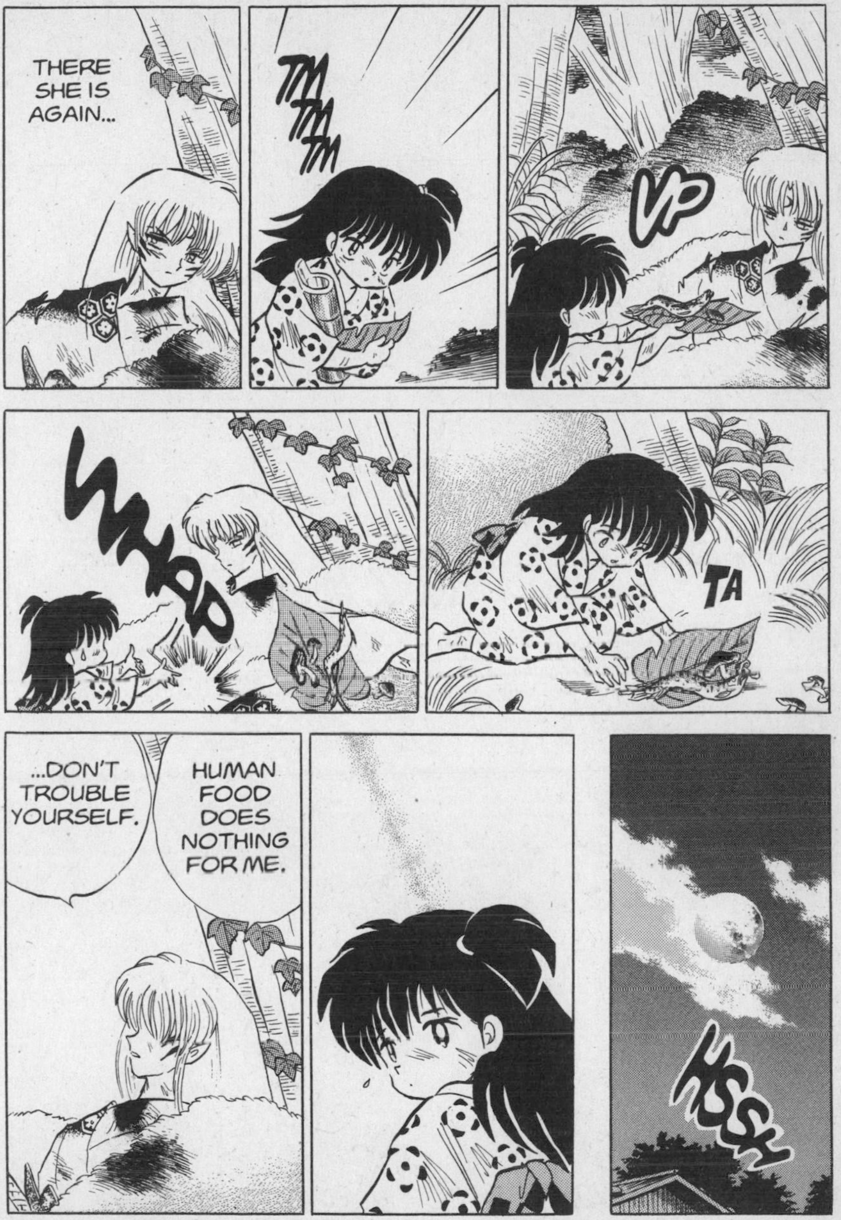
THERE SHE IS AGAIN...
TM TM TM TM
VP
WHAP
TA
...DON'T TROUBLE YOURSELF.
HUMAN FOOD DOES NOTHING FOR ME.
HSSH

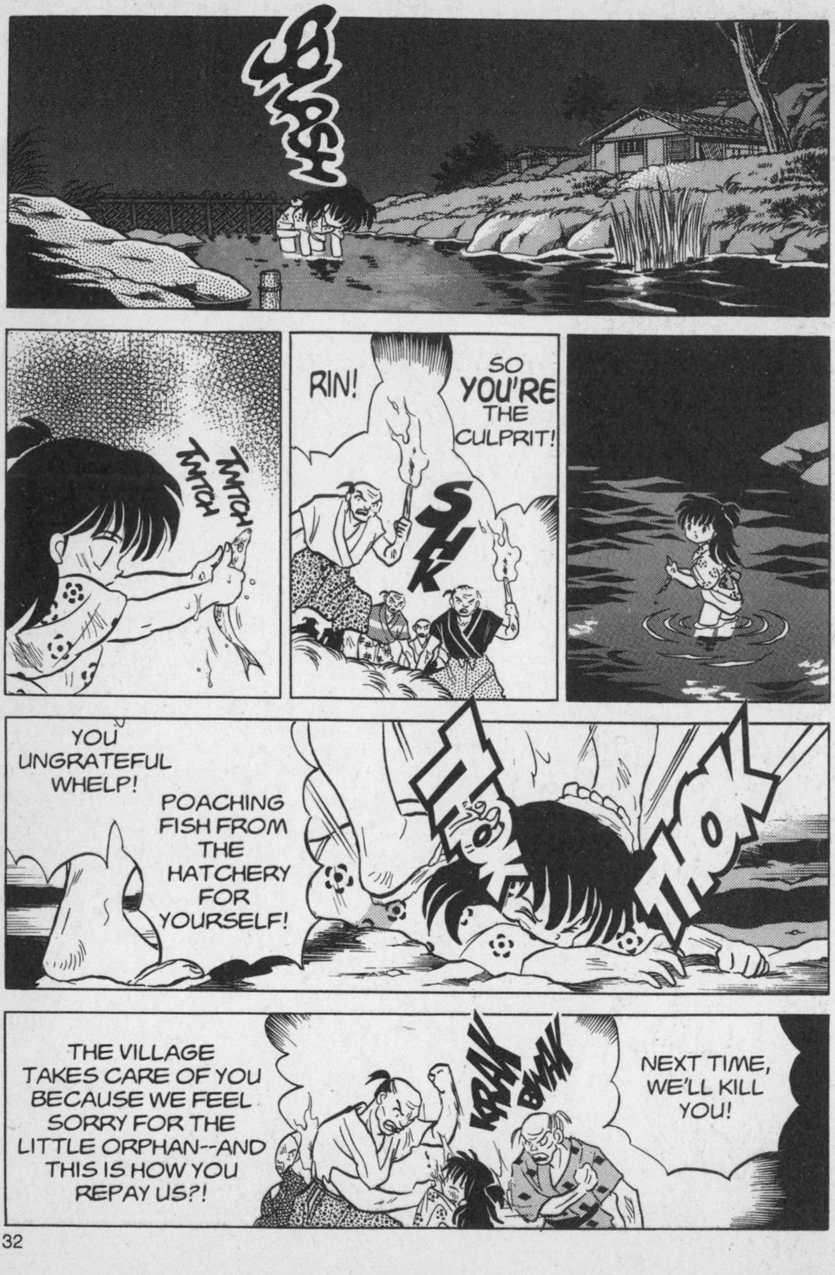
SPLOSH
TWITCH TWITCH
RIN!
SO YOU'RE THE CULPRIT!
SHUK
YOU UNGRATEFUL WHELP!
POACHING FISH FROM THE HATCHERY FOR YOURSELF!
THOK THOK
THE VILLAGE TAKES CARE OF YOU BECAUSE WE FEEL SORRY FOR THE LITTLE ORPHAN--AND THIS IS HOW YOU REPAY US?!
KRAK BAMAK
NEXT TIME, WE'LL KILL YOU!

HMPH.... SHE'S A STRANGE ONE....

NOT EVEN A WHIMPER...

EVER SINCE SHE WATCHED THOSE BANDITS SLAUGHTER HER FAMILY...

...SHE'S BEEN MUTE.

SHE CAN'T HELP IT.

STAGGER

SHHH

RUSTLE

POIP

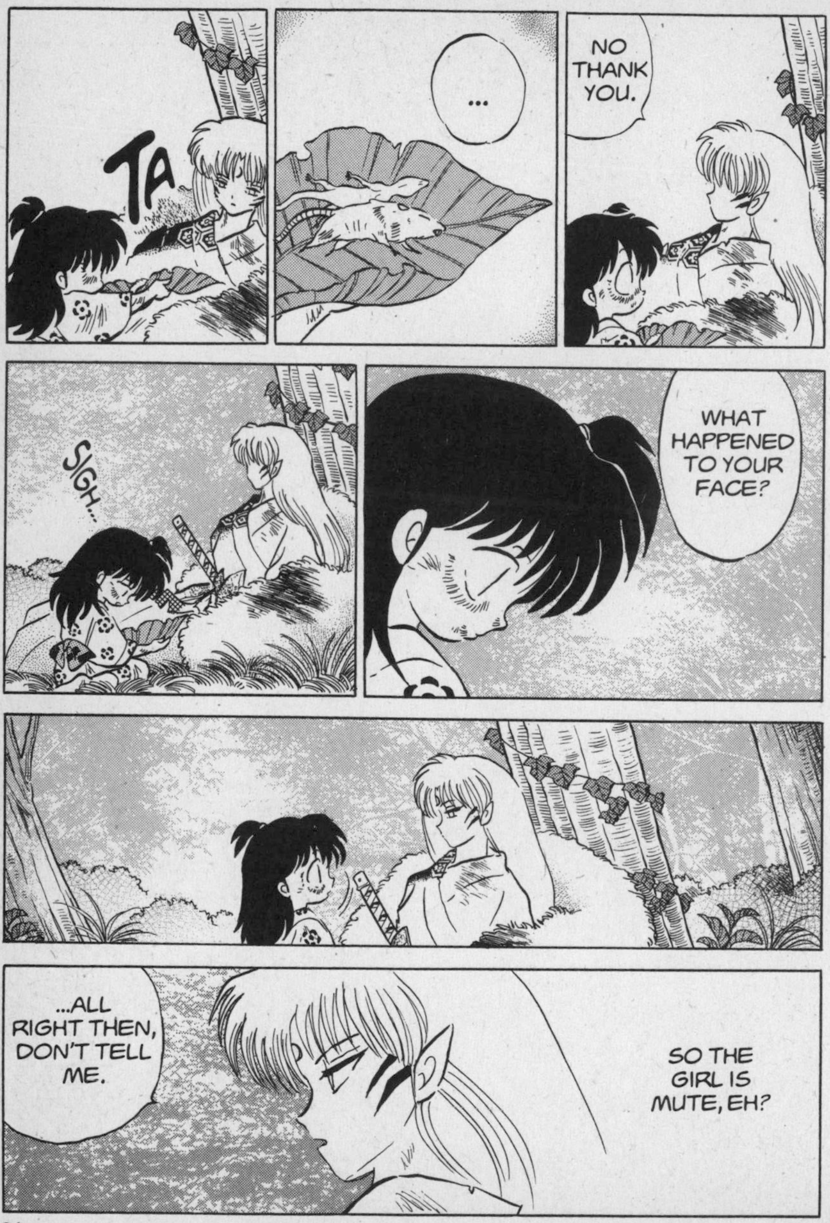
TA
...
NO THANK YOU.
SIGH...
WHAT HAPPENED TO YOUR FACE?
...ALL RIGHT THEN, DON'T TELL ME.
SO THE GIRL IS MUTE, EH?

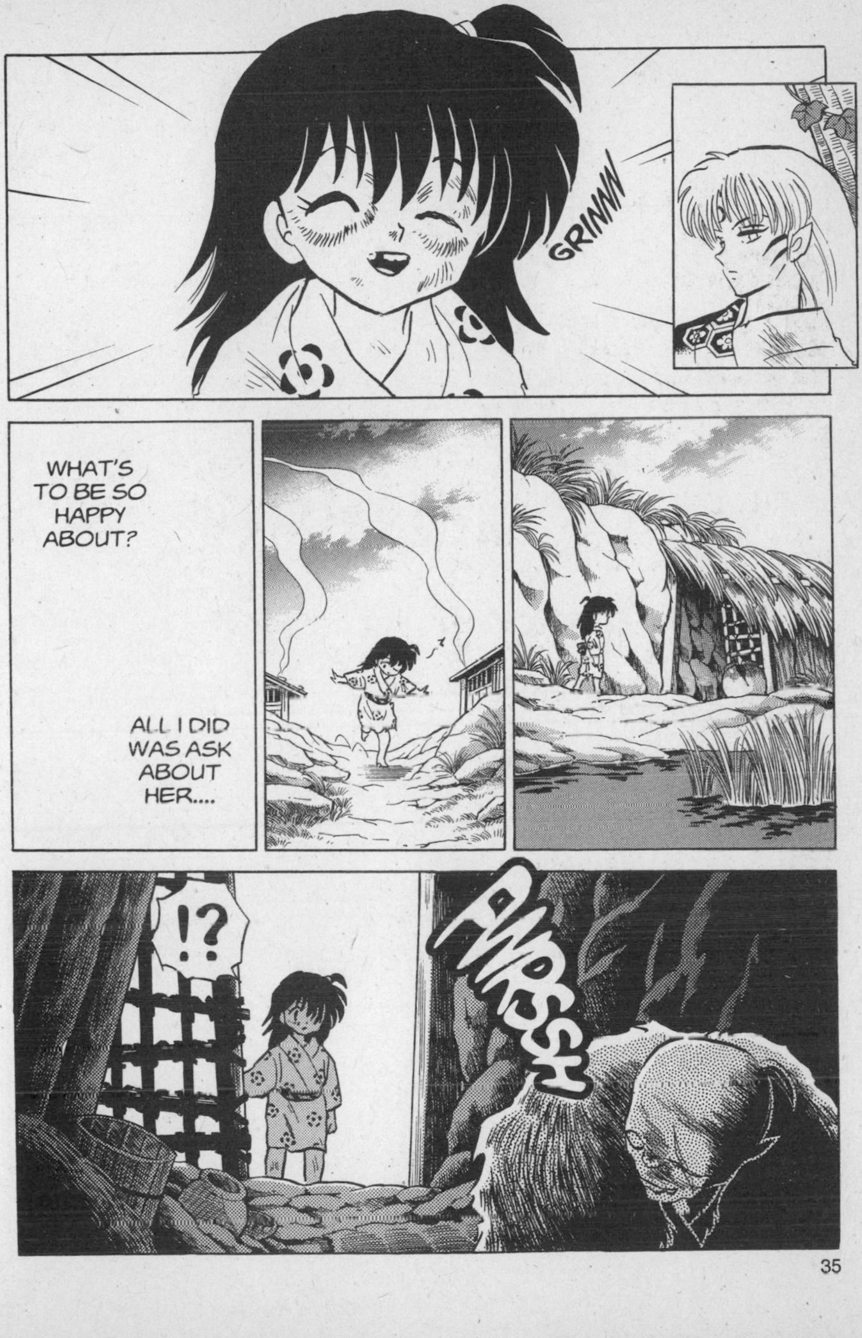
GRINNN
WHAT'S TO BE SO HAPPY ABOUT?
ALL I DID WAS ASK ABOUT HER....
!?
PWOSSH

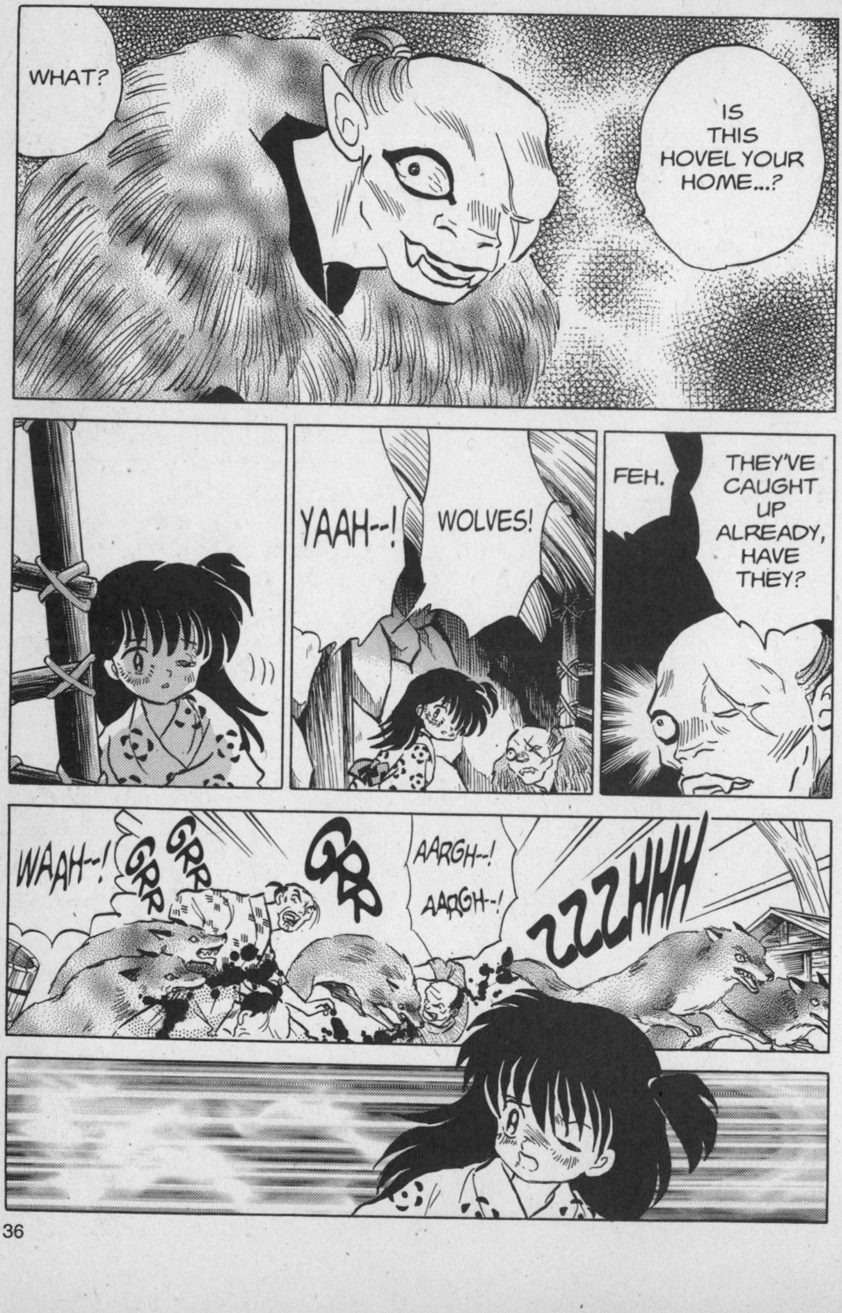

WHAT?
IS THIS HOVEL YOUR HOME...?
YAAH--!
WOLVES!
FEH.
THEY'VE CAUGHT UP ALREADY, HAVE THEY?
WAAH--!
GRR GRR
GRR
AARGH--!
AARGH--!
ZZZSHHH

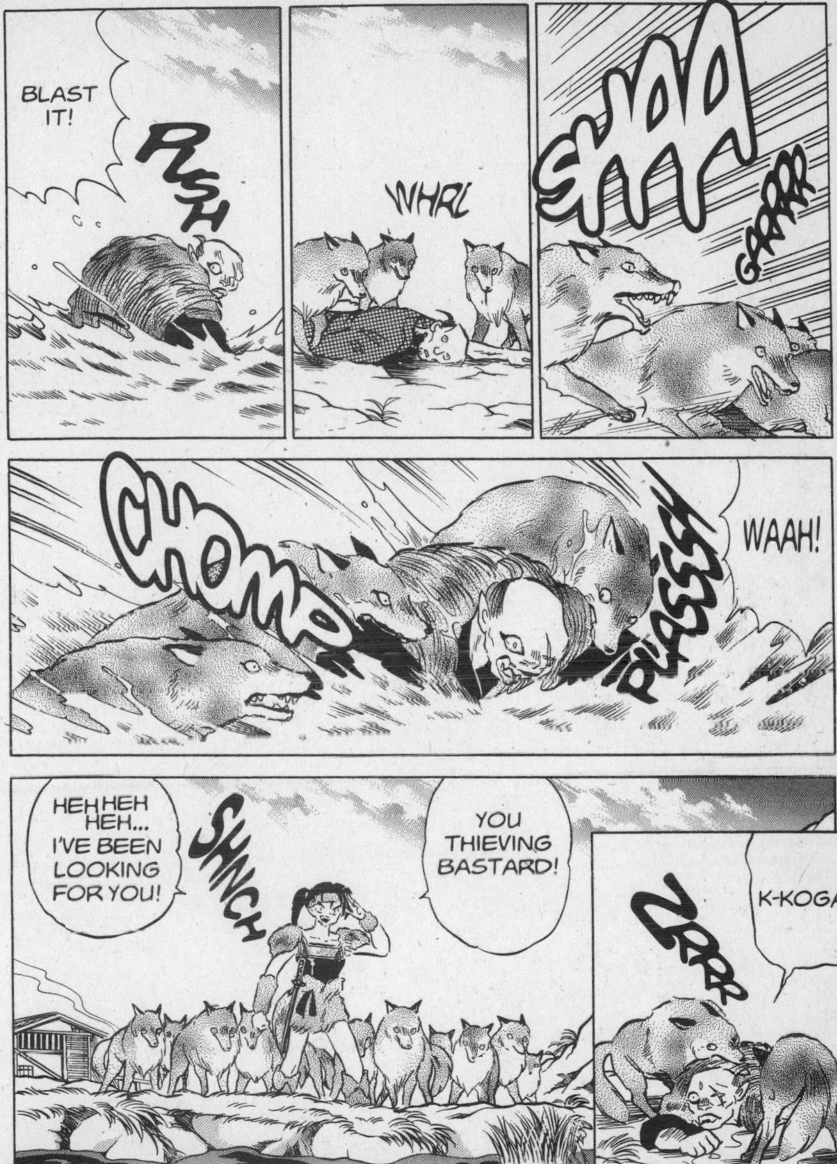
BLAST IT!
RUSH
WHRL
SHAAA
GRRRR
CHOMP
WAAH!
PLASSSH
HEH HEH HEH... I'VE BEEN LOOKING FOR YOU!
SHNCH
YOU THIEVING BASTARD!
K-KOGA...
ZRRR

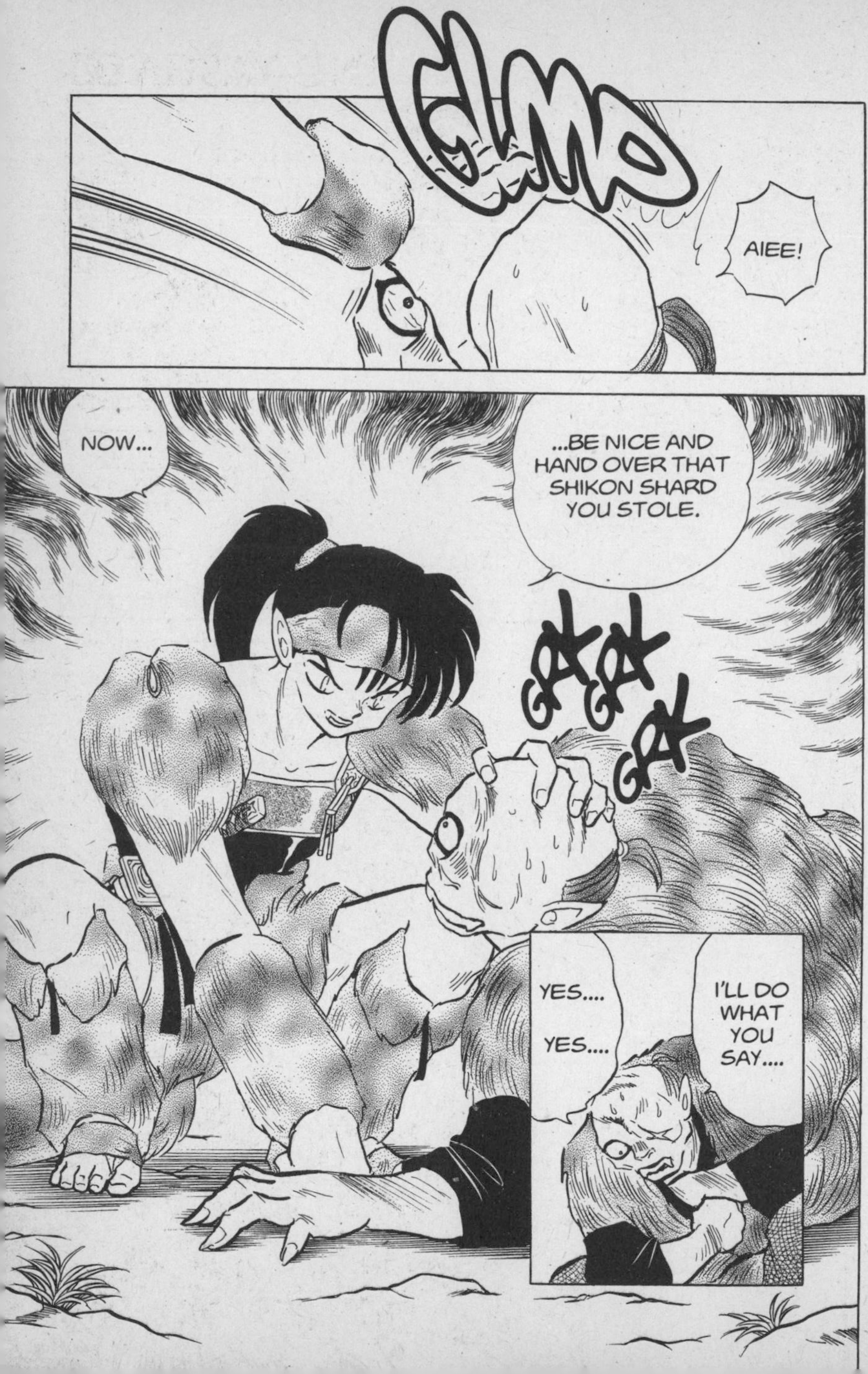
CLMP
AIEE!
NOW...
...BE NICE AND HAND OVER THAT SHIKON SHARD YOU STOLE.
GRAK GRAK GRAK
YES....
YES....
I'LL DO WHAT YOU SAY....

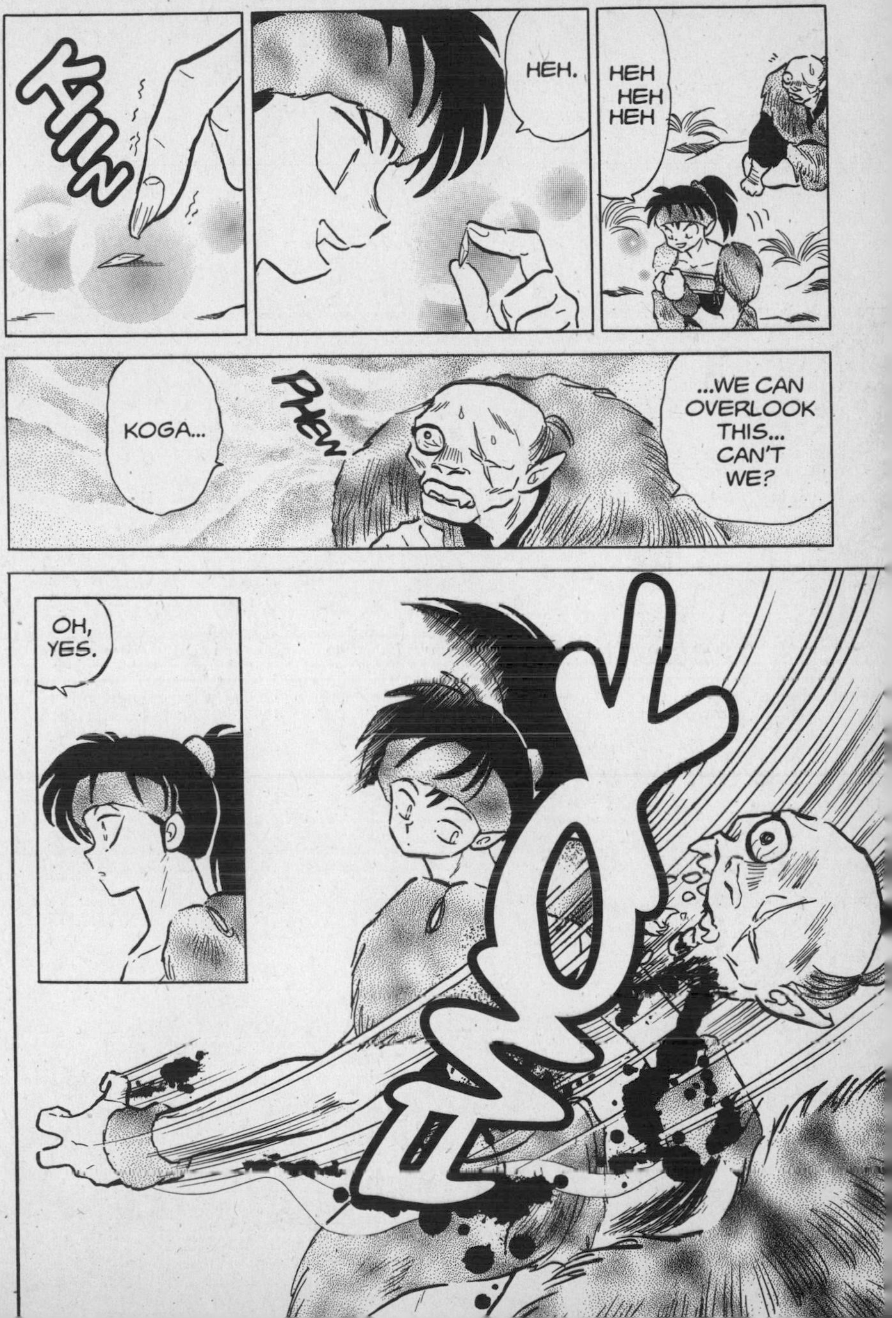
KAIIN
HEH.
HEH HEH HEH
KOGA...
PHEW
...WE CAN OVERLOOK THIS... CAN'T WE?
OH, YES.

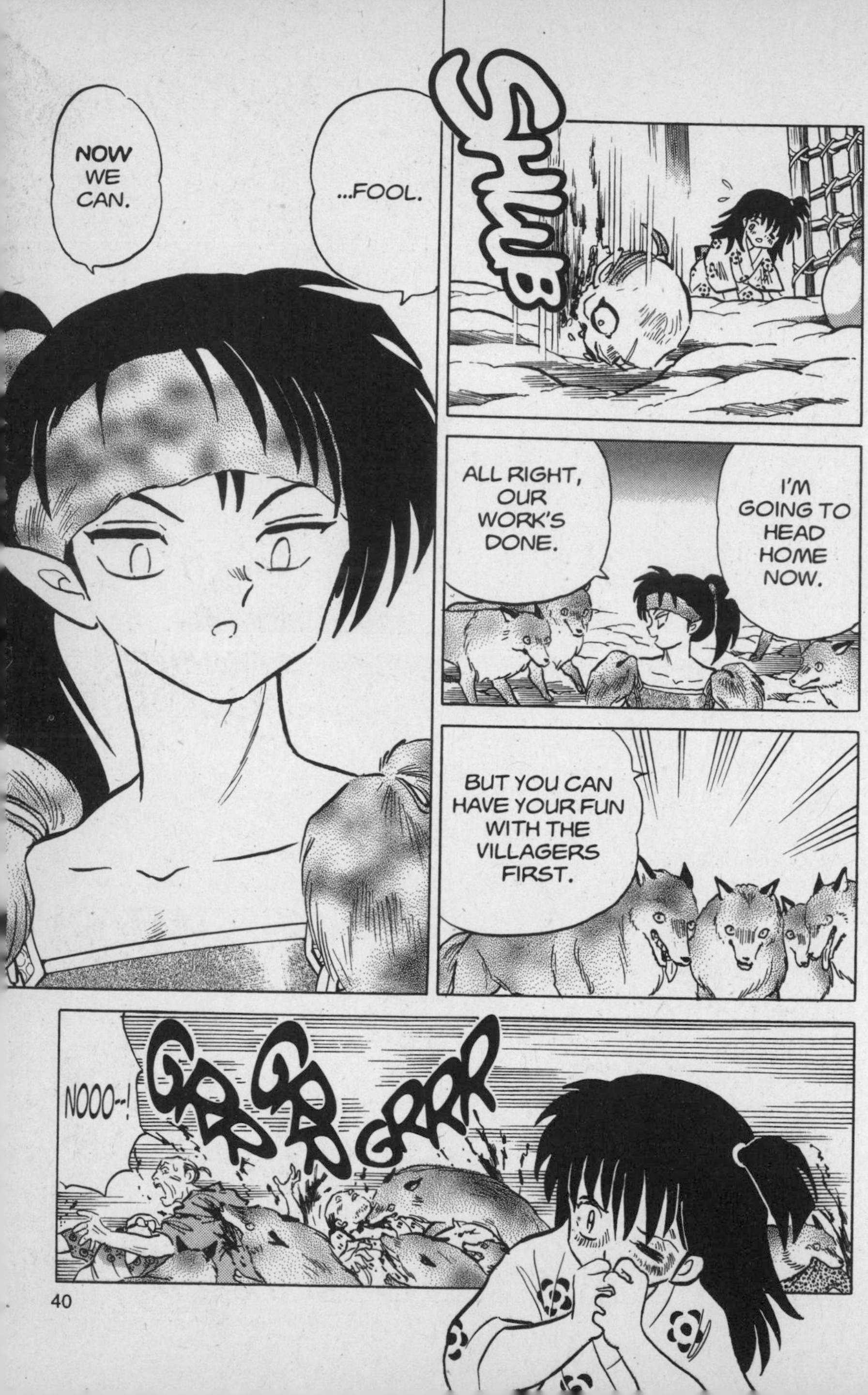
NOW WE CAN.
...FOOL.
ALL RIGHT, OUR WORK'S DONE.
I'M GOING TO HEAD HOME NOW.
BUT YOU CAN HAVE YOUR FUN WITH THE VILLAGERS FIRST.
NOOO--!
GRR GRR GRRR

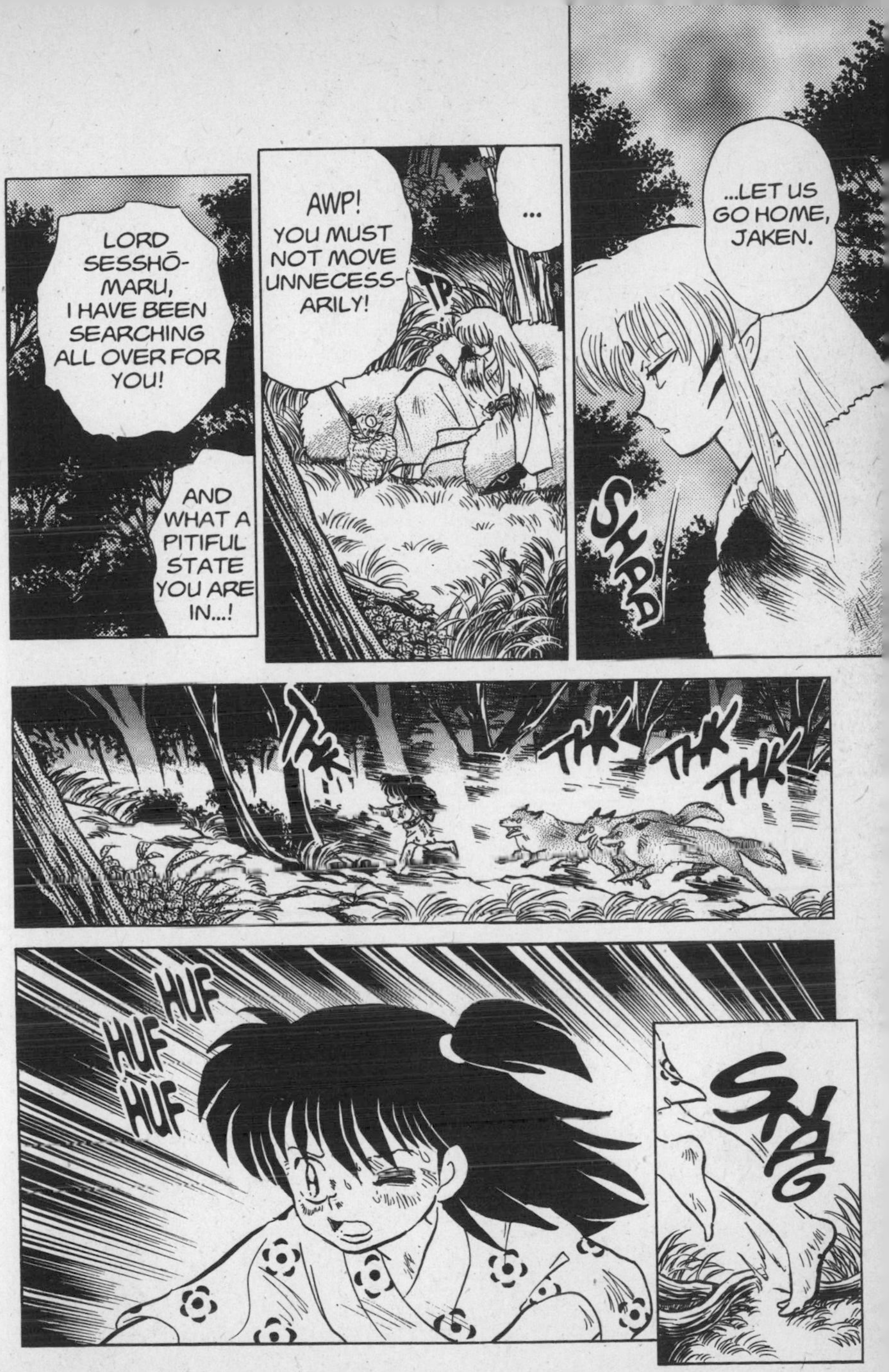

LORD SESSHŌ-MARU, I HAVE BEEN SEARCHING ALL OVER FOR YOU!
AND WHAT A PITIFUL STATE YOU ARE IN...!
AWP! YOU MUST NOT MOVE UNNECESS-ARILY!
TP
...
...LET US GO HOME, JAKEN.
SHAA
THK
THK
THK
THK
HUF
HUF
HUF
SHNG

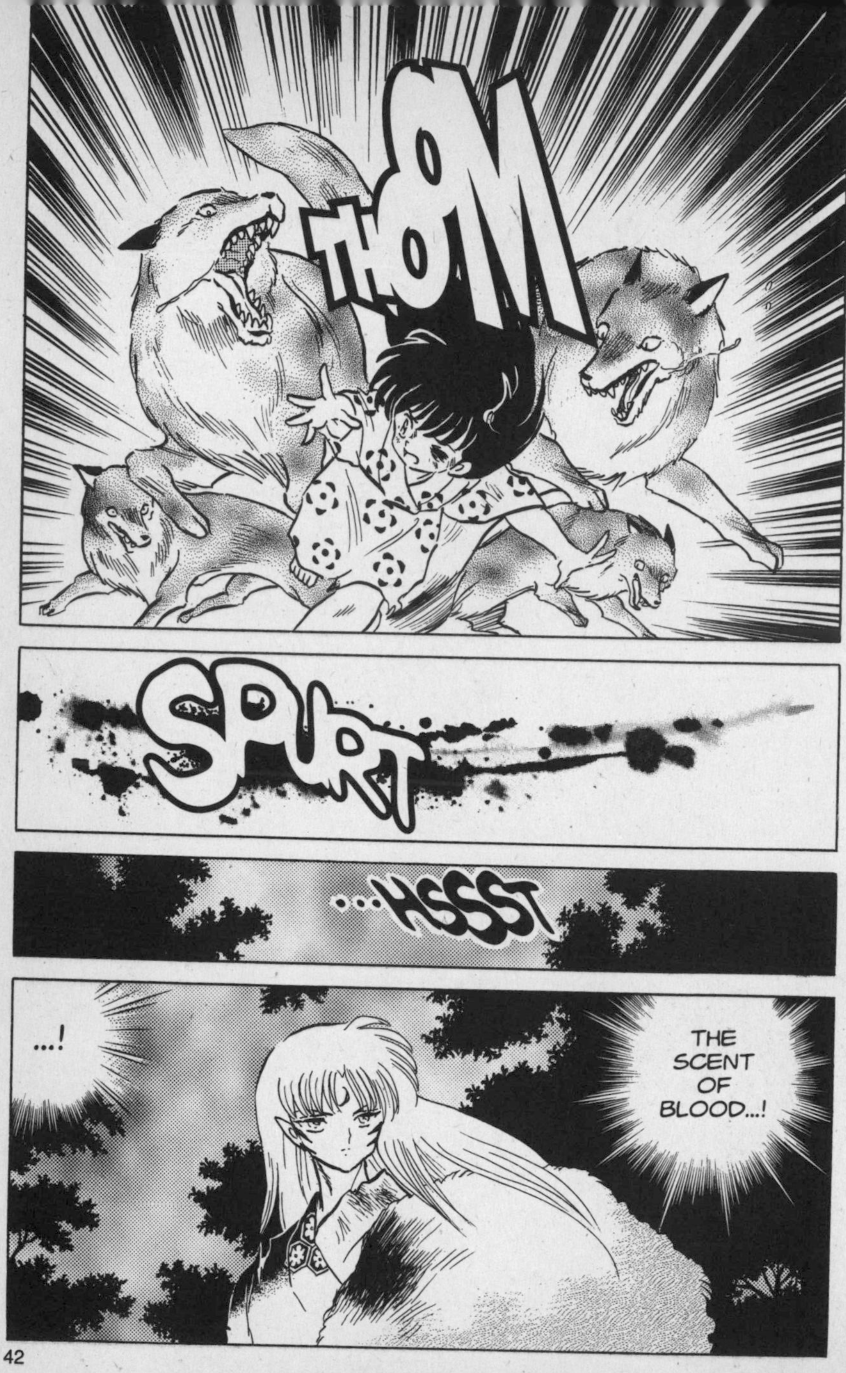
THOOM
SPURT
...HSSST
...!
THE SCENT OF BLOOD...!

SCROLL THREE

THE MAIDEN'S LIFE

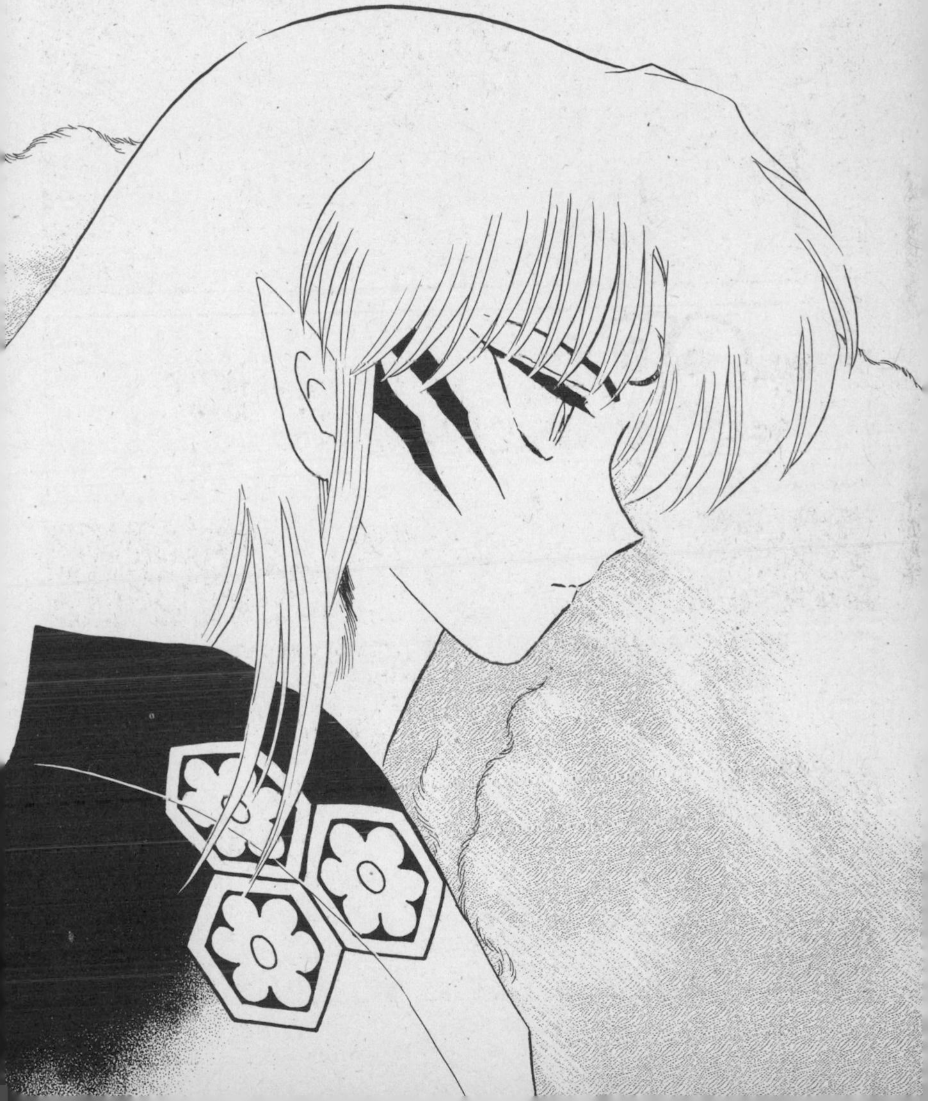

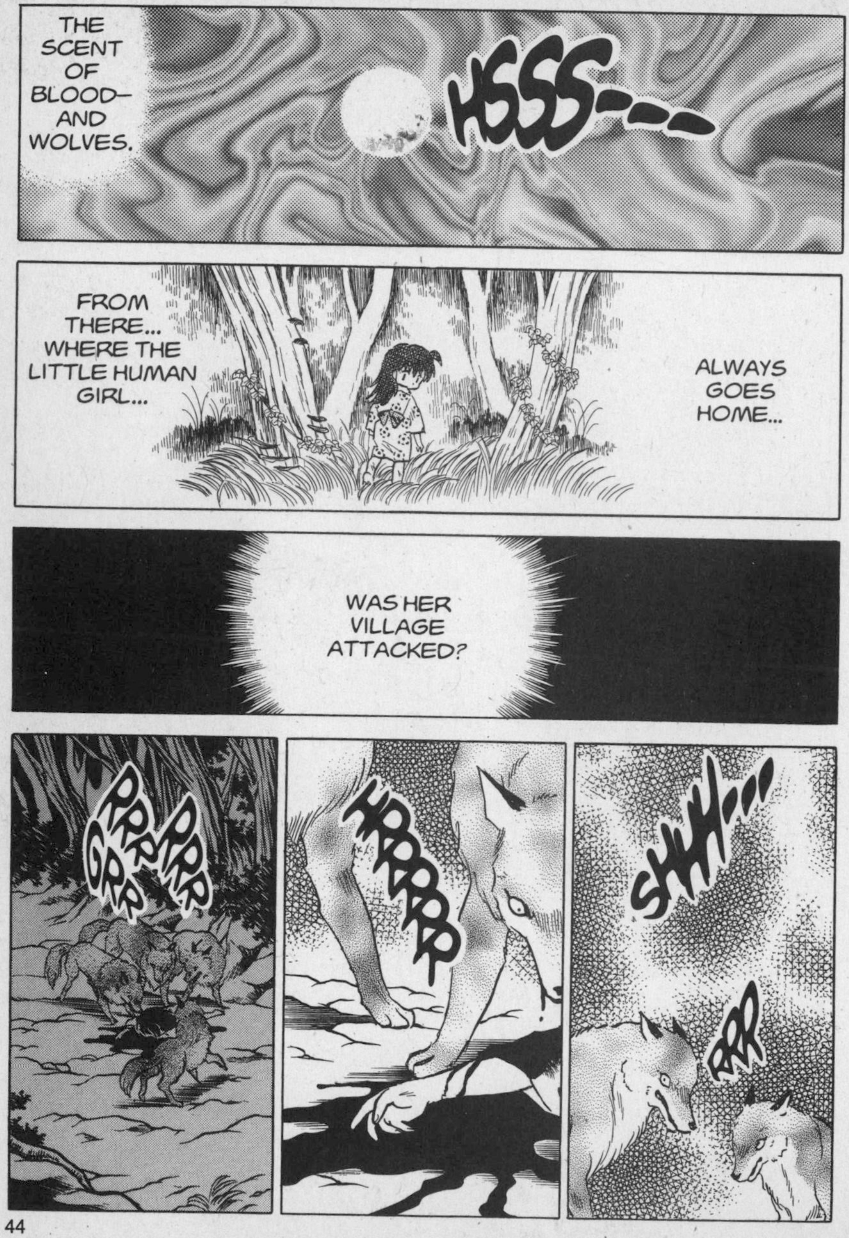
THE SCENT OF BLOOD— AND WOLVES.
HSSS---
FROM THERE... WHERE THE LITTLE HUMAN GIRL...
ALWAYS GOES HOME...
WAS HER VILLAGE ATTACKED?
RRRRRR
GRR
HRRRRR
SHH...
RRR

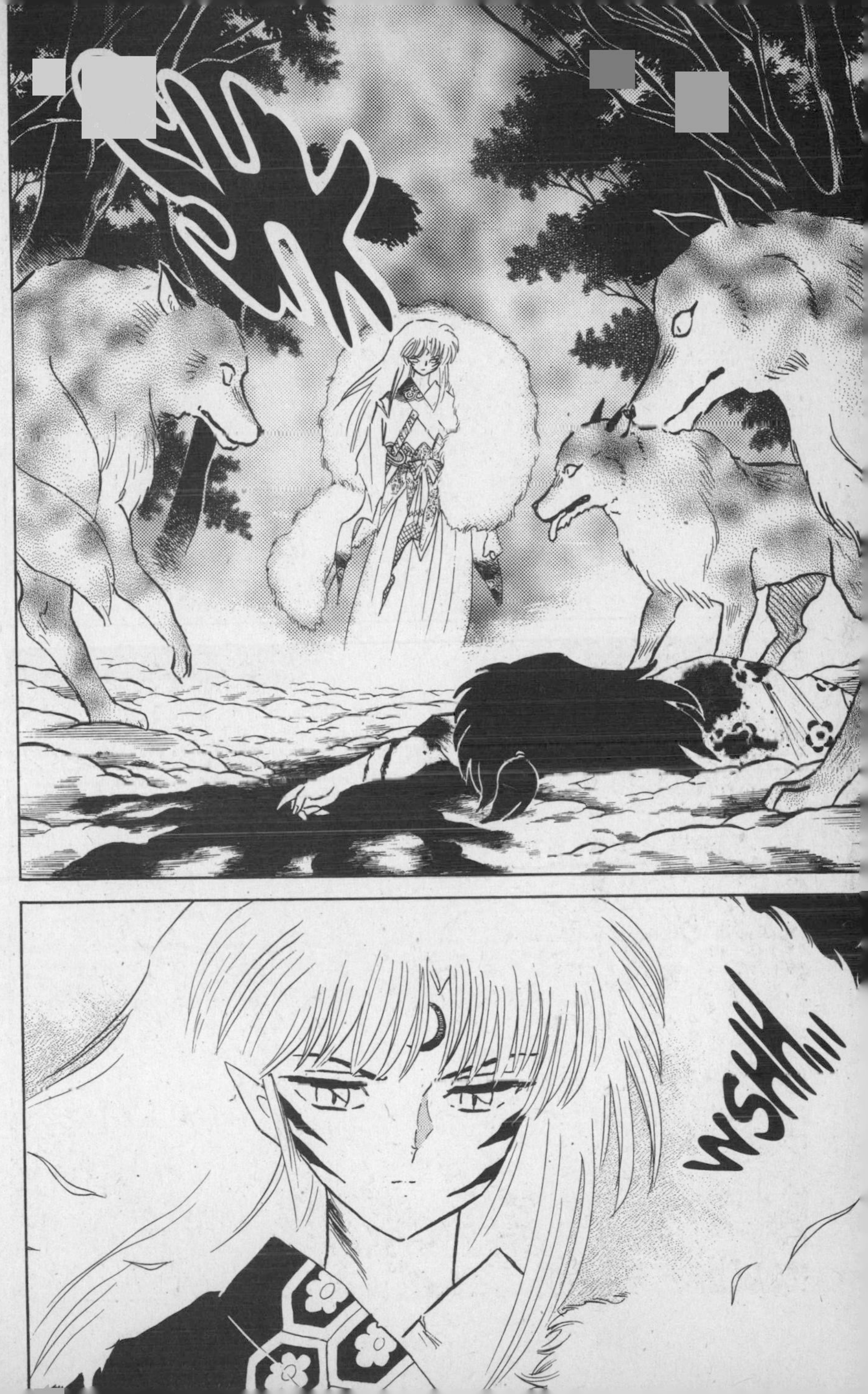
WSHH...

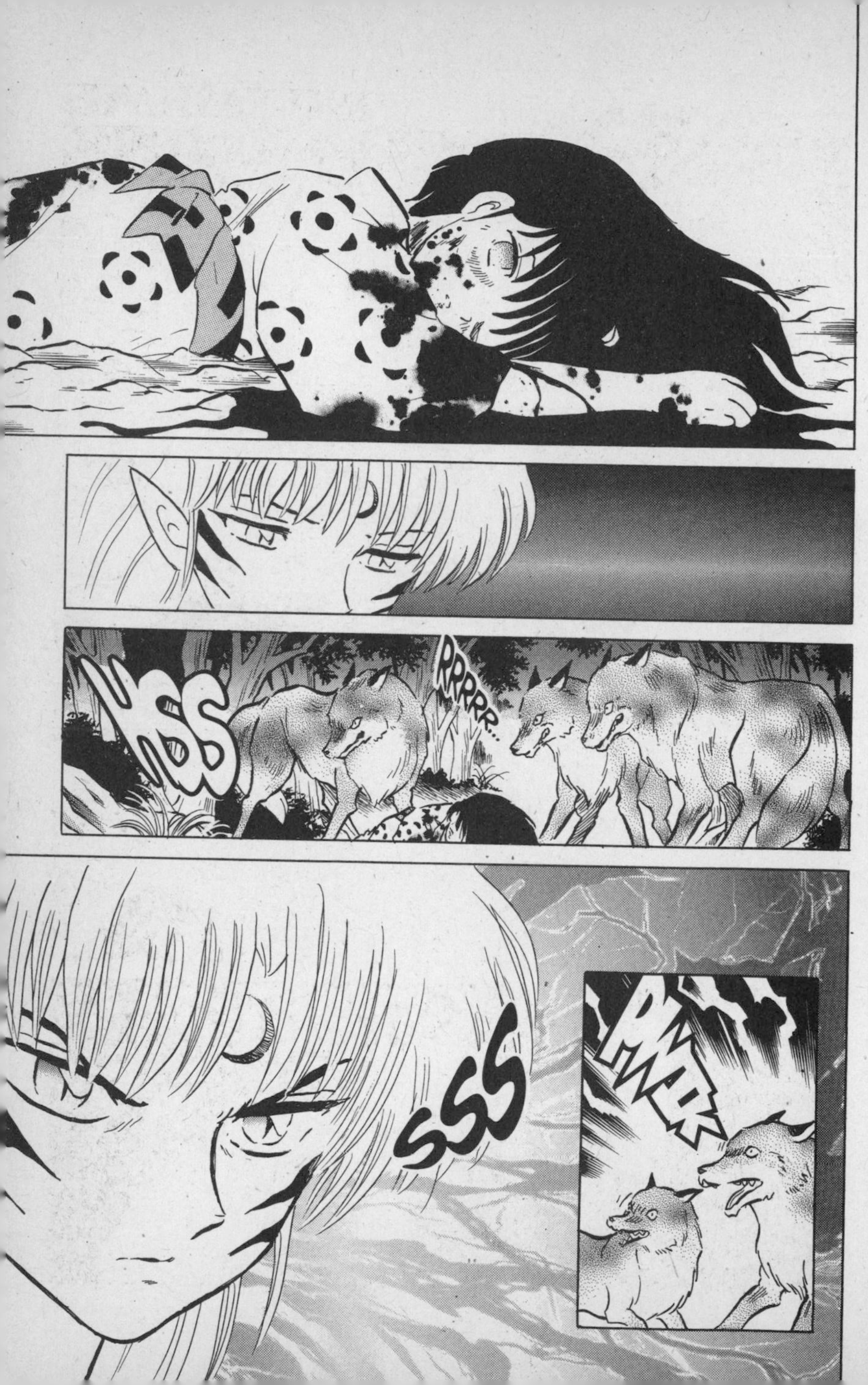
HSS
RRRRR...
SSS
PWAK

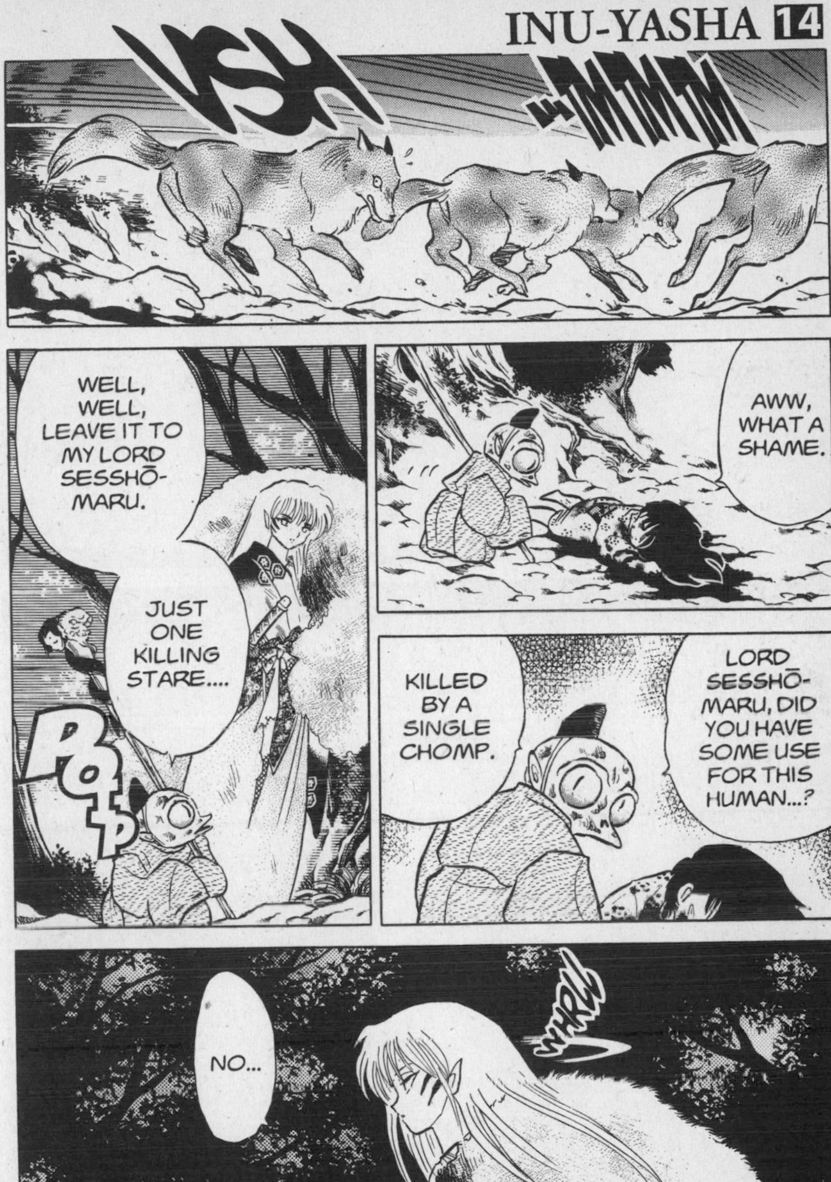
VSH
WELL, WELL, LEAVE IT TO MY LORD SESSHŌ-MARU.
JUST ONE KILLING STARE....
POP
AWW, WHAT A SHAME.
KILLED BY A SINGLE CHOMP.
LORD SESSHŌ-MARU, DID YOU HAVE SOME USE FOR THIS HUMAN...?
NO...

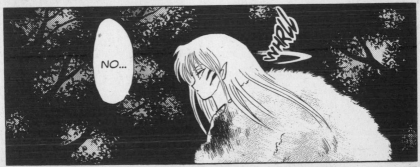

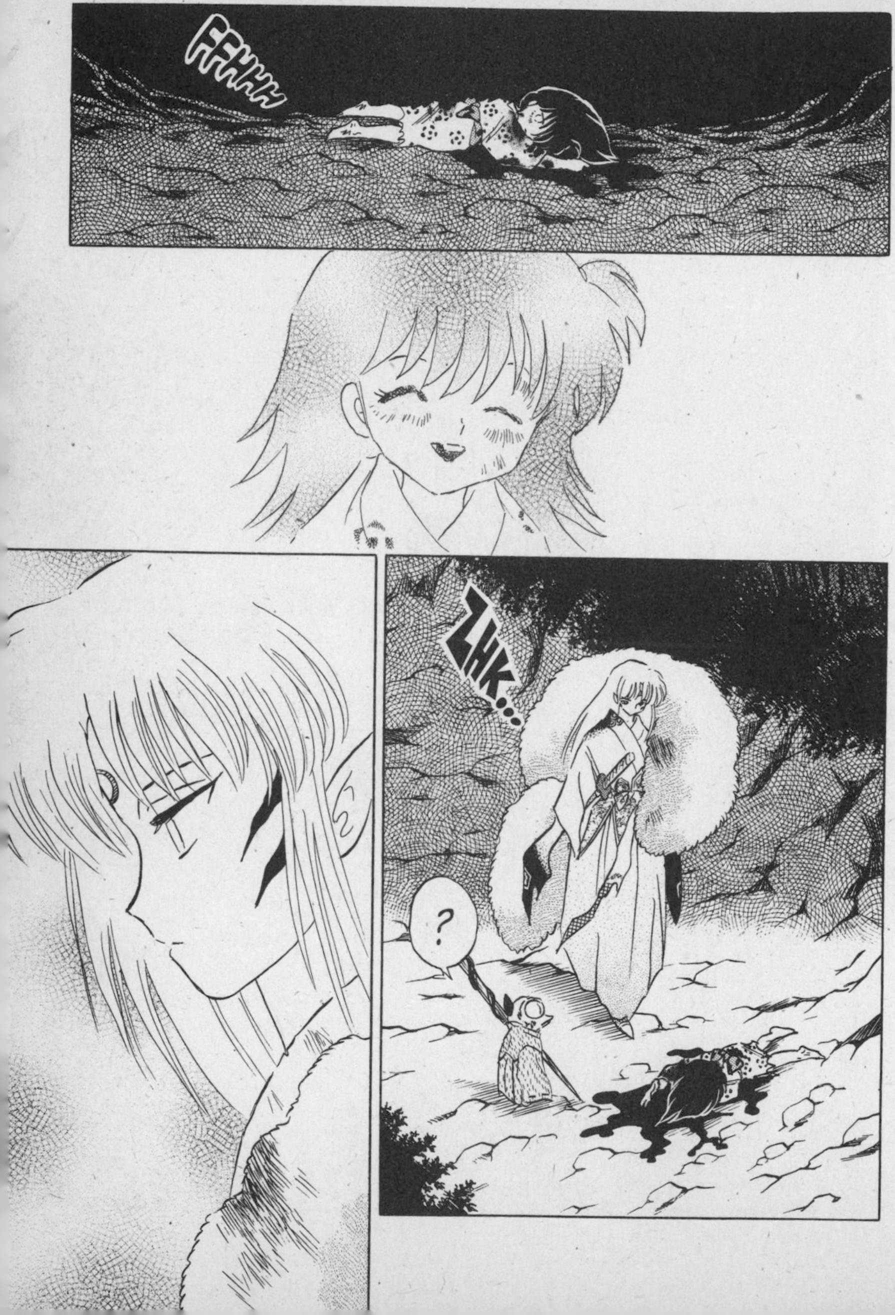
FFHHHH
ZHK...
?

...?

LORD SESSHŌ-MARU?

BBMP

MMM...

49

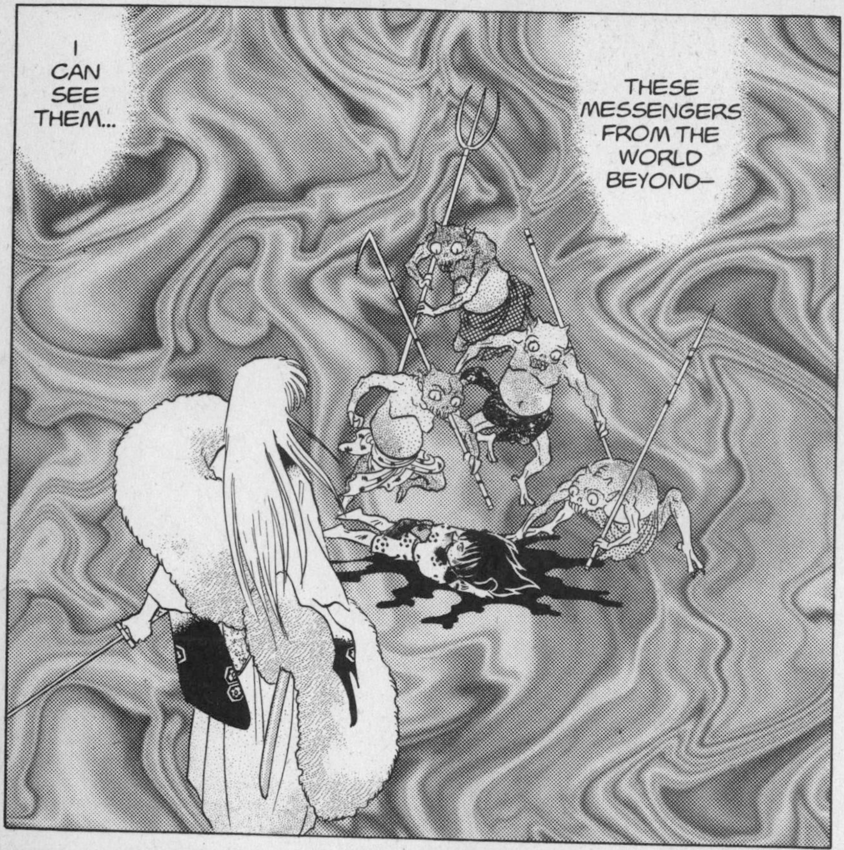
I CAN SEE THEM...
THESE MESSENGERS FROM THE WORLD BEYOND—
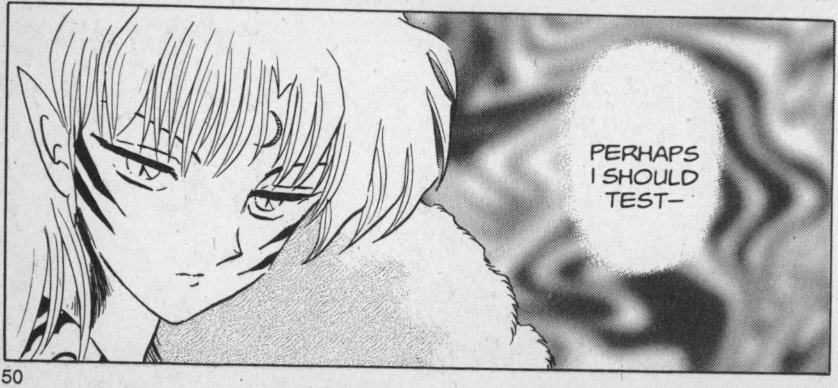
PERHAPS I SHOULD TEST—

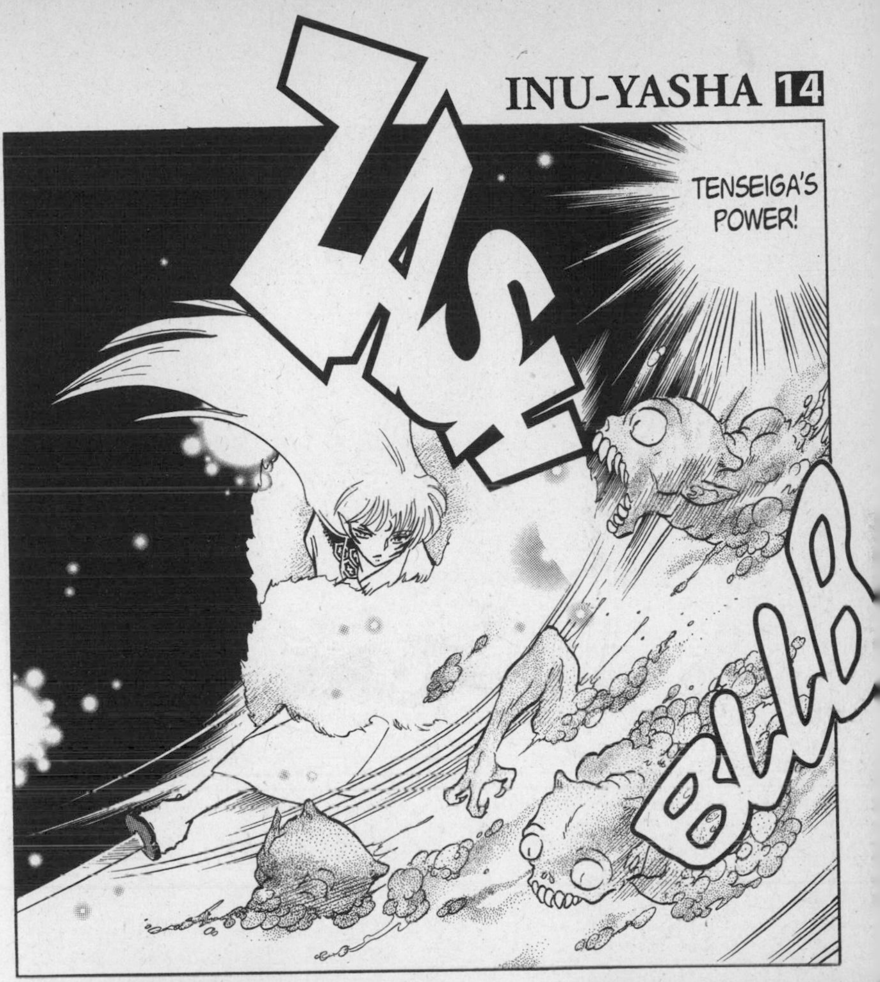
ZAS
TENSEIGA'S POWER!
BLUB

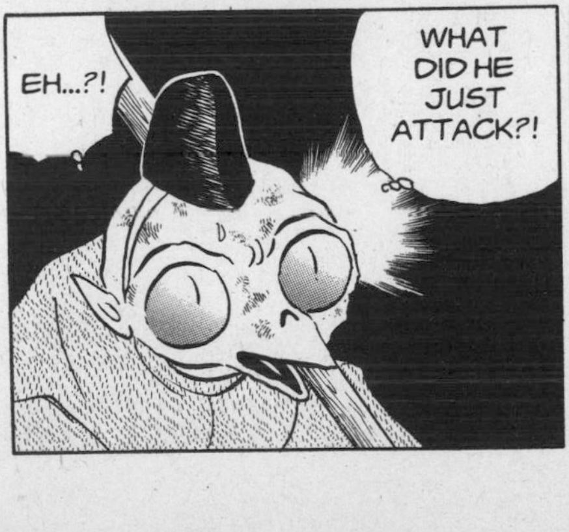
EH...?!
WHAT DID HE JUST ATTACK?!

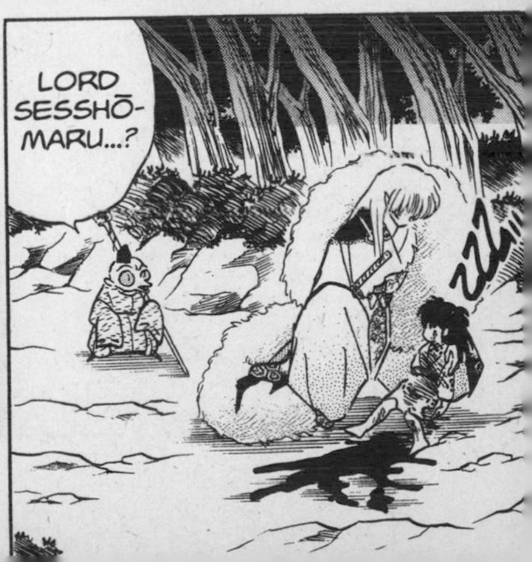
LORD SESSHŌ-MARU...?
ZZZ

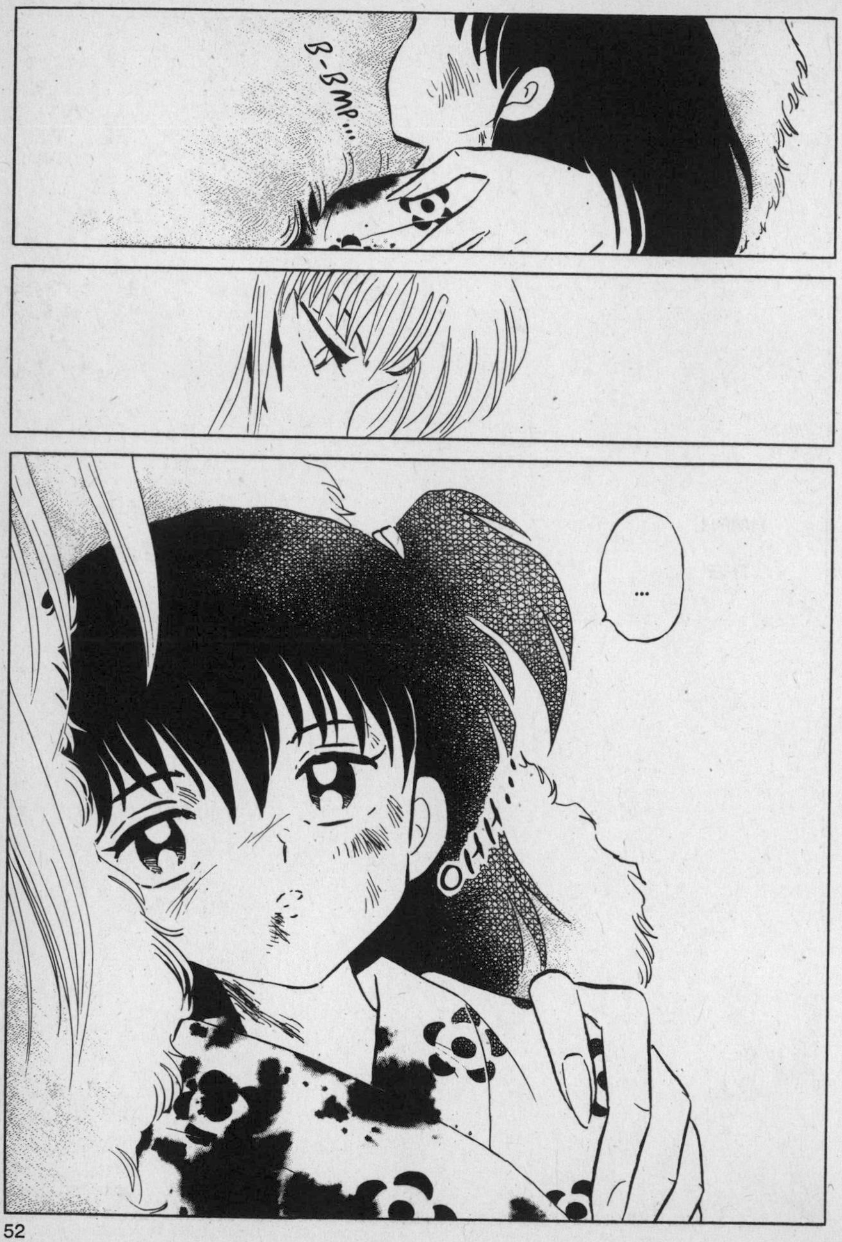
B-BMP...
...
OHH...

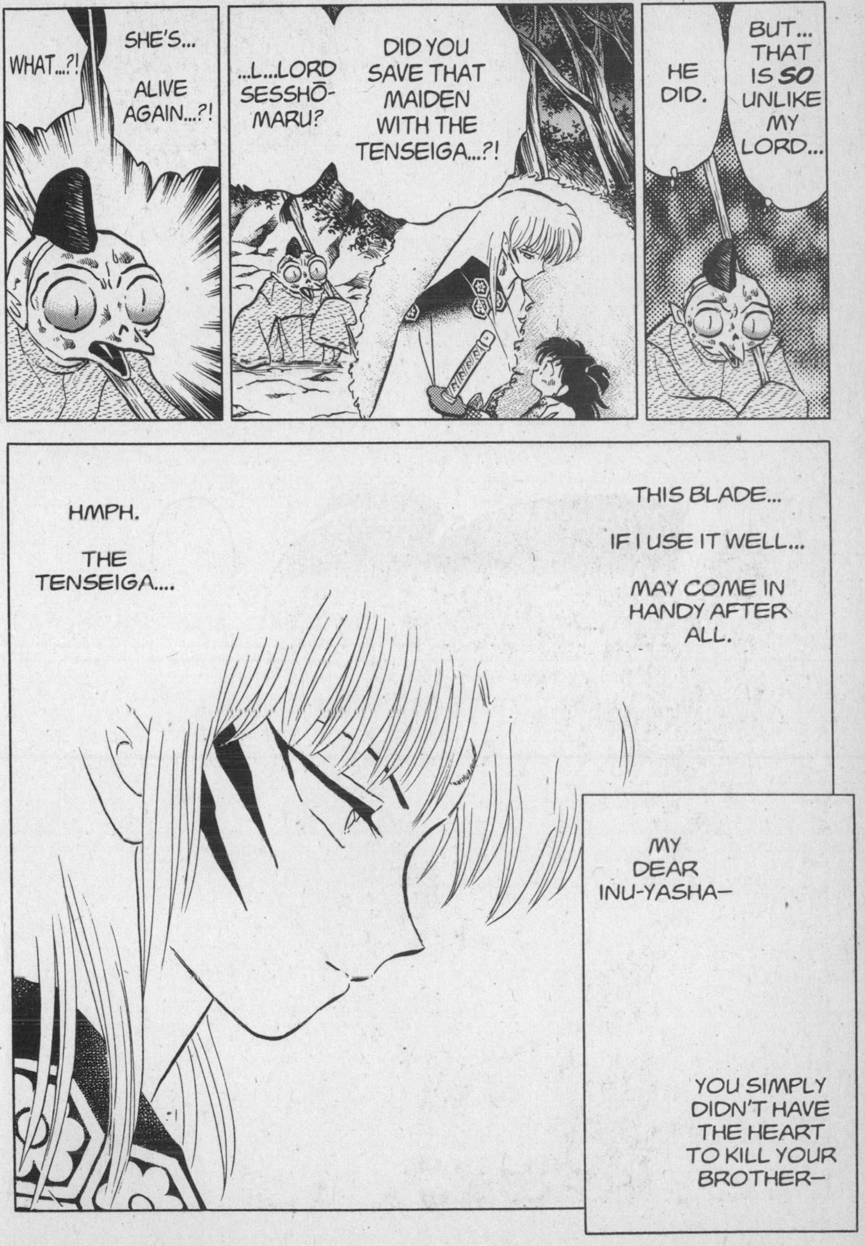
WHAT...?!
SHE'S... ALIVE AGAIN...?!
...L...LORD SESSHŌMARU?
DID YOU SAVE THAT MAIDEN WITH THE TENSEIGA...?!
HE DID.
BUT... THAT IS SO UNLIKE MY LORD...
HMPH.
THE TENSEIGA....
THIS BLADE...
IF I USE IT WELL...
MAY COME IN HANDY AFTER ALL.
MY DEAR INU-YASHA—
YOU SIMPLY DIDN'T HAVE THE HEART TO KILL YOUR BROTHER—

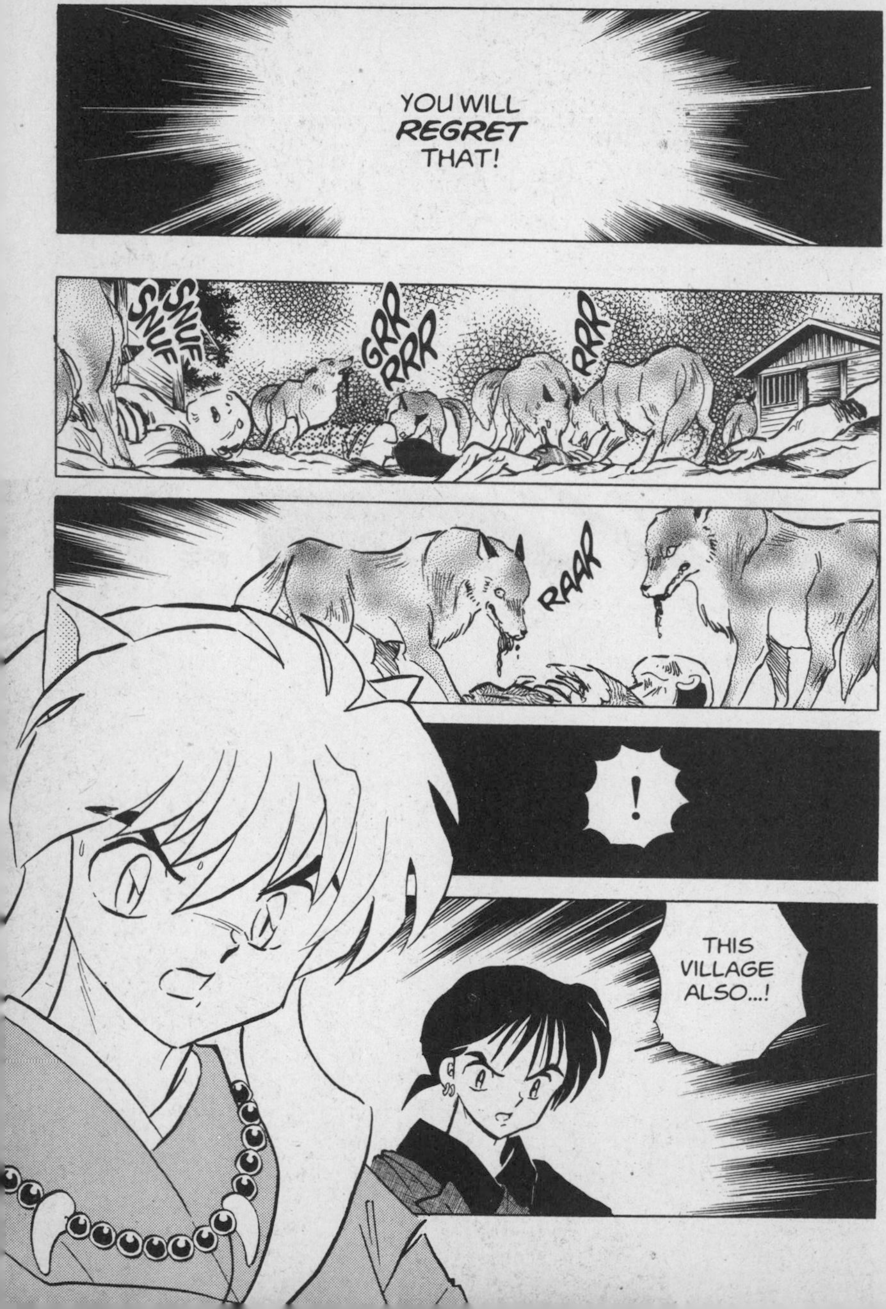
YOU WILL REGRET THAT!
SNUF SNUF
GRR RRR
RRR
RAAR
!
THIS VILLAGE ALSO...!

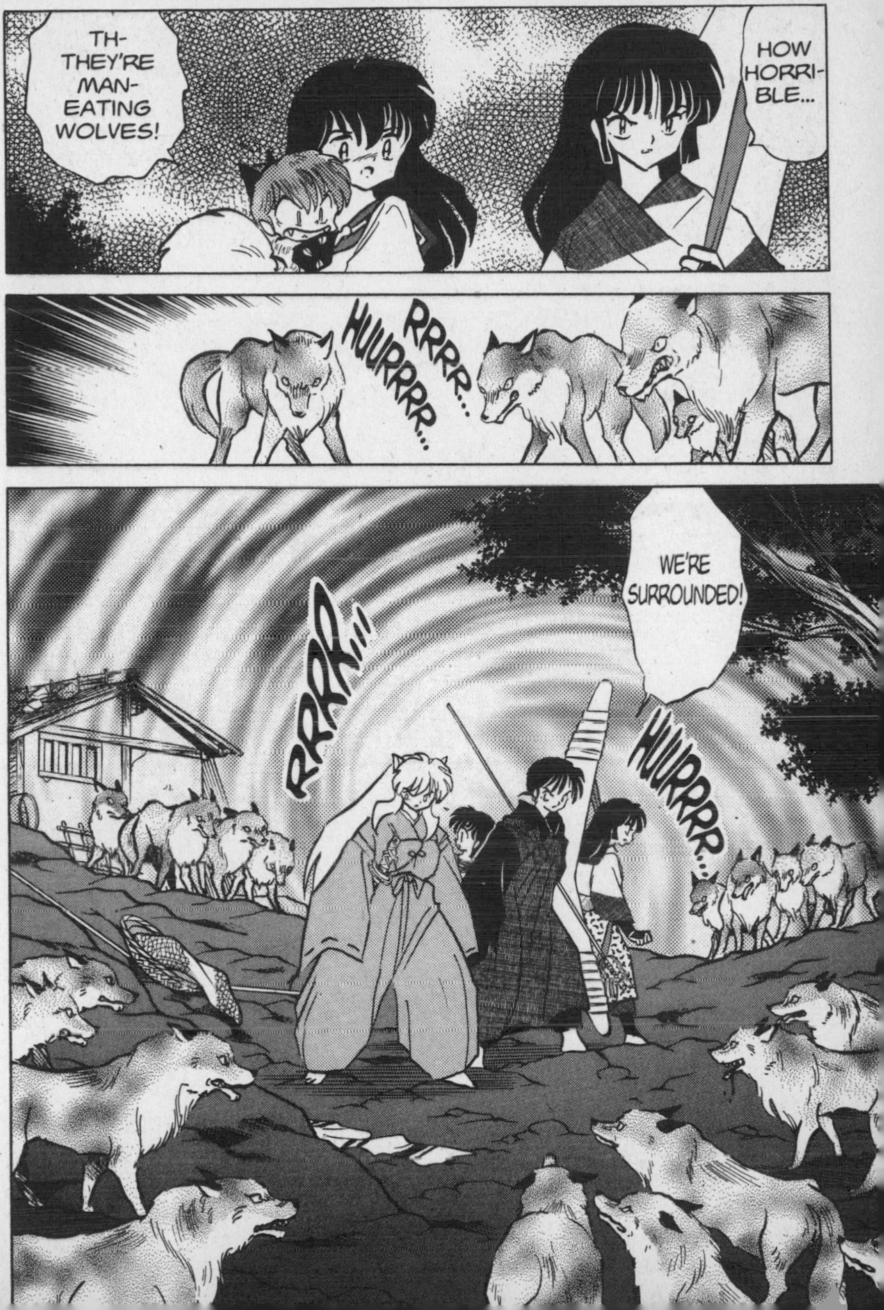
TH-
THEY'RE
MAN-
EATING
WOLVES!
HOW
HORRI-
BLE...
HUURRRRR...
RRRR...
RRRR...!!
WE'RE
SURROUNDED!
HUURRRR...

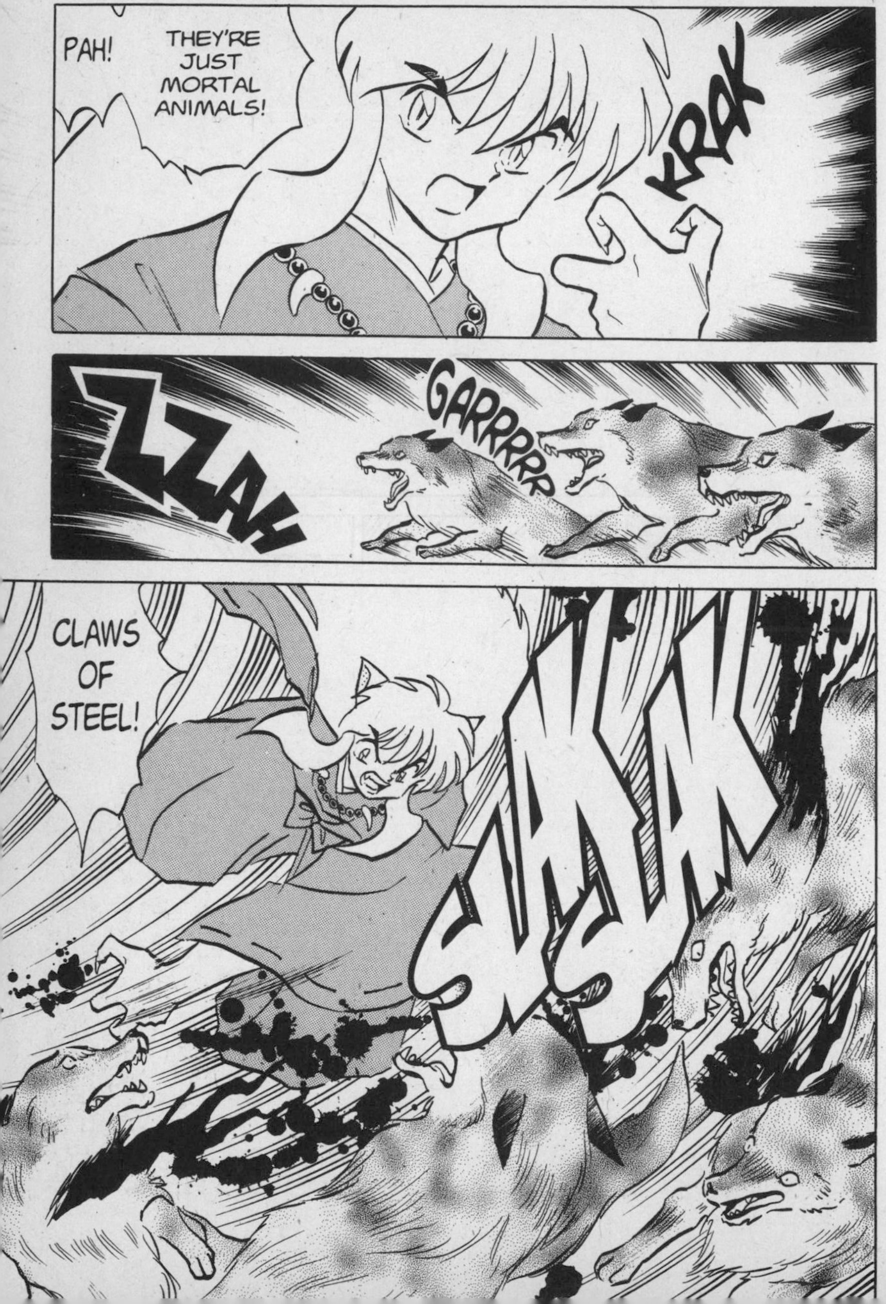
PAH!
THEY'RE JUST MORTAL ANIMALS!
KRAK
ZZAH
GARRRRR
CLAWS OF STEEL!

BOOMERANG BONE!

BOOK BOOK YELP

DRRFF

TMTM

THEY'RE RUNNING AWAY?!

VSSSH ONOOOOO

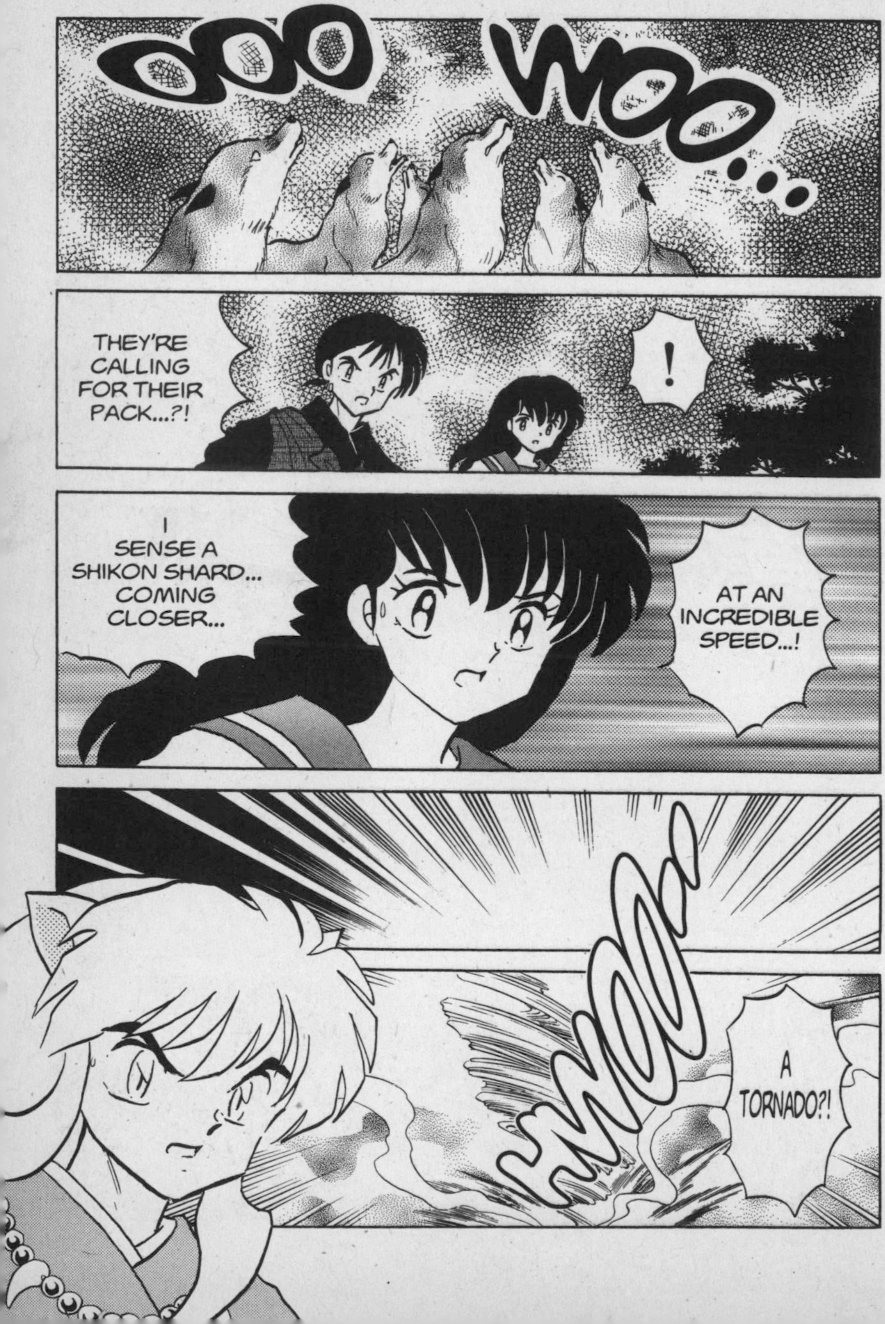
OOO WOO...
THEY'RE CALLING FOR THEIR PACK...?!
!
I SENSE A SHIKON SHARD... COMING CLOSER...
AT AN INCREDIBLE SPEED...!
A TORNADO?!

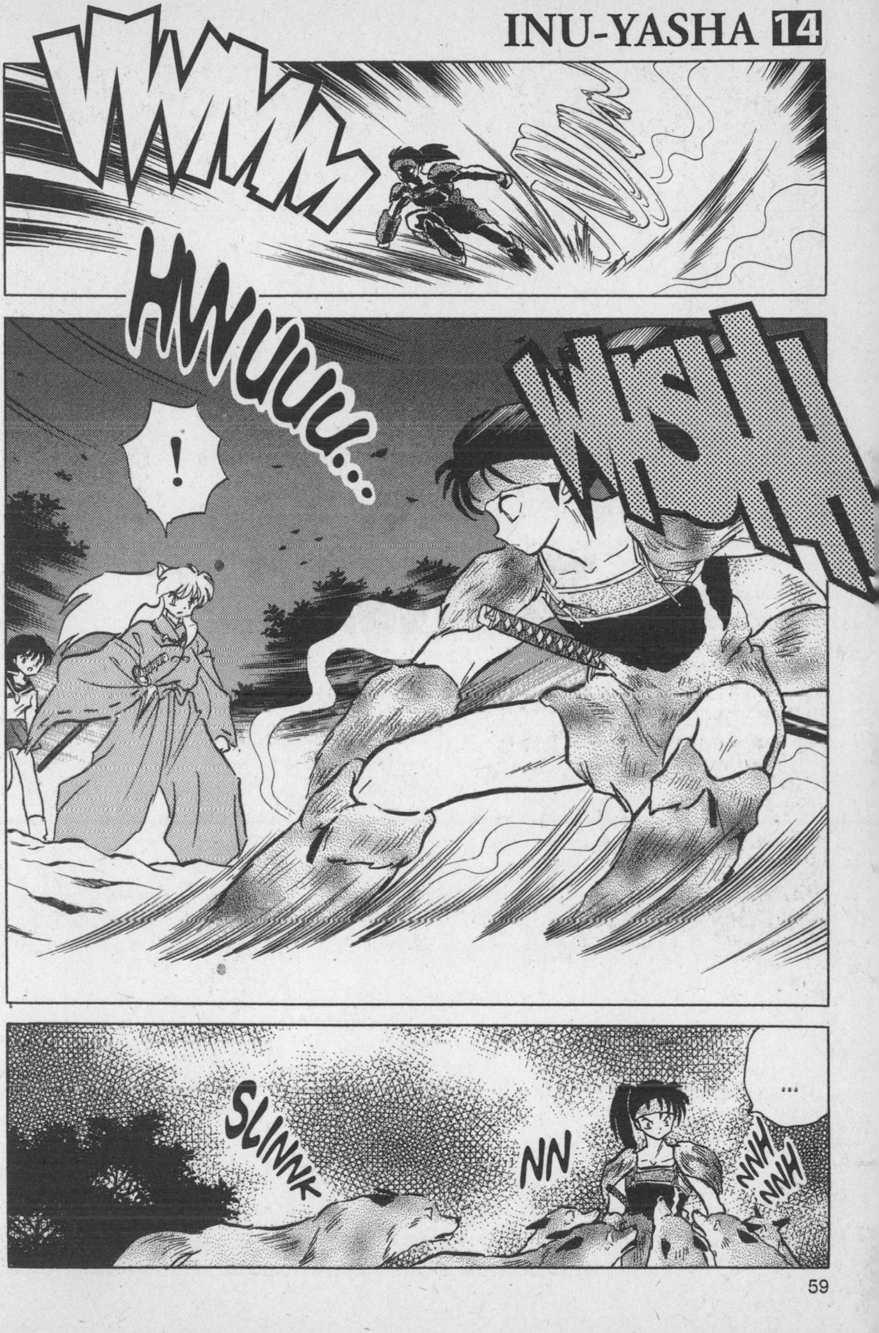
WMM
HWUUUU...
!
WISH
SLINNK
NN
...
NNH NNH

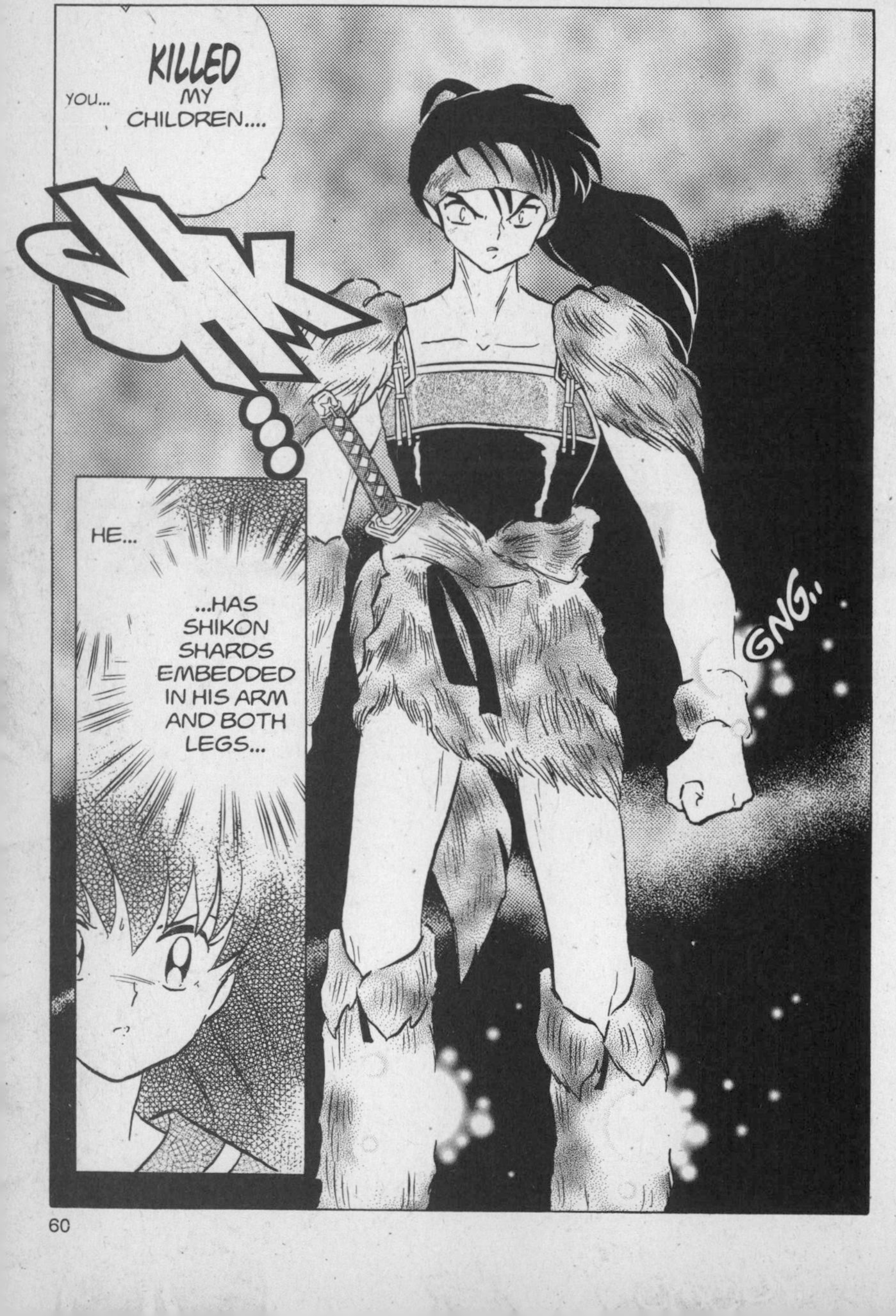
YOU... KILLED MY CHILDREN....
SHK...
HE...
...HAS SHIKON SHARDS EMBEDDED IN HIS ARM AND BOTH LEGS...
GNG..

SCROLL FOUR

KOGA

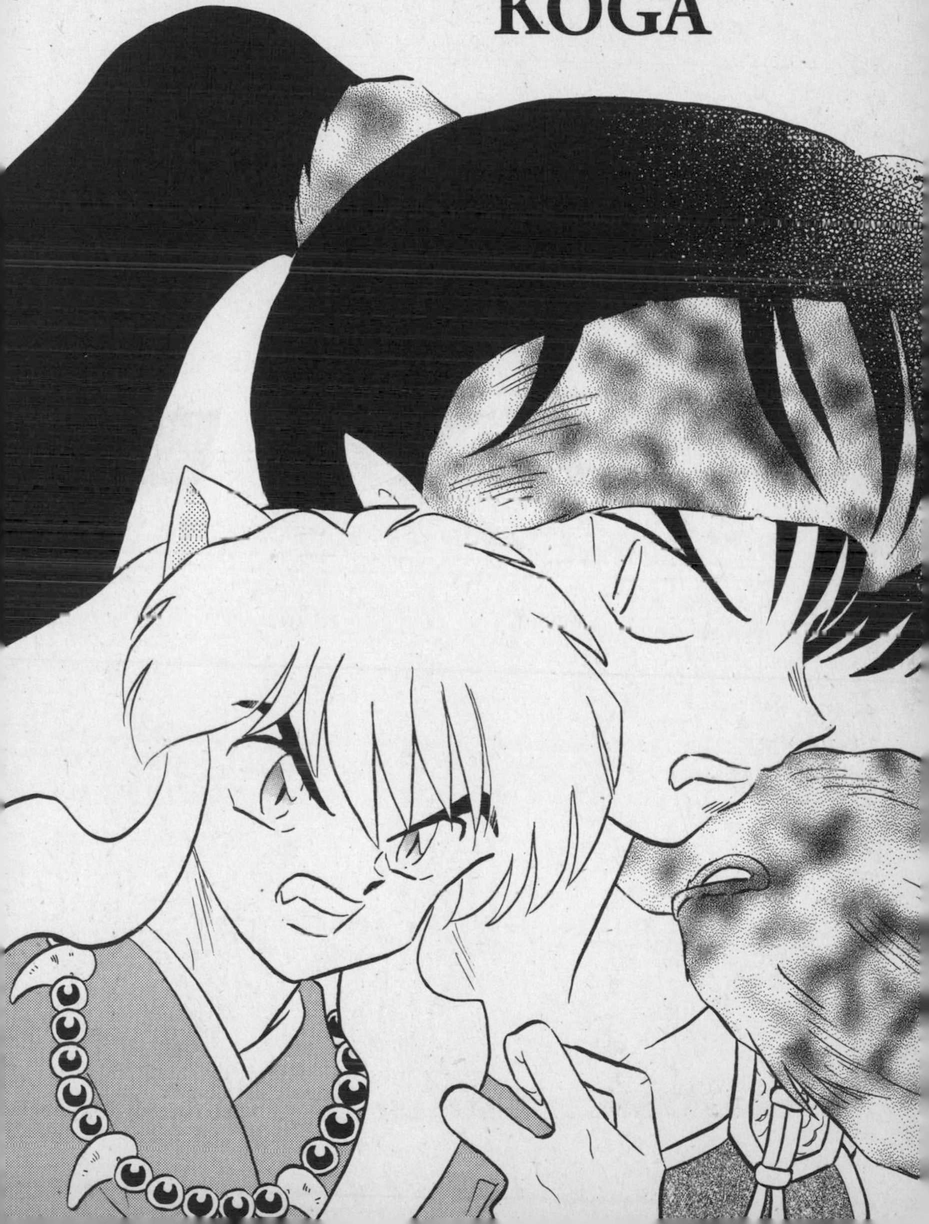

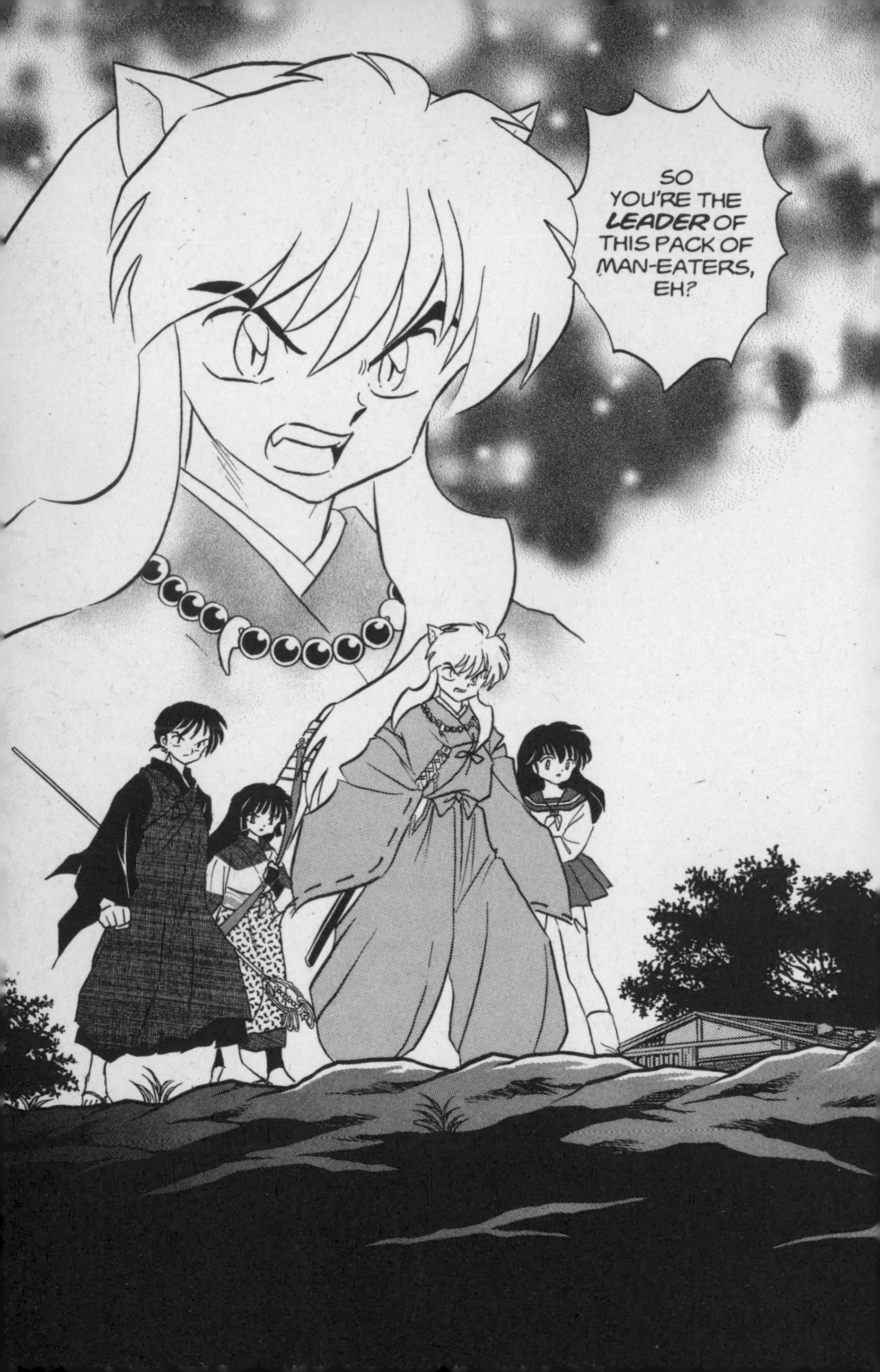
SO YOU'RE THE **LEADER** OF THIS PACK OF MAN-EATERS, EH?

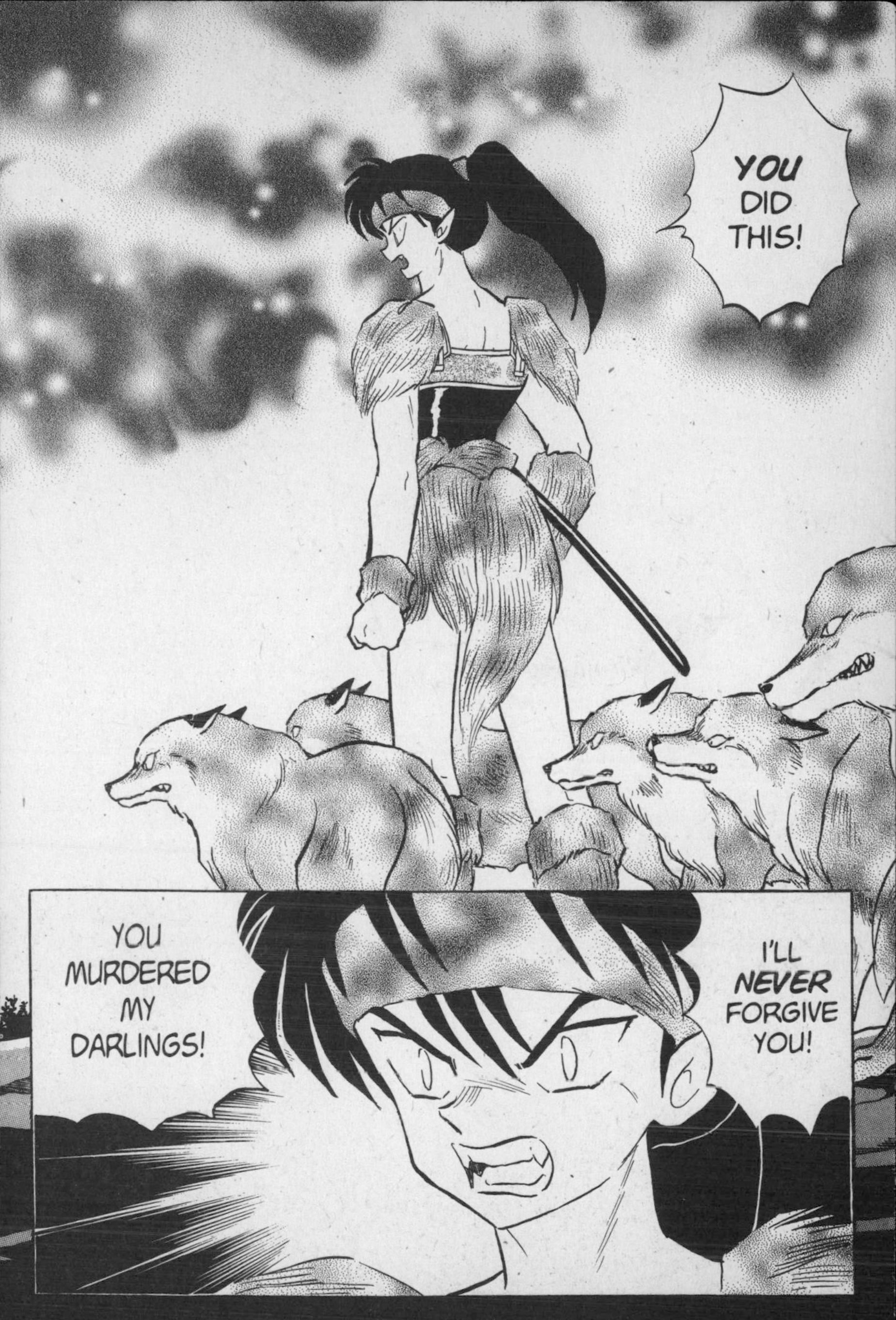

YOU DID THIS!
YOU MURDERED MY DARLINGS!
I'LL ***NEVER*** FORGIVE YOU!

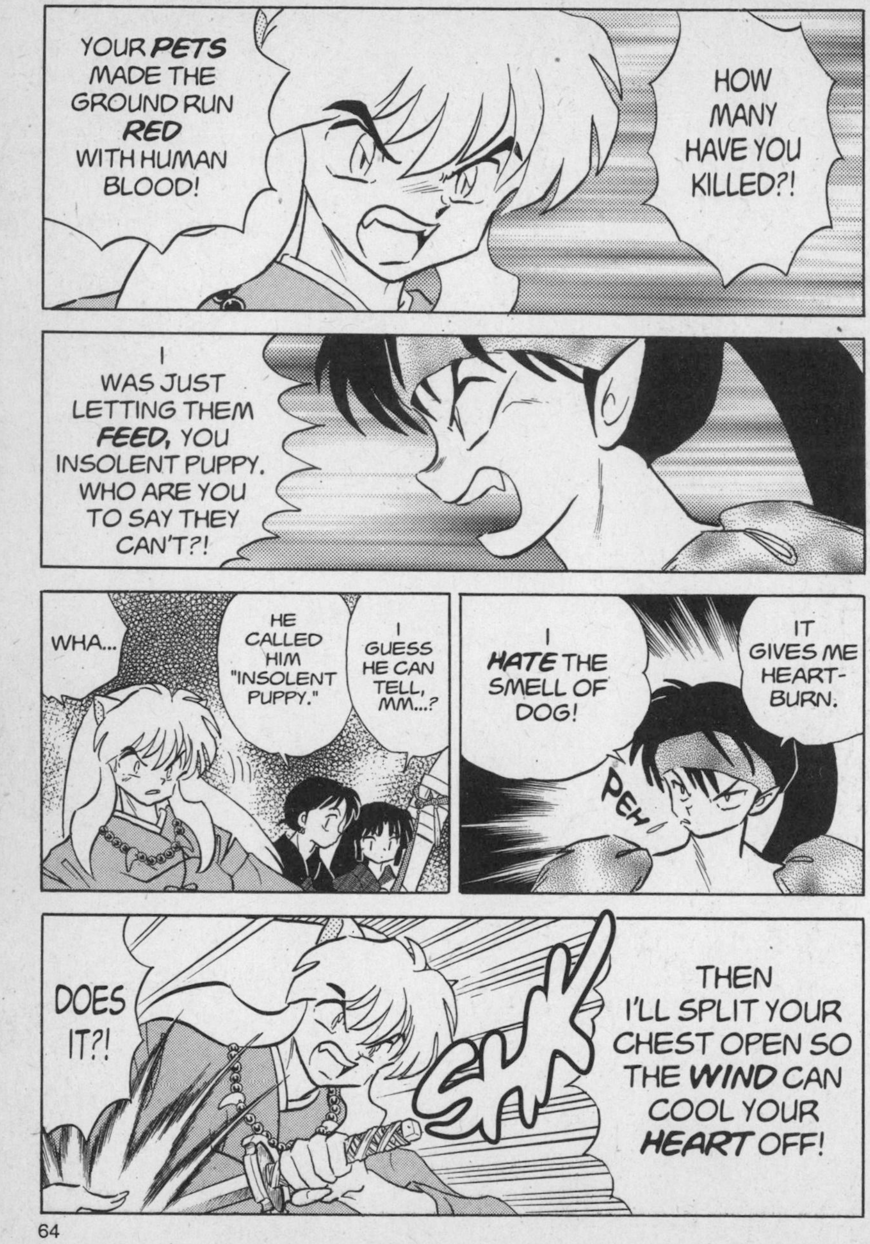
YOUR PETS MADE THE GROUND RUN RED WITH HUMAN BLOOD!
HOW MANY HAVE YOU KILLED?!
I WAS JUST LETTING THEM FEED, YOU INSOLENT PUPPY. WHO ARE YOU TO SAY THEY CAN'T?!
WHA...
HE CALLED HIM "INSOLENT PUPPY."
I GUESS HE CAN TELL, MM...?
I HATE THE SMELL OF DOG!
IT GIVES ME HEART-BURN.
PEH
DOES IT?!
THEN I'LL SPLIT YOUR CHEST OPEN SO THE WIND CAN COOL YOUR HEART OFF!

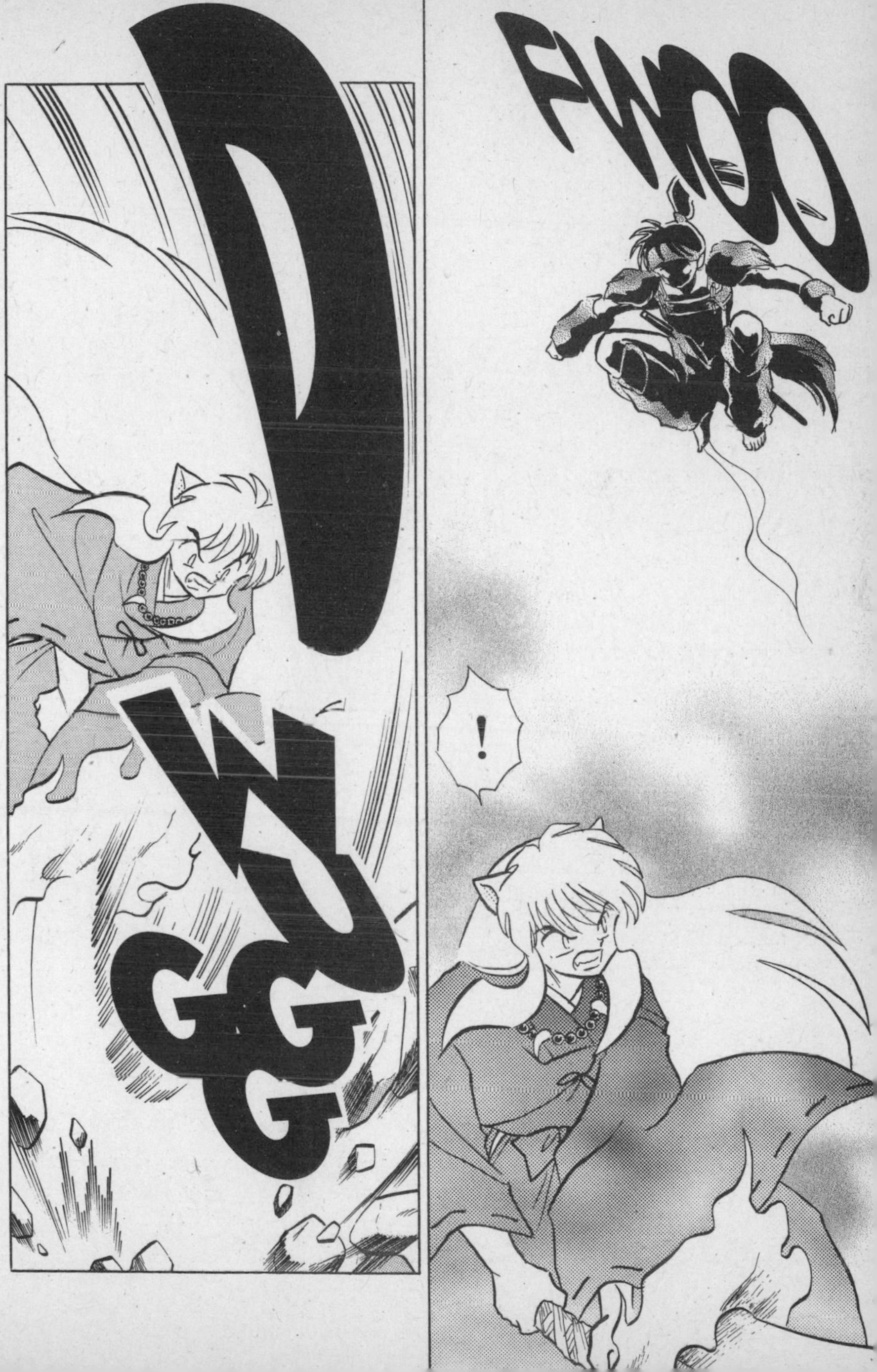
FWOO
!

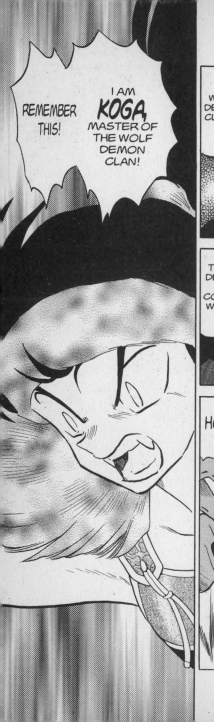

REMEMBER THIS!

I AM **KOGA**, MASTER OF THE WOLF DEMON CLAN!

WOLF DEMON CLAN...?

DO YOU KNOW OF THEM, SANGO?

I DID ONCE HEAR ABOUT THEM FROM A FELLOW EXTERMIN-ATOR.

THEY'RE DEMONS WHO CONTROL WOLVES.

THEY MAY TAKE A HUMAN **FORM**, BUT THEIR TRUE NATURE IS THAT OF THEIR BEASTS-- WILD AND VIOLENT--

HCH!

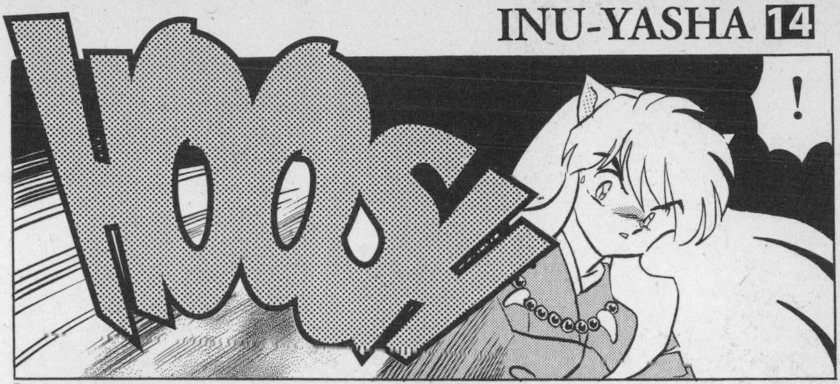
WOOOSH
!

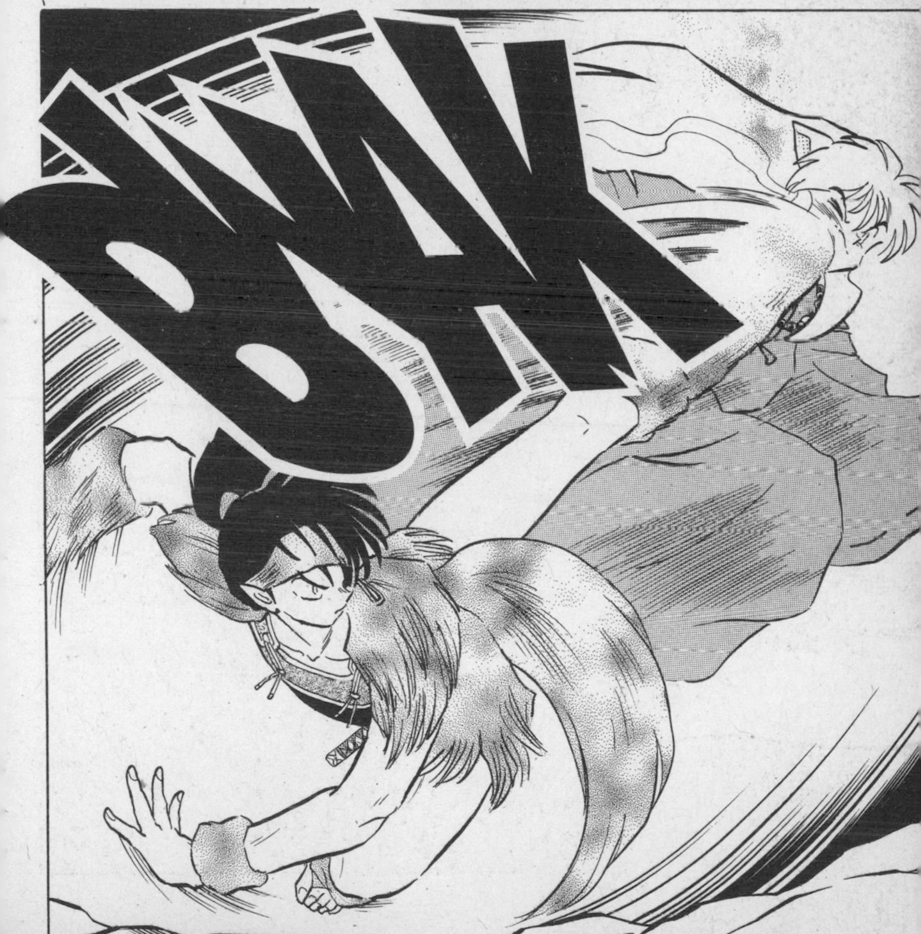

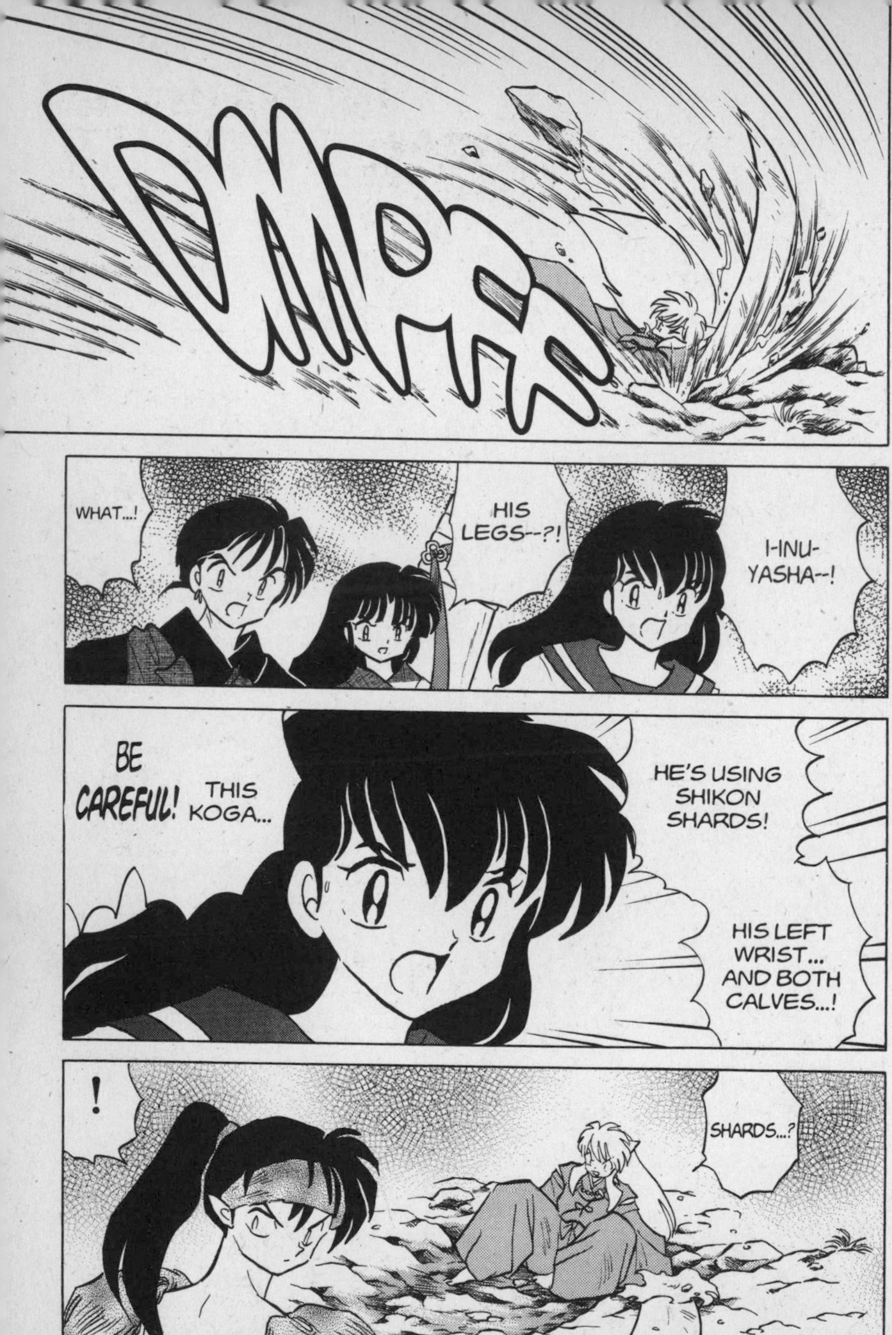
WHAT...!
HIS LEGS--?!
I-INU-YASHA--!
BE CAREFUL!
THIS KOGA...
HE'S USING SHIKON SHARDS!
HIS LEFT WRIST... AND BOTH CALVES...!
!
SHARDS...?

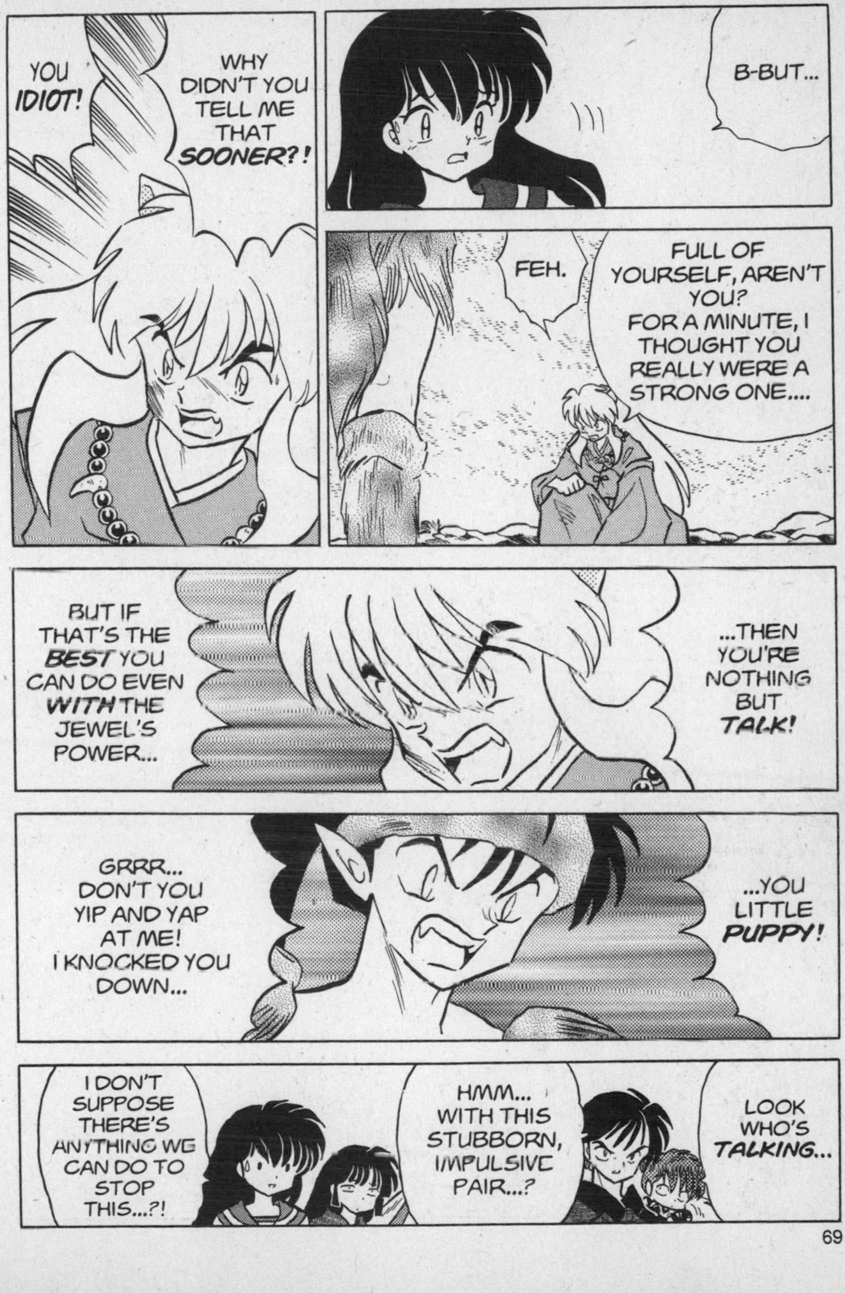
YOU IDIOT!
WHY DIDN'T YOU TELL ME THAT SOONER?!
B-BUT...
FEH.
FULL OF YOURSELF, AREN'T YOU? FOR A MINUTE, I THOUGHT YOU REALLY WERE A STRONG ONE....
BUT IF THAT'S THE BEST YOU CAN DO EVEN WITH THE JEWEL'S POWER...
...THEN YOU'RE NOTHING BUT TALK!
GRRR... DON'T YOU YIP AND YAP AT ME! I KNOCKED YOU DOWN...
...YOU LITTLE PUPPY!
I DON'T SUPPOSE THERE'S ANYTHING WE CAN DO TO STOP THIS...?!
HMM... WITH THIS STUBBORN, IMPULSIVE PAIR...?
LOOK WHO'S TALKING...

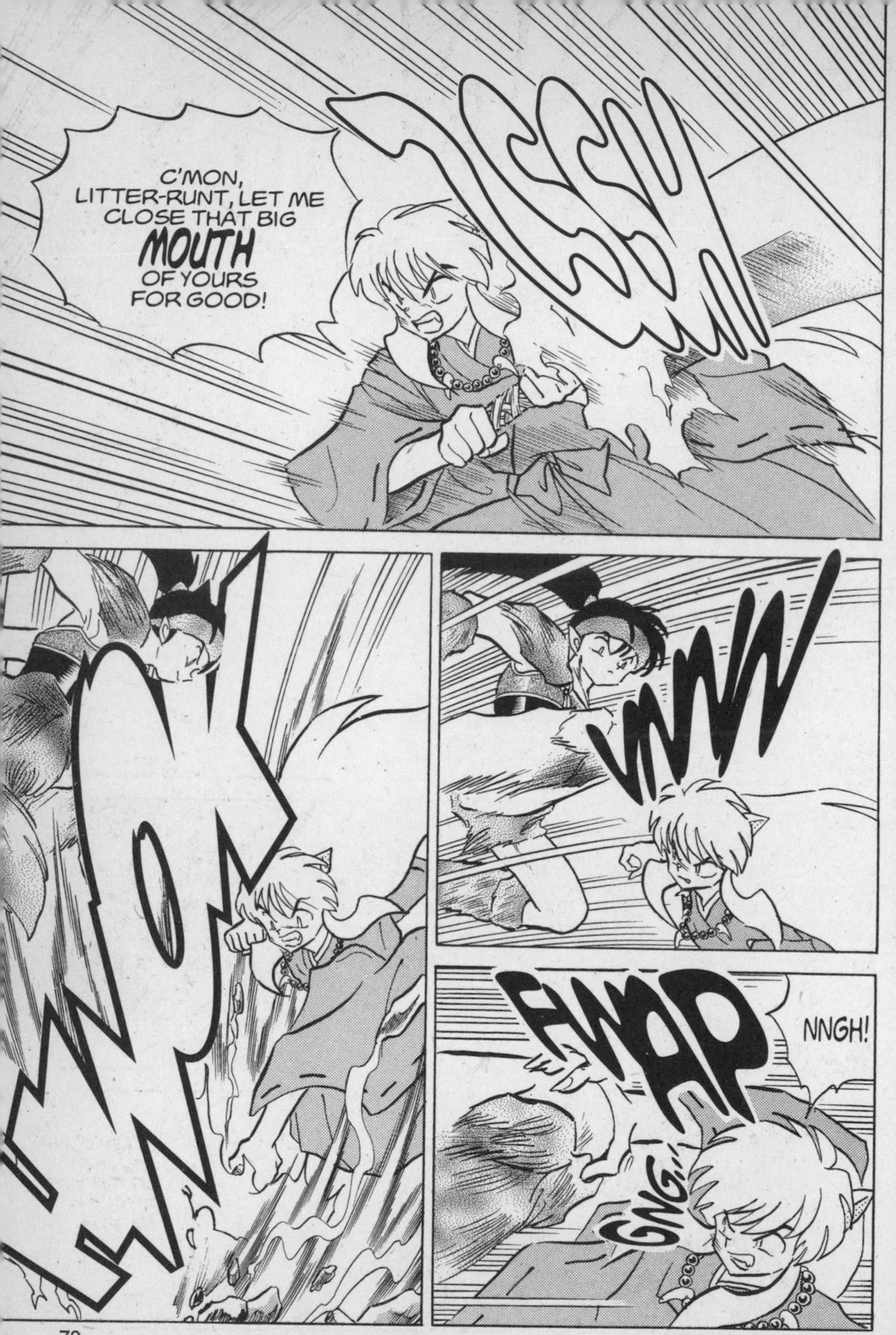
C'MON, LITTER-RUNT, LET ME CLOSE THAT BIG MOUTH OF YOURS FOR GOOD!
FWAP
NNGH!
GNG..!

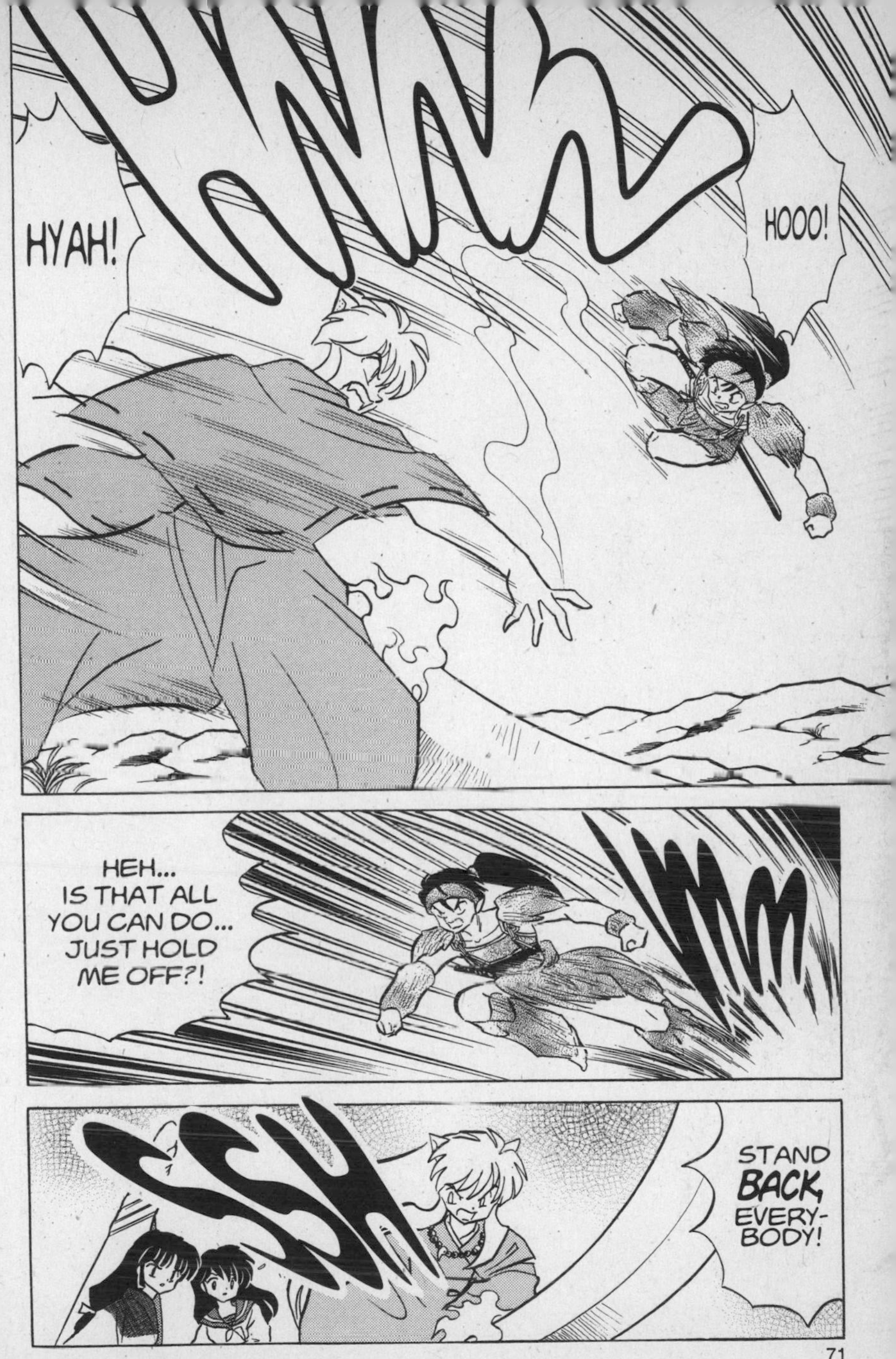
HYAH!
HOOO!
HEH... IS THAT ALL YOU CAN DO... JUST HOLD ME OFF?!
STAND BACK, EVERY-BODY!

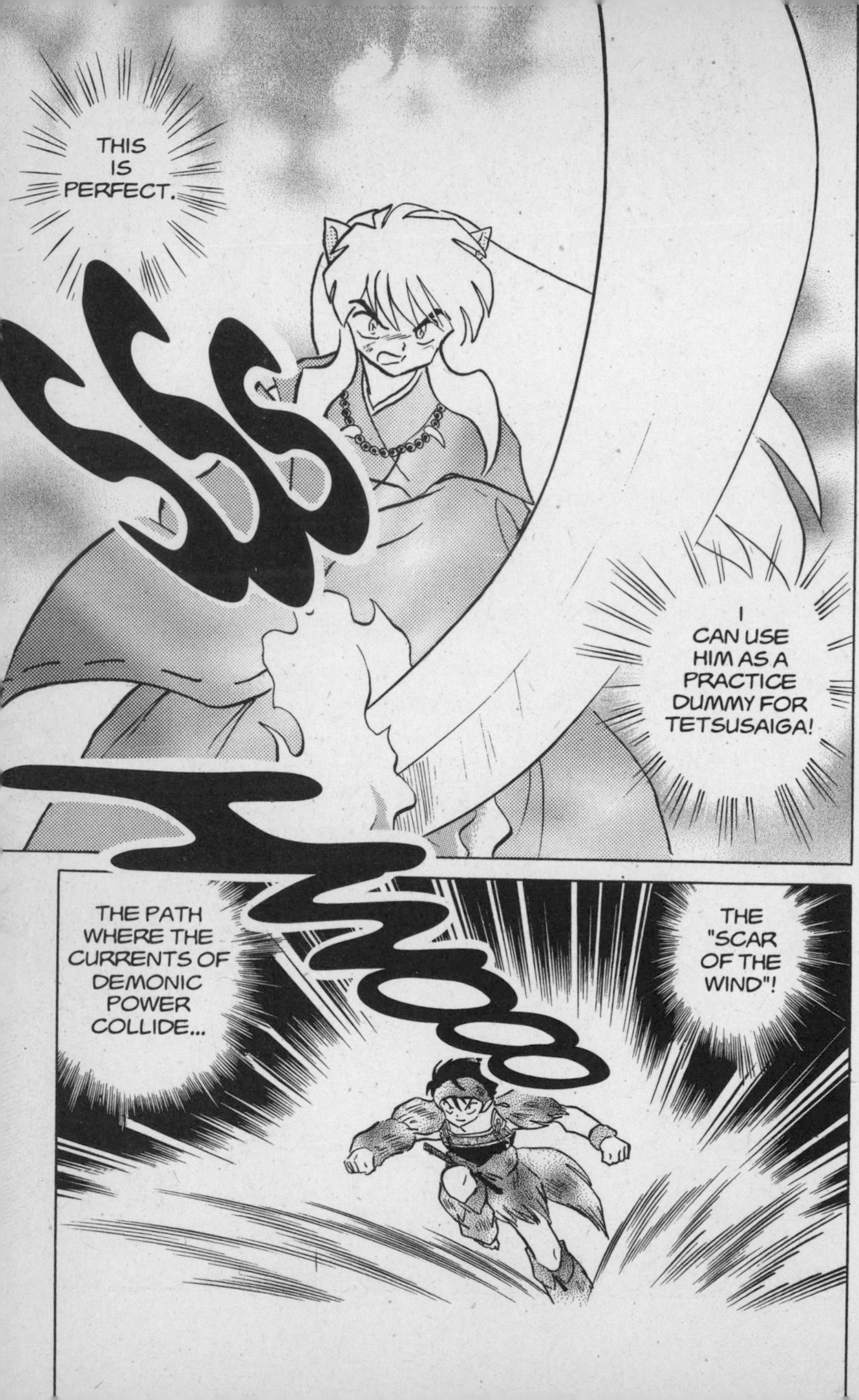
THIS IS PERFECT.
SSSHWOOO
I CAN USE HIM AS A PRACTICE DUMMY FOR TETSUSAIGA!
THE PATH WHERE THE CURRENTS OF DEMONIC POWER COLLIDE...
THE "SCAR OF THE WIND"!

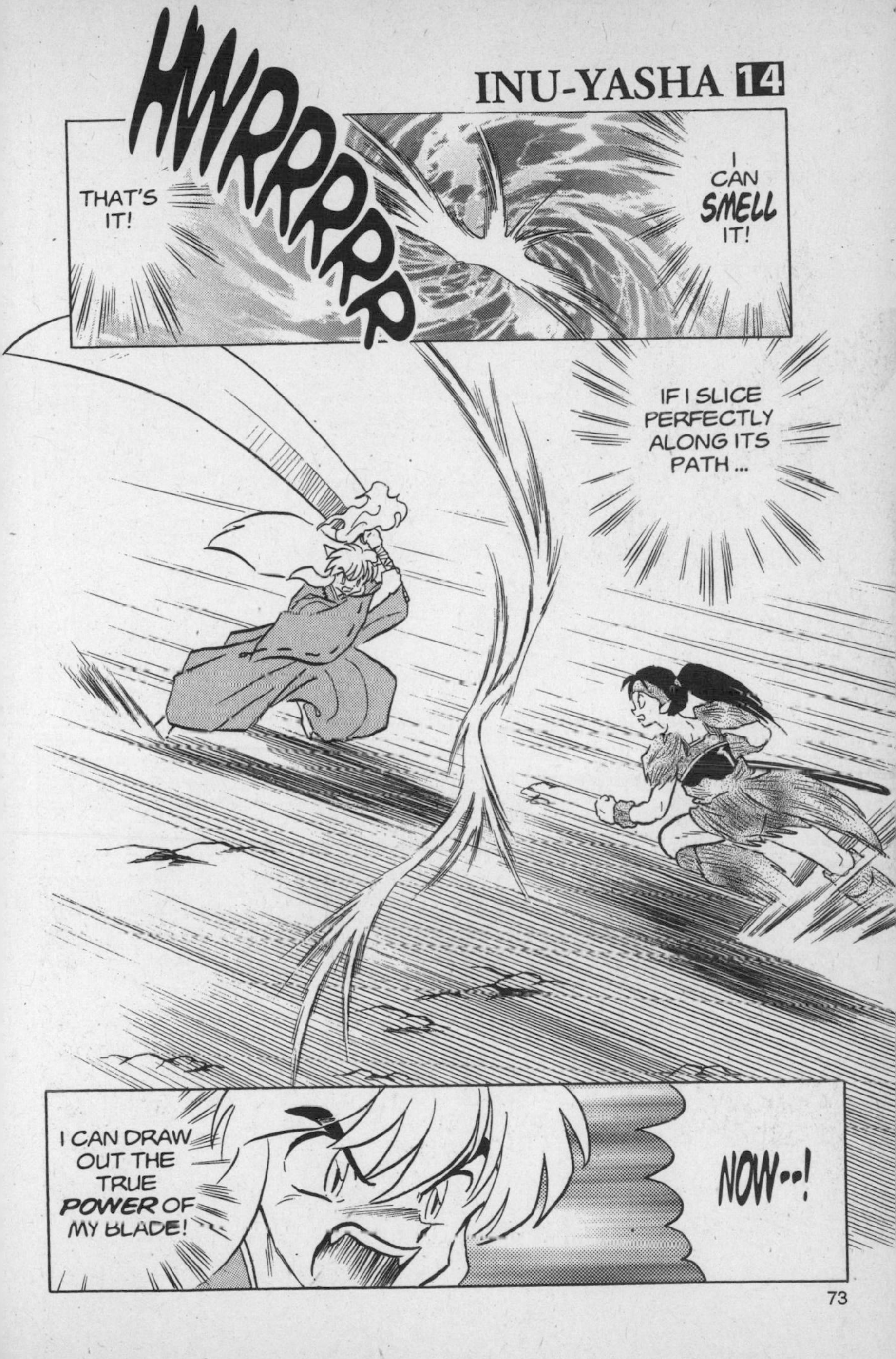
HWRRRRR
THAT'S IT!
I CAN SMELL IT!
IF I SLICE PERFECTLY ALONG ITS PATH ...
I CAN DRAW OUT THE TRUE POWER OF MY BLADE!
NOW--!

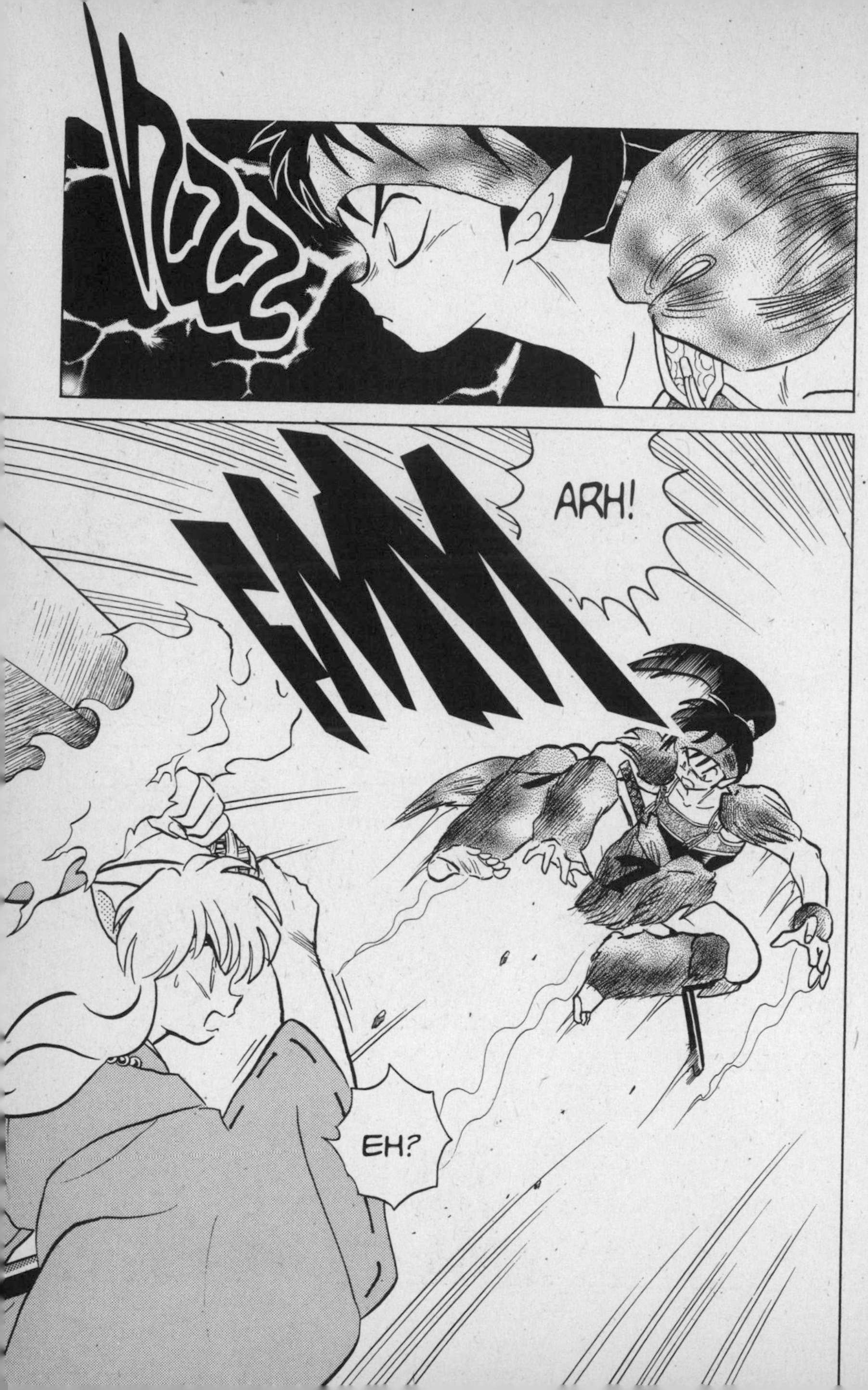
ARH!
EH?

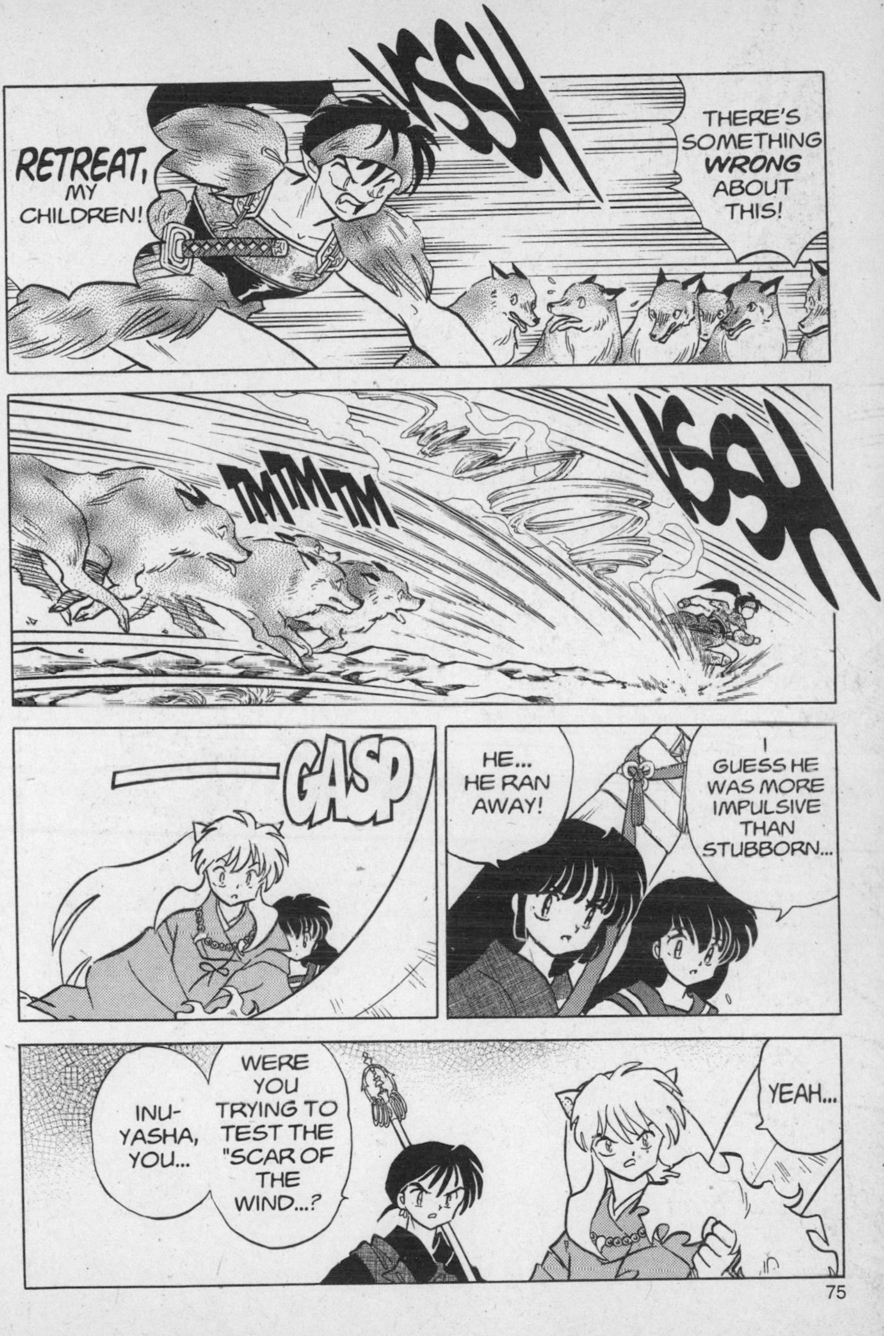
RETREAT, MY CHILDREN!
VSSH
THERE'S SOMETHING WRONG ABOUT THIS!
TMTMTMTM
VSSH
GASP
HE... HE RAN AWAY!
I GUESS HE WAS MORE IMPULSIVE THAN STUBBORN...
INU-YASHA, YOU...
WERE YOU TRYING TO TEST THE "SCAR OF THE WIND...?
YEAH...

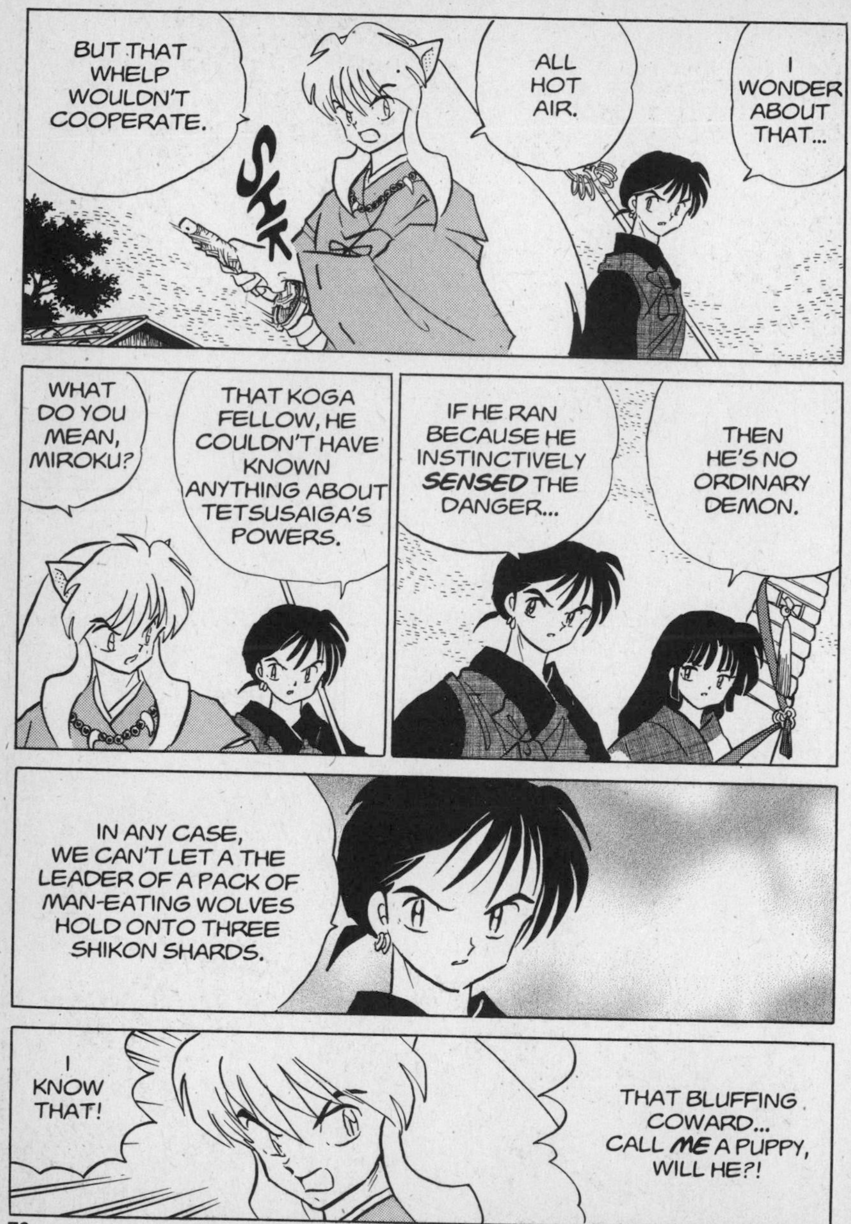
BUT THAT WHELP WOULDN'T COOPERATE.
SHK
ALL HOT AIR.
I WONDER ABOUT THAT...
WHAT DO YOU MEAN, MIROKU?
THAT KOGA FELLOW, HE COULDN'T HAVE KNOWN ANYTHING ABOUT TETSUSAIGA'S POWERS.
IF HE RAN BECAUSE HE INSTINCTIVELY *SENSED* THE DANGER...
THEN HE'S NO ORDINARY DEMON.
IN ANY CASE, WE CAN'T LET A THE LEADER OF A PACK OF MAN-EATING WOLVES HOLD ONTO THREE SHIKON SHARDS.
I KNOW THAT!
THAT BLUFFING COWARD... CALL *ME* A PUPPY, WILL HE?!

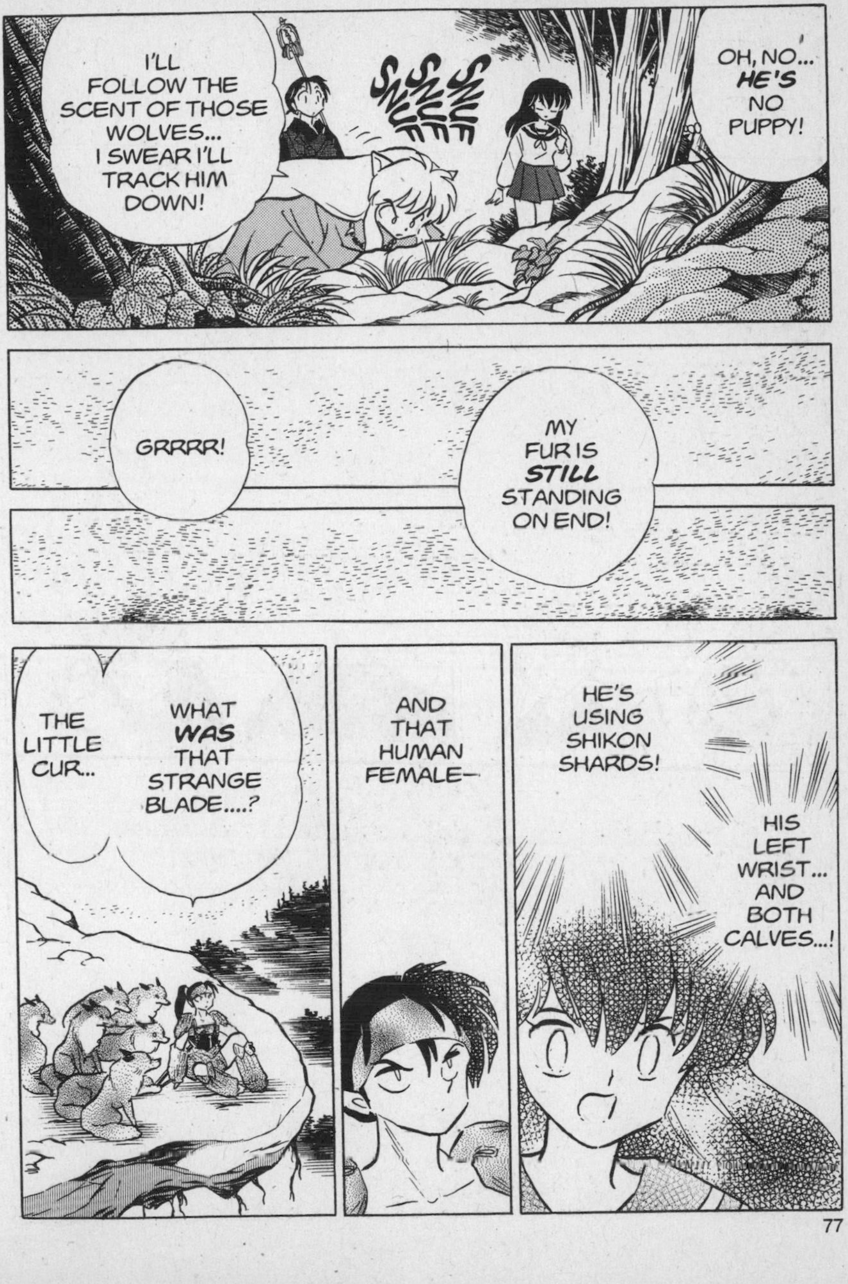
I'LL FOLLOW THE SCENT OF THOSE WOLVES... I SWEAR I'LL TRACK HIM DOWN!
SNUF SNUF SNUF
OH, NO... **HE'S** NO PUPPY!
GRRRR!
MY FUR IS **STILL** STANDING ON END!
THE LITTLE CUR...
WHAT **WAS** THAT STRANGE BLADE....?
AND THAT HUMAN FEMALE—
HE'S USING SHIKON SHARDS!
HIS LEFT WRIST... AND BOTH CALVES...!

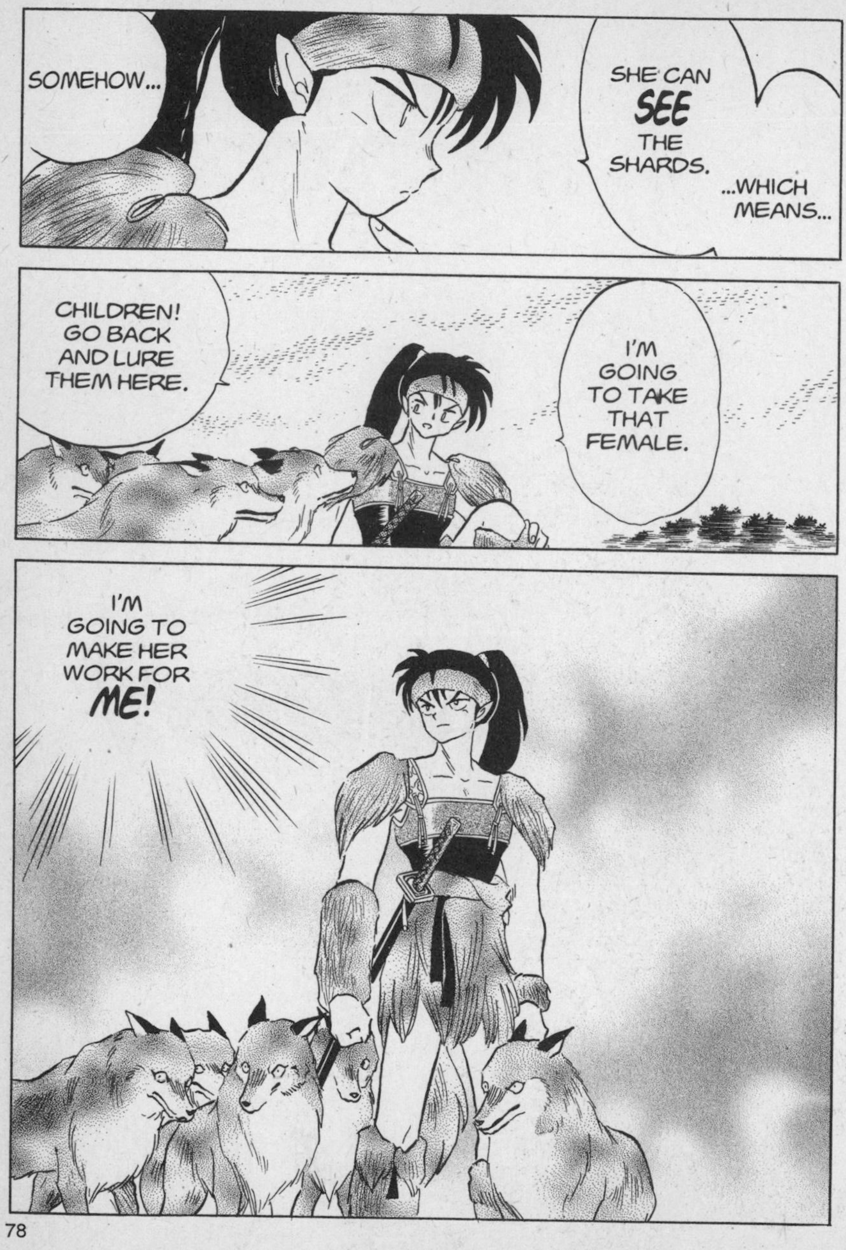

SOMEHOW...
SHE CAN SEE THE SHARDS.
...WHICH MEANS...
CHILDREN! GO BACK AND LURE THEM HERE.
I'M GOING TO TAKE THAT FEMALE.
I'M GOING TO MAKE HER WORK FOR ME!

SCROLL FIVE
HOSTAGE

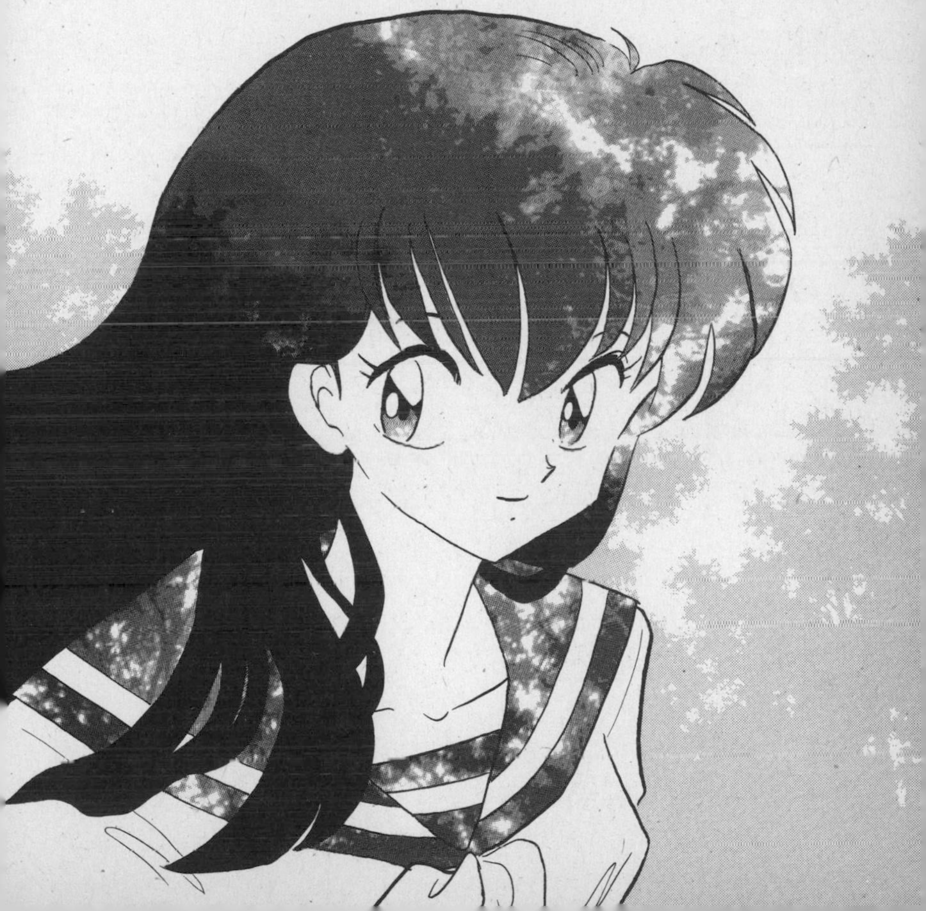

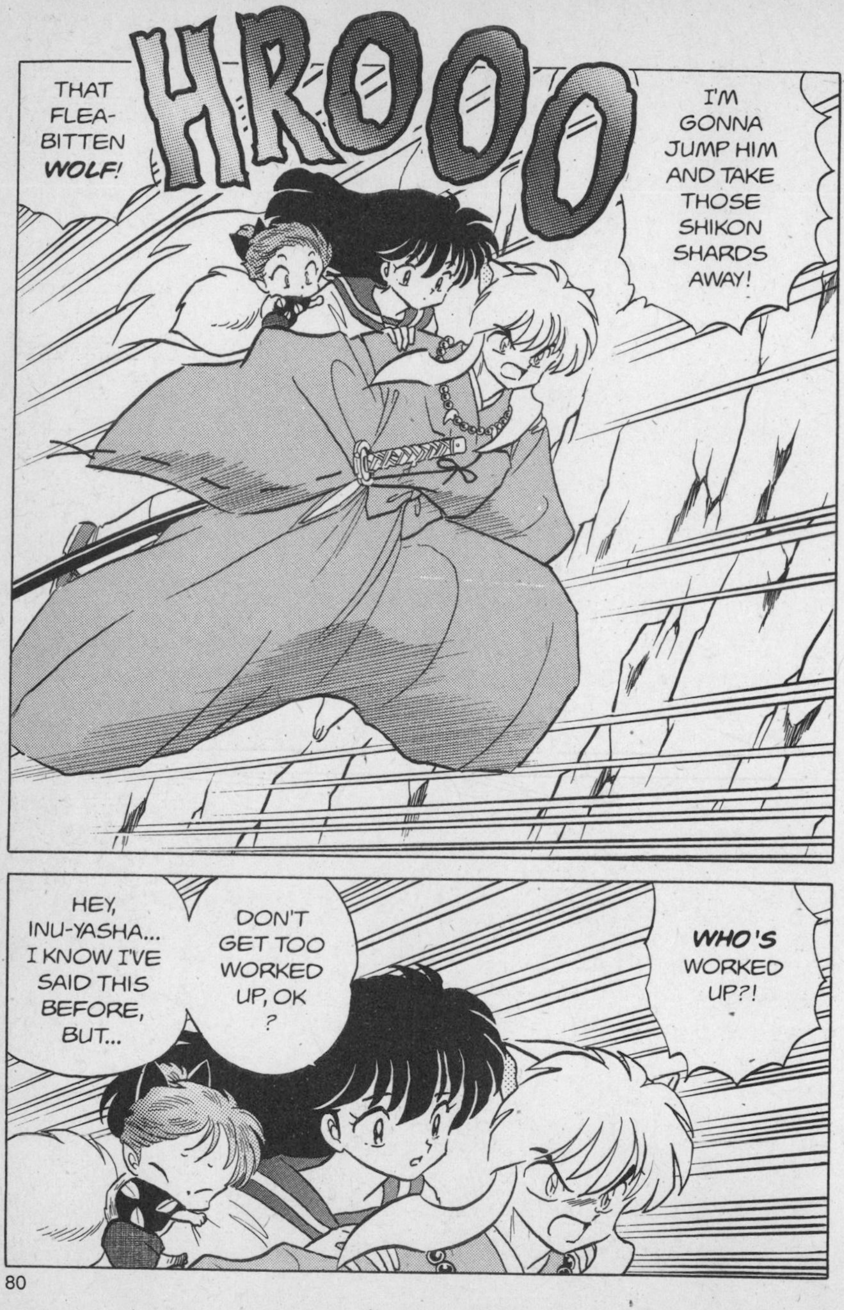
HROOO
THAT FLEA-BITTEN *WOLF!*
I'M GONNA JUMP HIM AND TAKE THOSE SHIKON SHARDS AWAY!
HEY, INU-YASHA... I KNOW I'VE SAID THIS BEFORE, BUT...
DON'T GET TOO WORKED UP, OK ?
WHO'S WORKED UP?!

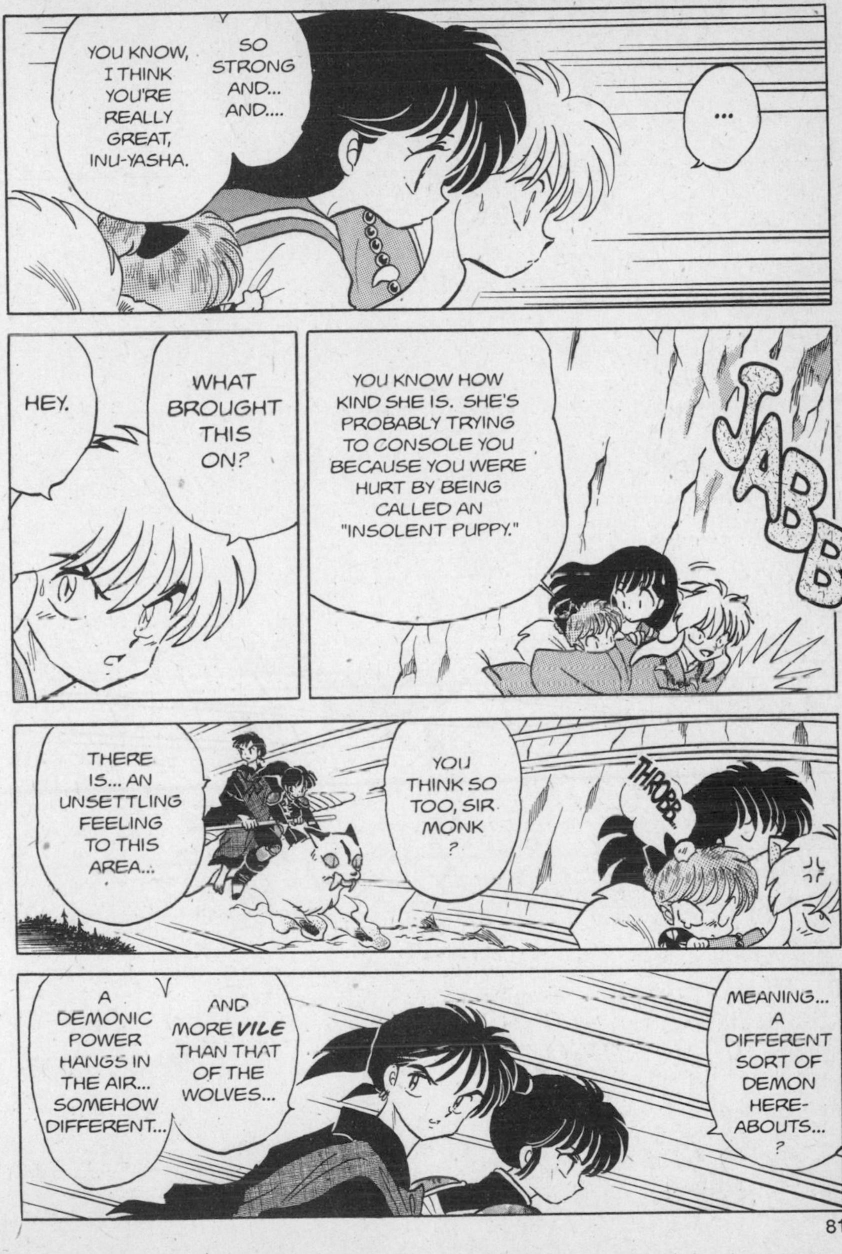
YOU KNOW, I THINK YOU'RE REALLY GREAT, INU-YASHA.
SO STRONG AND... AND....
...
HEY.
WHAT BROUGHT THIS ON?
YOU KNOW HOW KIND SHE IS. SHE'S PROBABLY TRYING TO CONSOLE YOU BECAUSE YOU WERE HURT BY BEING CALLED AN "INSOLENT PUPPY."
JABB
THERE IS... AN UNSETTLING FEELING TO THIS AREA...
YOU THINK SO TOO, SIR MONK?
THROBB...
A DEMONIC POWER HANGS IN THE AIR... SOMEHOW DIFFERENT...
AND MORE **VILE** THAN THAT OF THE WOLVES...
MEANING... A DIFFERENT SORT OF DEMON HERE-ABOUTS...?

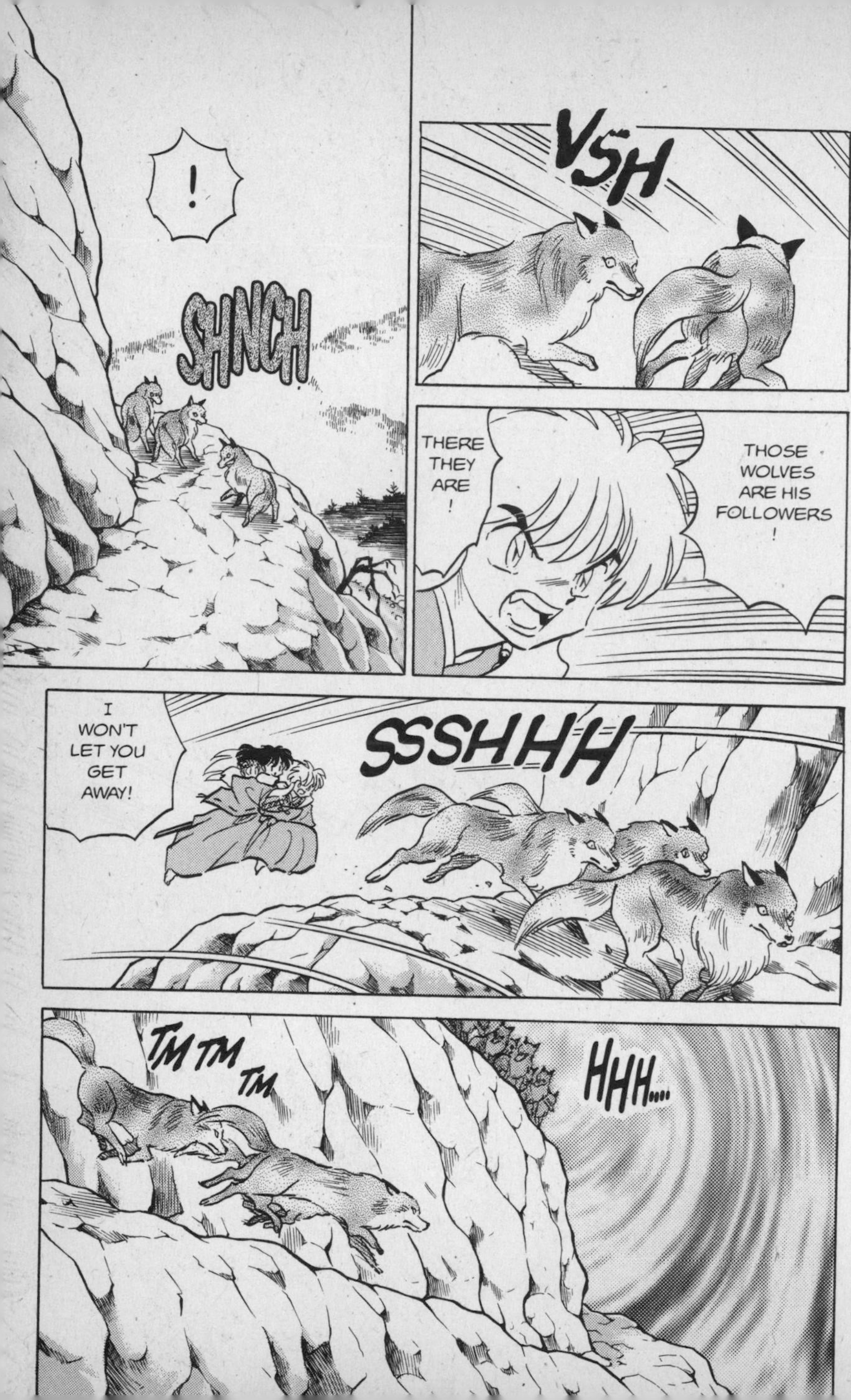
!
SHNCH
VSH
THERE THEY ARE!
THOSE WOLVES ARE HIS FOLLOWERS!
I WON'T LET YOU GET AWAY!
SSSHHH
TM TM TM
HHH....

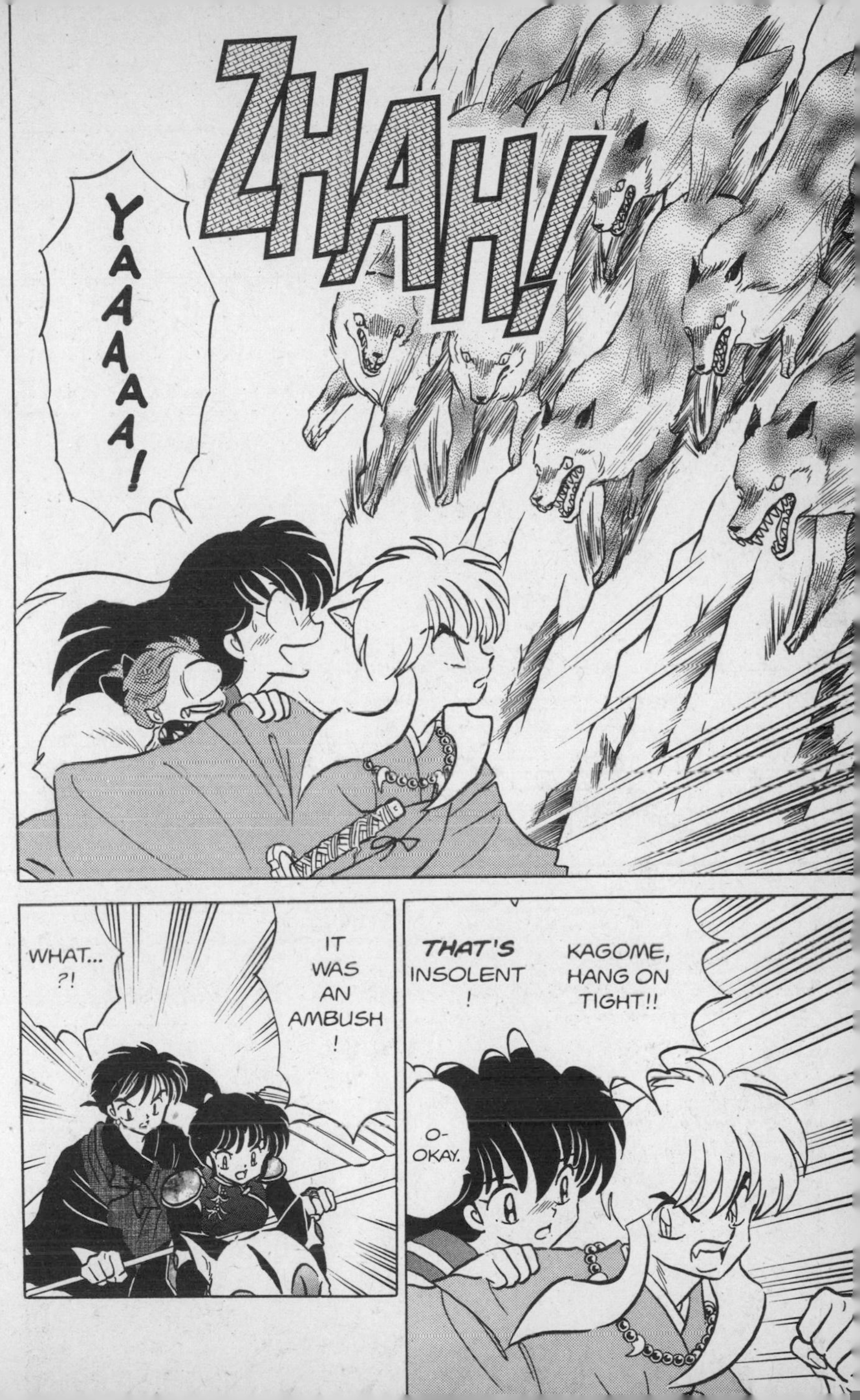
ZHAH!
YAAAAAA!
WHAT... ?!
IT WAS AN AMBUSH!
THAT'S INSOLENT!
KAGOME, HANG ON TIGHT!!
O-OKAY.

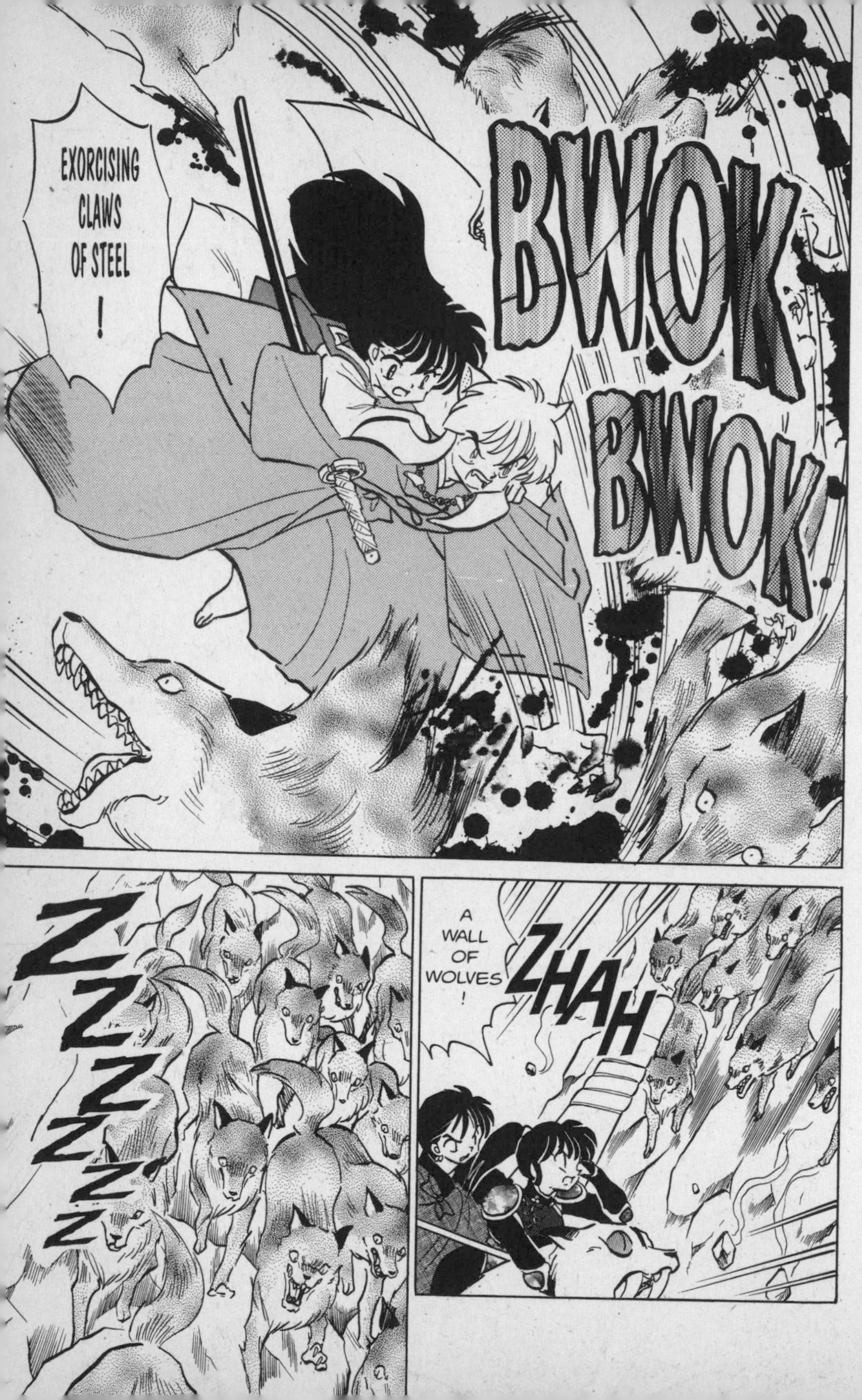
EXORCISING CLAWS OF STEEL !
BWOK
BWOK
ZZZZZZZ
A WALL OF WOLVES !
ZHAH

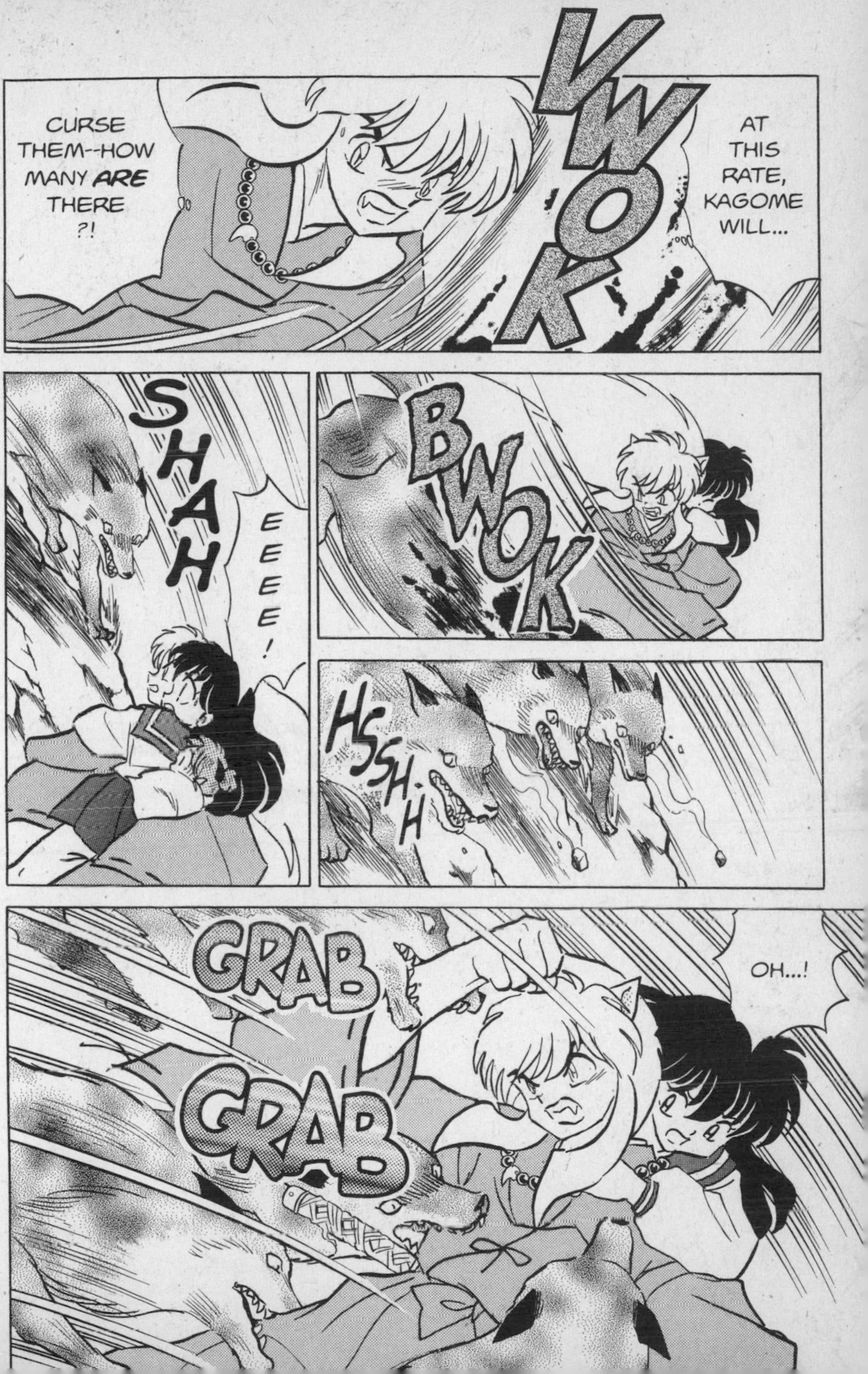
CURSE THEM--HOW MANY **ARE** THERE ?!
VWOK
AT THIS RATE, KAGOME WILL...
SHAH
EEEEE!
BWOK
HSSSHH
GRAB
GRAB
OH...!

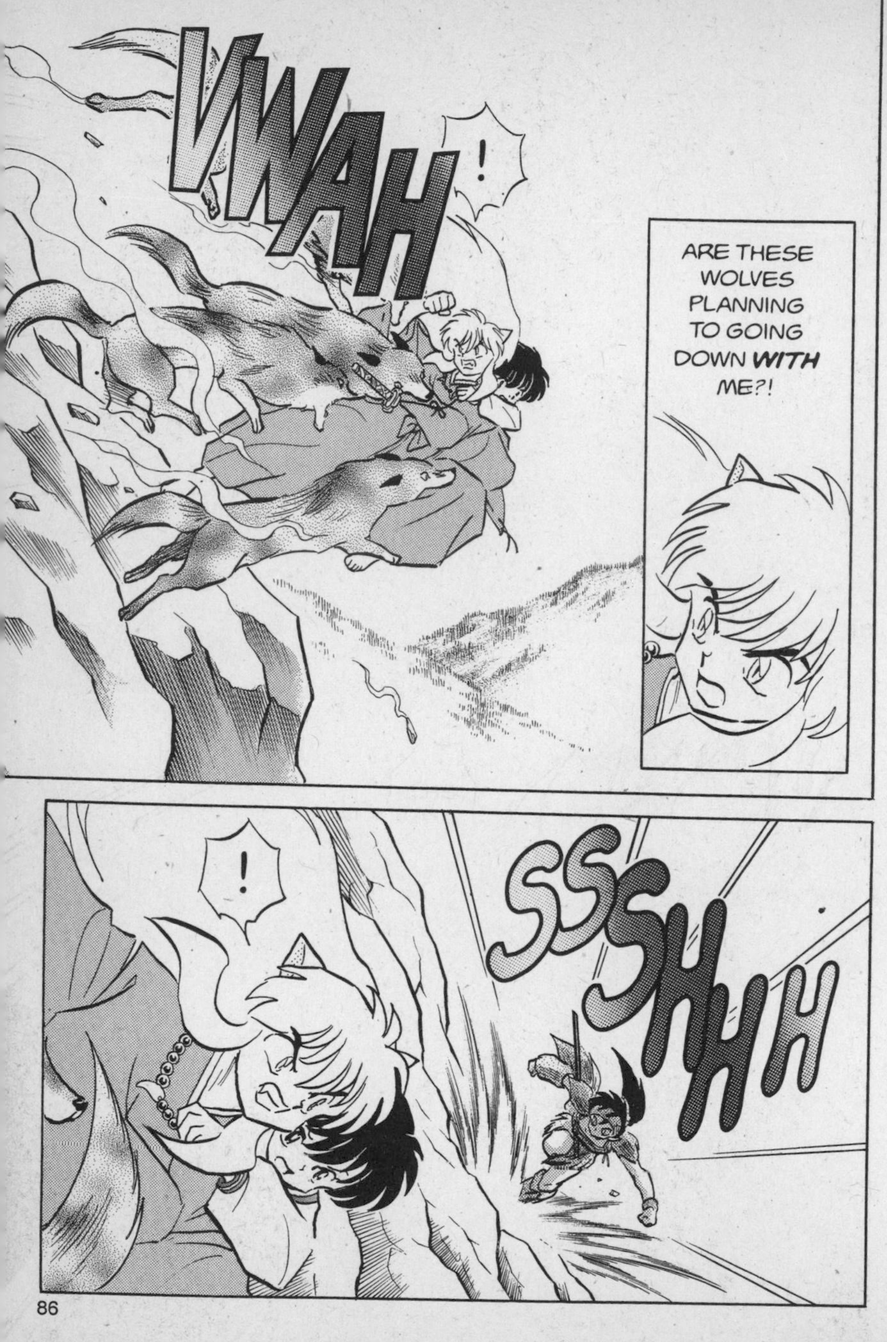

VWAH
!
ARE THESE WOLVES PLANNING TO GOING DOWN **WITH** ME?!
!
SSSHHHH

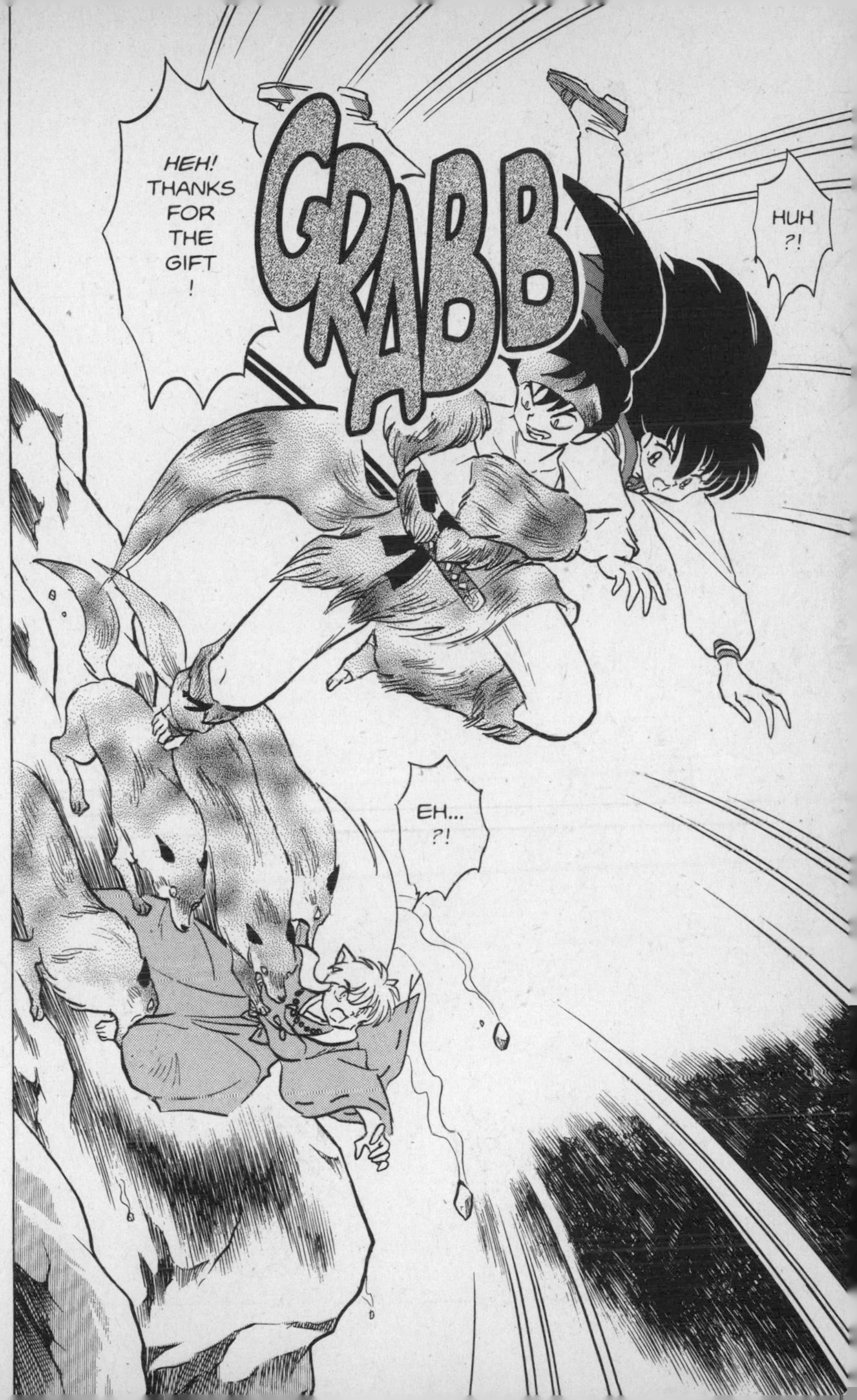
HEH! THANKS FOR THE GIFT !
GRABB
HUH ?!
EH... ?!

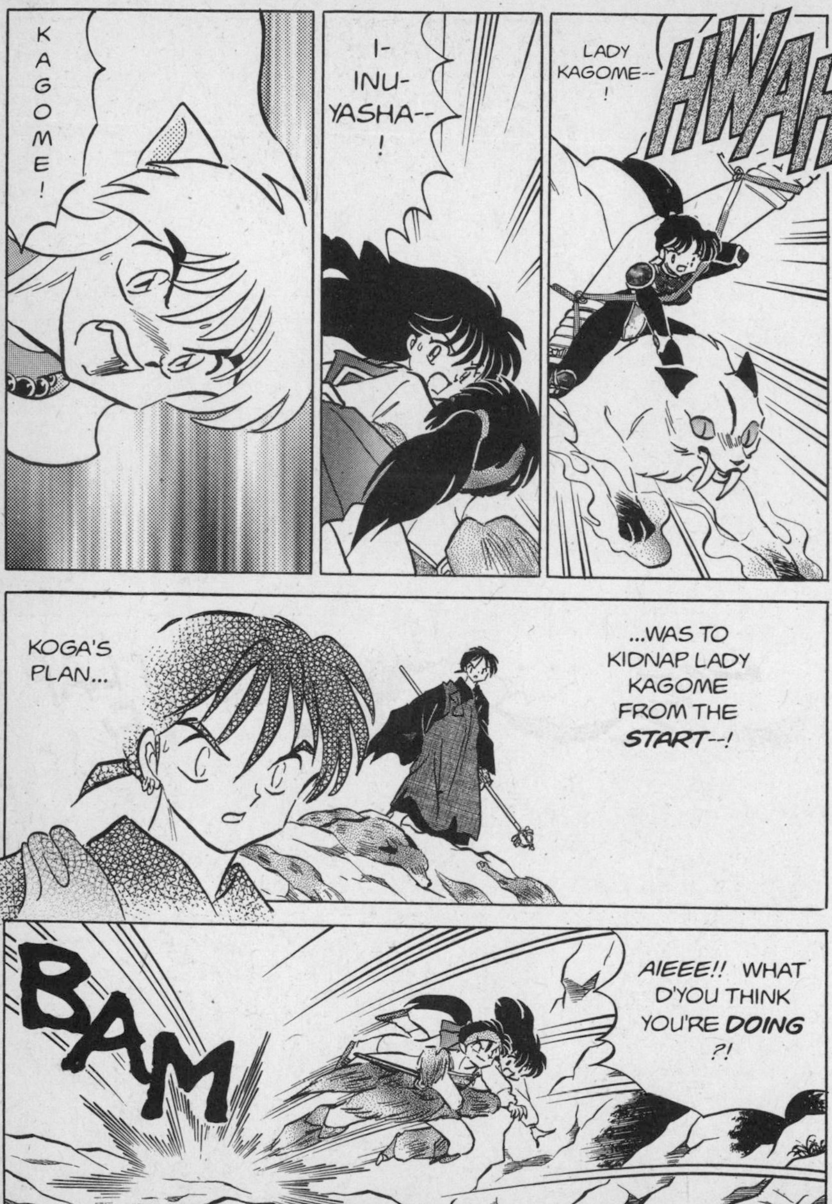
KAGOME!
I-INU-YASHA--!
LADY KAGOME--!
HWAH
KOGA'S PLAN...
...WAS TO KIDNAP LADY KAGOME FROM THE START--!
BAM
AIEEE!! WHAT D'YOU THINK YOU'RE DOING?!

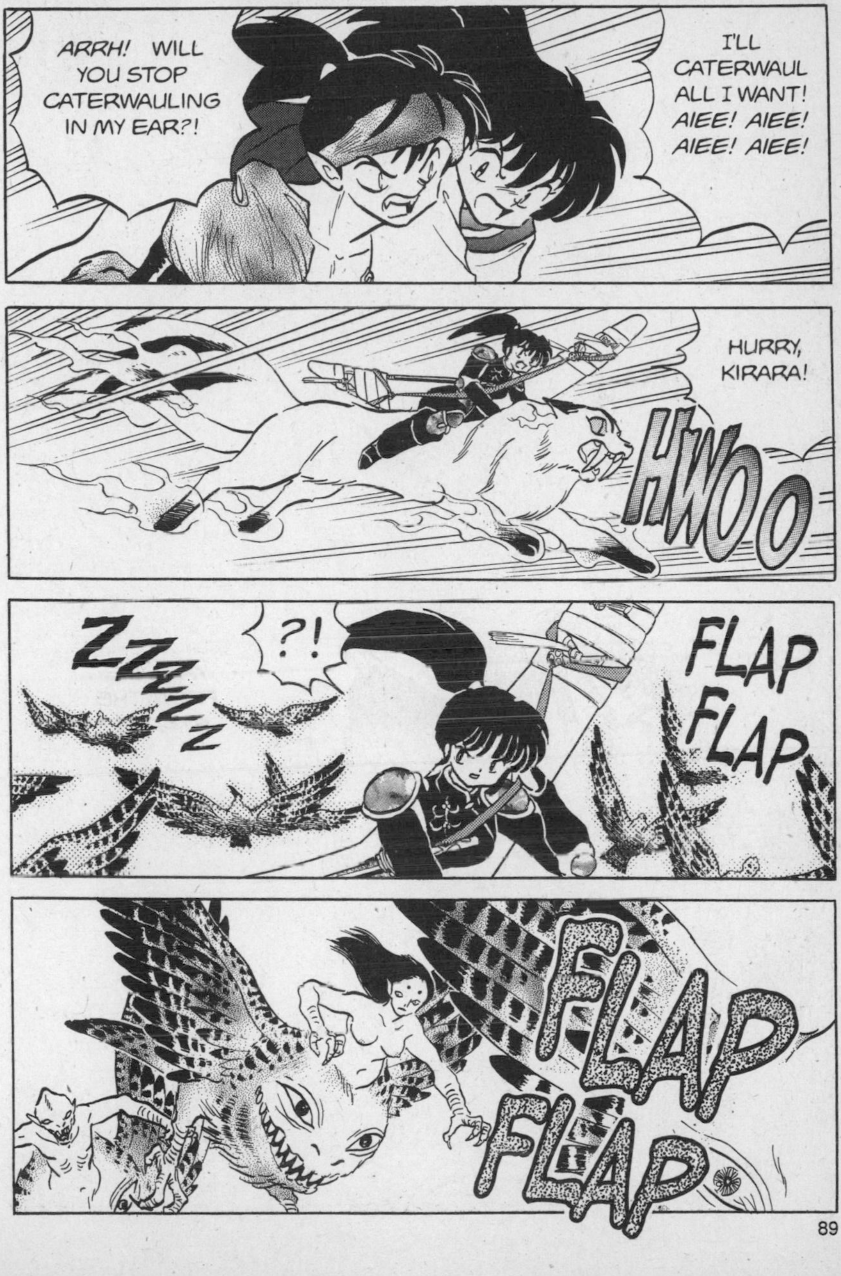
ARRH! WILL YOU STOP CATERWAULING IN MY EAR?!
I'LL CATERWAUL ALL I WANT! AIEE! AIEE! AIEE! AIEE!
HURRY, KIRARA!
HWOO
ZZZZZZ
?!
FLAP FLAP
FLAP FLAP

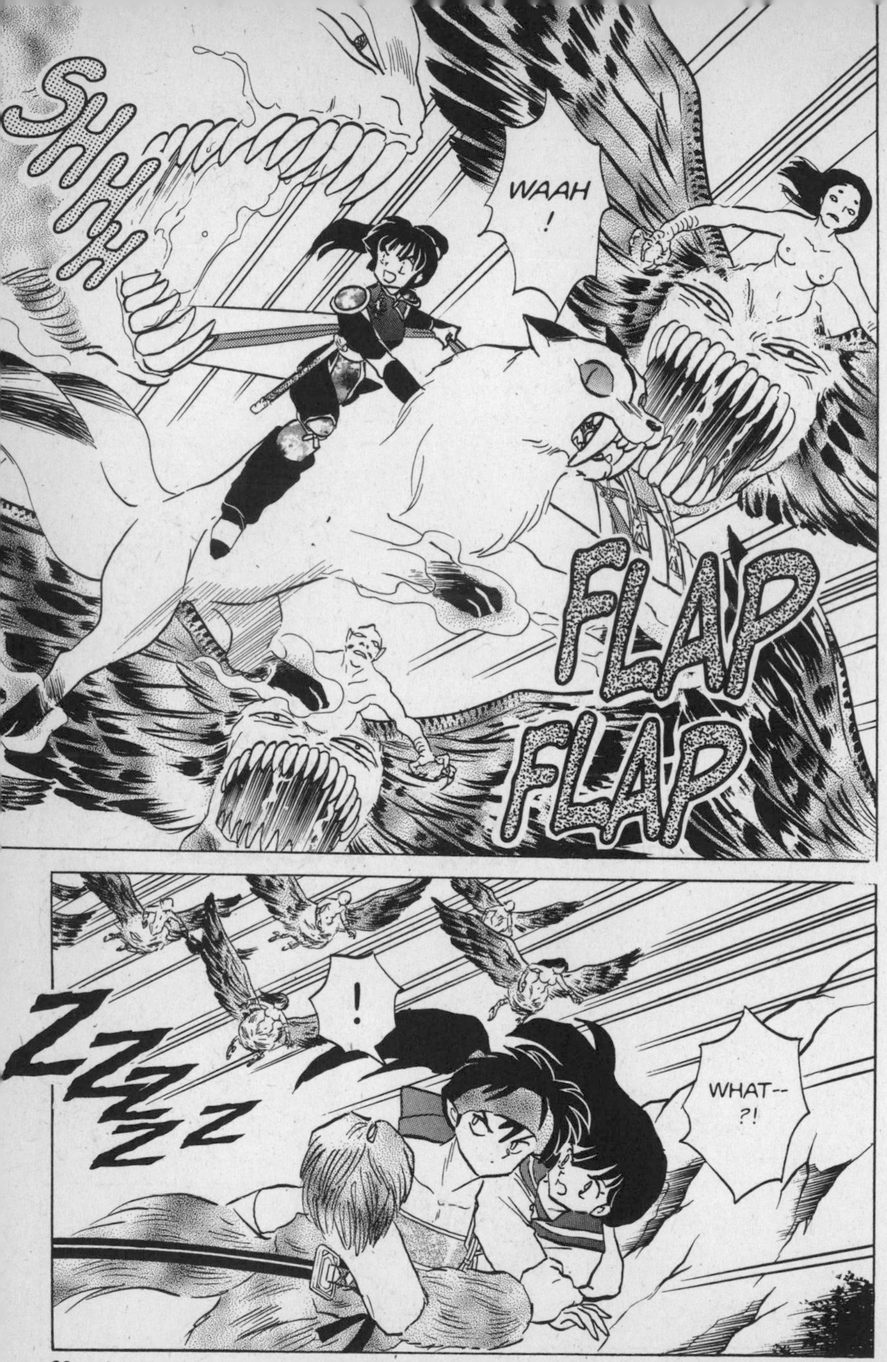
SHHHH
WAAH!
FLAP FLAP
!
ZZZZZZ
WHAT--?!

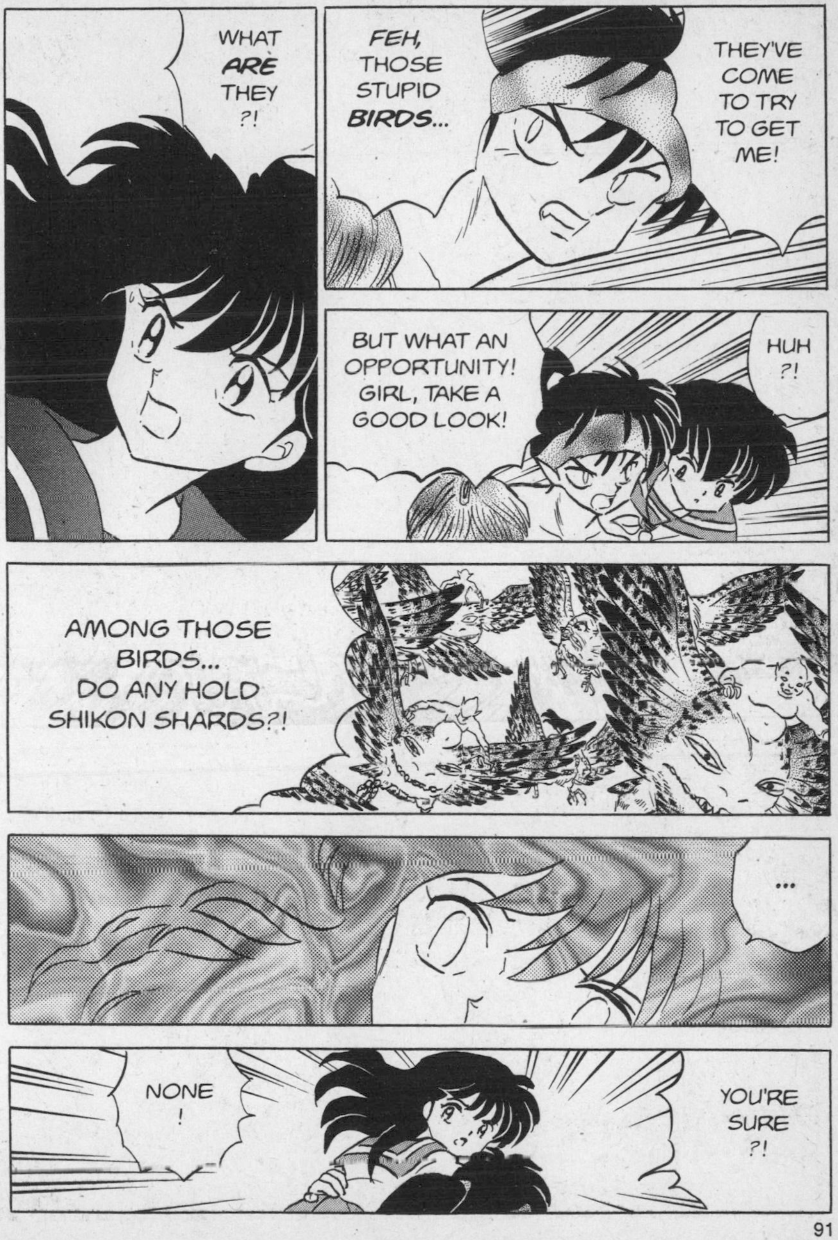
WHAT *ARE* THEY ?!
FEH, THOSE STUPID *BIRDS*...
THEY'VE COME TO TRY TO GET ME!
BUT WHAT AN OPPORTUNITY! GIRL, TAKE A GOOD LOOK!
HUH ?!
AMONG THOSE BIRDS... DO ANY HOLD SHIKON SHARDS?!
...
NONE !
YOU'RE SURE ?!

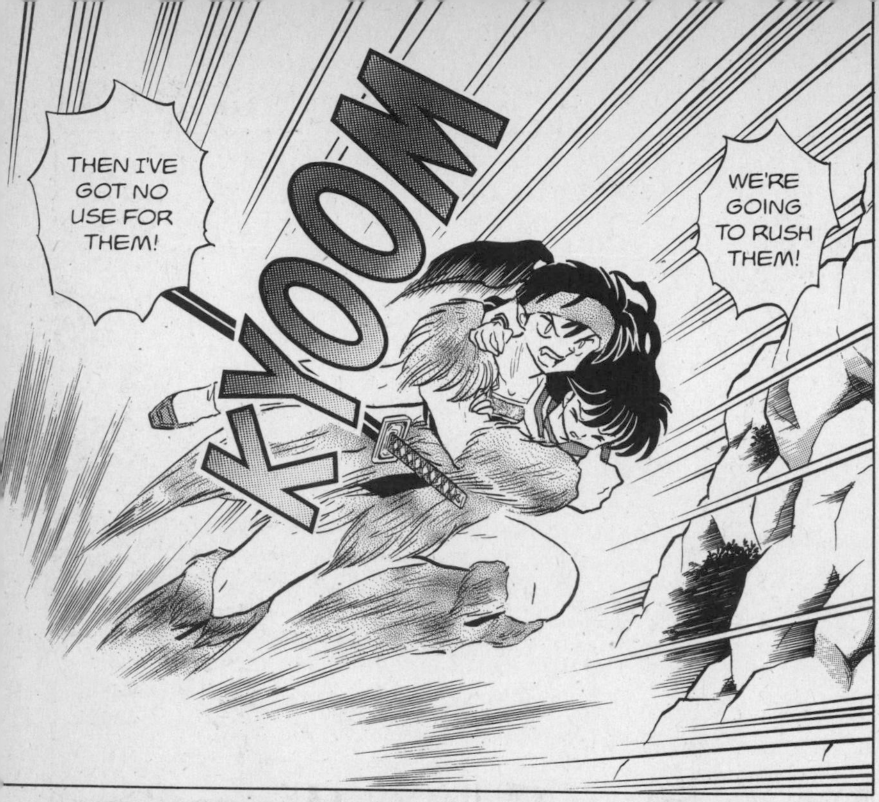
THEN I'VE GOT NO USE FOR THEM!
KYOOM
WE'RE GOING TO RUSH THEM!

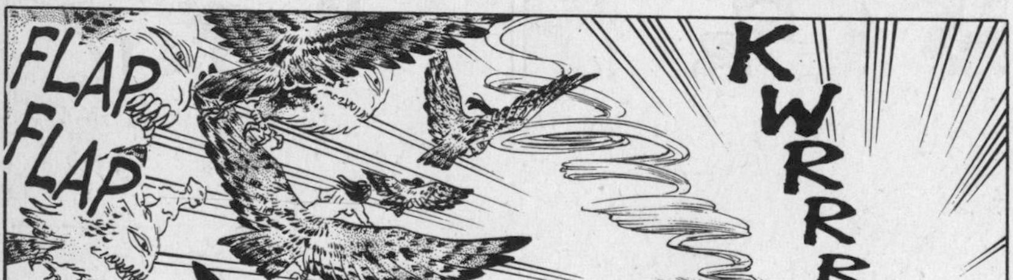
FLAP FLAP
KWRRR

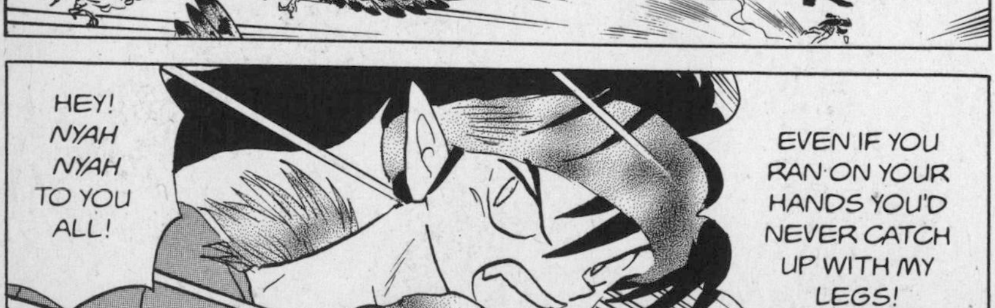
HEY! NYAH NYAH TO YOU ALL!
EVEN IF YOU RAN ON YOUR HANDS YOU'D NEVER CATCH UP WITH MY LEGS!

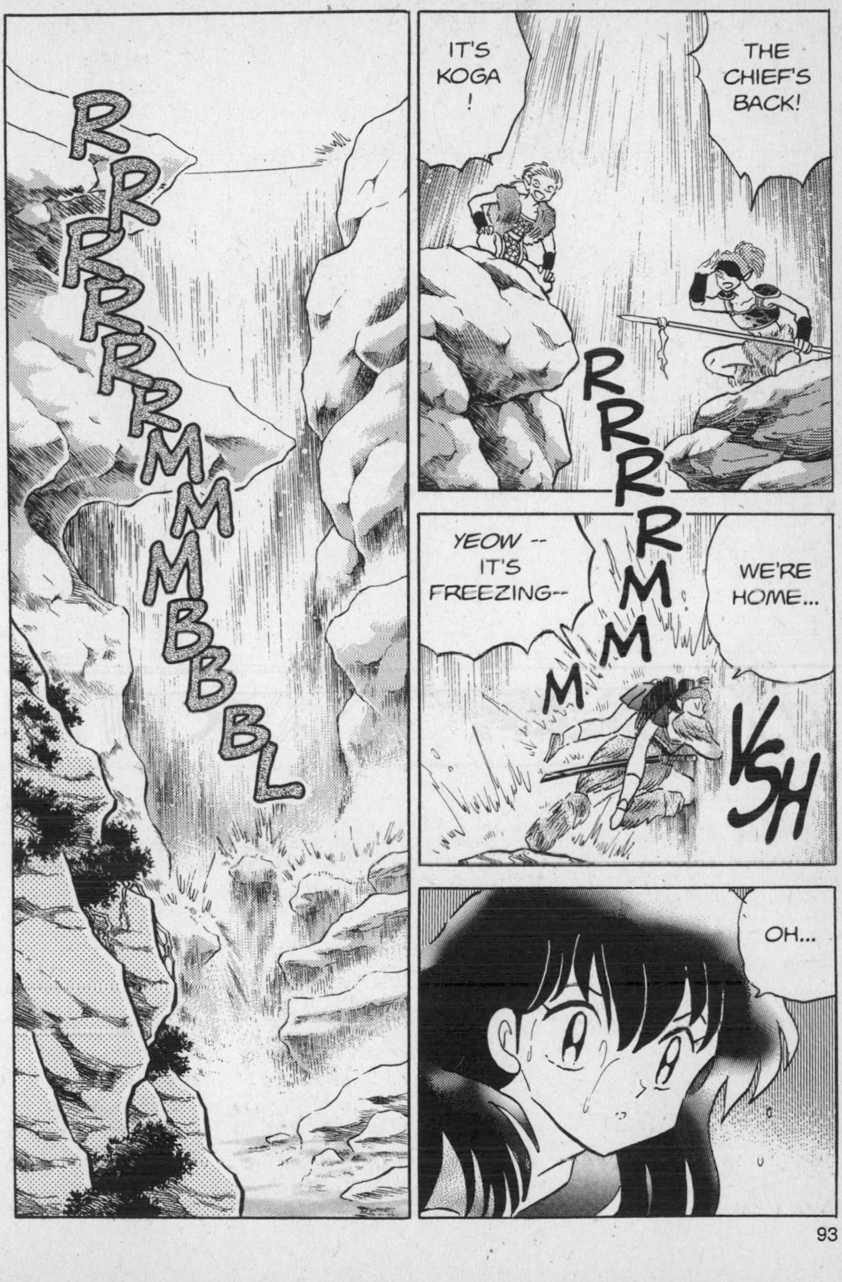
RRRRRRMMMBBBL
IT'S KOGA!
THE CHIEF'S BACK!
RRRRMMMM
YEOW -- IT'S FREEZING--
WE'RE HOME...
VSH
OH...

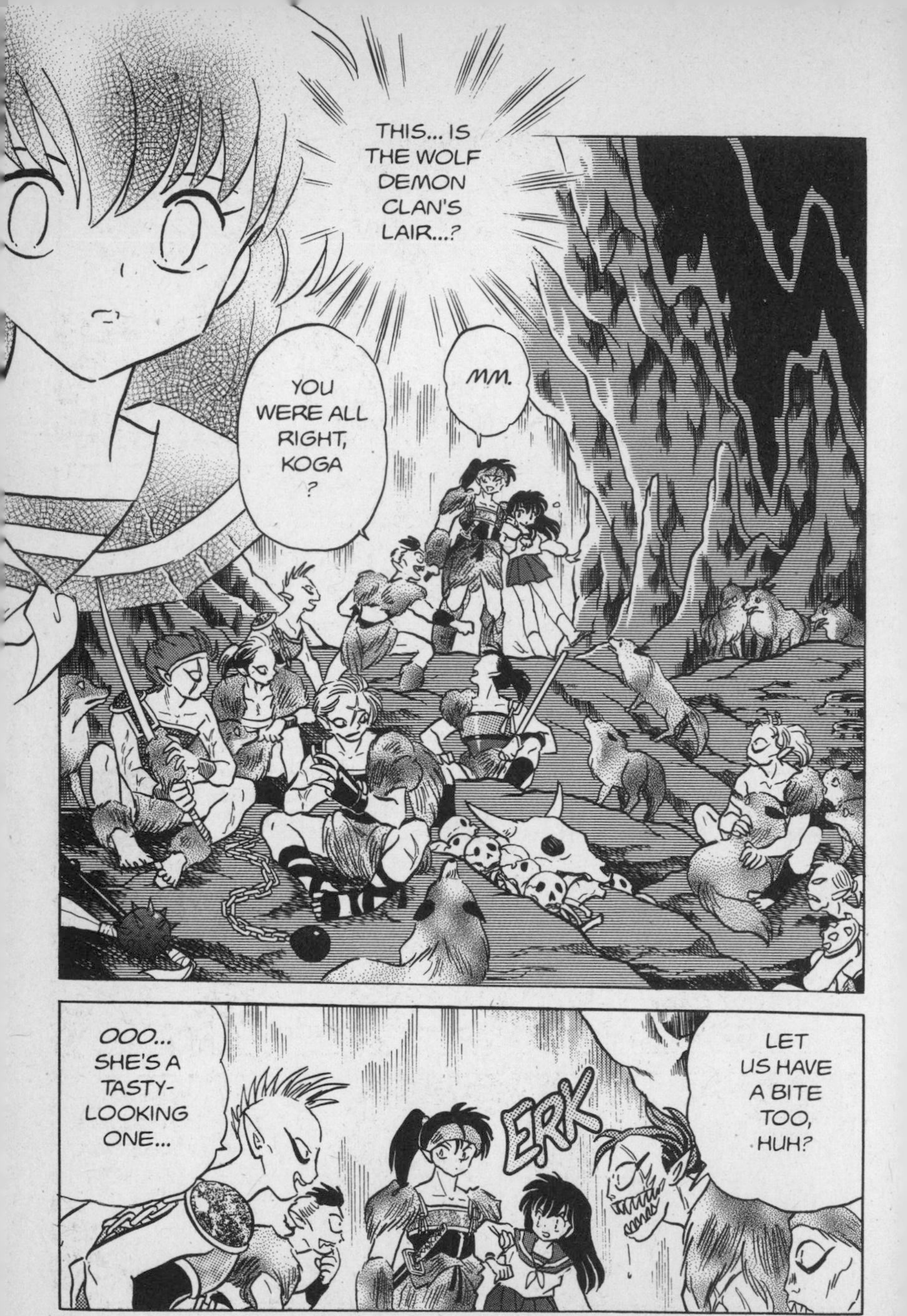
THIS... IS THE WOLF DEMON CLAN'S LAIR...?
YOU WERE ALL RIGHT, KOGA?
MM.
OOO... SHE'S A TASTY-LOOKING ONE...
ERK
LET US HAVE A BITE TOO, HUH?

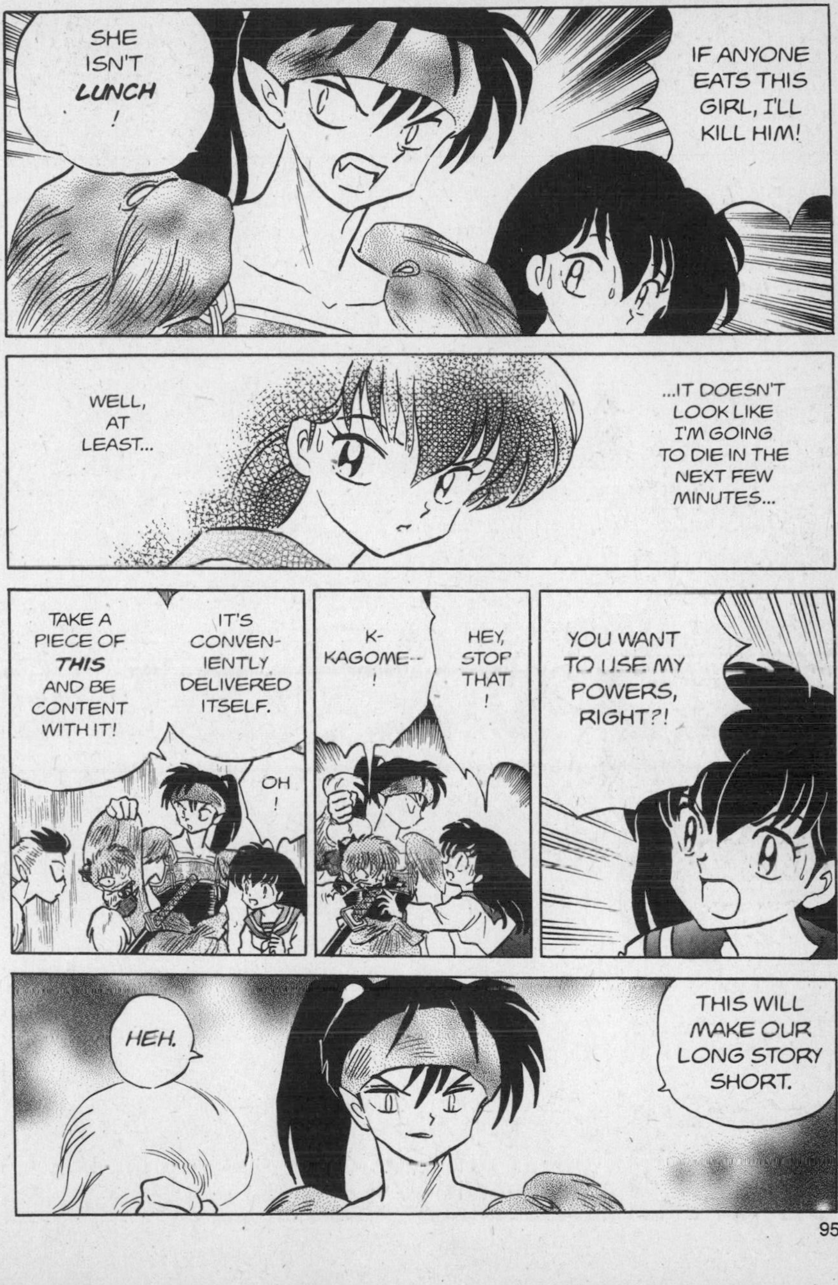
SHE ISN'T *LUNCH* !
IF ANYONE EATS THIS GIRL, I'LL KILL HIM!
WELL, AT LEAST...
...IT DOESN'T LOOK LIKE I'M GOING TO DIE IN THE NEXT FEW MINUTES...
TAKE A PIECE OF *THIS* AND BE CONTENT WITH IT!
IT'S CONVEN-IENTLY DELIVERED ITSELF.
OH !
K-KAGOME-- !
HEY, STOP THAT !
YOU WANT TO USE MY POWERS, RIGHT?!
HEH.
THIS WILL MAKE OUR LONG STORY SHORT.

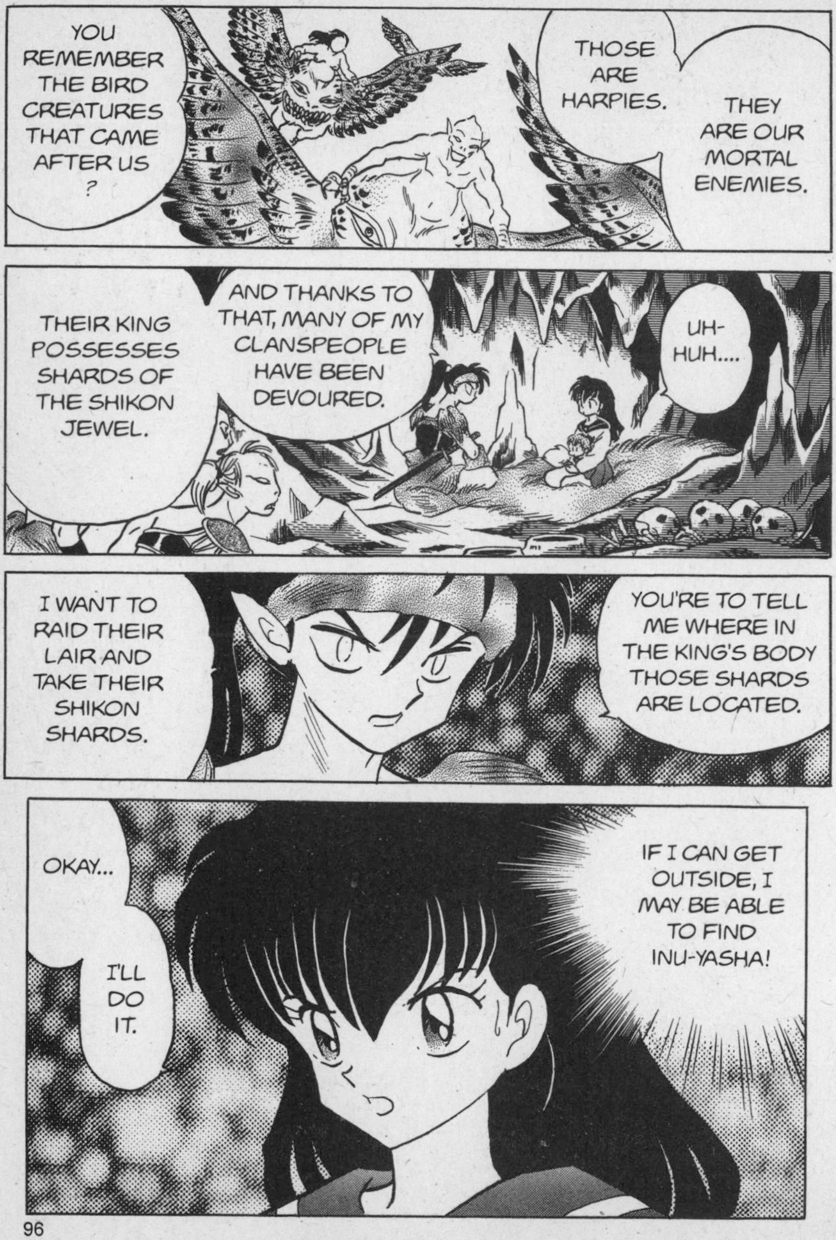

YOU REMEMBER THE BIRD CREATURES THAT CAME AFTER US ?
THOSE ARE HARPIES.
THEY ARE OUR MORTAL ENEMIES.
THEIR KING POSSESSES SHARDS OF THE SHIKON JEWEL.
AND THANKS TO THAT, MANY OF MY CLANSPEOPLE HAVE BEEN DEVOURED.
UH-HUH....
I WANT TO RAID THEIR LAIR AND TAKE THEIR SHIKON SHARDS.
YOU'RE TO TELL ME WHERE IN THE KING'S BODY THOSE SHARDS ARE LOCATED.
OKAY...
I'LL DO IT.
IF I CAN GET OUTSIDE, I MAY BE ABLE TO FIND INU-YASHA!

SCROLL SIX
THE WOLVES' CAVE

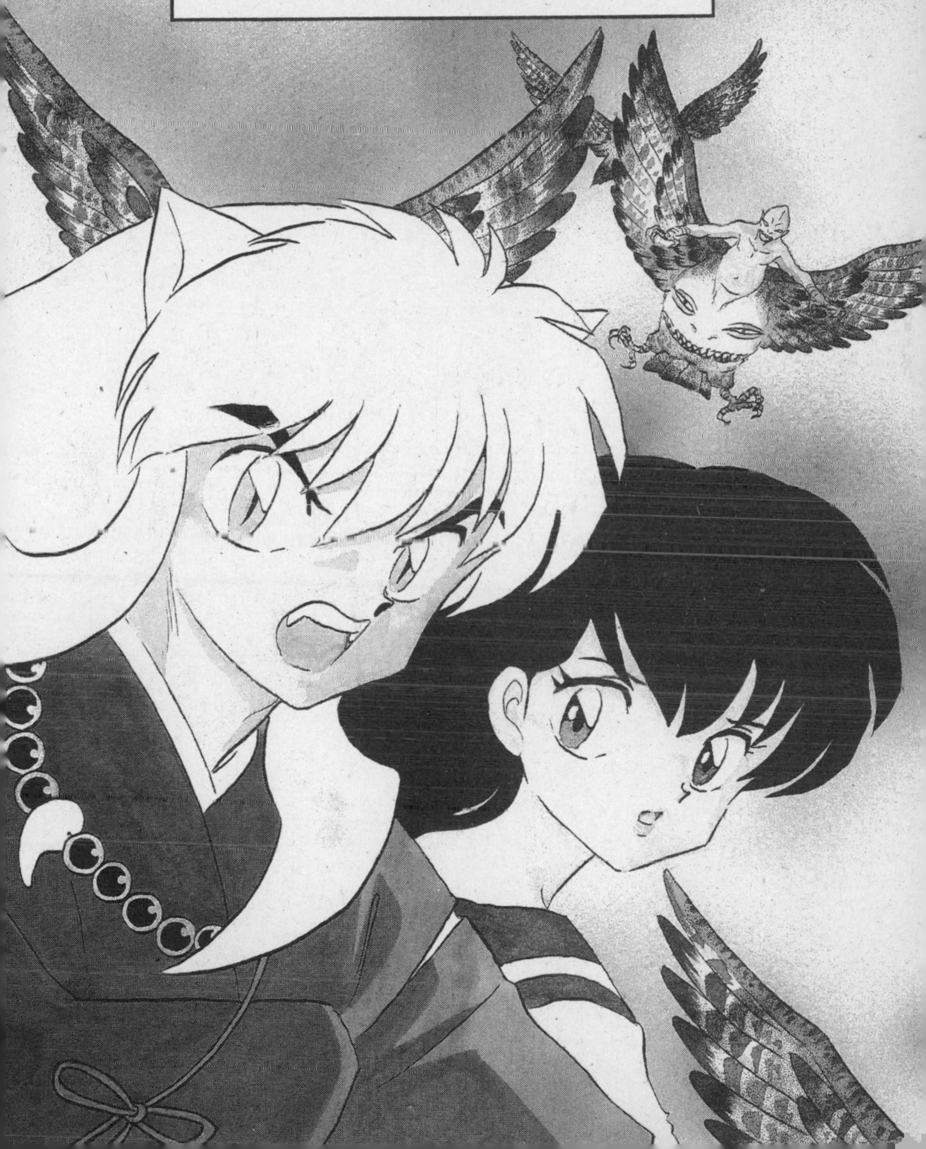

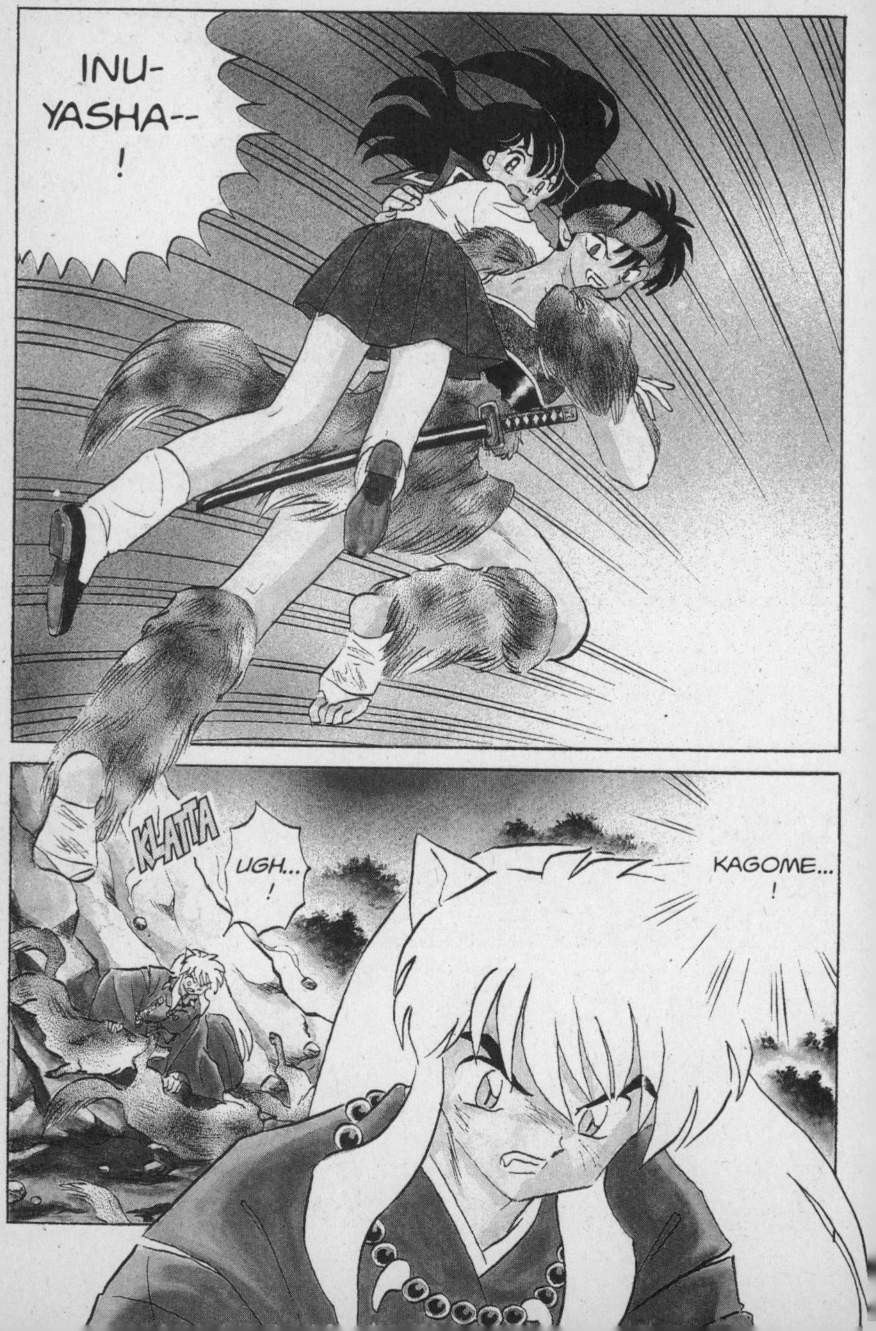
INU-
YASHA--
!
KLATTA
UGH...
!
KAGOME...
!

KOGA'S TRUE AIM, IT SEEMS, WAS TO TAKE LADY KAGOME.

SHCH

INU-YASHA, ARE YOU ALL RIGHT?!

MIROKU...

IF YOU DOUBT ME, NOTE THAT ALL THE WOLVES THAT WERE SWARMING AROUND US...

...HAVE SUDDENLY DIS-PERSED.

GRR HRR

SANGO!

WHERE'S LADY KAGOME...?!

SNCH

OH...

SORRY...

THEY ESCAPED WHILE I WAS DEALING WITH THESE ...

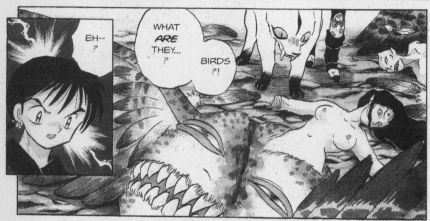

EH--?

WHAT *ARE* THEY...?

BIRDS?!

RRRMMMBBLL

I-I'VE *GOT* TO PROTECT KAGOME...!

B-DMP B-DMP

B-DMP

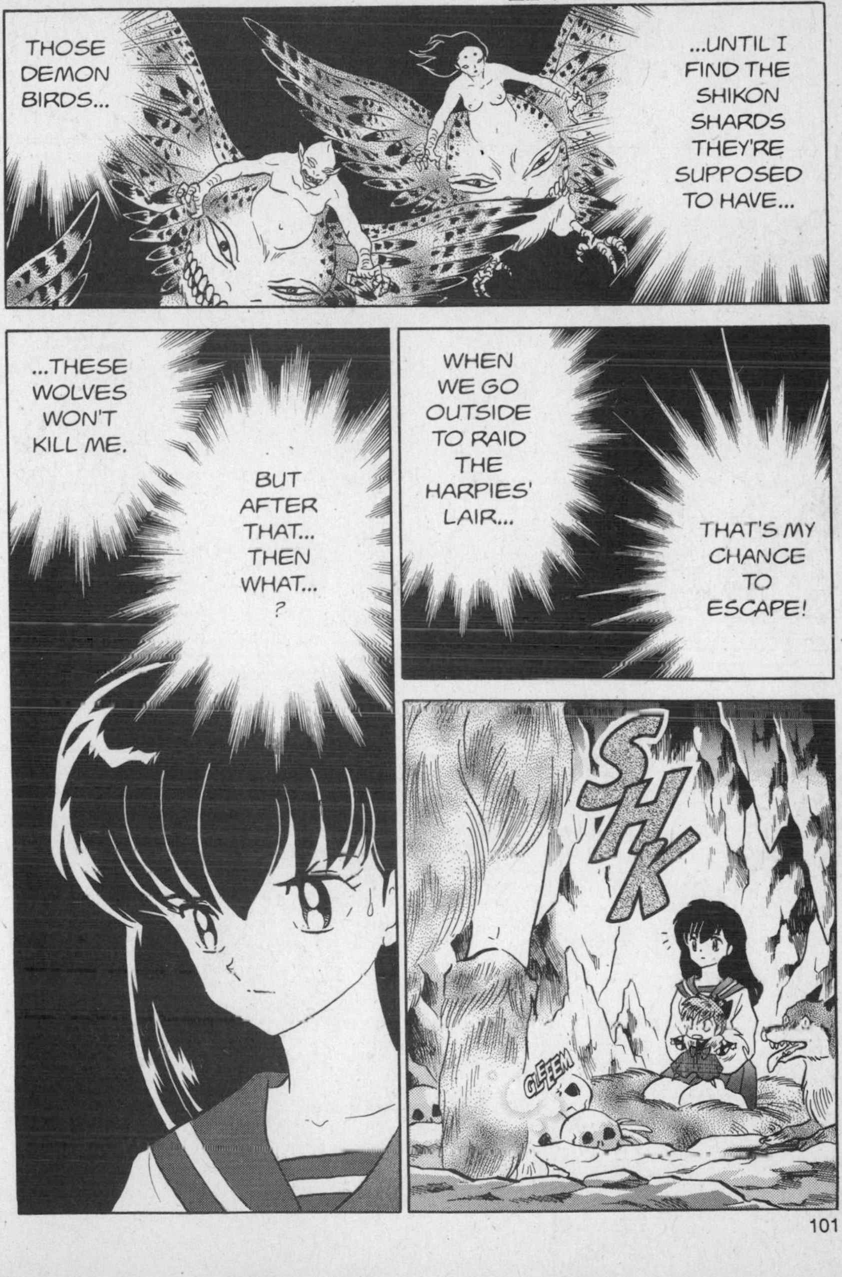
THOSE DEMON BIRDS...
...UNTIL I FIND THE SHIKON SHARDS THEY'RE SUPPOSED TO HAVE...
...THESE WOLVES WON'T KILL ME.
BUT AFTER THAT... THEN WHAT...?
WHEN WE GO OUTSIDE TO RAID THE HARPIES' LAIR...
THAT'S MY CHANCE TO ESCAPE!
SHK
GLEEEM

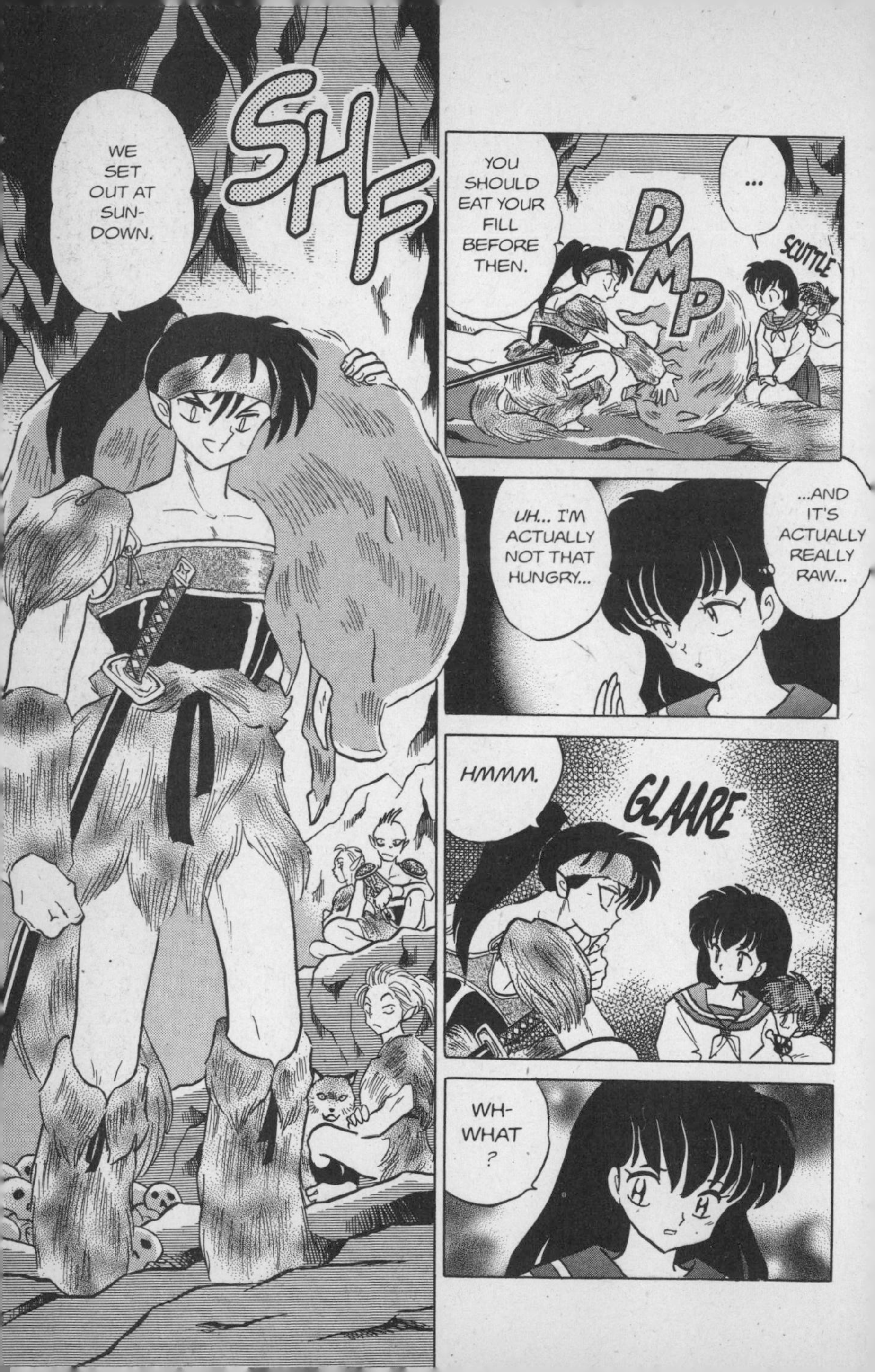
WE SET OUT AT SUN-DOWN.
SHF
YOU SHOULD EAT YOUR FILL BEFORE THEN.
DMP
...
SCUTTLE
UH... I'M ACTUALLY NOT THAT HUNGRY...
...AND IT'S ACTUALLY REALLY RAW...
HMMM.
GLAARE
WH-WHAT?

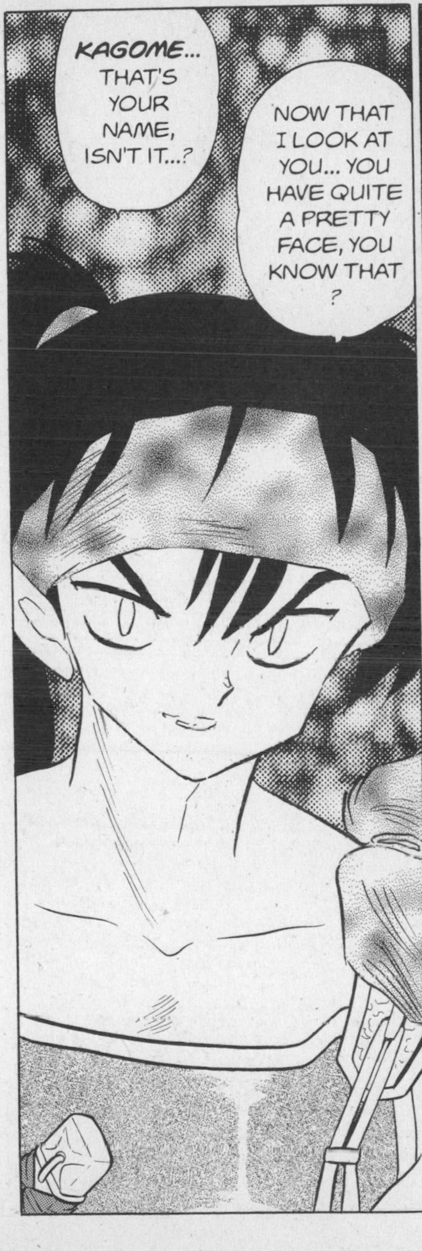
KAGOME... THAT'S YOUR NAME, ISN'T IT...?
NOW THAT I LOOK AT YOU... YOU HAVE QUITE A PRETTY FACE, YOU KNOW THAT?

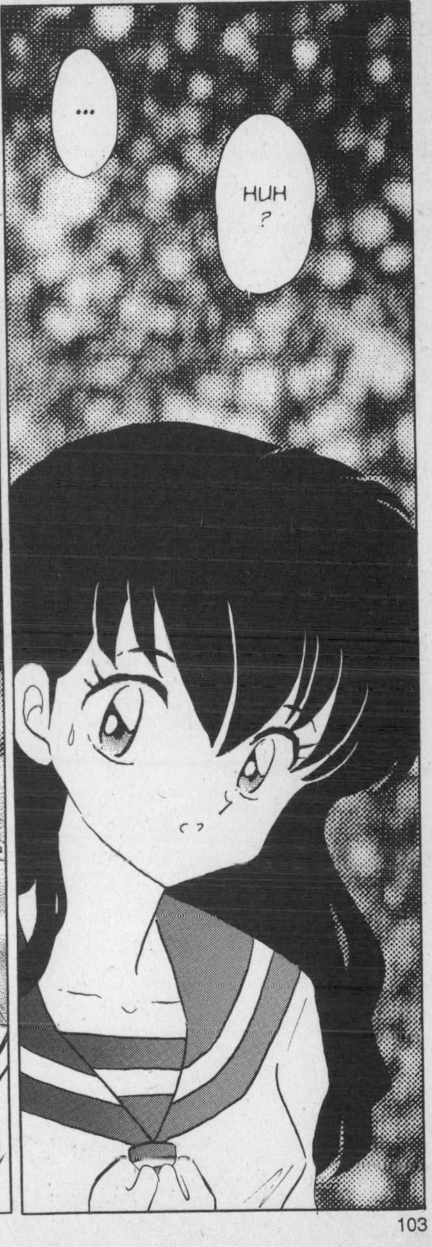
...
HUH?

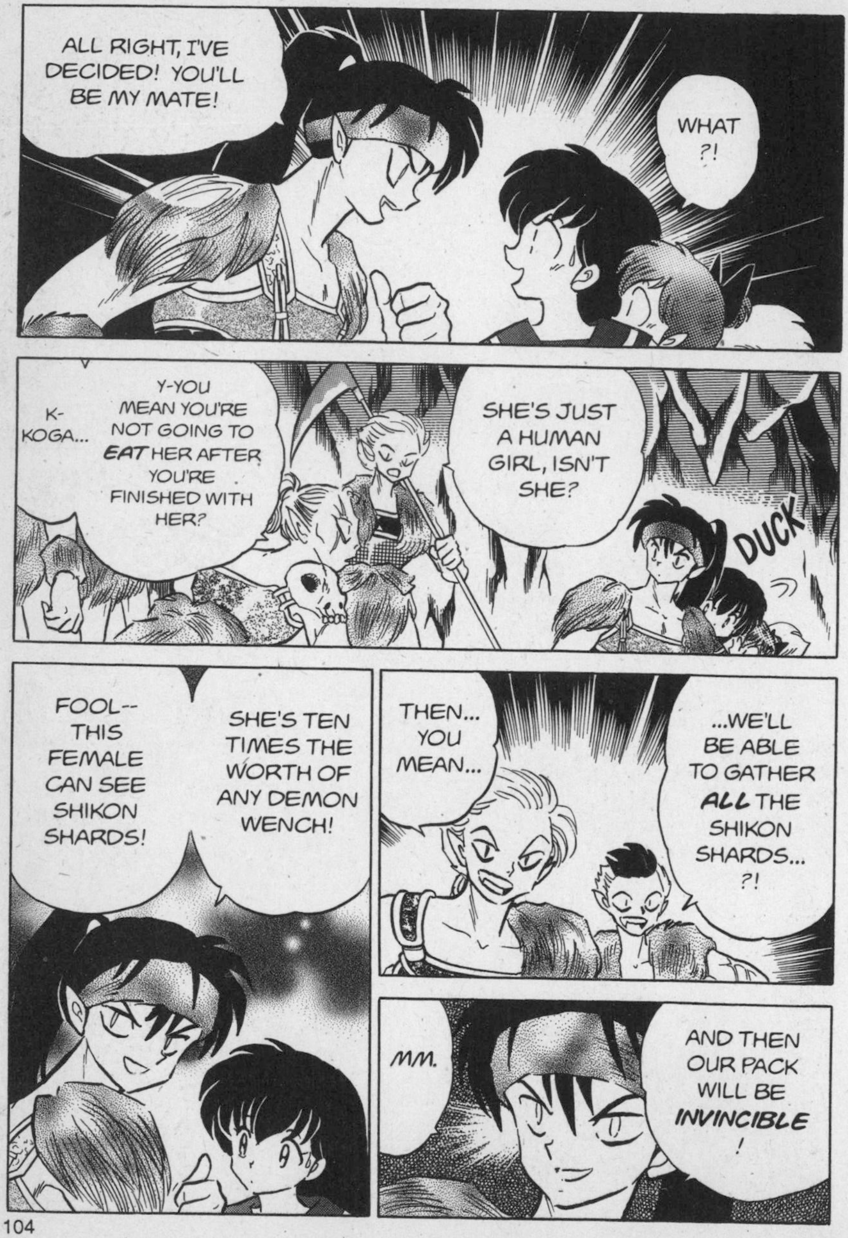
ALL RIGHT, I'VE DECIDED! YOU'LL BE MY MATE!
WHAT ?!
K-KOGA...
Y-YOU MEAN YOU'RE NOT GOING TO *EAT* HER AFTER YOU'RE FINISHED WITH HER?
SHE'S JUST A HUMAN GIRL, ISN'T SHE?
DUCK
FOOL-- THIS FEMALE CAN SEE SHIKON SHARDS!
SHE'S TEN TIMES THE WORTH OF ANY DEMON WENCH!
THEN... YOU MEAN...
...WE'LL BE ABLE TO GATHER *ALL* THE SHIKON SHARDS... ?!
MM.
AND THEN OUR PACK WILL BE *INVINCIBLE* !

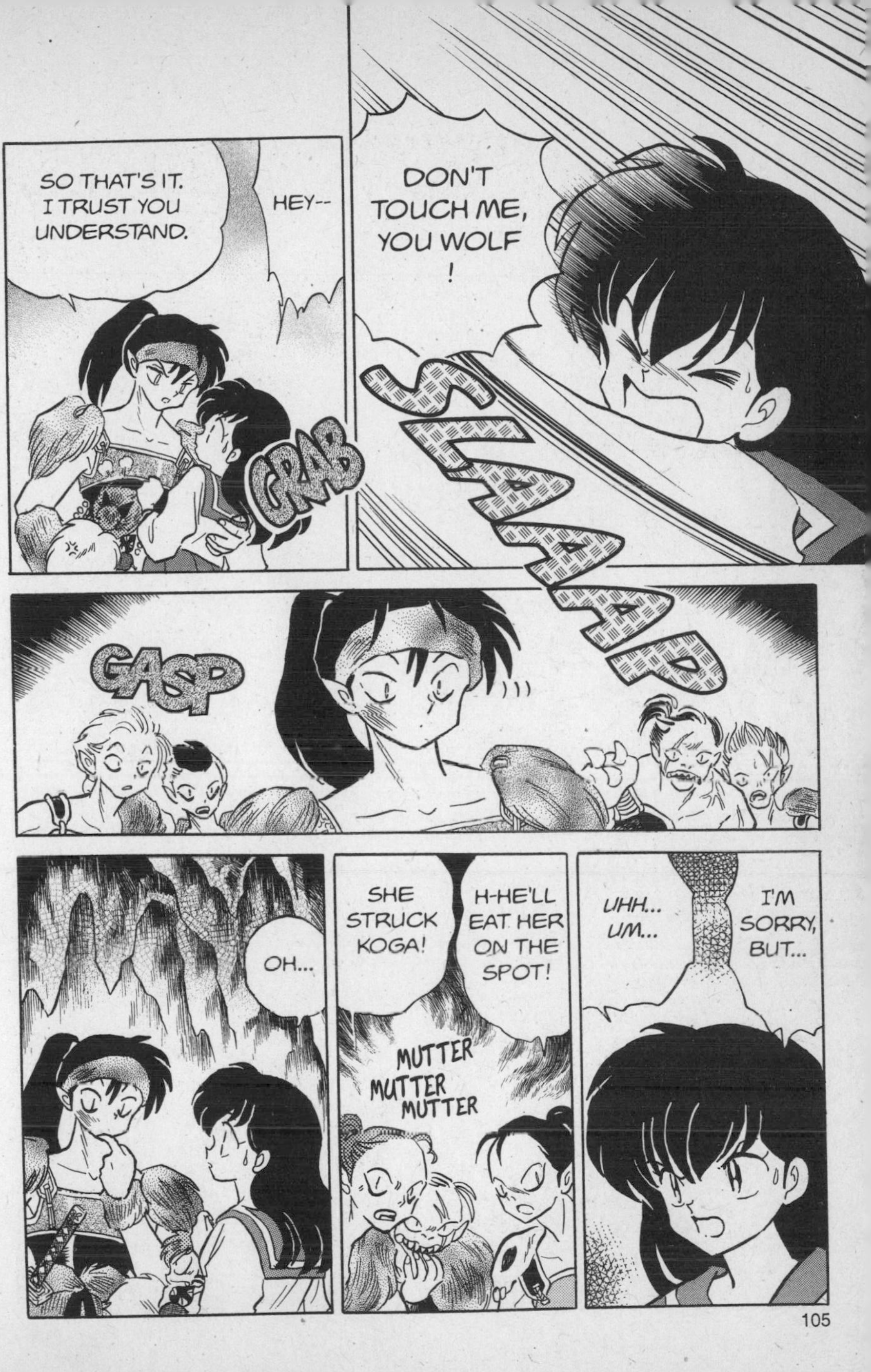

SO THAT'S IT. I TRUST YOU UNDERSTAND.
HEY--
GRAB
DON'T TOUCH ME, YOU WOLF !
SLAAAAP
GASP
OH...
SHE STRUCK KOGA!
H-HE'LL EAT HER ON THE SPOT!
MUTTER MUTTER MUTTER
UHH... UM...
I'M SORRY, BUT...

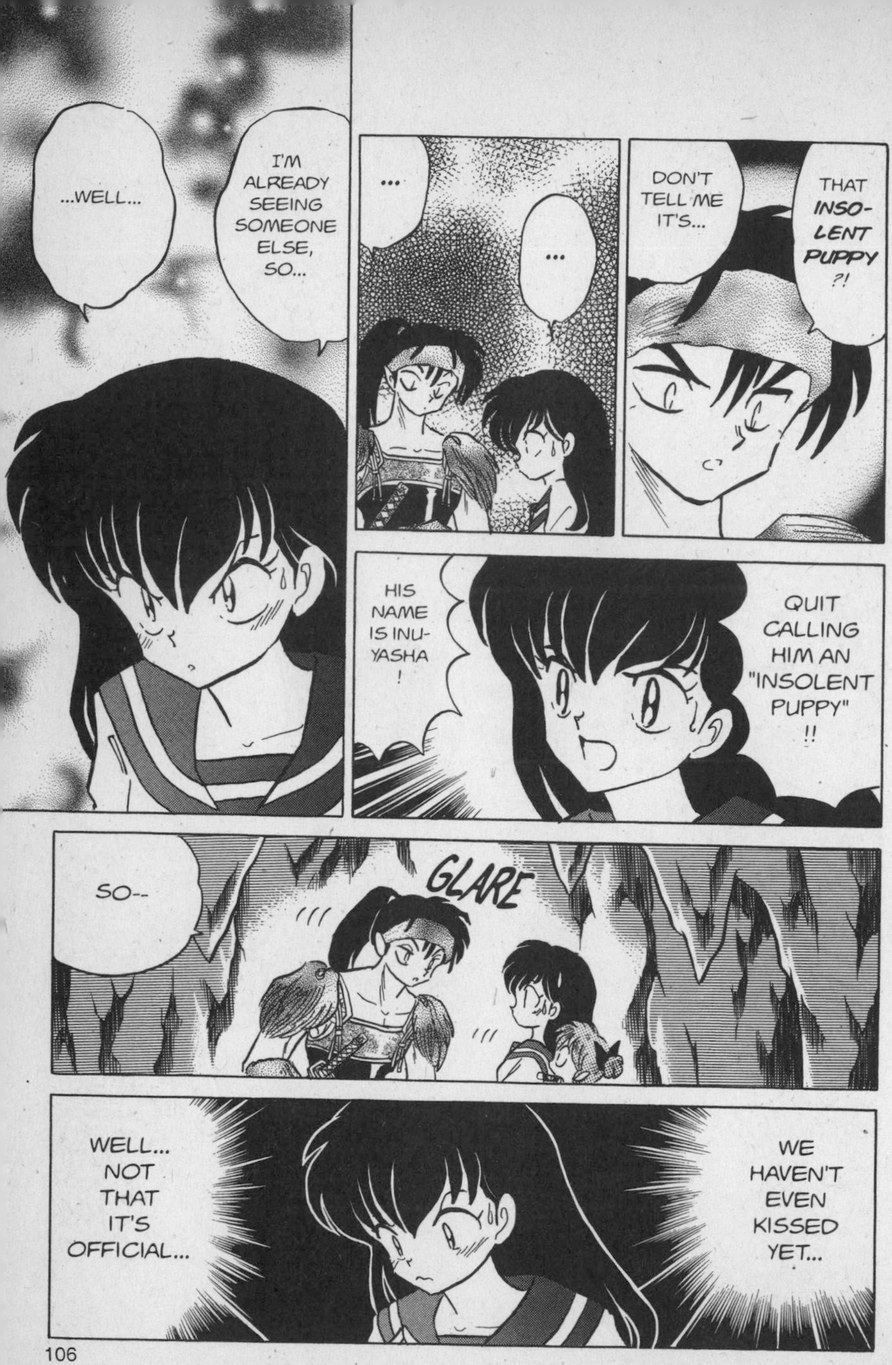
...WELL...
I'M ALREADY SEEING SOMEONE ELSE, SO...
...
...
DON'T TELL ME IT'S...
THAT INSOLENT PUPPY ?!
HIS NAME IS INU-YASHA !
QUIT CALLING HIM AN "INSOLENT PUPPY" !!
SO--
GLARE
WELL... NOT THAT IT'S OFFICIAL...
WE HAVEN'T EVEN KISSED YET...

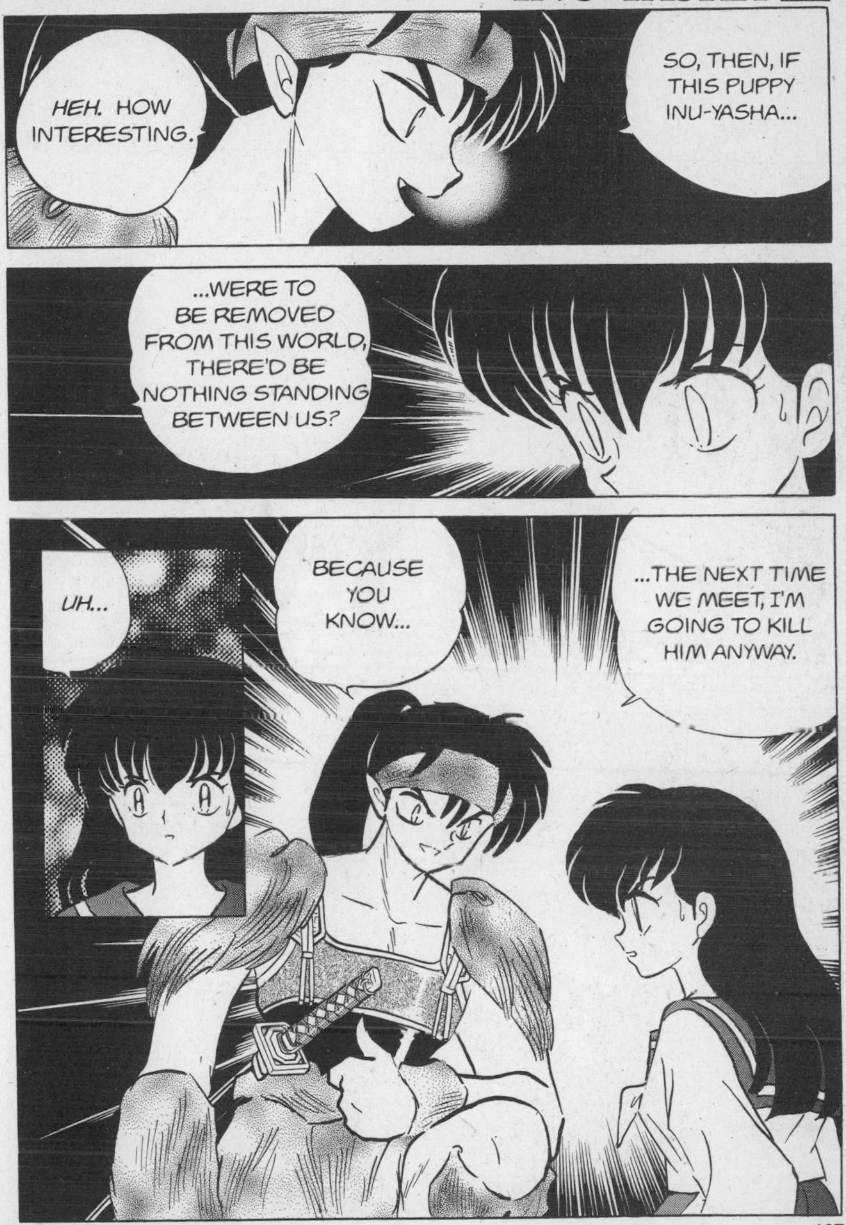
HEH. HOW INTERESTING.
SO, THEN, IF THIS PUPPY INU-YASHA...
...WERE TO BE REMOVED FROM THIS WORLD, THERE'D BE NOTHING STANDING BETWEEN US?
UH...
BECAUSE YOU KNOW...
...THE NEXT TIME WE MEET, I'M GOING TO KILL HIM ANYWAY.

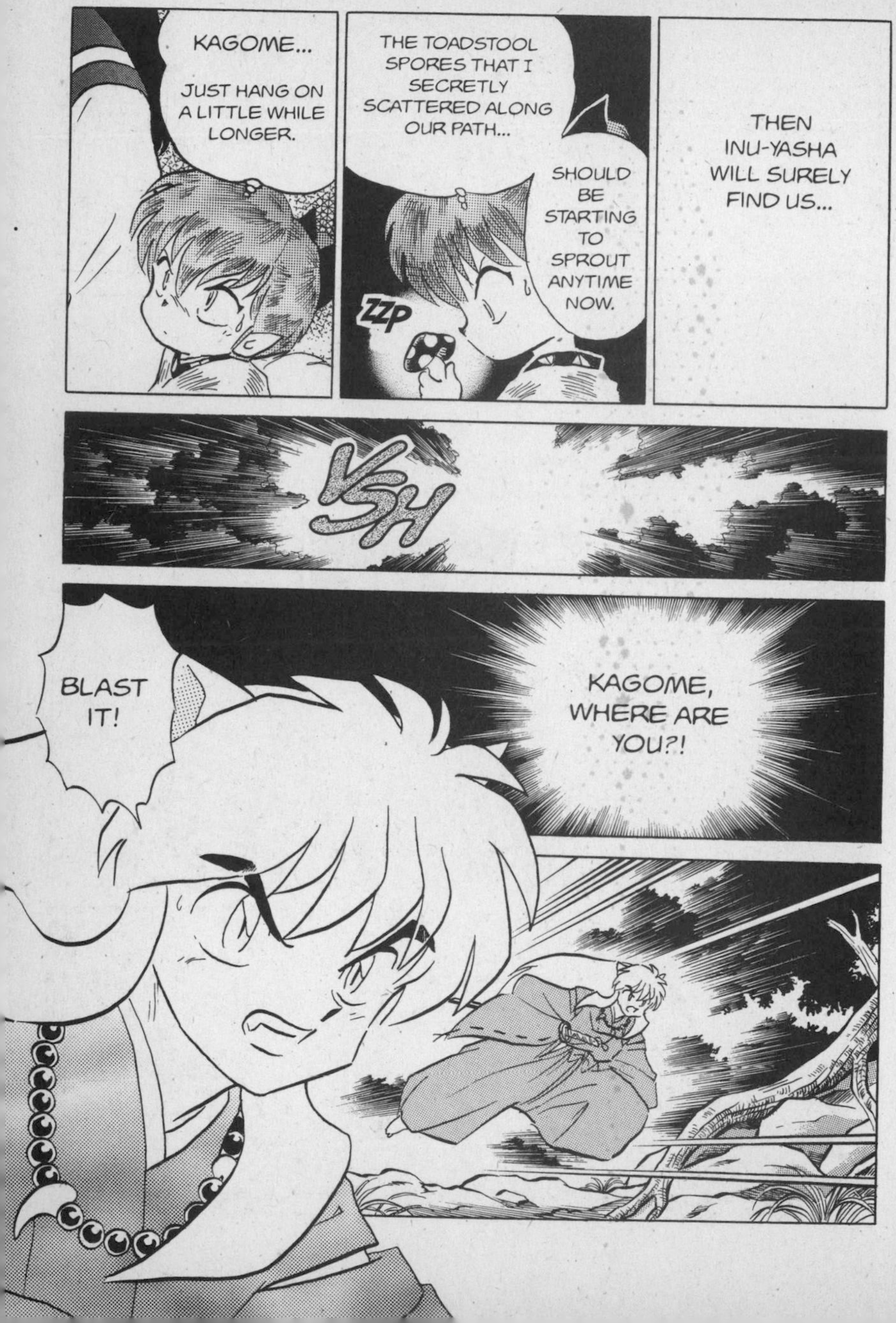
KAGOME...
JUST HANG ON A LITTLE WHILE LONGER.
THE TOADSTOOL SPORES THAT I SECRETLY SCATTERED ALONG OUR PATH...
SHOULD BE STARTING TO SPROUT ANYTIME NOW.
ZZP
THEN INU-YASHA WILL SURELY FIND US...
VSH
BLAST IT!
KAGOME, WHERE ARE YOU?!

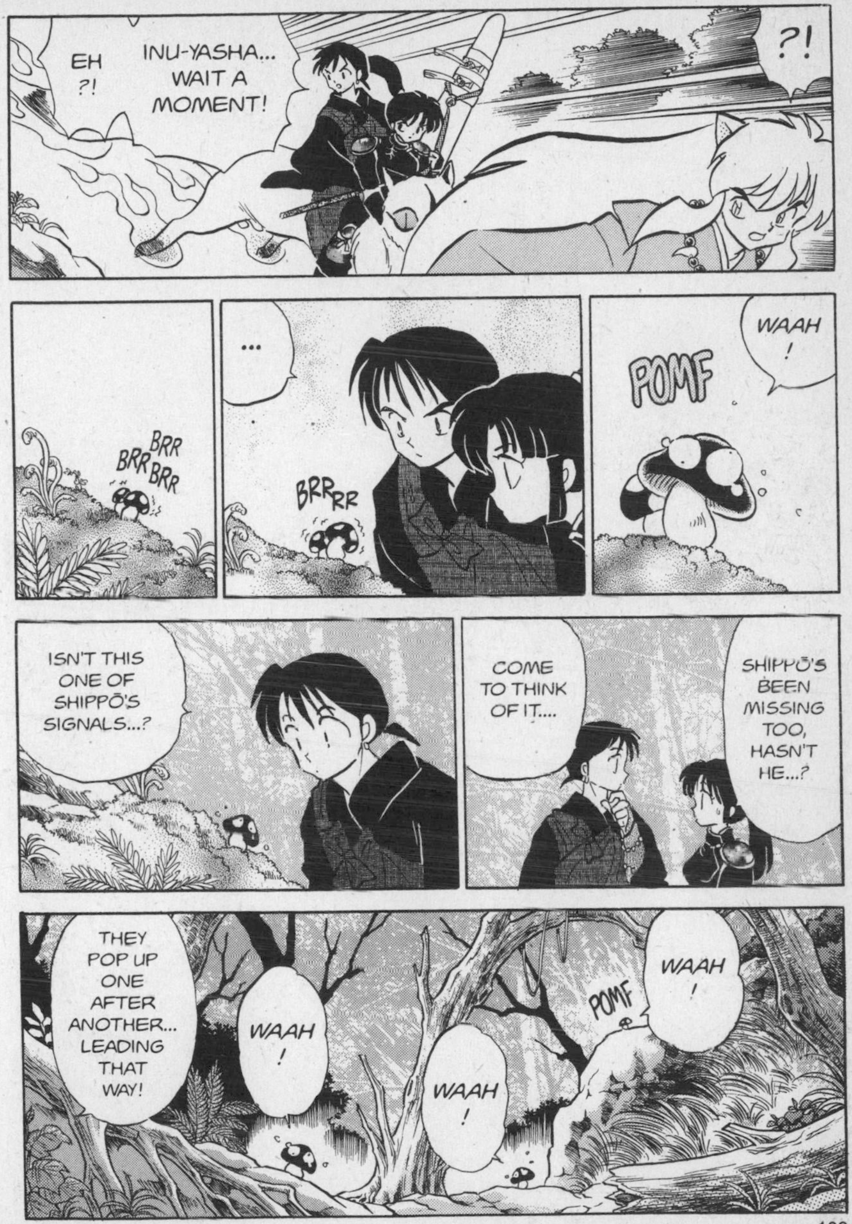
EH ?!
INU-YASHA... WAIT A MOMENT!
?!
BRR BRR BRR
...
BRRRR
POMF
WAAH !
ISN'T THIS ONE OF SHIPPŌ'S SIGNALS...?
COME TO THINK OF IT....
SHIPPŌ'S BEEN MISSING TOO, HASN'T HE...?
THEY POP UP ONE AFTER ANOTHER... LEADING THAT WAY!
WAAH !
WAAH !
POMF
WAAH !

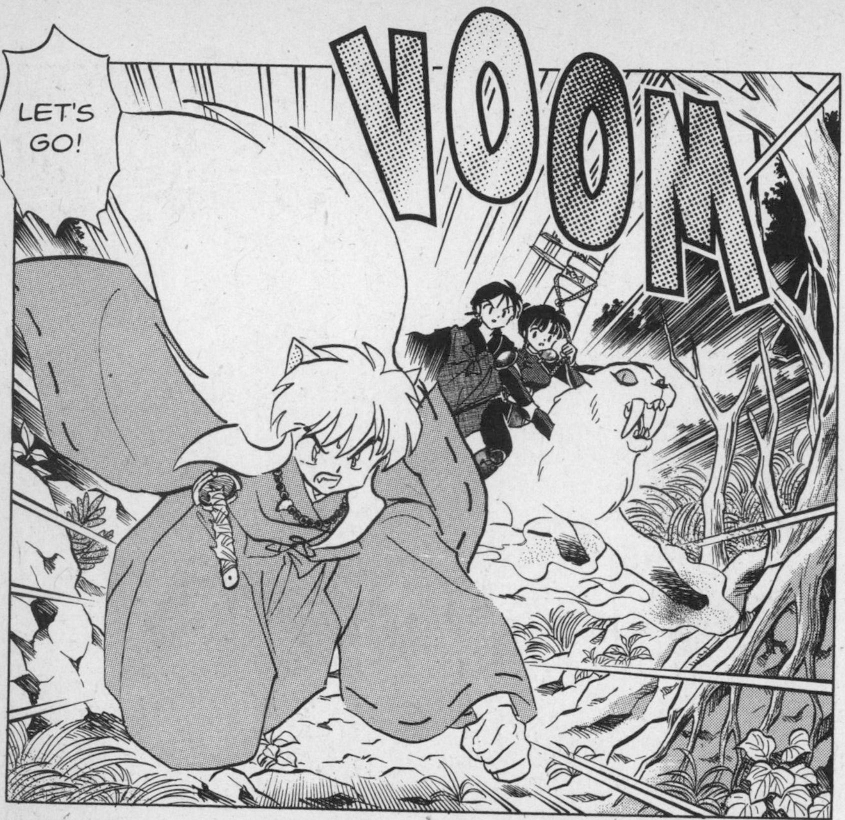
LET'S GO!
VOOM
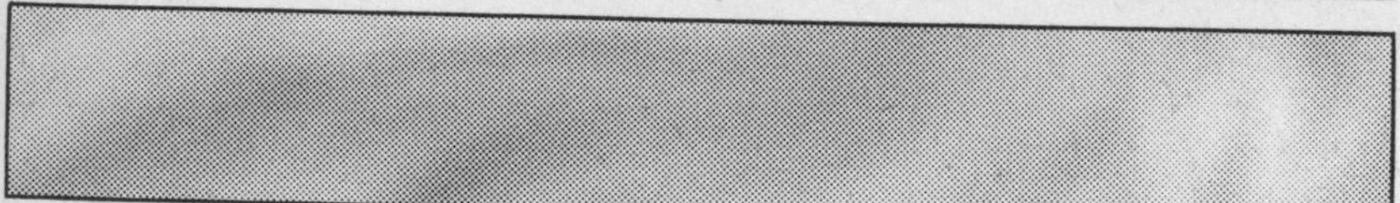
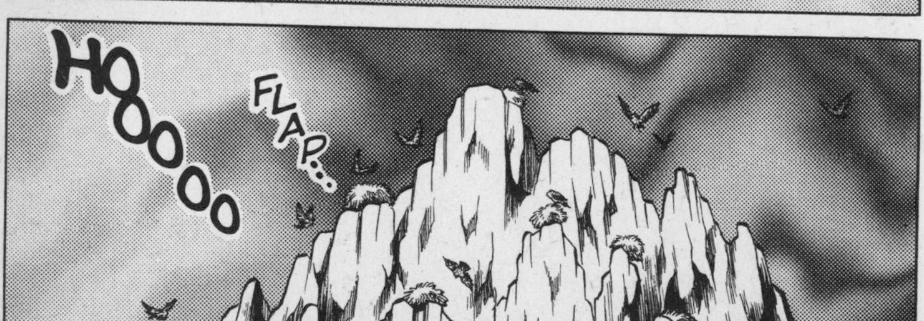
HOOOOO
FLAP...

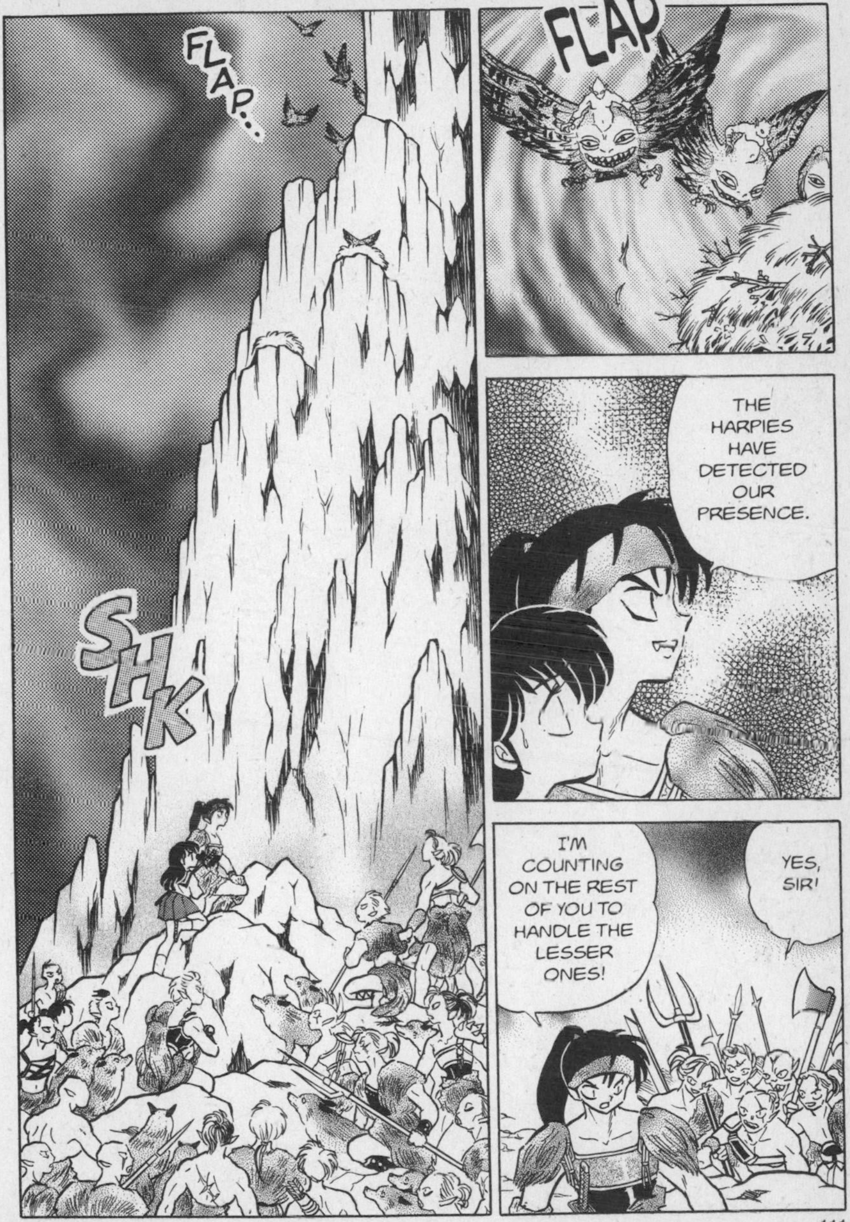
FLAP...
SHK
FLAP
THE HARPIES HAVE DETECTED OUR PRESENCE.
I'M COUNTING ON THE REST OF YOU TO HANDLE THE LESSER ONES!
YES, SIR!

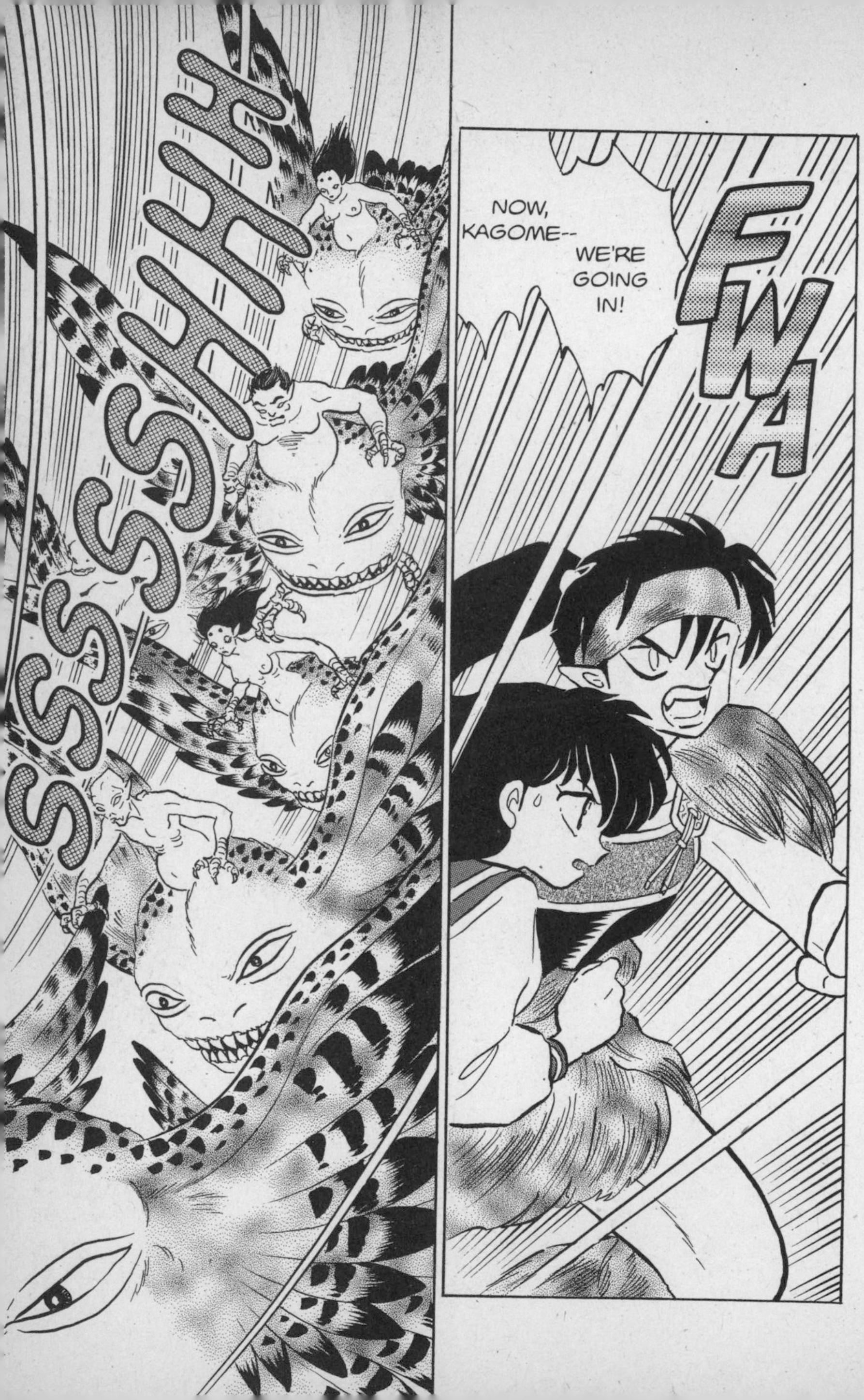
SSSSSHHH
NOW, KAGOME--
WE'RE GOING IN!
FWA

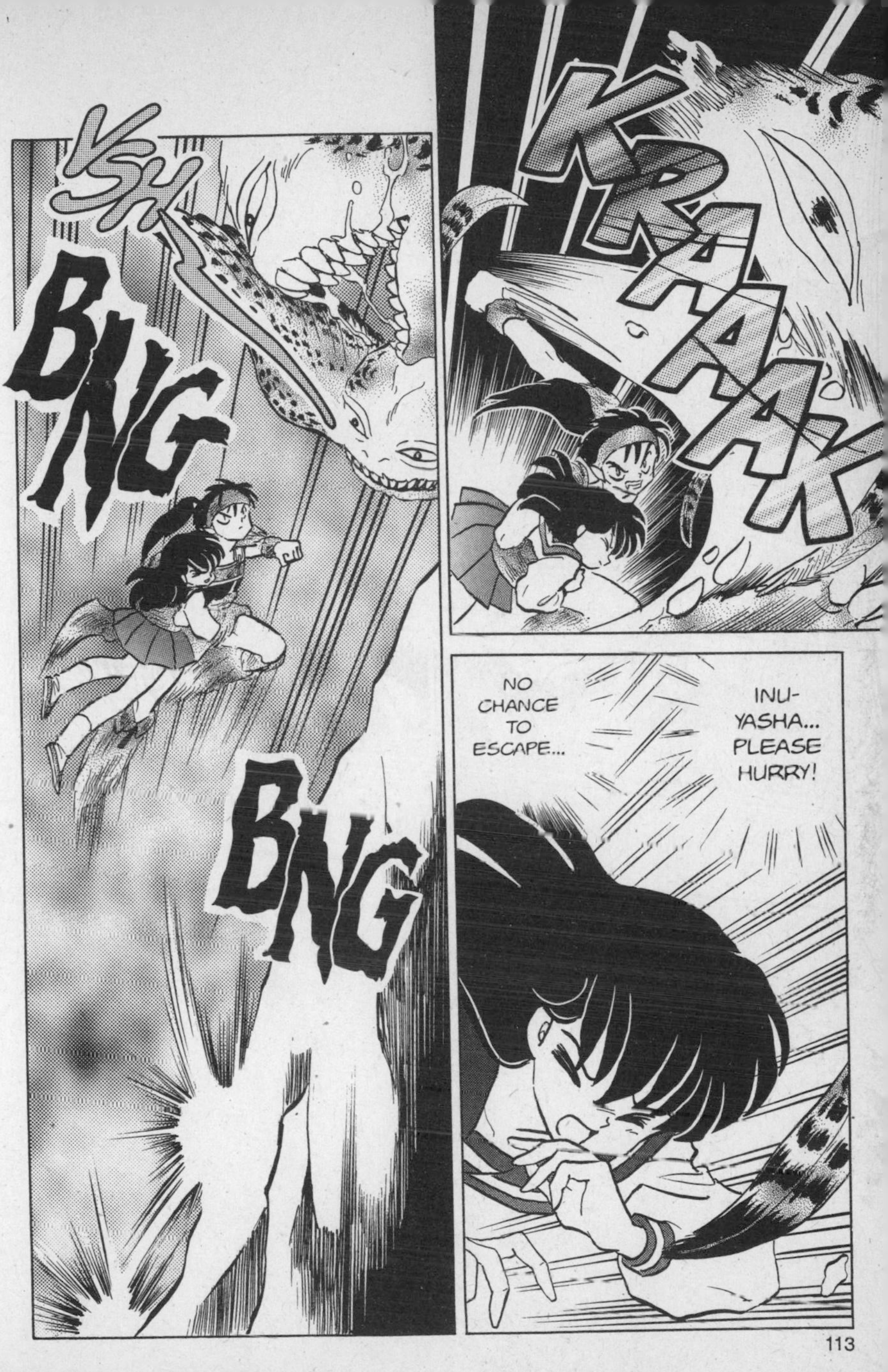
VSH
BNG
BNG
KRAAAK
NO CHANCE TO ESCAPE...
INU-YASHA... PLEASE HURRY!

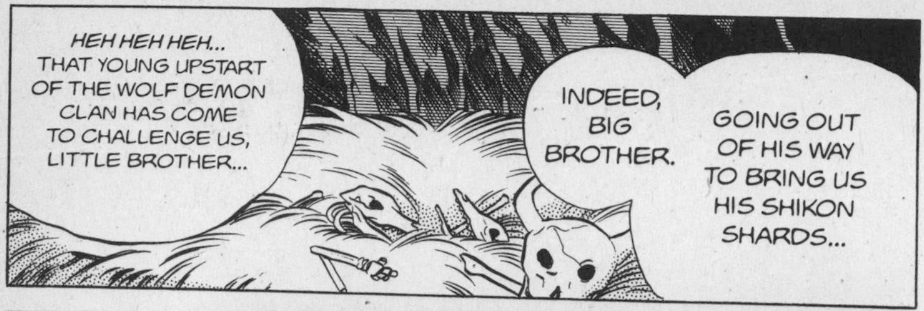
HEH HEH HEH... THAT YOUNG UPSTART OF THE WOLF DEMON CLAN HAS COME TO CHALLENGE US, LITTLE BROTHER...
INDEED, BIG BROTHER.
GOING OUT OF HIS WAY TO BRING US HIS SHIKON SHARDS...

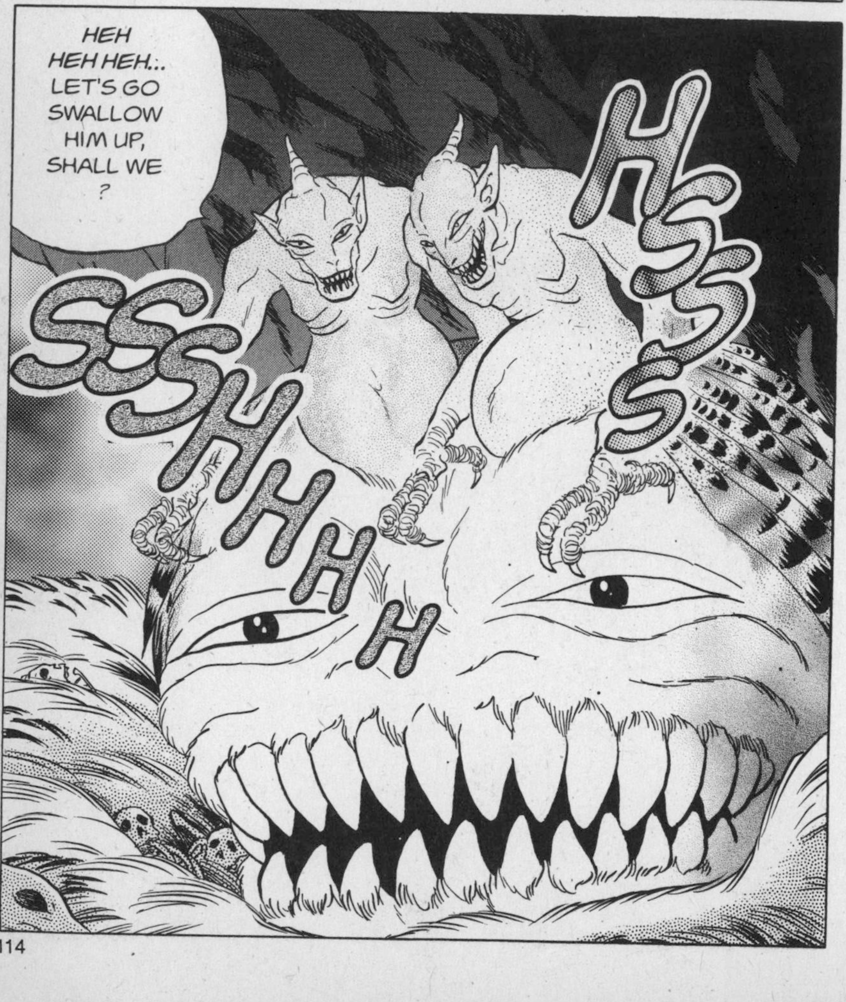
HEH HEH HEH... LET'S GO SWALLOW HIM UP, SHALL WE ?
SSSHHHHH
HISSS

SCROLL SEVEN

THE HARPIES

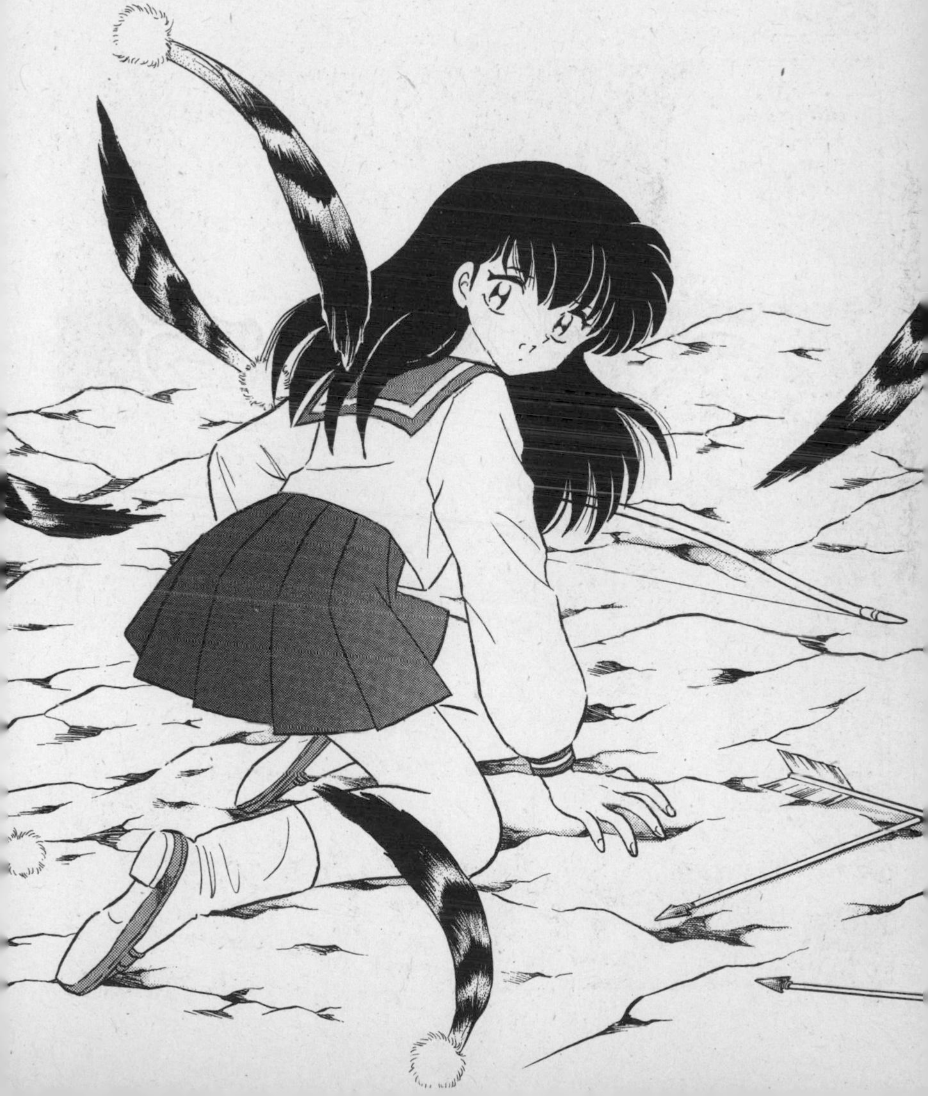

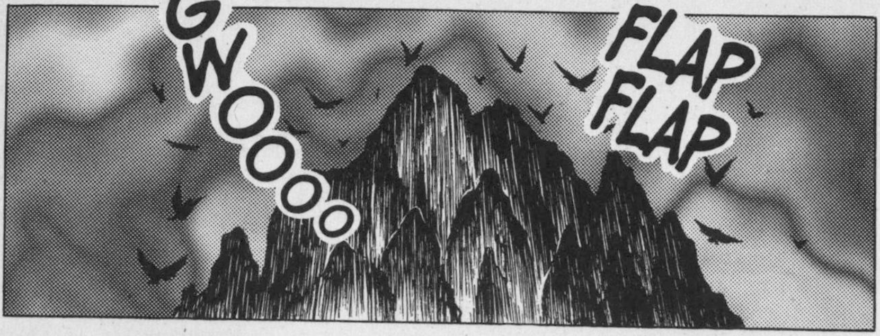
GWOOOOO
FLAP FLAP
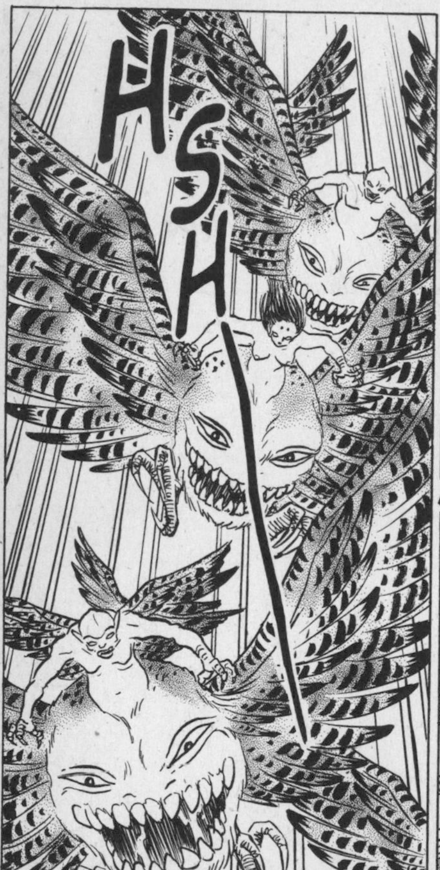
HSH
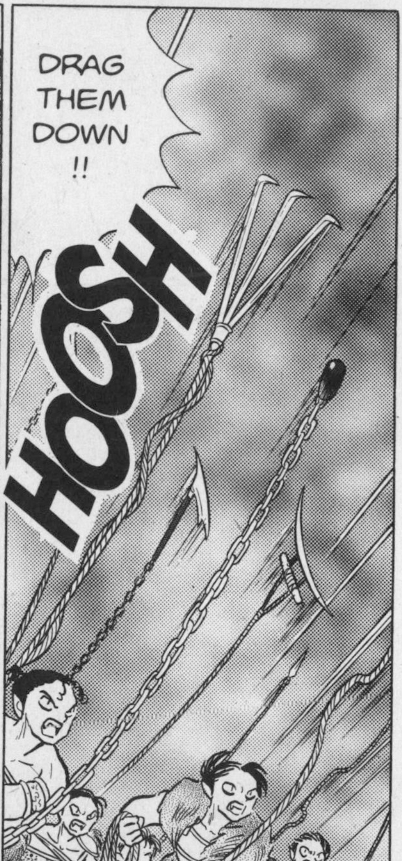
DRAG THEM DOWN !!
HOOSH

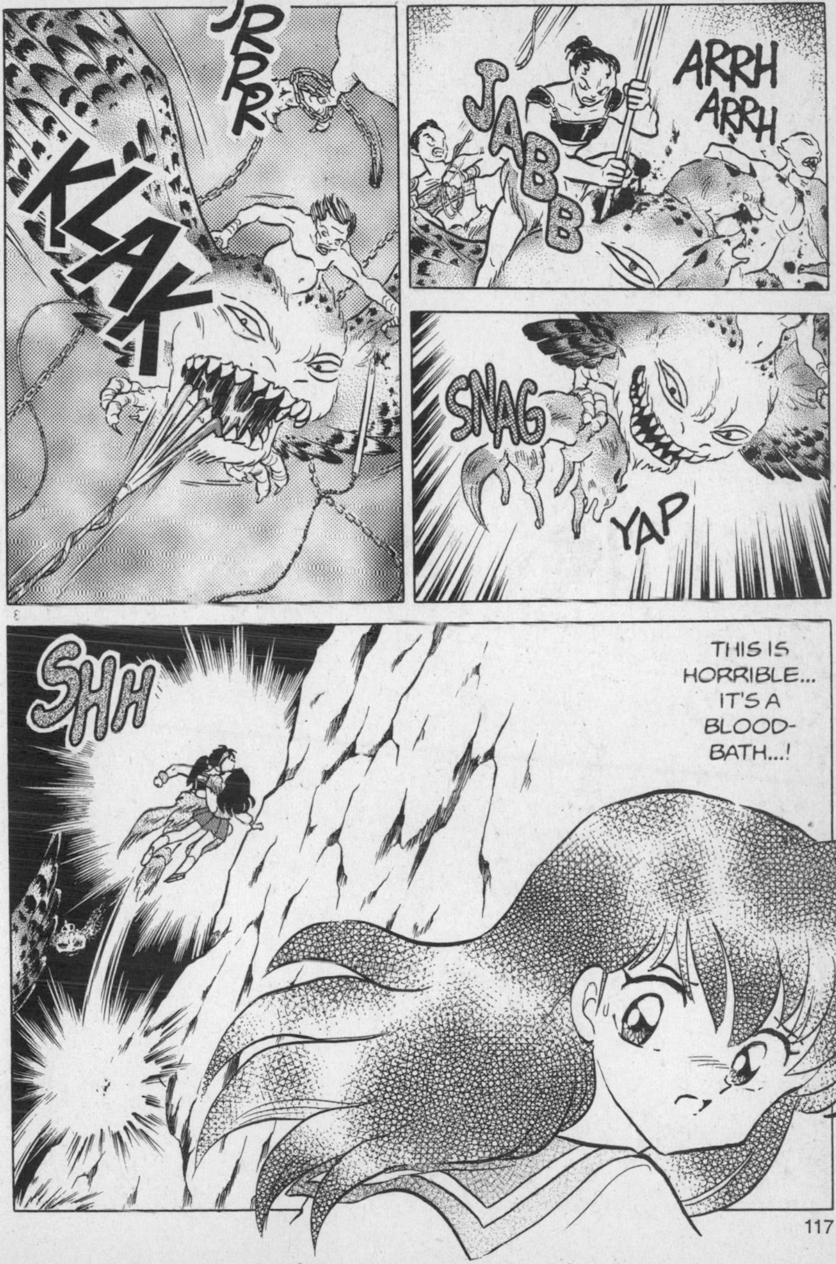
JRRR
KLAK
JABB
ARRH ARRH
SNAG
YAP
SHH
THIS IS HORRIBLE... IT'S A BLOOD-BATH...!

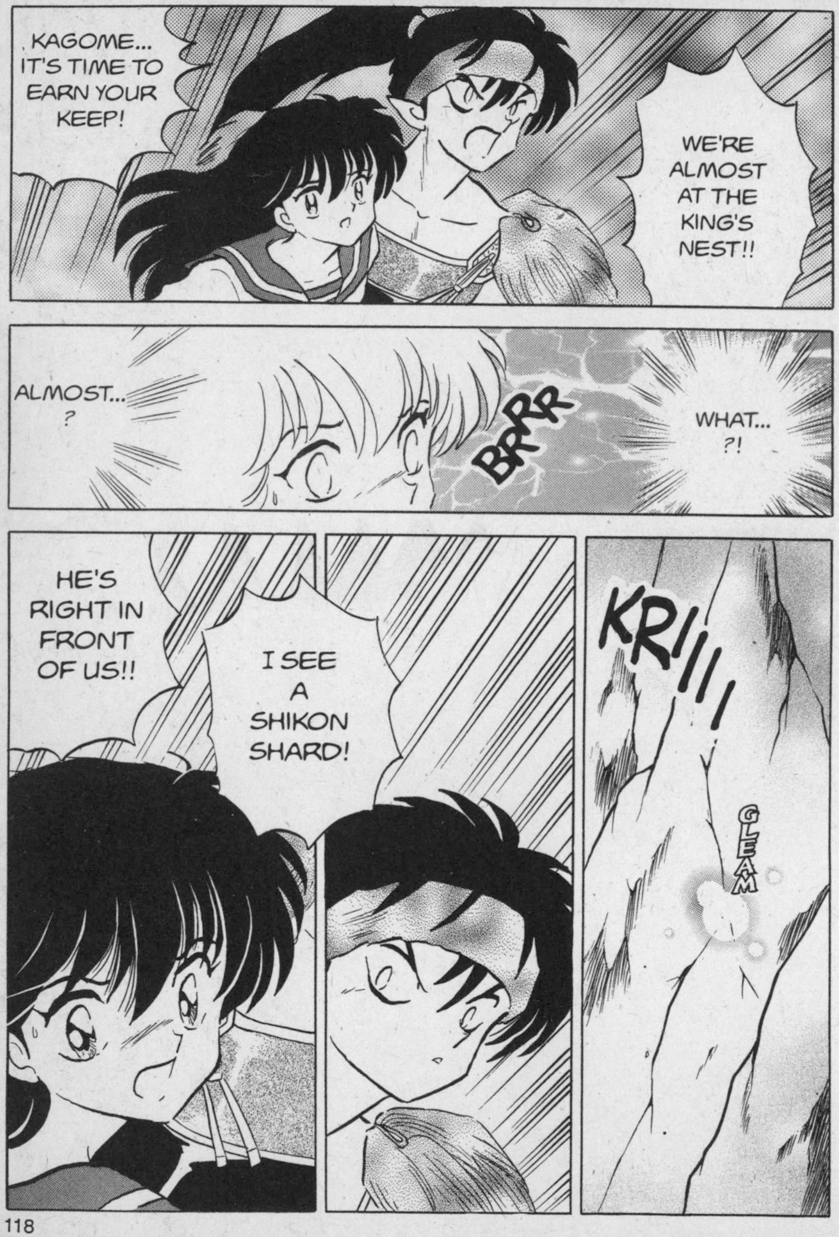
KAGOME... IT'S TIME TO EARN YOUR KEEP!
WE'RE ALMOST AT THE KING'S NEST!!
ALMOST... ?
BRRR
WHAT... ?!
HE'S RIGHT IN FRONT OF US!!
I SEE A SHIKON SHARD!
KRIIII
GLEAM

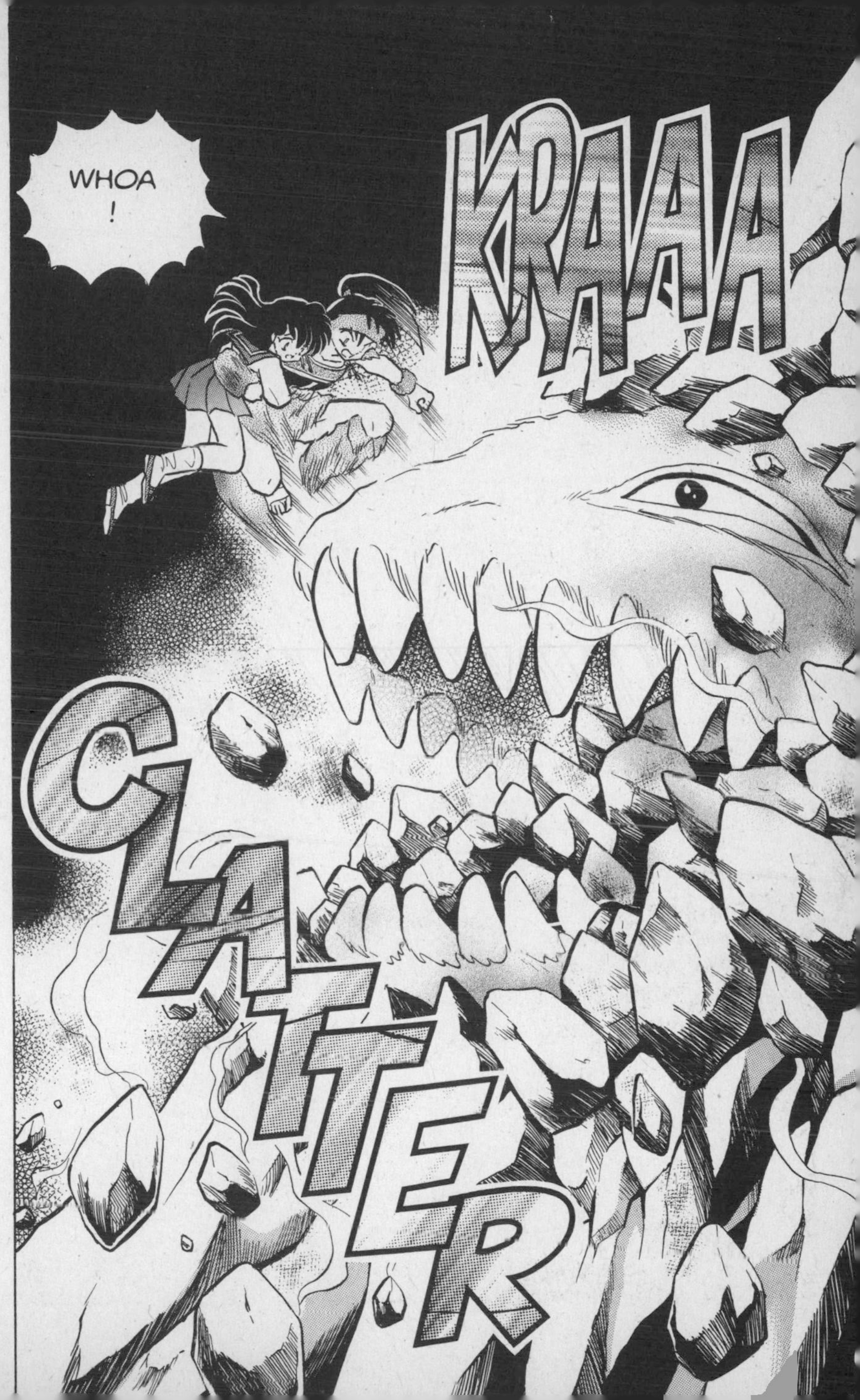
WHOA
!
KRAAA
CLATTER

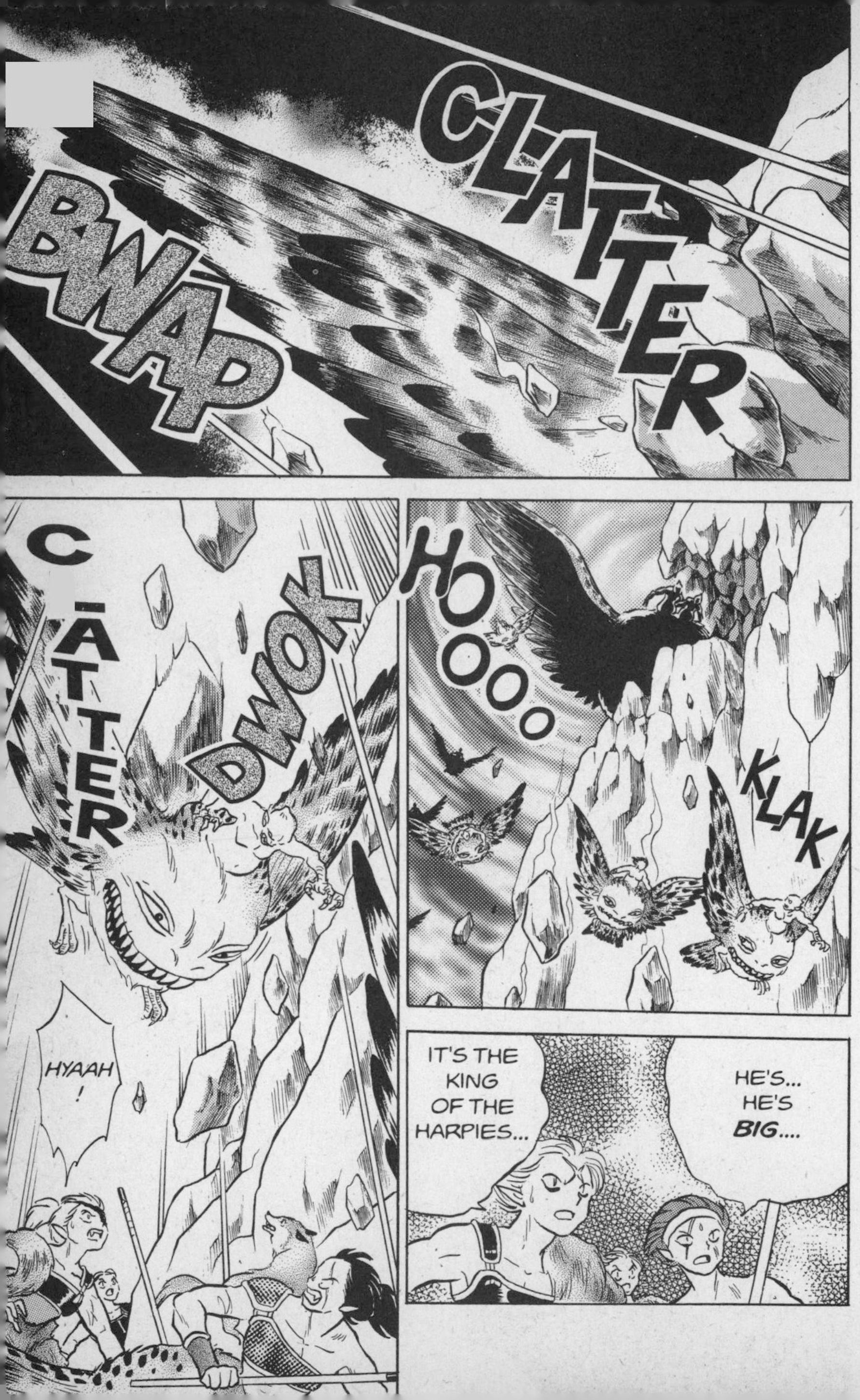
BWAP
CLATTER
C ATTER
DWOK
HYAAH!
HOOOO
KLAK
IT'S THE KING OF THE HARPIES...
HE'S... HE'S *BIG*....

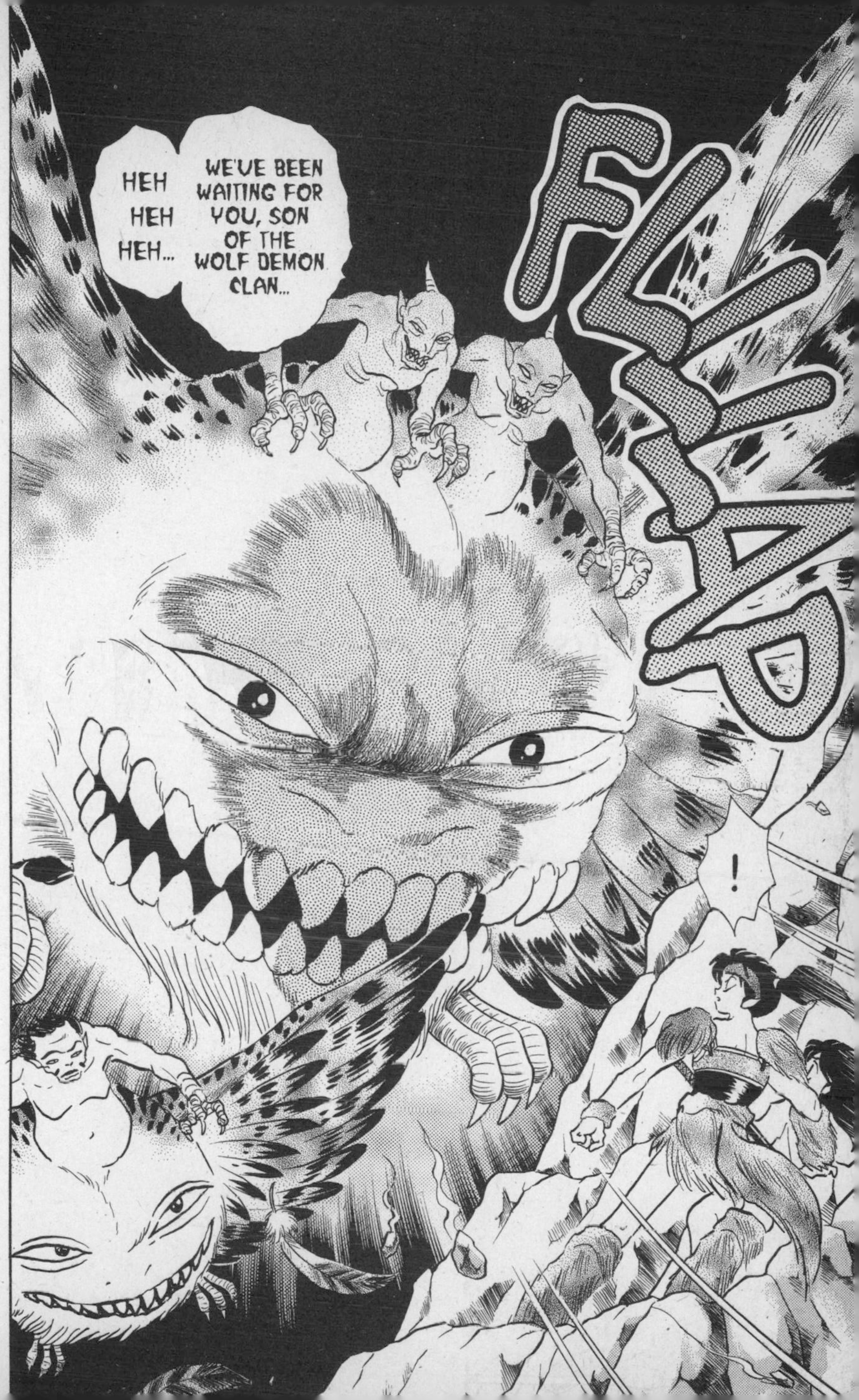
HEH HEH HEH...
WE'VE BEEN WAITING FOR YOU, SON OF THE WOLF DEMON CLAN...
FLAP
!

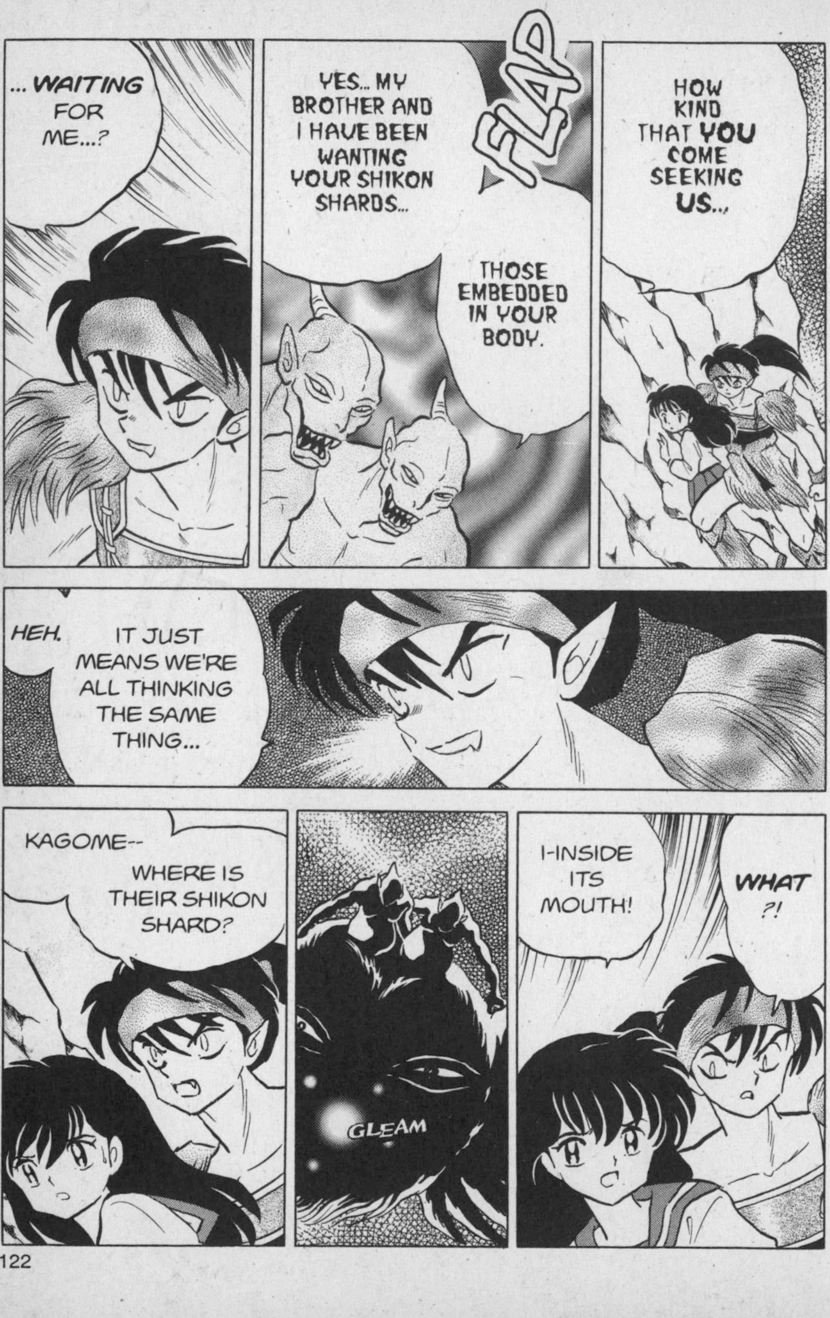
...WAITING FOR ME...?
YES... MY BROTHER AND I HAVE BEEN WANTING YOUR SHIKON SHARDS...
FLAP
THOSE EMBEDDED IN YOUR BODY.
HOW KIND THAT YOU COME SEEKING US...
HEH.
IT JUST MEANS WE'RE ALL THINKING THE SAME THING...
KAGOME--
WHERE IS THEIR SHIKON SHARD?
GLEAM
I-INSIDE ITS MOUTH!
WHAT?!

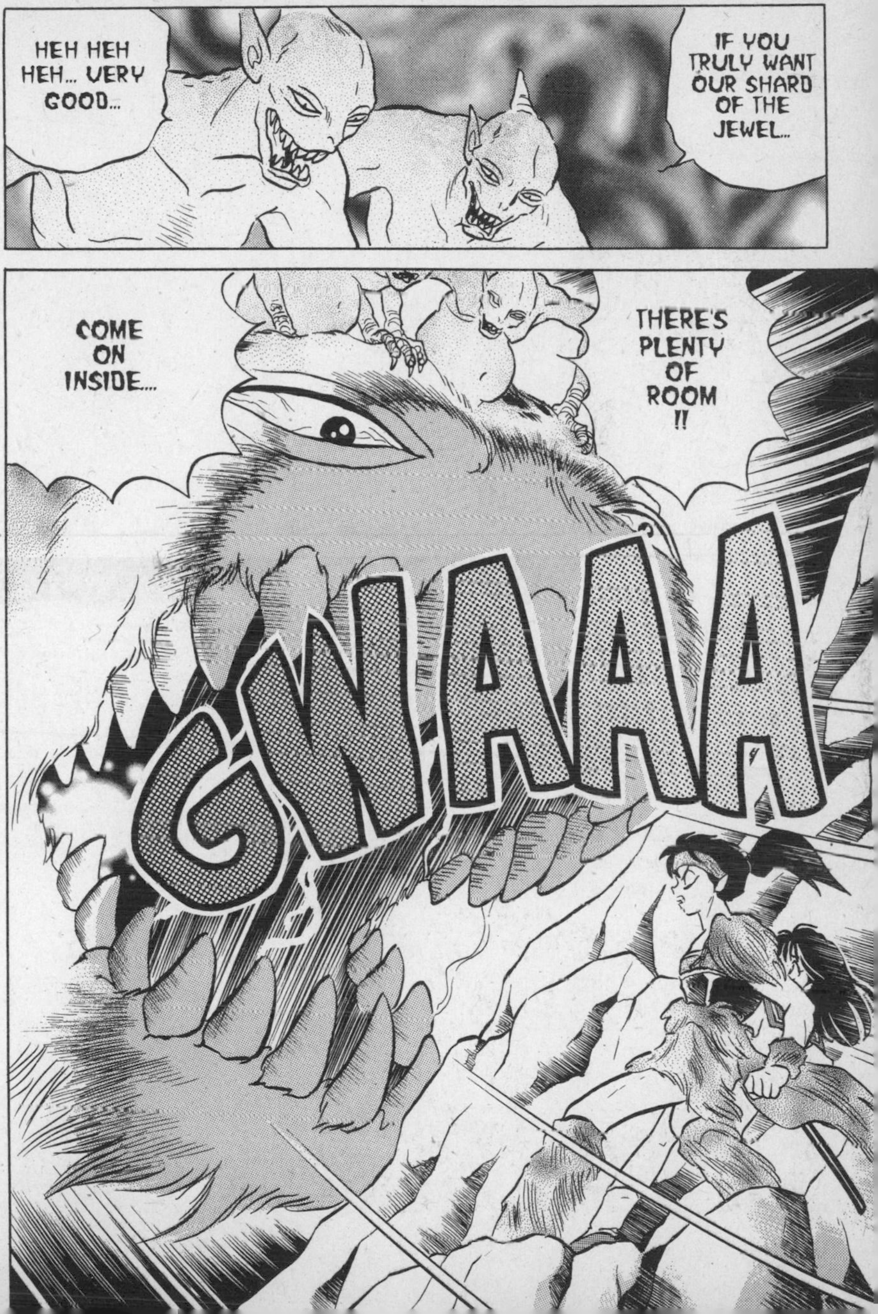
HEH HEH HEH... VERY GOOD...
IF YOU TRULY WANT OUR SHARD OF THE JEWEL...
COME ON INSIDE...
THERE'S PLENTY OF ROOM !!
GWAAA

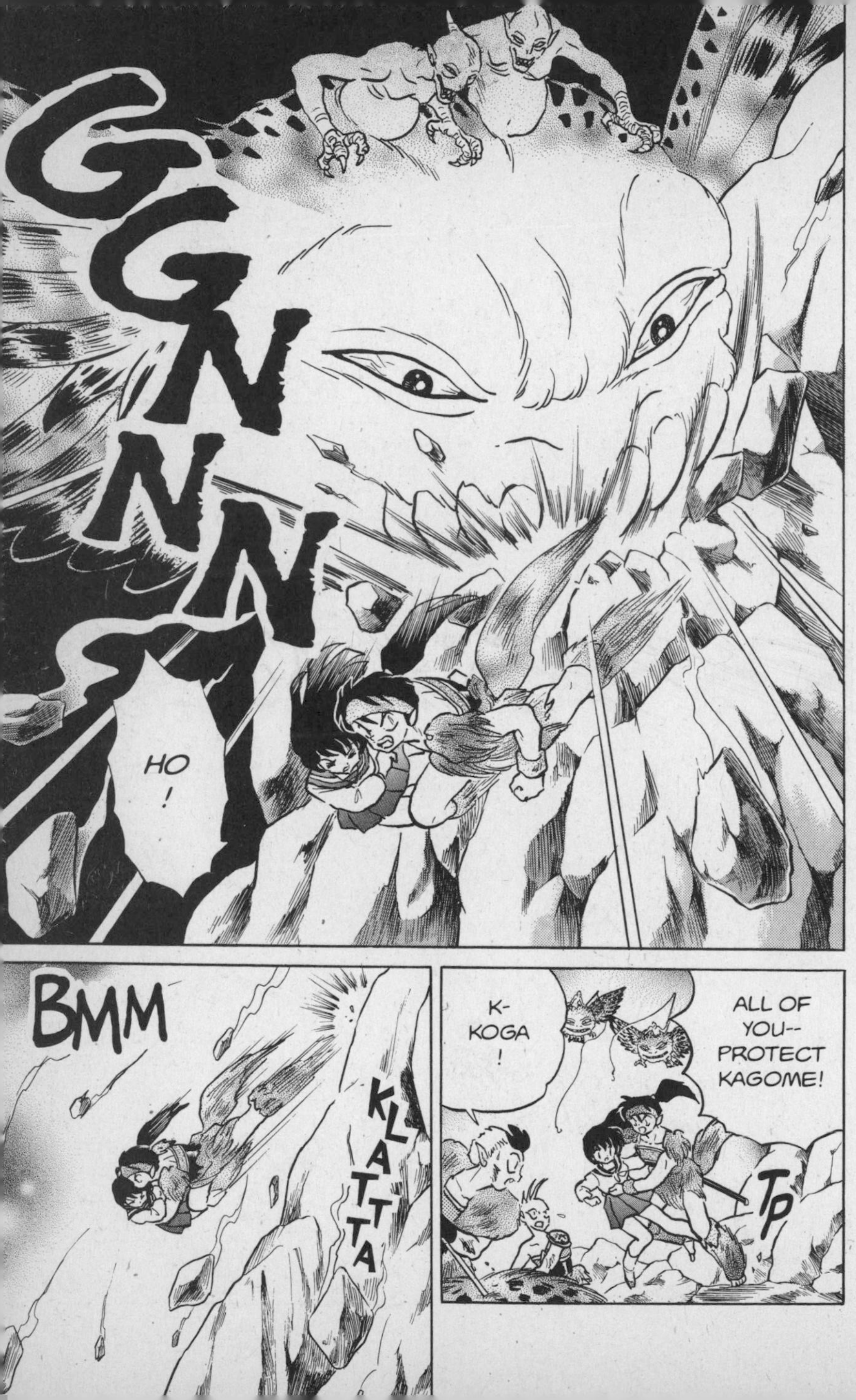
GGNNNS
HO!
BMM
KLATTTTA
K-KOGA!
ALL OF YOU-- PROTECT KAGOME!
TP

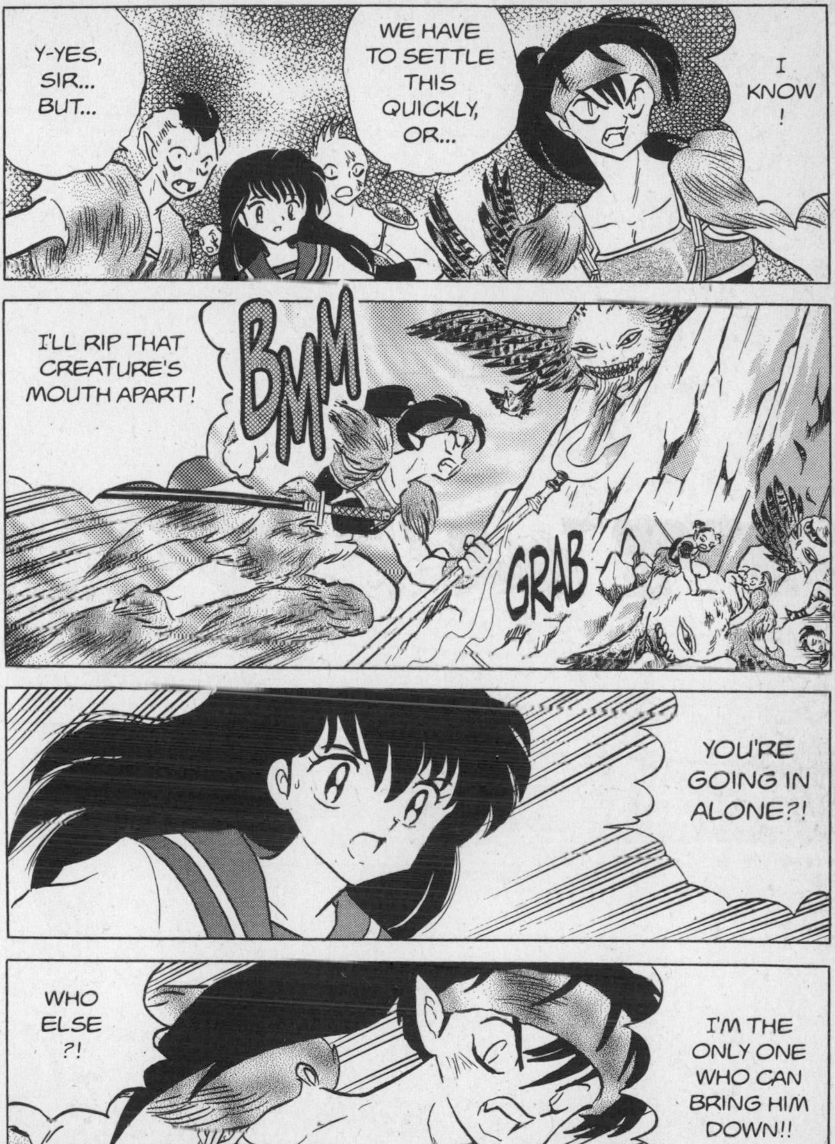
Y-YES, SIR... BUT...
WE HAVE TO SETTLE THIS QUICKLY, OR...
I KNOW!
I'LL RIP THAT CREATURE'S MOUTH APART!
BMM
GRAB
YOU'RE GOING IN ALONE?!
WHO ELSE?!
I'M THE ONLY ONE WHO CAN BRING HIM DOWN!!

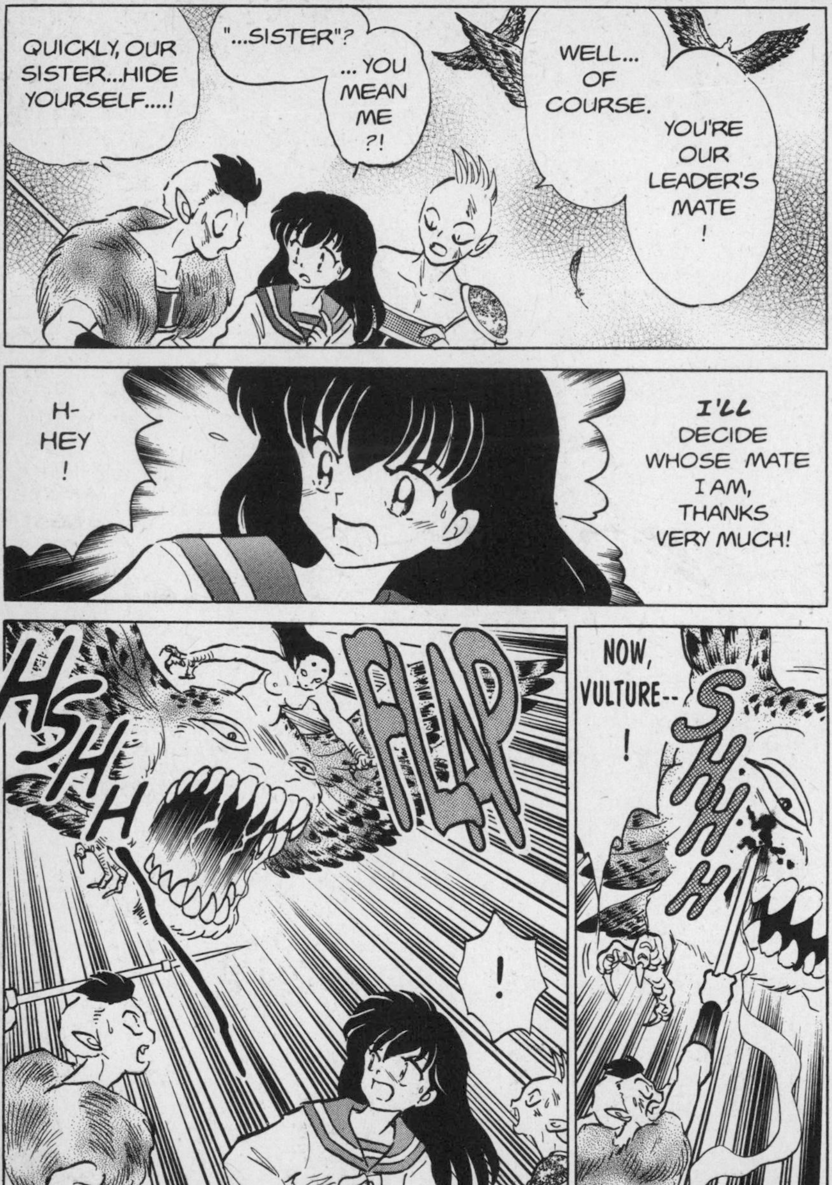
QUICKLY, OUR SISTER...HIDE YOURSELF....!
"...SISTER"?
... YOU MEAN ME ?!
WELL... OF COURSE.
YOU'RE OUR LEADER'S MATE !
H- HEY !
I'LL DECIDE WHOSE MATE I AM, THANKS VERY MUCH!
HSHHH
FLAP
!
NOW, VULTURE-- !
SHHHH

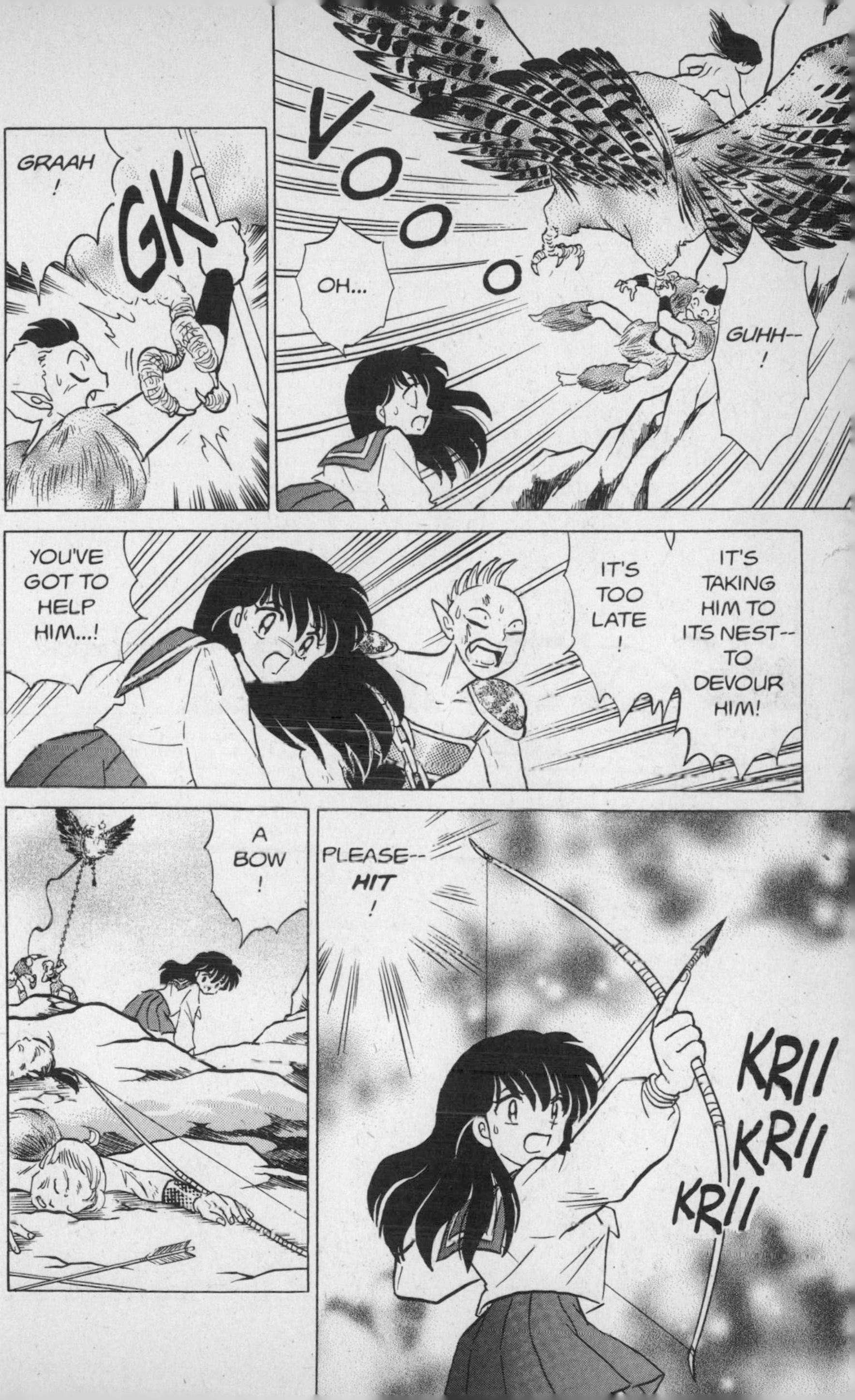

GRAAH !
GK
VOOOO
OH...
GUHH-- !
YOU'VE GOT TO HELP HIM...!
IT'S TOO LATE !
IT'S TAKING HIM TO ITS NEST-- TO DEVOUR HIM!
A BOW !
PLEASE-- HIT !
KRII KRII KRII

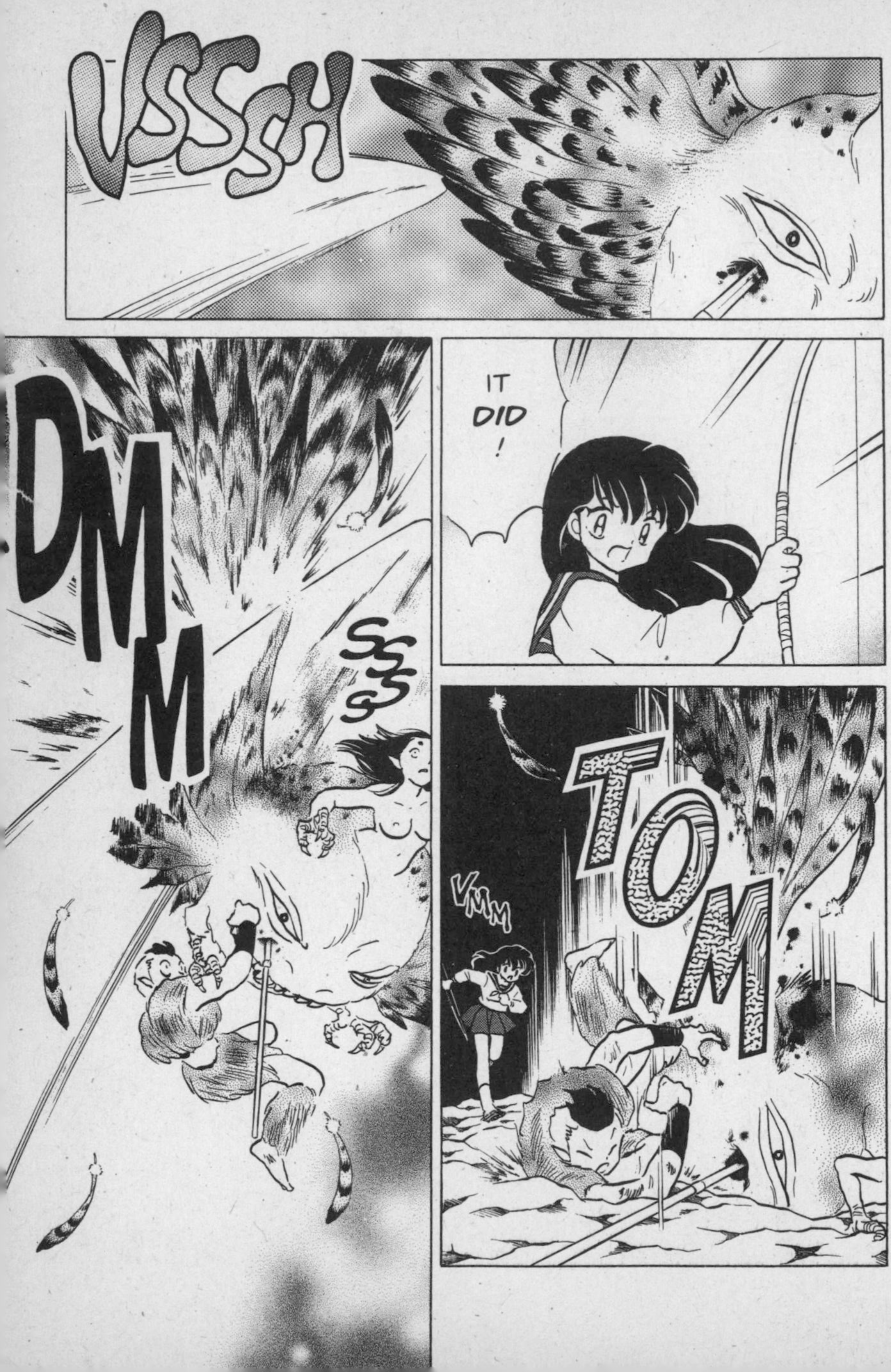
VSSSH
DMM
SSSS
IT DID!
VMM
TOM

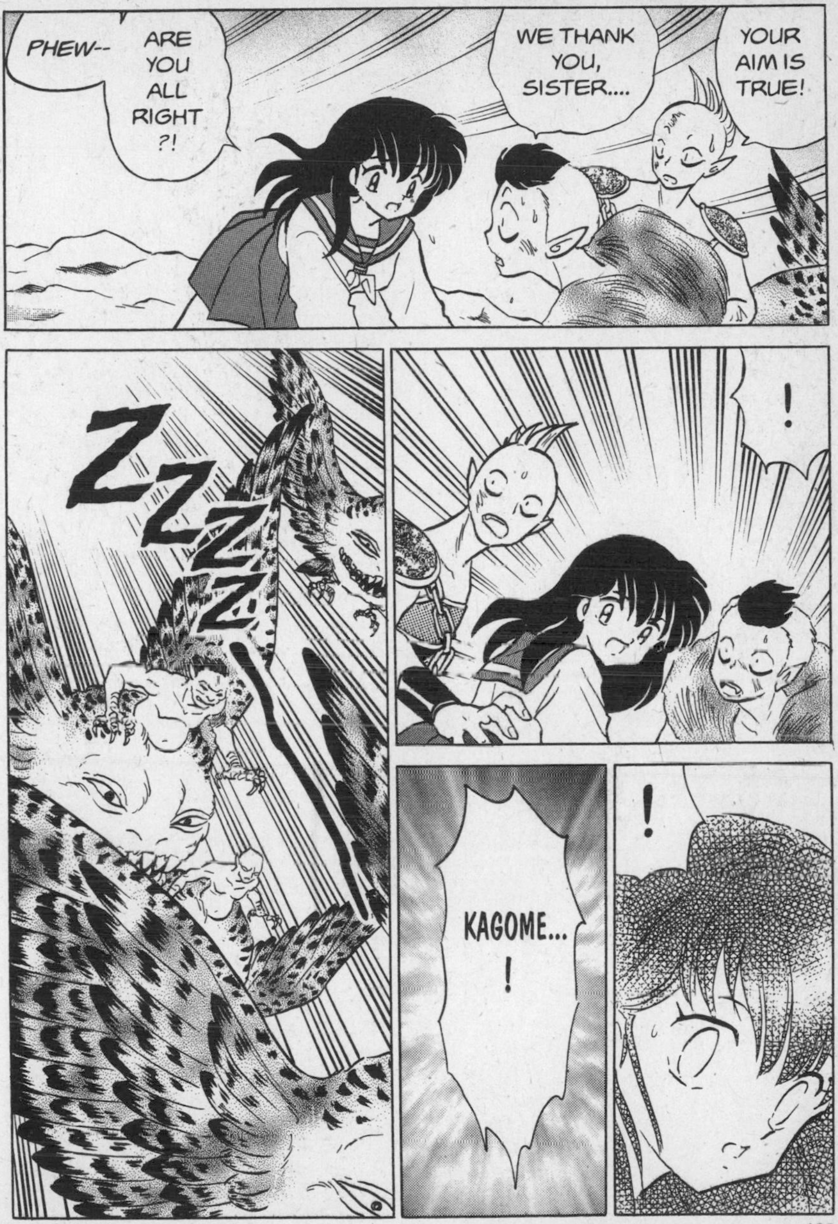
PHEW--
ARE YOU ALL RIGHT ?!
WE THANK YOU, SISTER....
YOUR AIM IS TRUE!
ZZZZZ
!
KAGOME... !
!

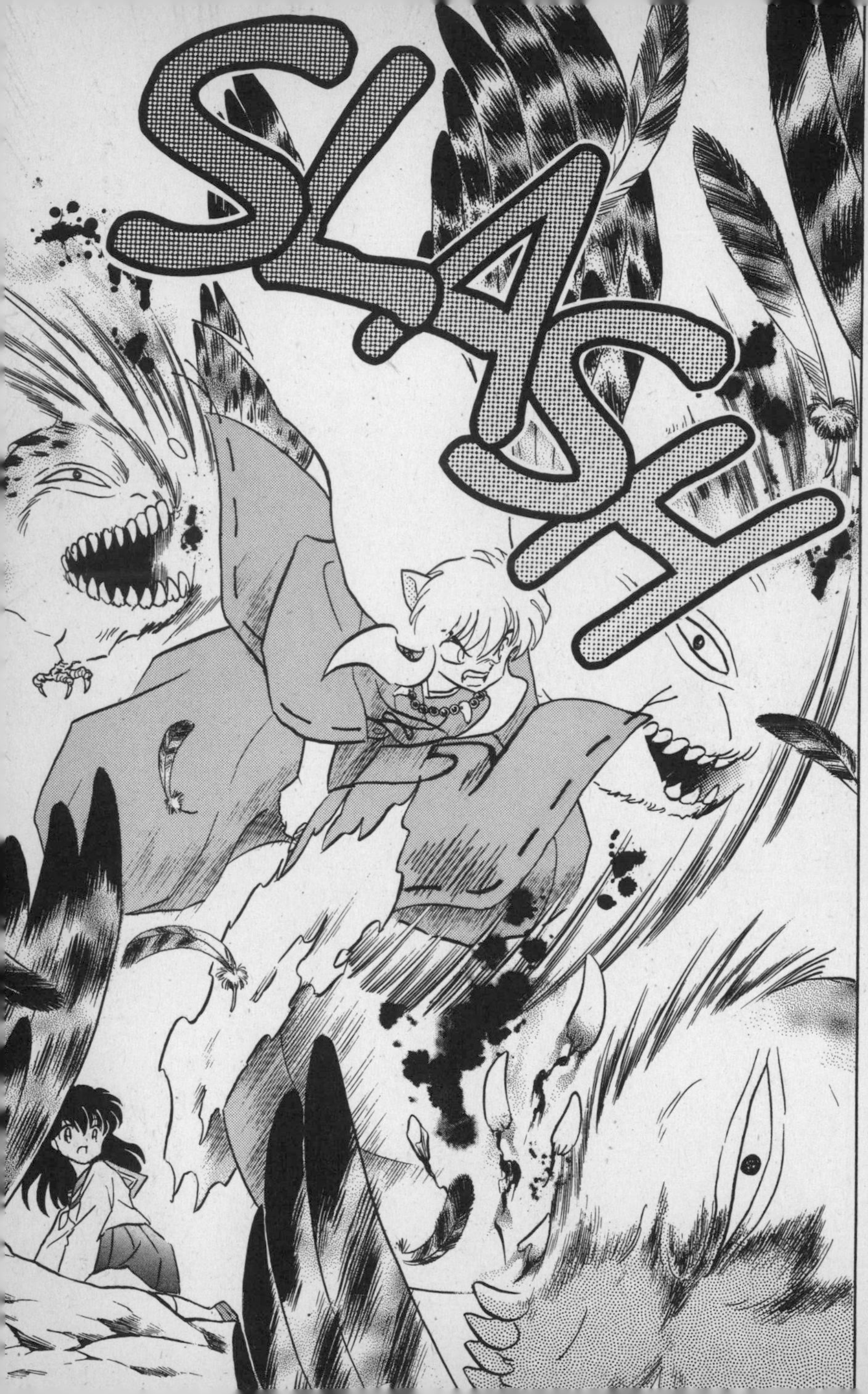
SLASH

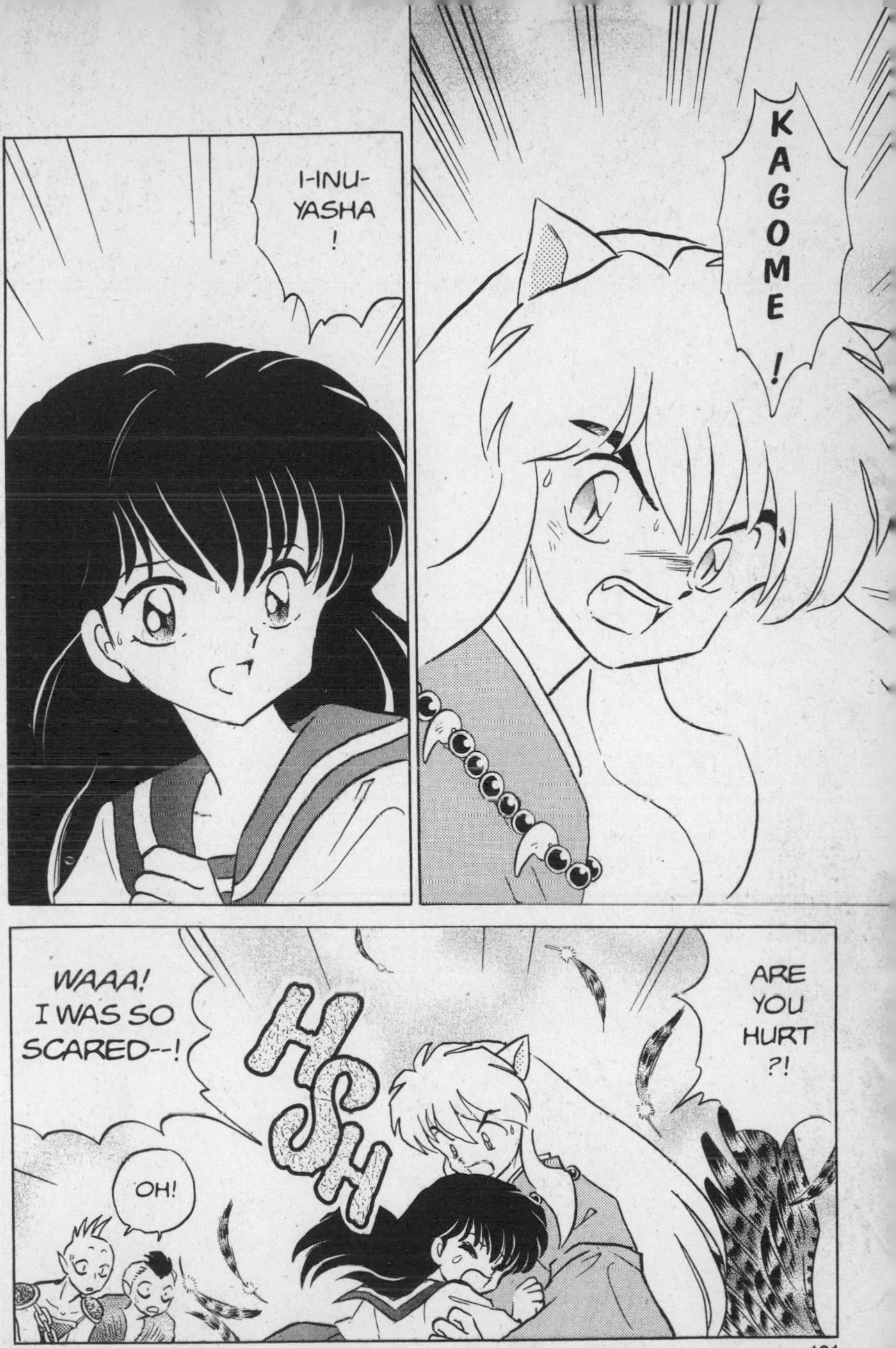
I-INU-YASHA !
KAGOME !
WAAA! I WAS SO SCARED--!
ARE YOU HURT ?!
HSH
OH!

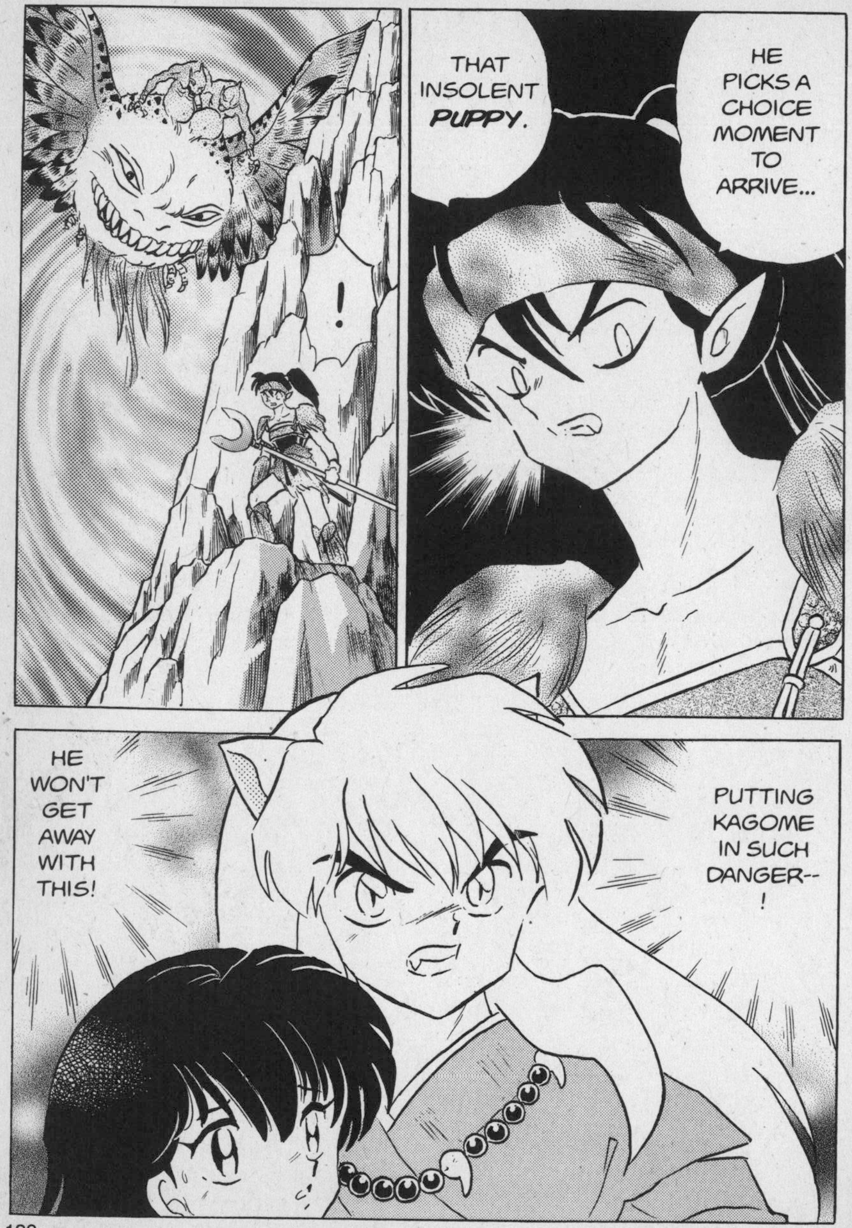
!
THAT INSOLENT PUPPY.
HE PICKS A CHOICE MOMENT TO ARRIVE...
HE WON'T GET AWAY WITH THIS!
PUTTING KAGOME IN SUCH DANGER--!

SCROLL EIGHT

THE THREE-WAY BATTLE

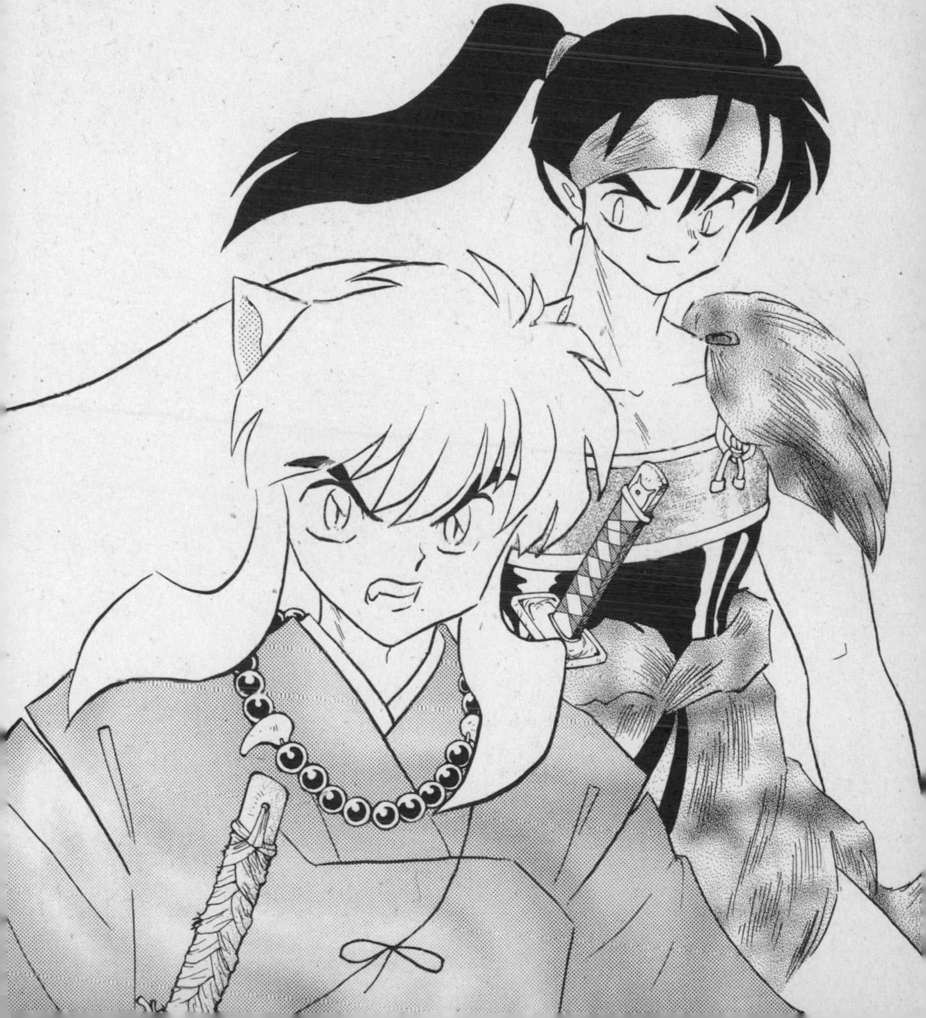

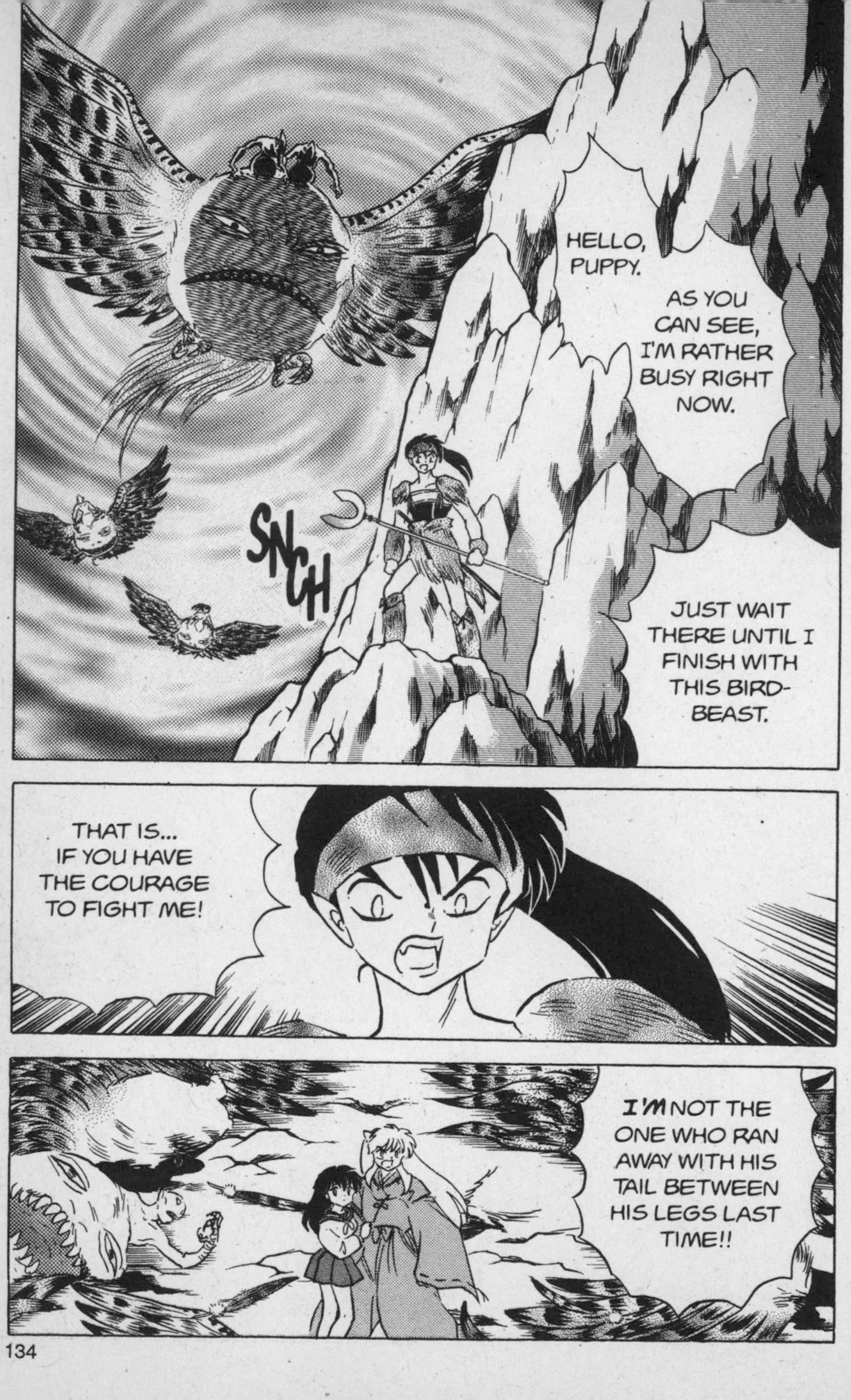
SNCH
HELLO, PUPPY.
AS YOU CAN SEE, I'M RATHER BUSY RIGHT NOW.
JUST WAIT THERE UNTIL I FINISH WITH THIS BIRD-BEAST.
THAT IS... IF YOU HAVE THE COURAGE TO FIGHT ME!
I'M NOT THE ONE WHO RAN AWAY WITH HIS TAIL BETWEEN HIS LEGS LAST TIME!!

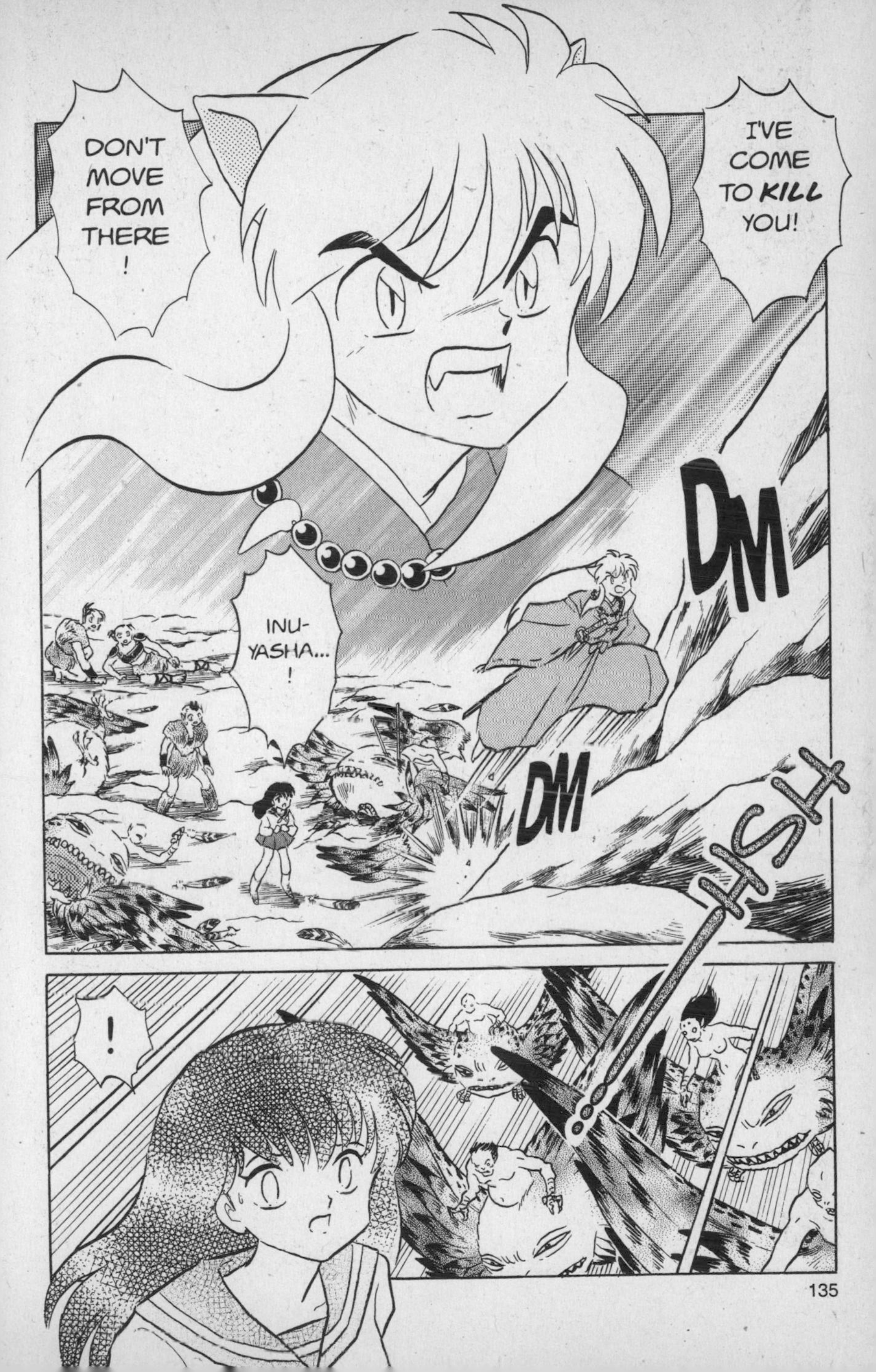
DON'T MOVE FROM THERE !
I'VE COME TO KILL YOU!
DM
INU-YASHA... !
DM
HSH
!

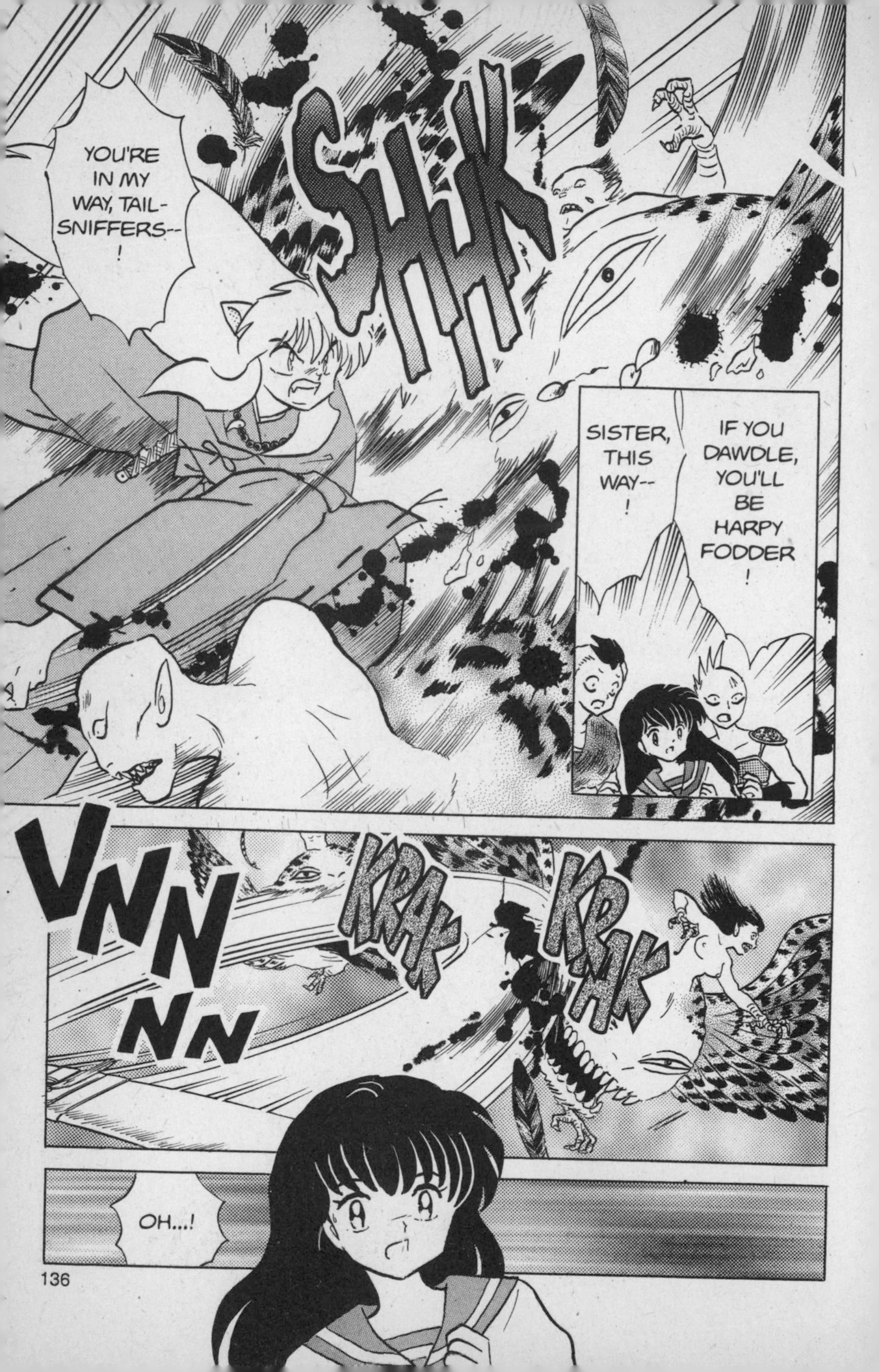
YOU'RE IN MY WAY, TAIL-SNIFFERS--!
SHHK
SISTER, THIS WAY--!
IF YOU DAWDLE, YOU'LL BE HARPY FODDER!
VNNNN
KRAK
KRAK
OH...!

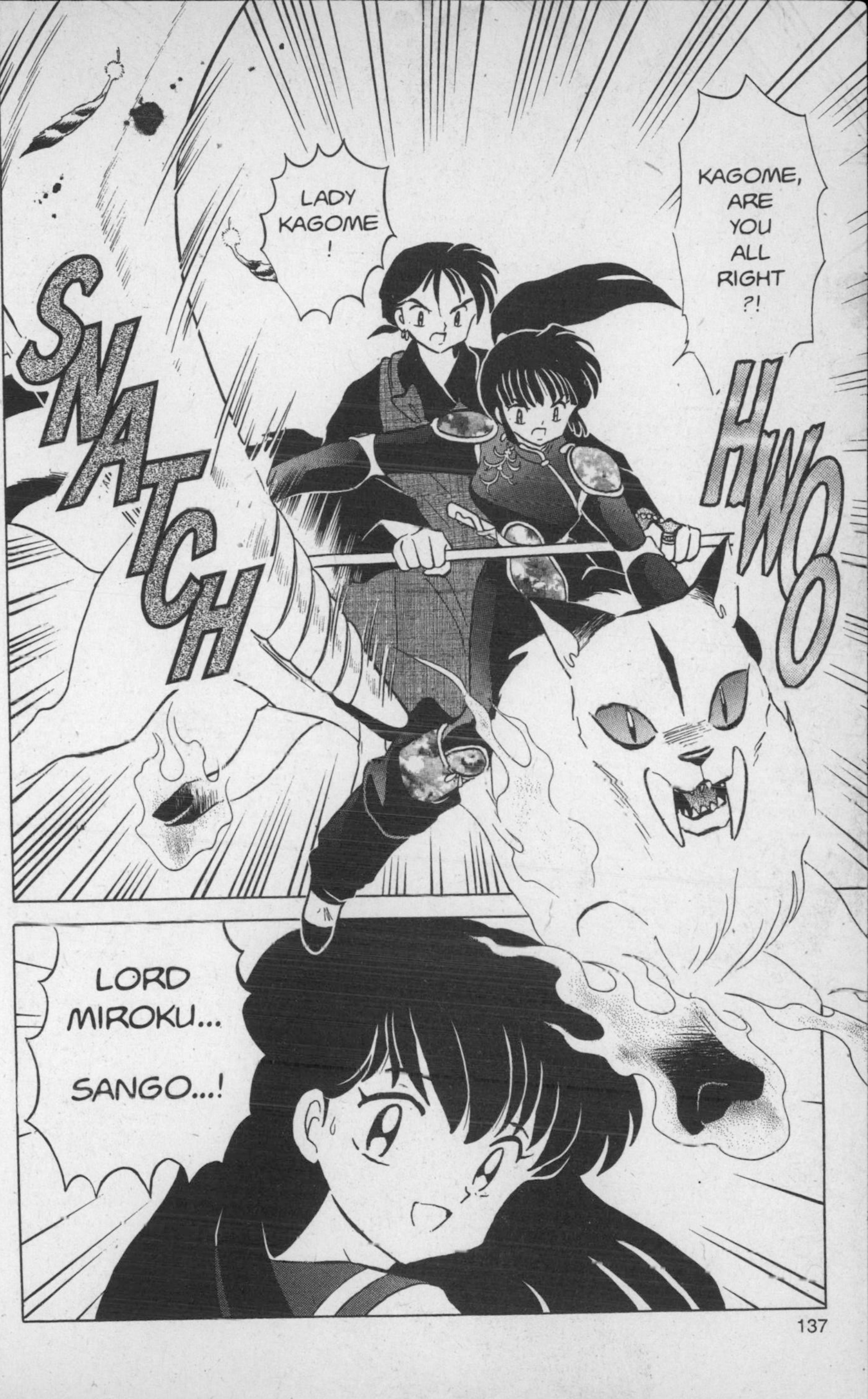
LADY KAGOME!
SNATCH
KAGOME, ARE YOU ALL RIGHT?!
HWOO
LORD MIROKU... SANGO...!

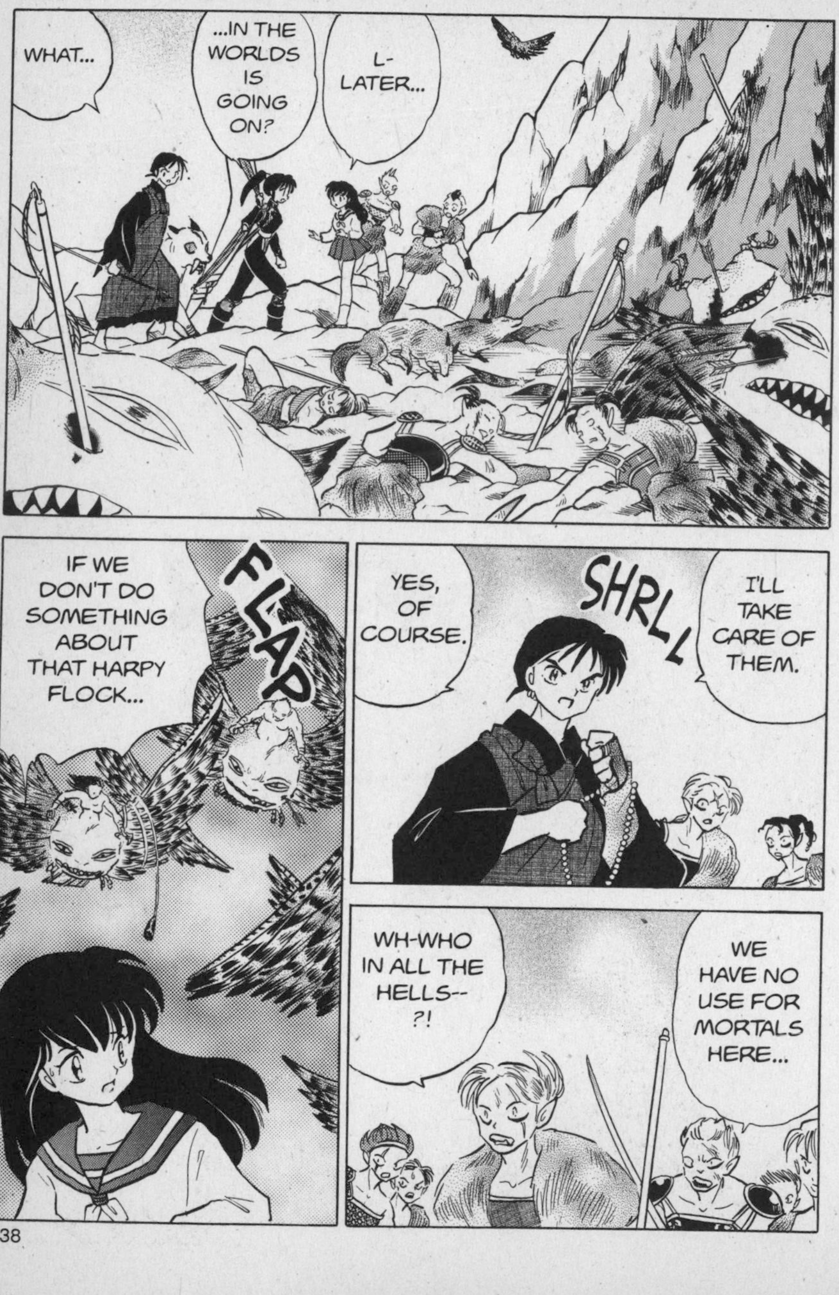
WHAT...
...IN THE WORLDS IS GOING ON?
L-LATER...
IF WE DON'T DO SOMETHING ABOUT THAT HARPY FLOCK...
FLAP
YES, OF COURSE.
SHRLL
I'LL TAKE CARE OF THEM.
WH-WHO IN ALL THE HELLS--?!
WE HAVE NO USE FOR MORTALS HERE...

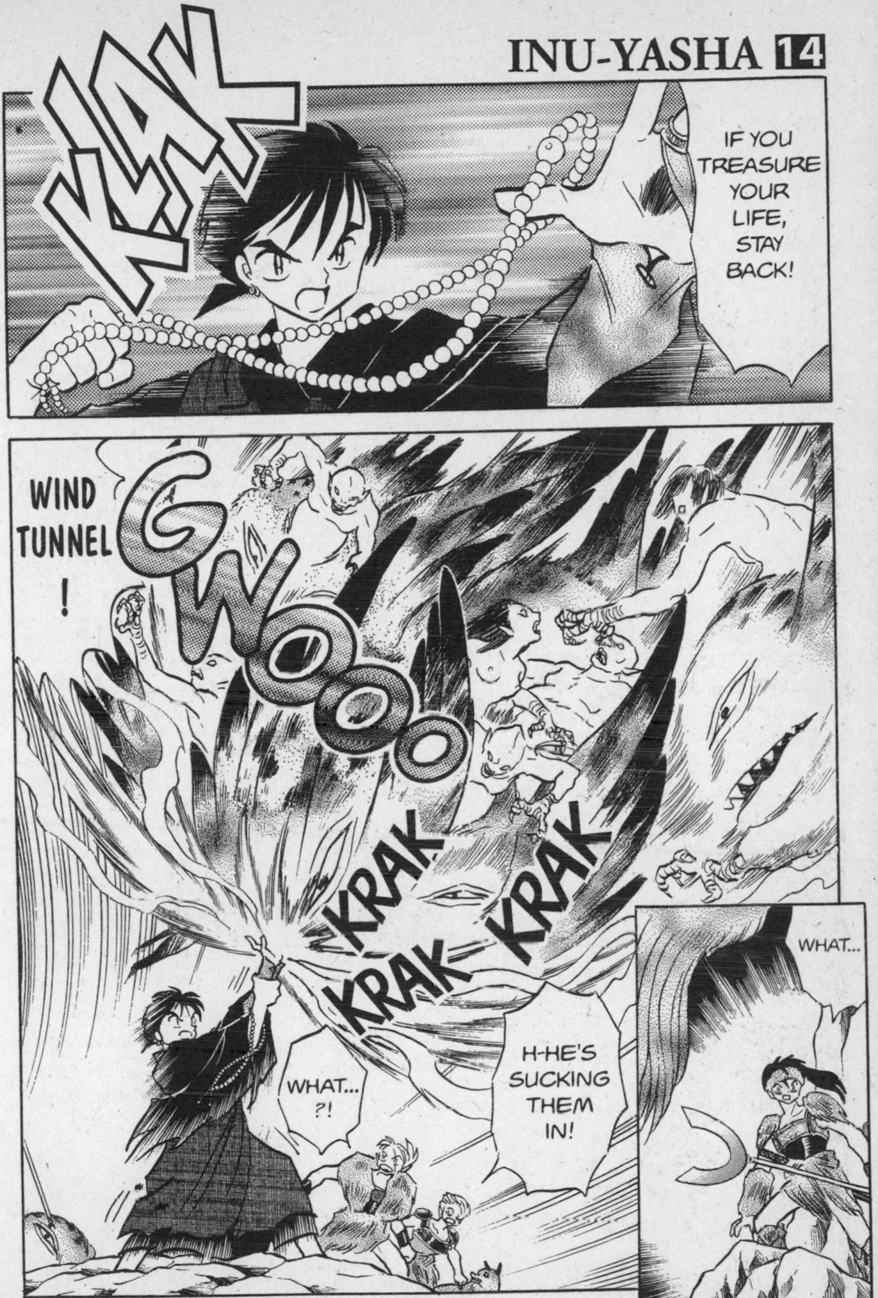
KLAK
IF YOU TREASURE YOUR LIFE, STAY BACK!
WIND TUNNEL!
GWOOOO
KRAK
KRAK
KRAK
WHAT... ?!
H-HE'S SUCKING THEM IN!
WHAT...

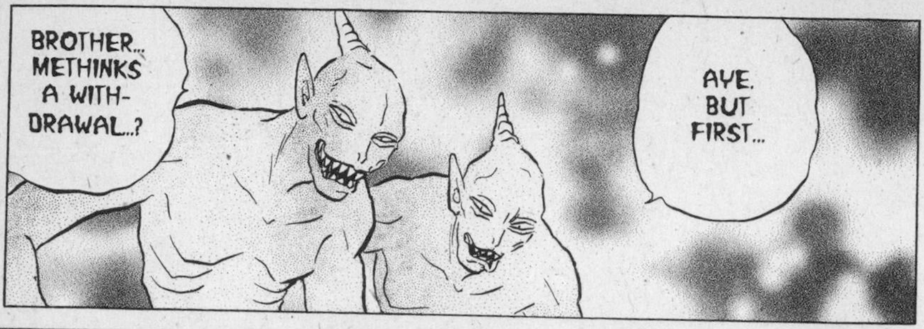
BROTHER... METHINKS A WITH-DRAWAL...?
AYE. BUT FIRST...

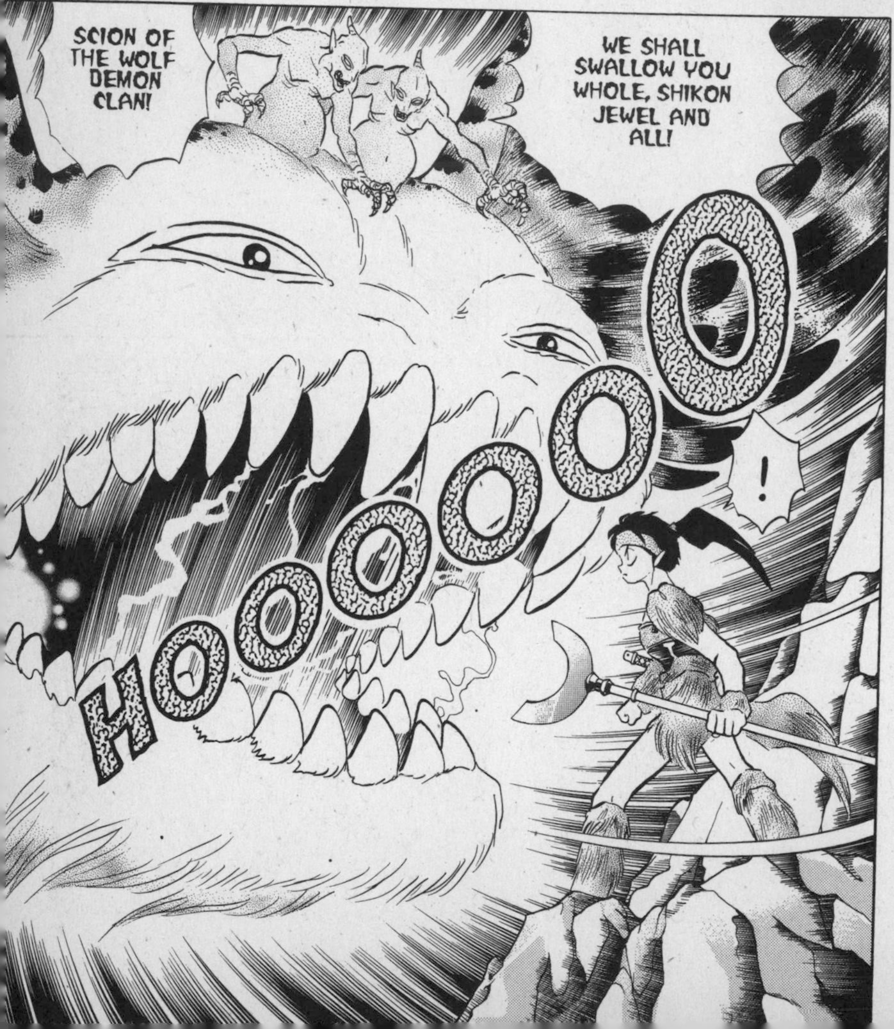
SCION OF THE WOLF DEMON CLAN!
WE SHALL SWALLOW YOU WHOLE, SHIKON JEWEL AND ALL!
HOOOOOO
!

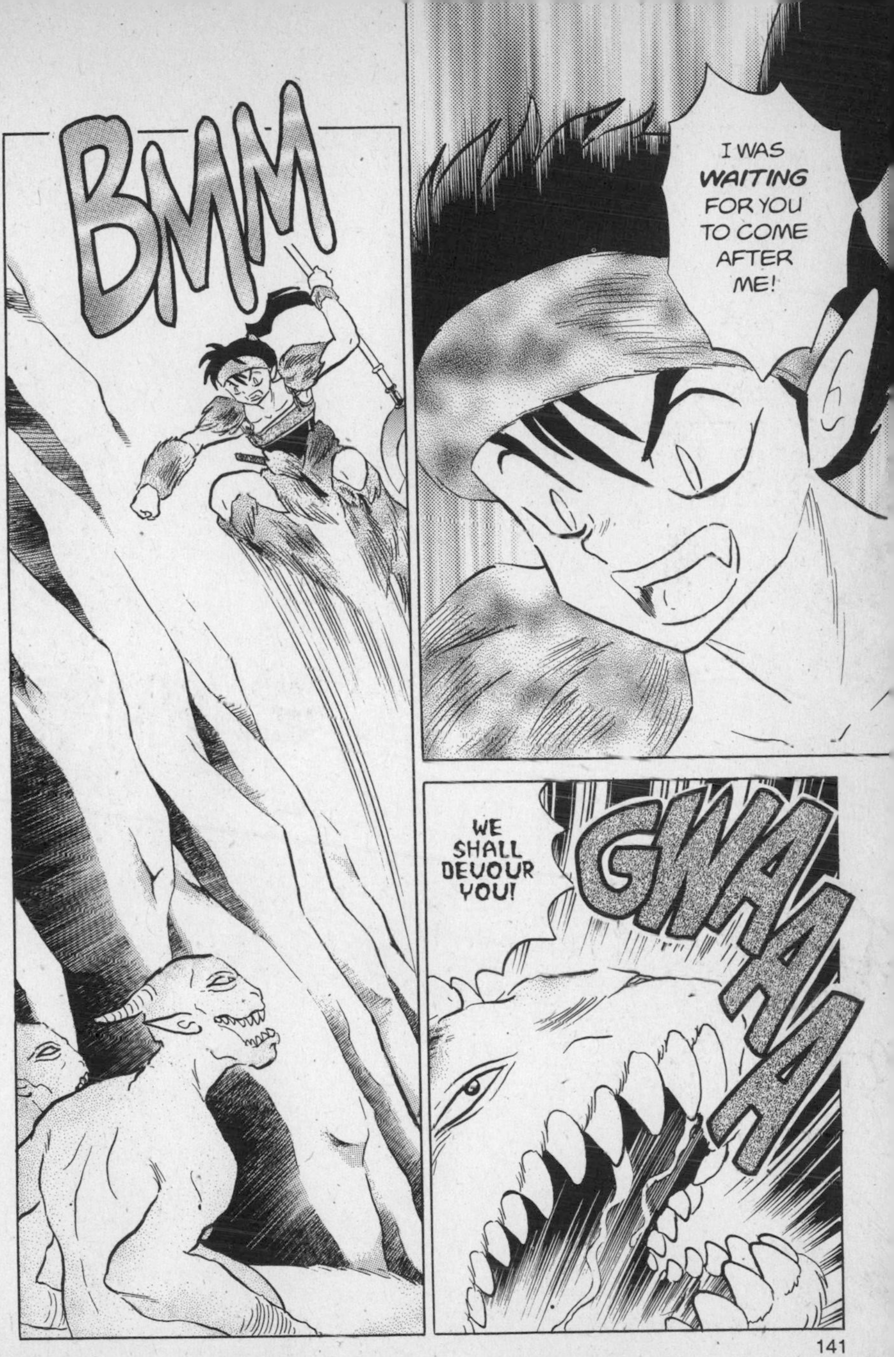
BMM
I WAS WAITING FOR YOU TO COME AFTER ME!
WE SHALL DEVOUR YOU!
GWAAAA

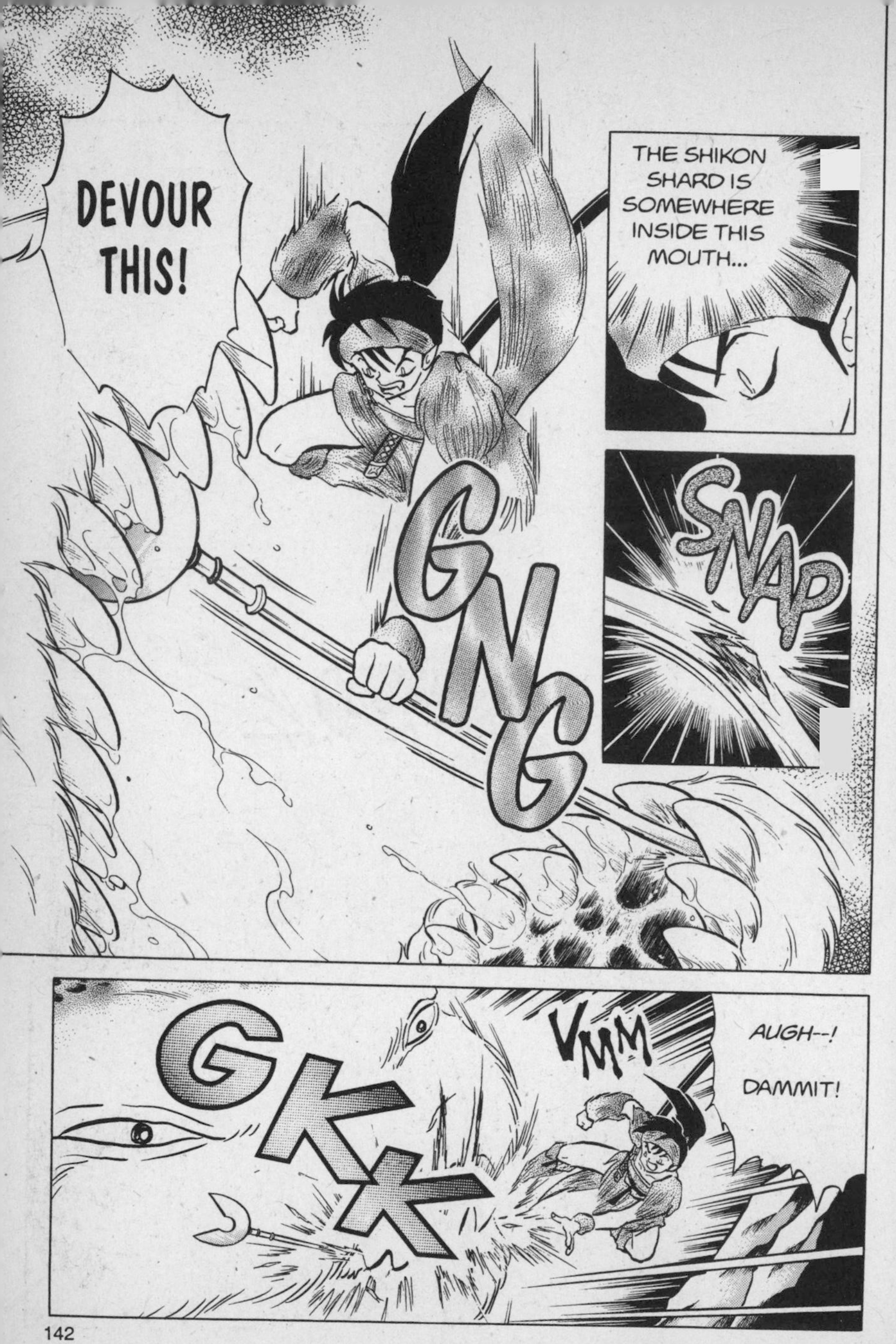
DEVOUR THIS!
GNG
THE SHIKON SHARD IS SOMEWHERE INSIDE THIS MOUTH...
SNAP
GKK
VMM
AUGH--!
DAMMIT!

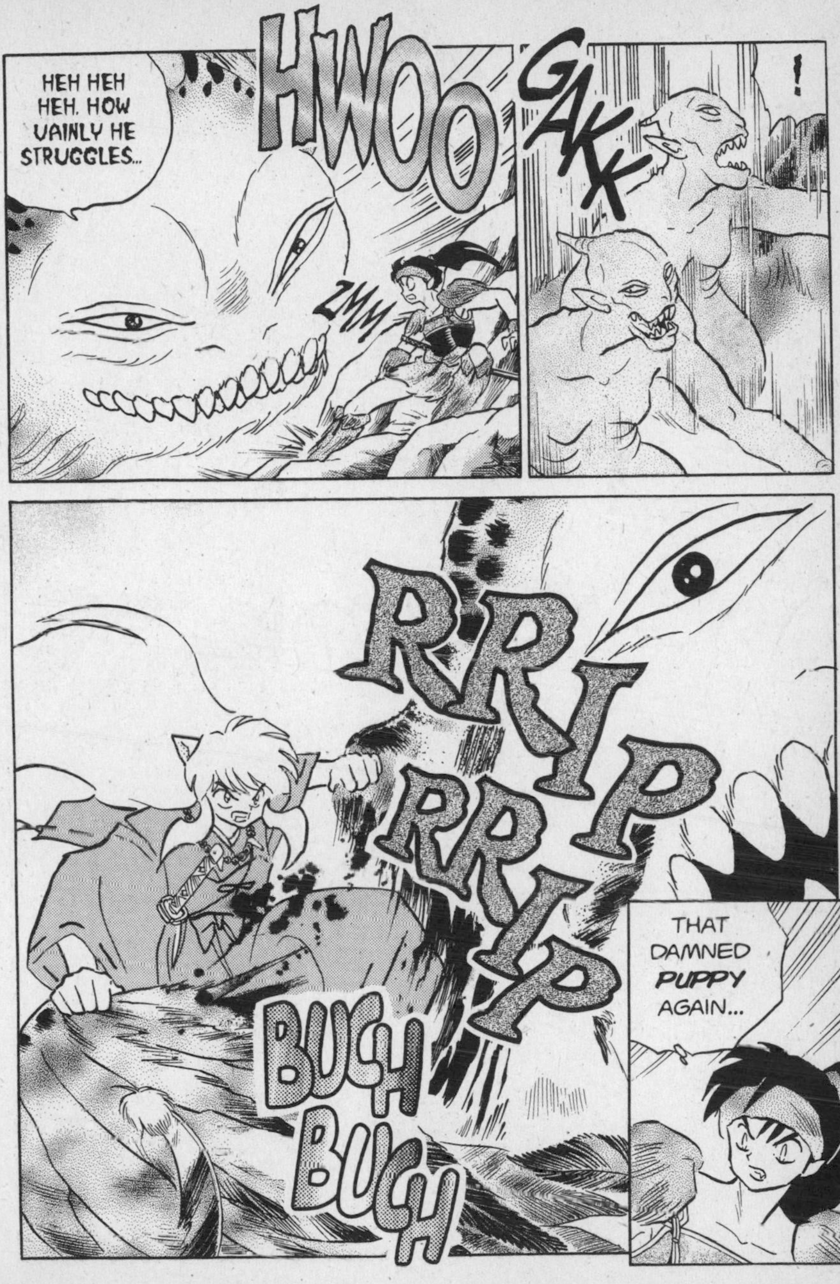
HEH HEH HEH. HOW VAINLY HE STRUGGLES...
HWOO
ZMM
GAKK
!
RRIP
RRIP
BUCH
BUCH
THAT DAMNED **PUPPY** AGAIN...

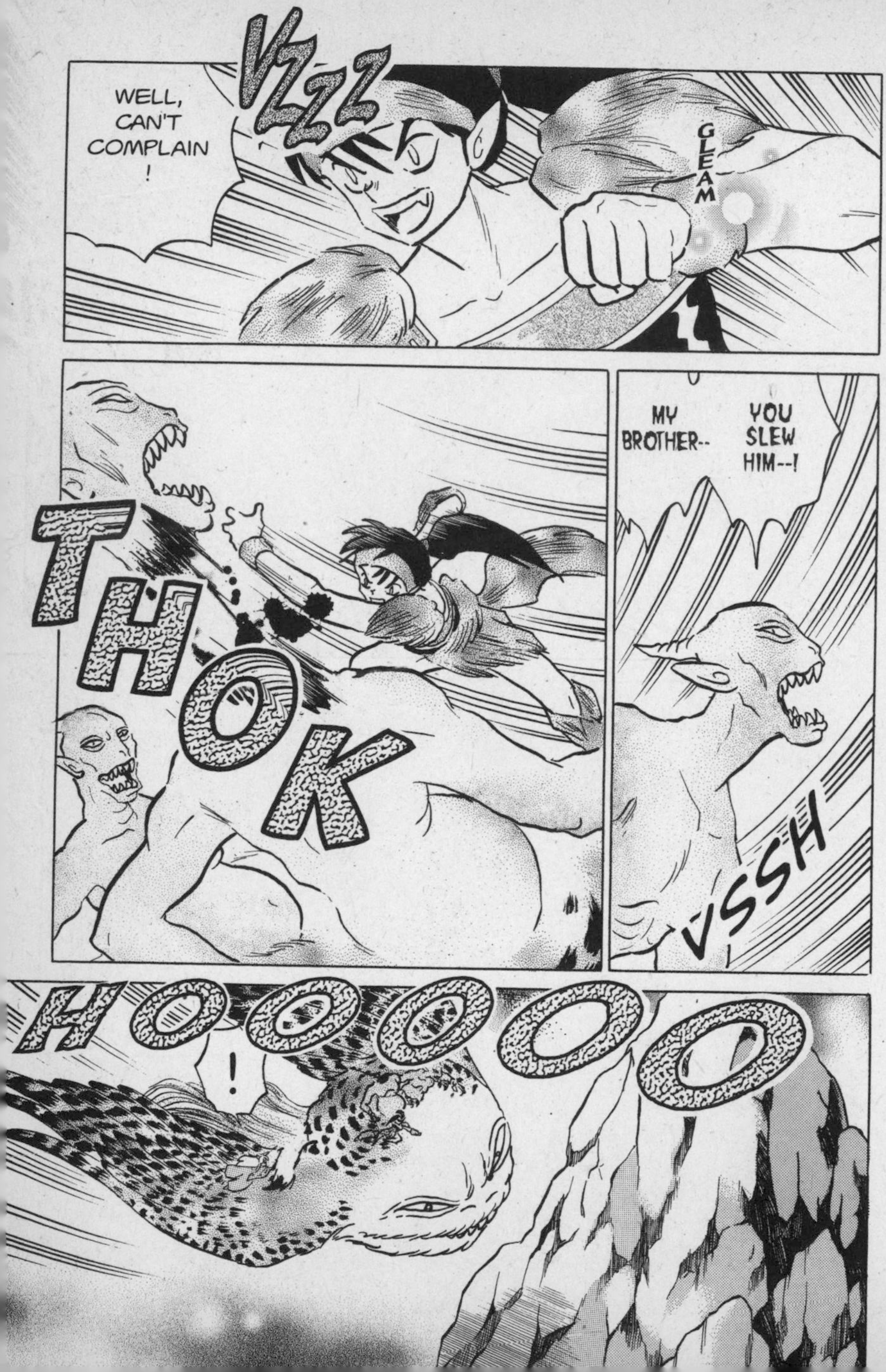
VZZZ
WELL, CAN'T COMPLAIN !
GLEAM
THOK
MY BROTHER--
YOU SLEW HIM--!
VSSH
HOOOOOO
!

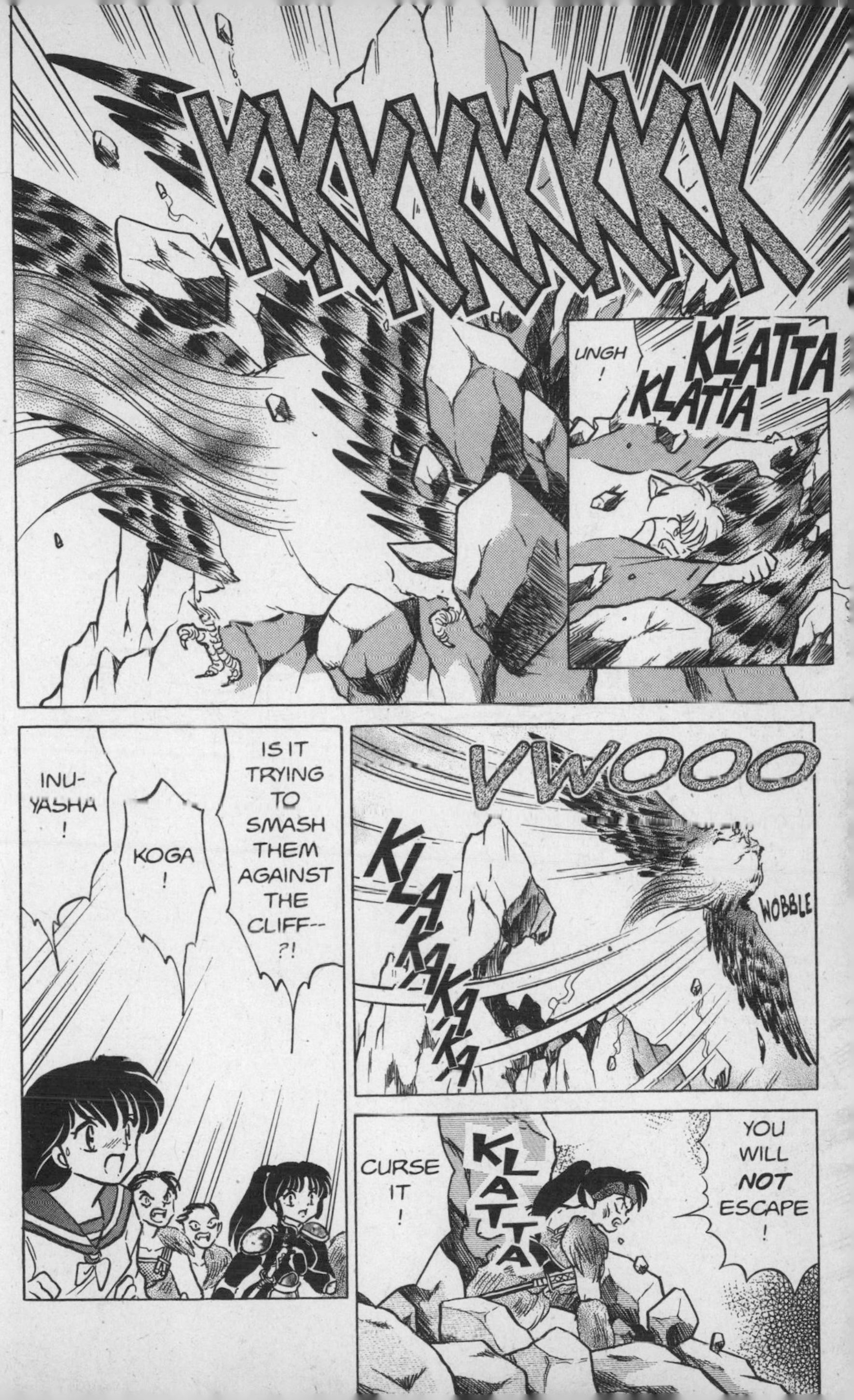
KKKKKKKKK
KLATTA KLATTA
UNGH!
VWOOO
WOBBLE
KLAKAKAKA
IS IT TRYING TO SMASH THEM AGAINST THE CLIFF--?!
KOGA!
INU-YASHA!
YOU WILL NOT ESCAPE!
KLATTA
CURSE IT!

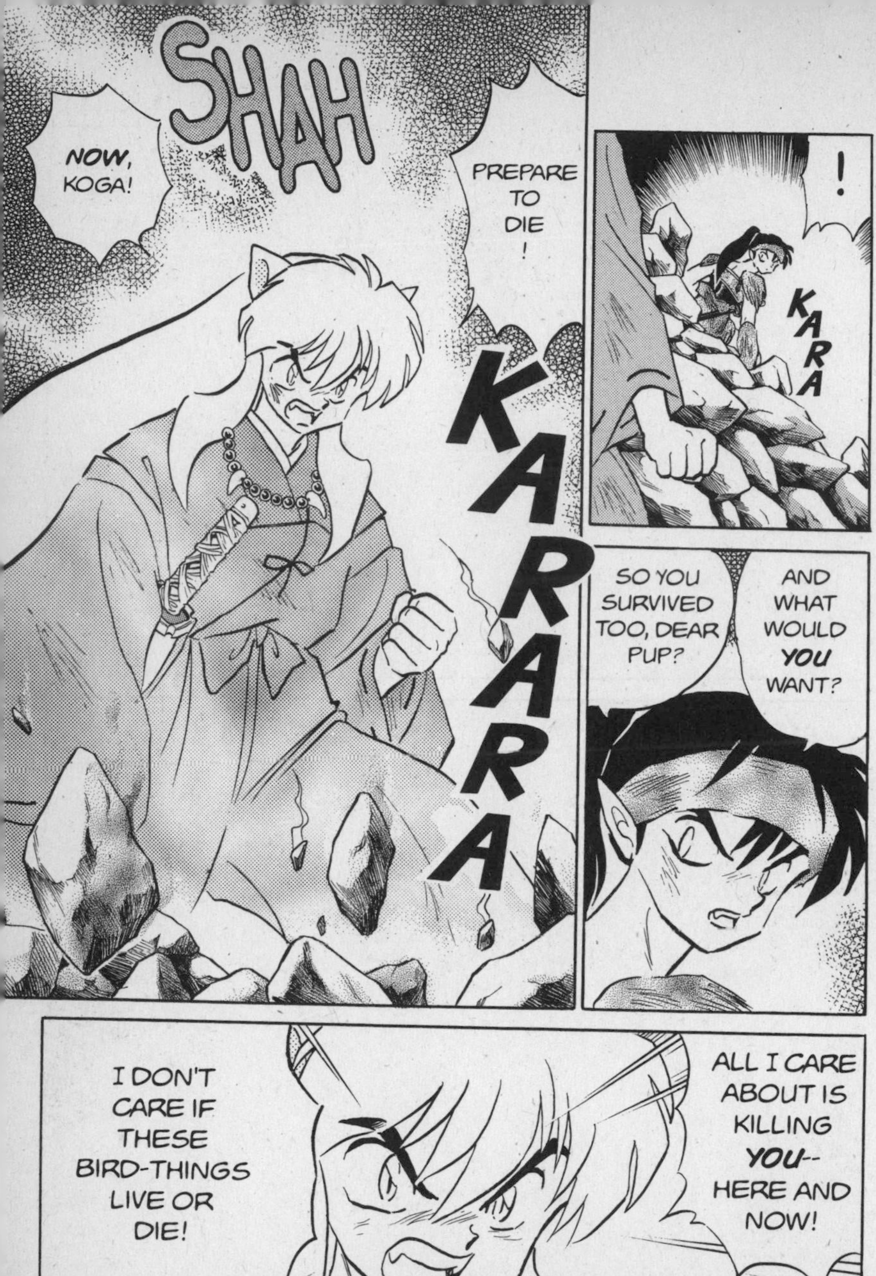
NOW, KOGA!
SHAH
PREPARE TO DIE!
KARARARA
!
KARA
SO YOU SURVIVED TOO, DEAR PUP?
AND WHAT WOULD YOU WANT?
I DON'T CARE IF THESE BIRD-THINGS LIVE OR DIE!
ALL I CARE ABOUT IS KILLING YOU-- HERE AND NOW!

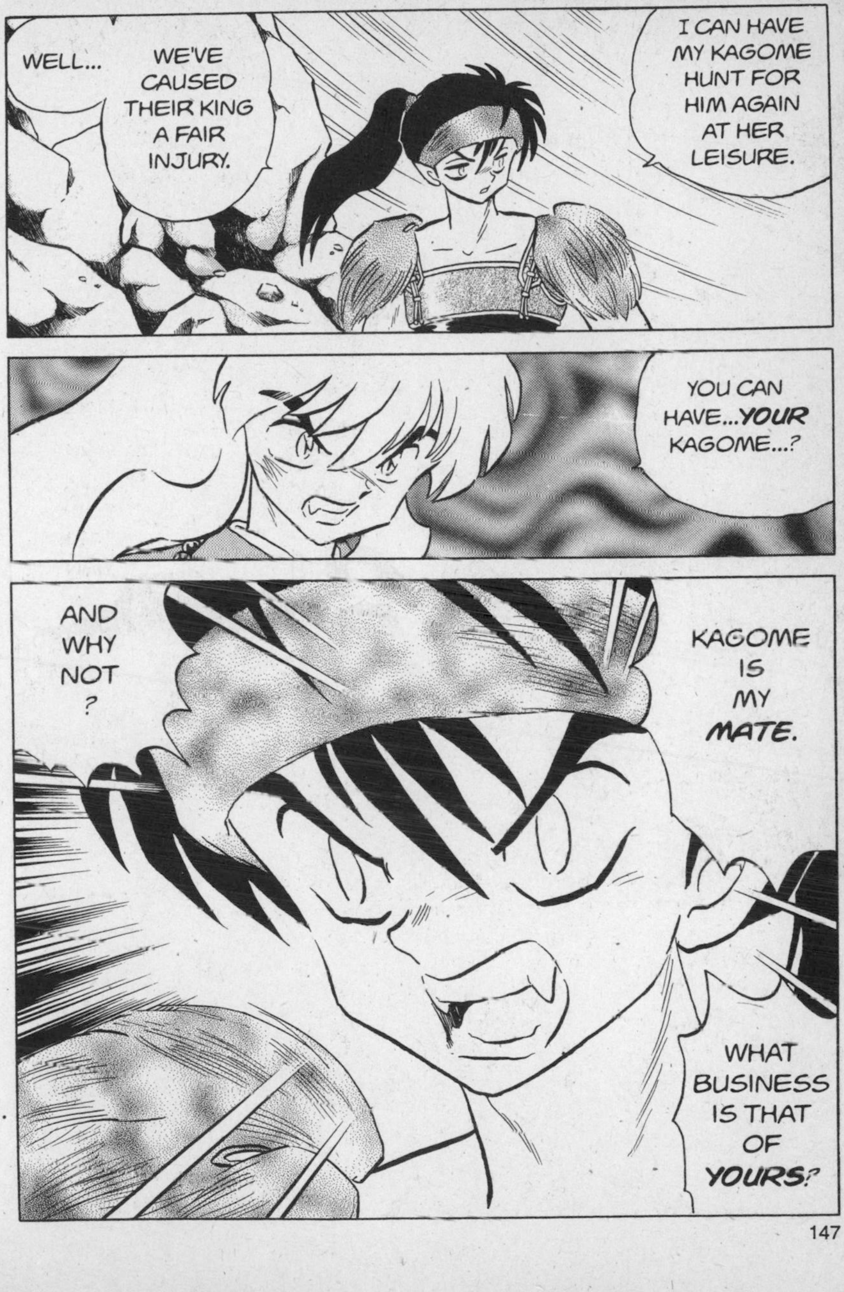
WELL...
WE'VE CAUSED THEIR KING A FAIR INJURY.
I CAN HAVE MY KAGOME HUNT FOR HIM AGAIN AT HER LEISURE.
YOU CAN HAVE...*YOUR* KAGOME...?
AND WHY NOT?
KAGOME IS MY *MATE.*
WHAT BUSINESS IS THAT OF *YOURS*?

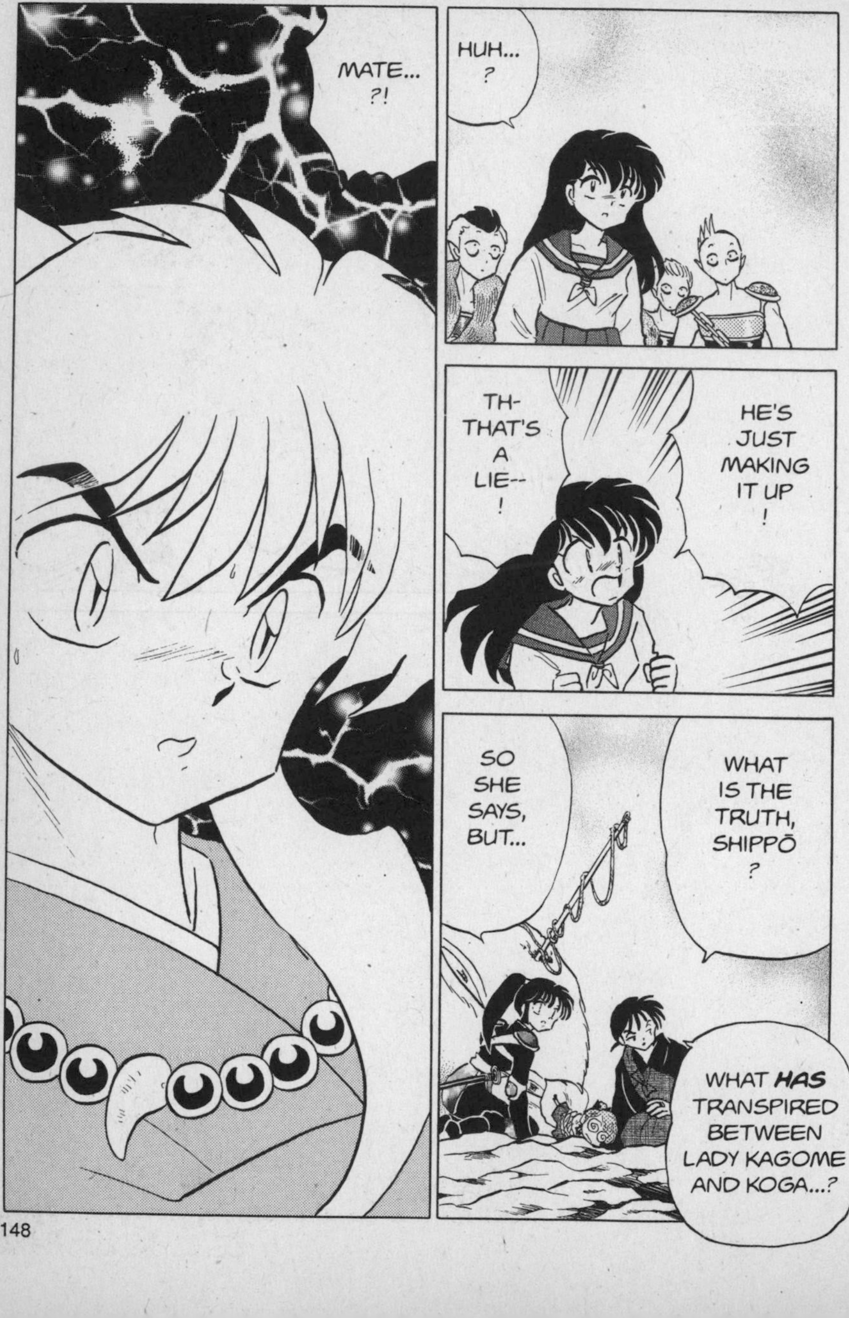
MATE... ?!
HUH... ?
TH- THAT'S A LIE-- !
HE'S JUST MAKING IT UP !
SO SHE SAYS, BUT...
WHAT IS THE TRUTH, SHIPPŌ ?
WHAT **HAS** TRANSPIRED BETWEEN LADY KAGOME AND KOGA...?

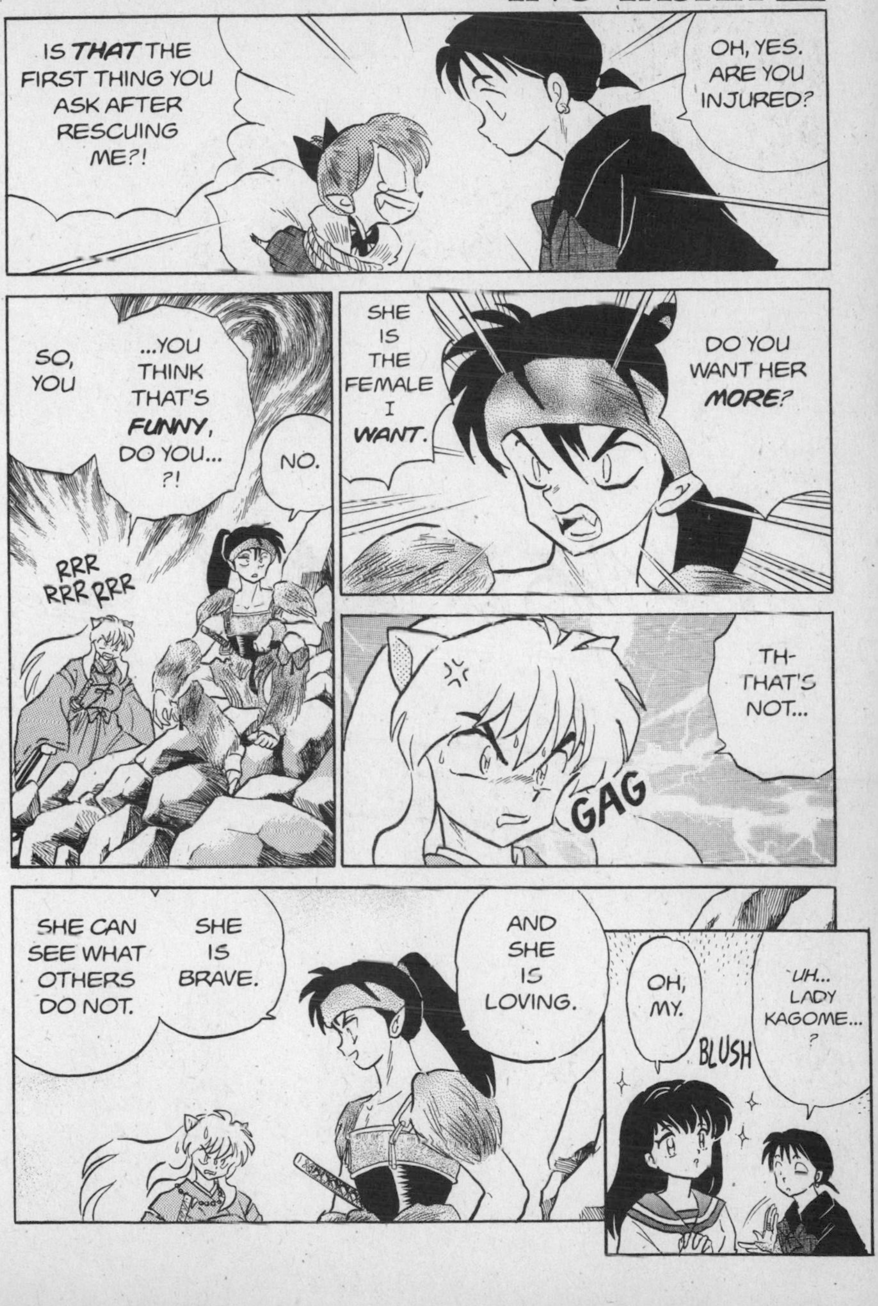
IS THAT THE FIRST THING YOU ASK AFTER RESCUING ME?!
OH, YES. ARE YOU INJURED?
SO, YOU
...YOU THINK THAT'S FUNNY, DO YOU...?!
NO.
RRR RRR RRR
SHE IS THE FEMALE I WANT.
DO YOU WANT HER MORE?
TH-THAT'S NOT...
GAG
SHE CAN SEE WHAT OTHERS DO NOT.
SHE IS BRAVE.
AND SHE IS LOVING.
OH, MY.
BLUSH
UH... LADY KAGOME...?

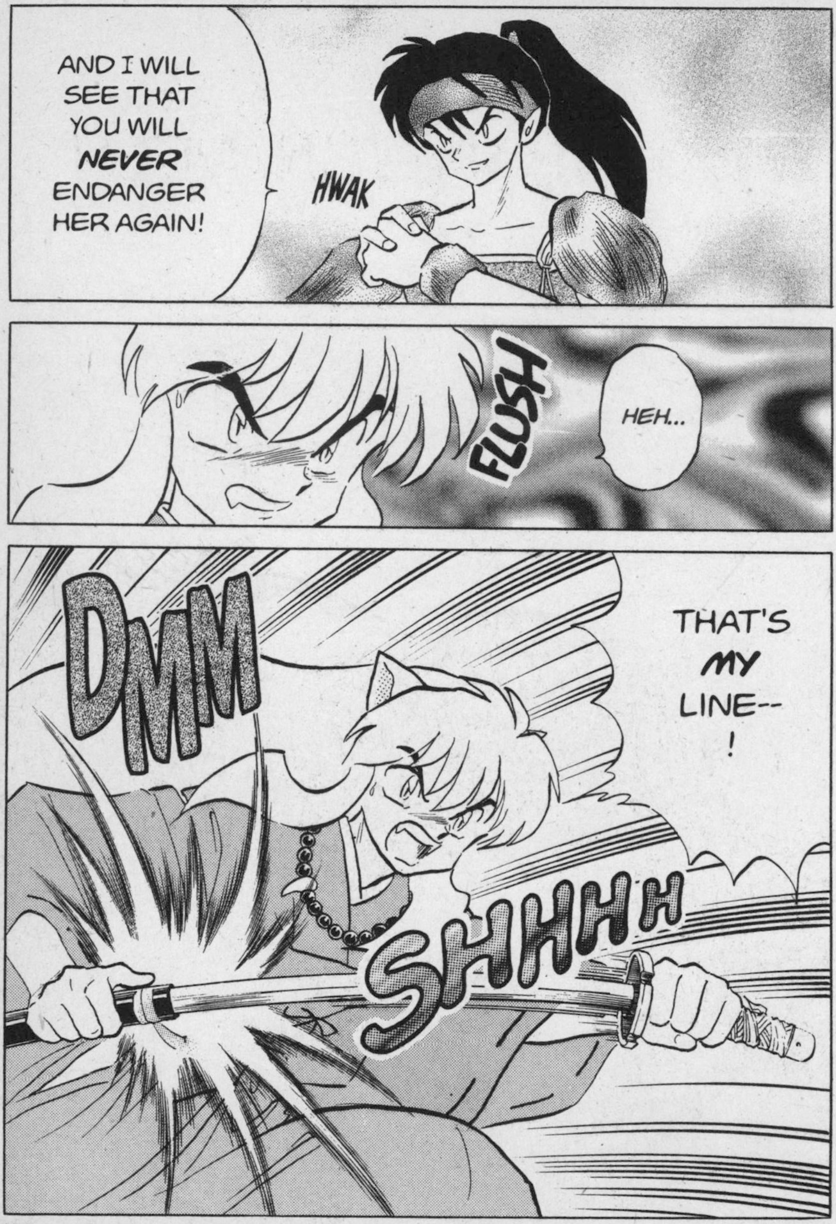

AND I WILL SEE THAT YOU WILL NEVER ENDANGER HER AGAIN!
HWAK
FLUSH
HEH...
DMM
THAT'S MY LINE-- !
SHHHH

SCROLL NINE

THE STRONGER MAN

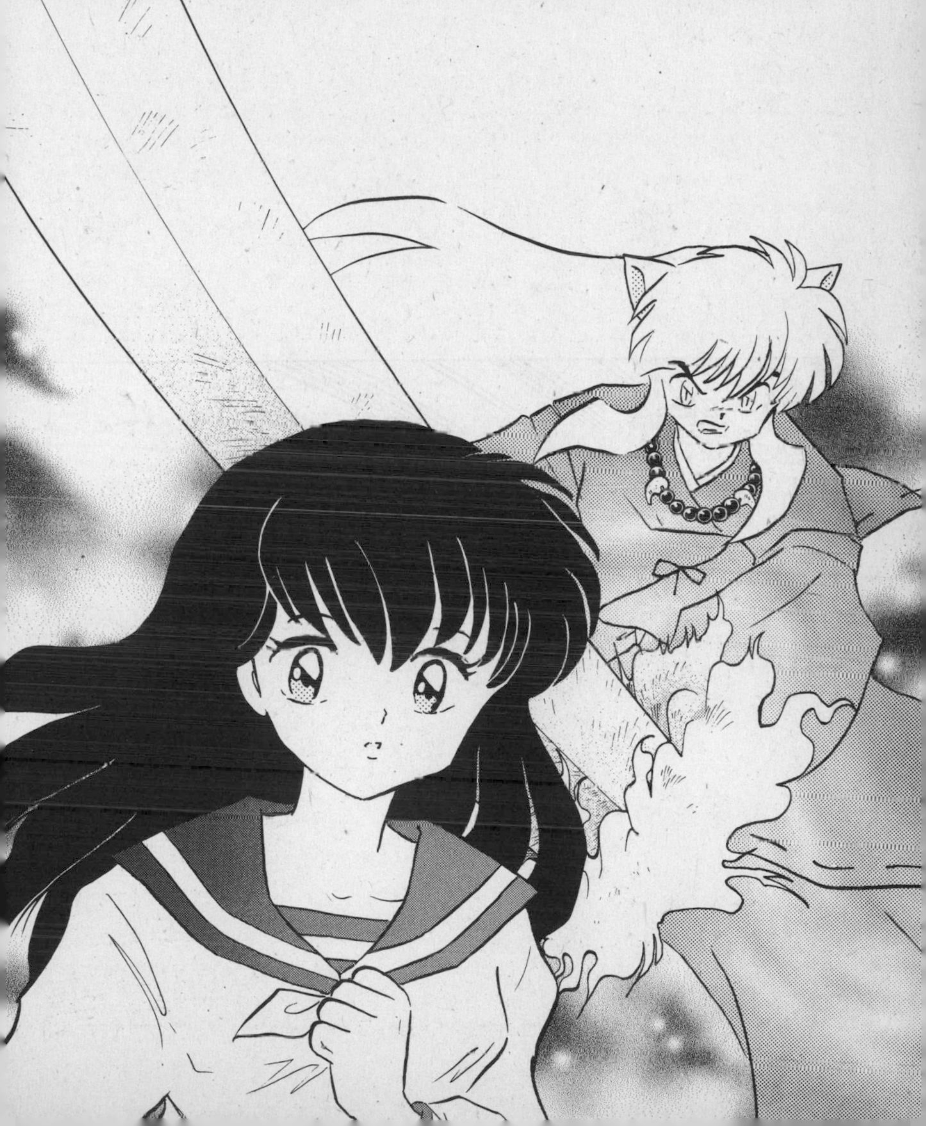

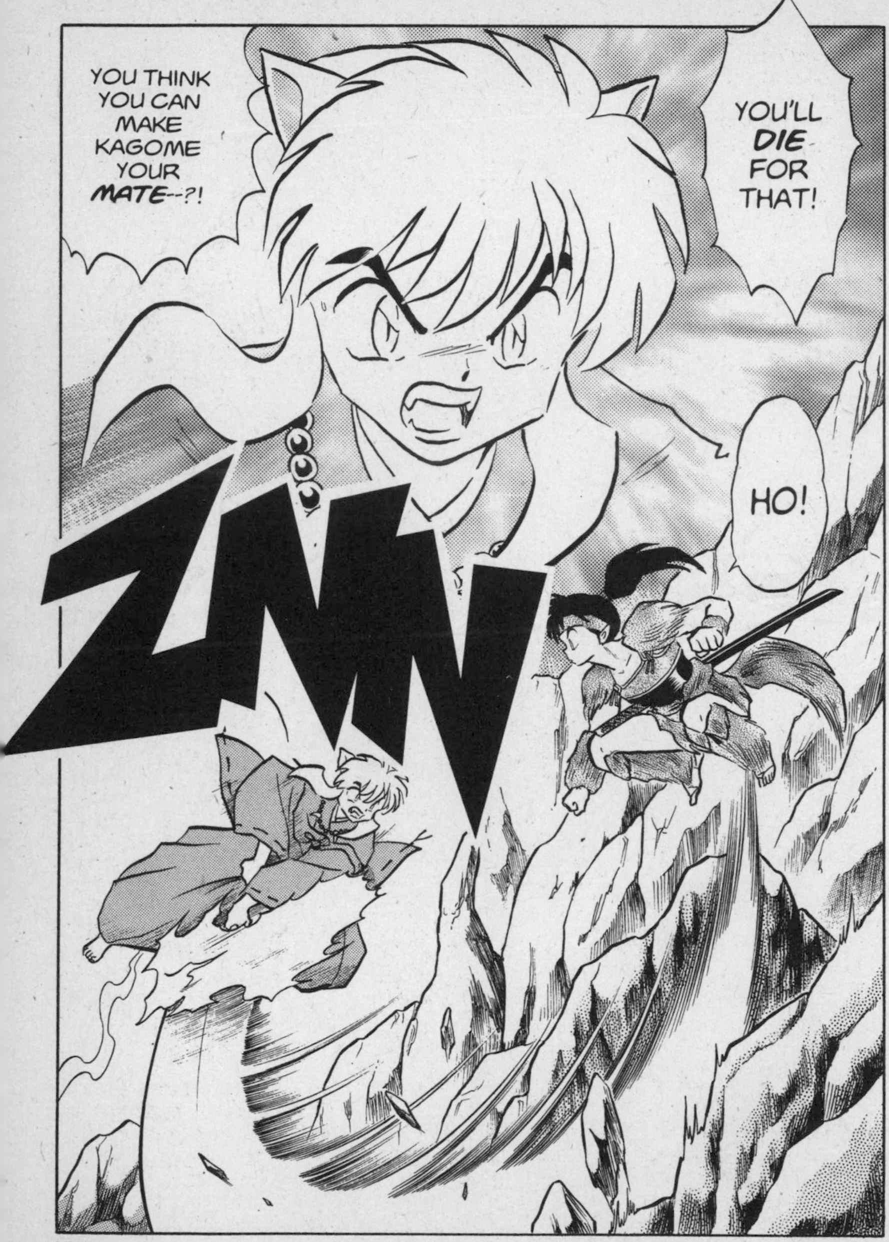
YOU THINK YOU CAN MAKE KAGOME YOUR MATE--?!
YOU'LL DIE FOR THAT!
HO!
ZMN

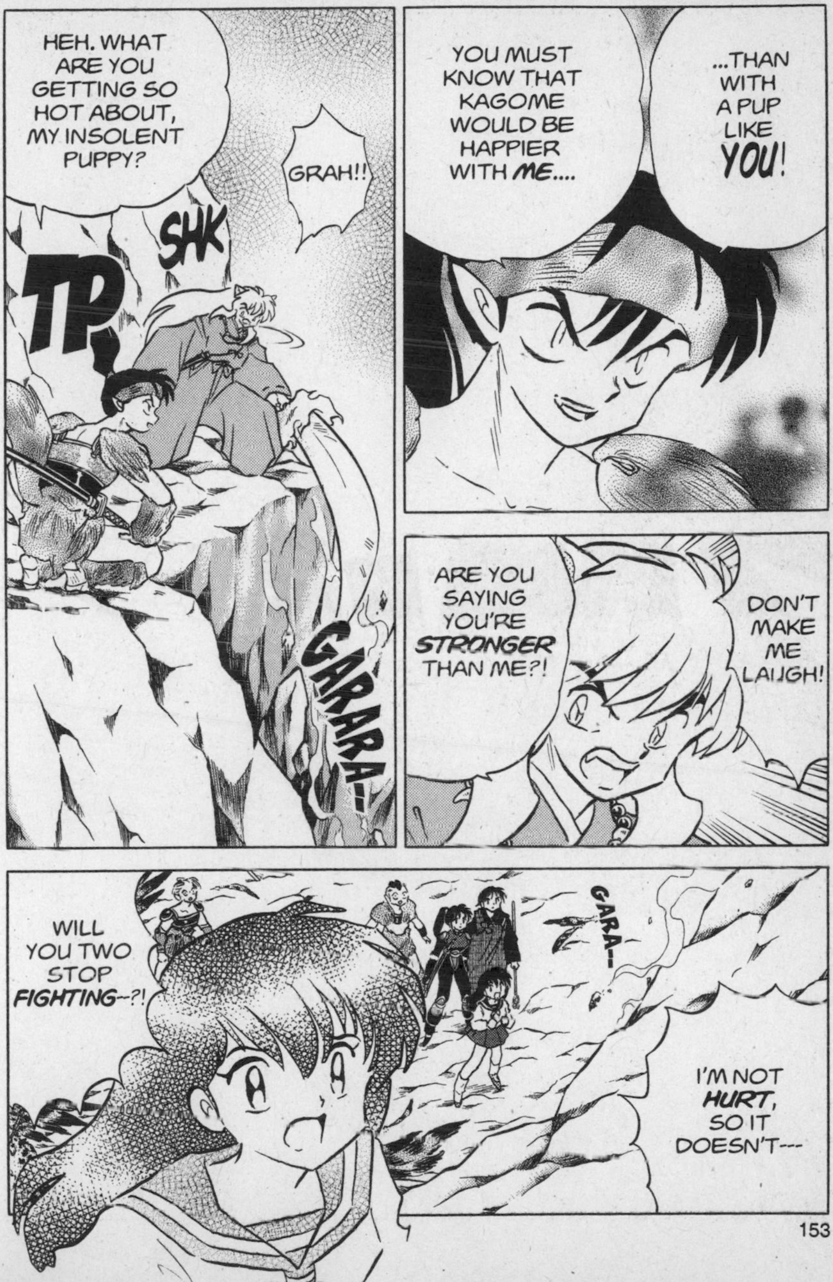
HEH. WHAT ARE YOU GETTING SO HOT ABOUT, MY INSOLENT PUPPY?
GRAH!!
SHK
TP
GARARA..
YOU MUST KNOW THAT KAGOME WOULD BE HAPPIER WITH ME....
...THAN WITH A PUP LIKE YOU!
ARE YOU SAYING YOU'RE STRONGER THAN ME?!
DON'T MAKE ME LAUGH!
WILL YOU TWO STOP FIGHTING--?!
GARA--
I'M NOT HURT, SO IT DOESN'T---

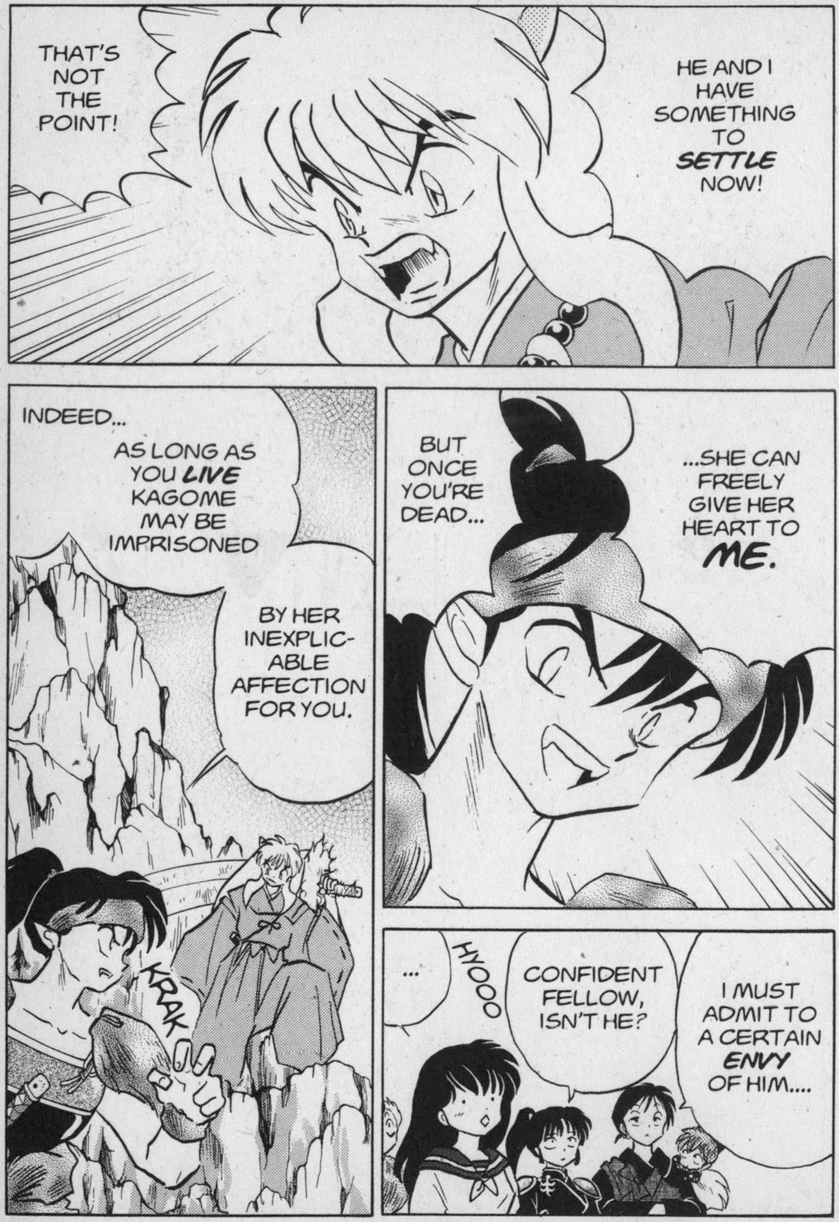
THAT'S NOT THE POINT!
HE AND I HAVE SOMETHING TO SETTLE NOW!
INDEED...
AS LONG AS YOU LIVE KAGOME MAY BE IMPRISONED
BY HER INEXPLICABLE AFFECTION FOR YOU.
KRAK
BUT ONCE YOU'RE DEAD...
...SHE CAN FREELY GIVE HER HEART TO ME.
...
HYOOO
CONFIDENT FELLOW, ISN'T HE?
I MUST ADMIT TO A CERTAIN ENVY OF HIM....

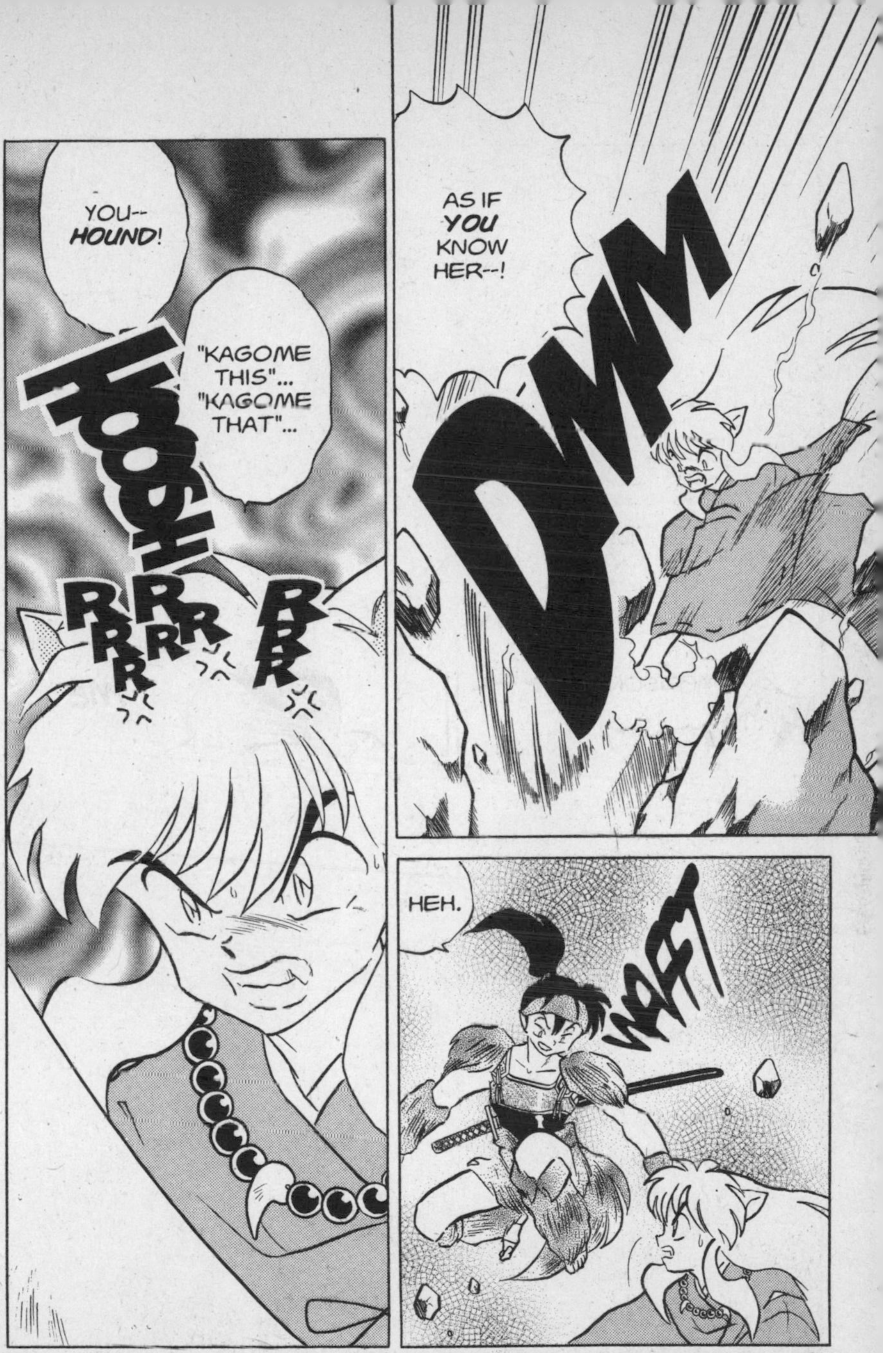
YOU--
HOUND!
"KAGOME THIS"... "KAGOME THAT"...
FOOSH
RRRRRRR
RRRR
AS IF YOU KNOW HER--!
DMM
HEH.
WAFFT

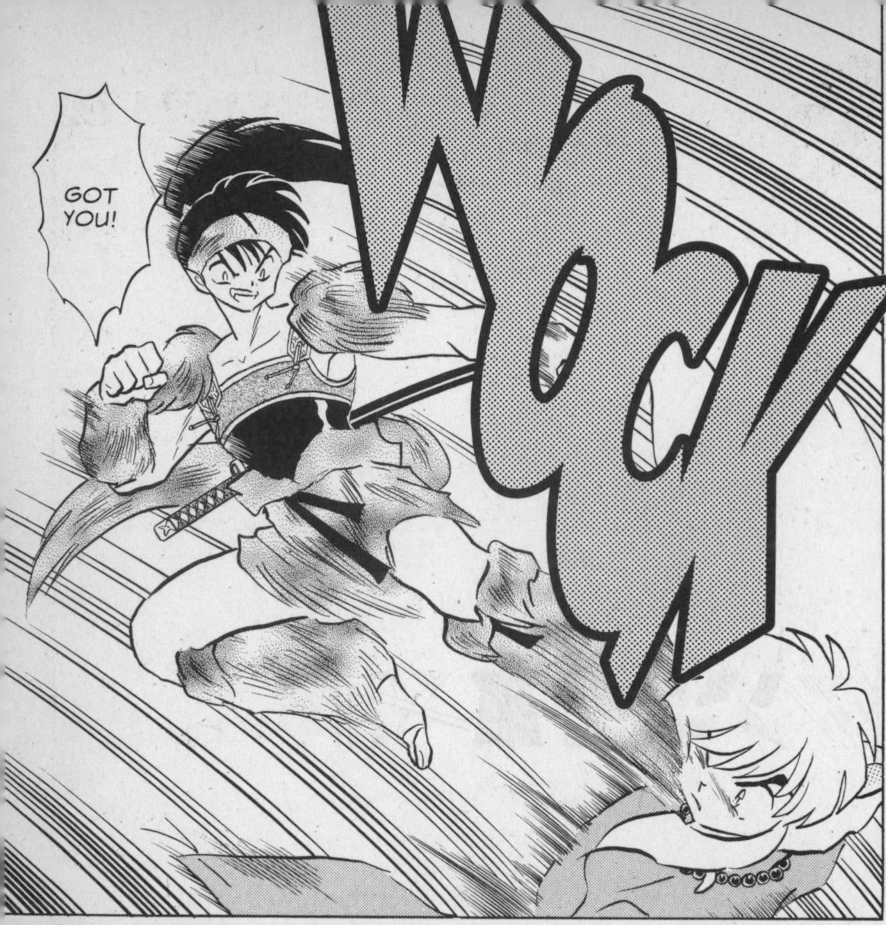
GOT YOU!
WOCK
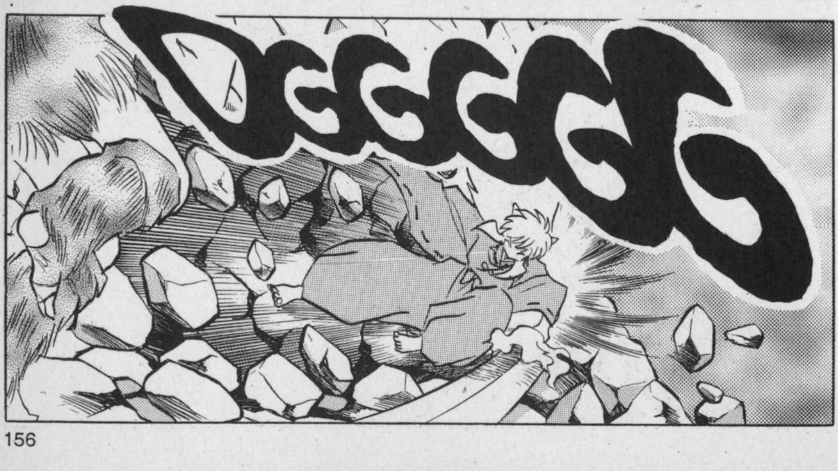

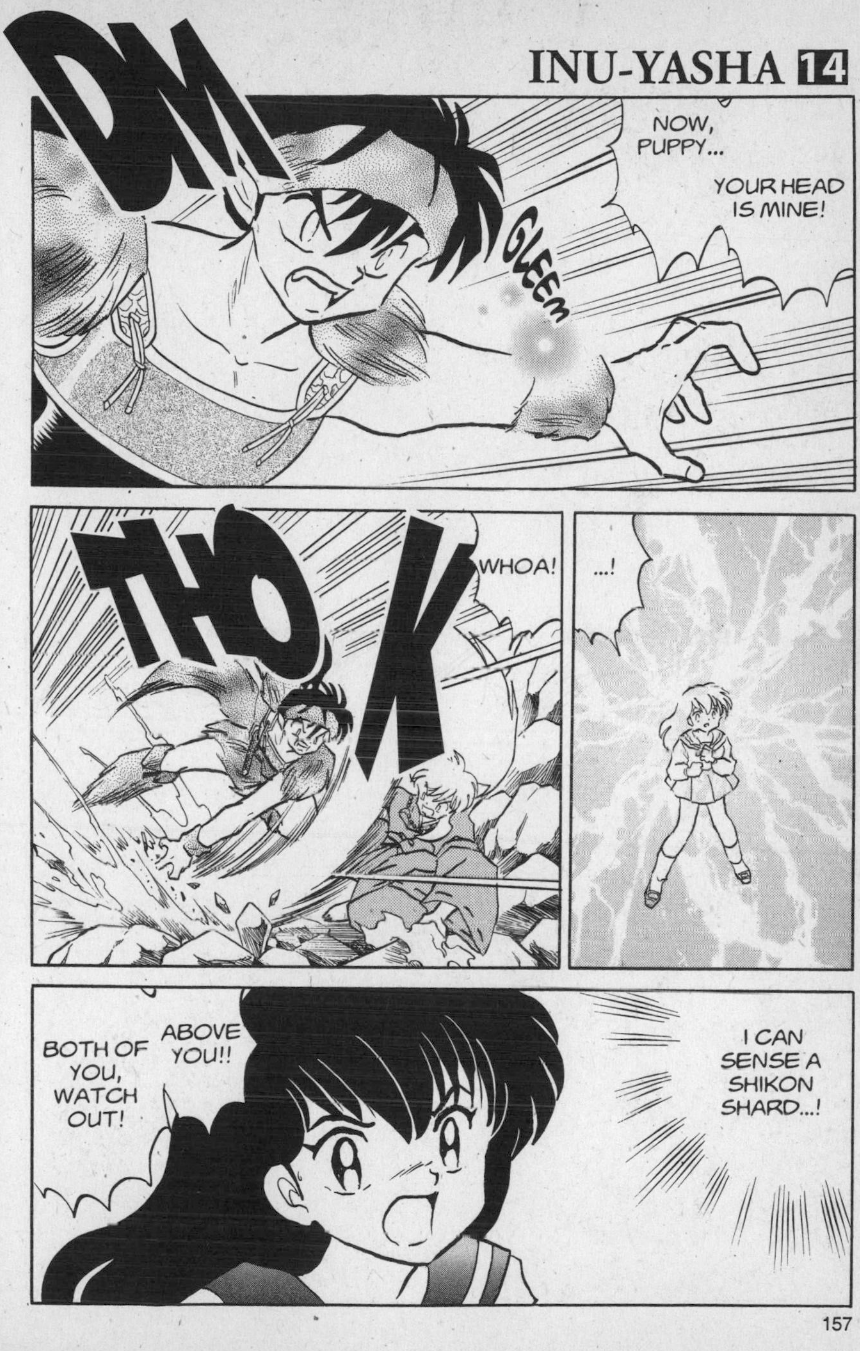
DM
NOW, PUPPY...
YOUR HEAD IS MINE!
GLEEM
THOK
WHOA!
...!
BOTH OF YOU, WATCH OUT!
ABOVE YOU!!
I CAN SENSE A SHIKON SHARD...!

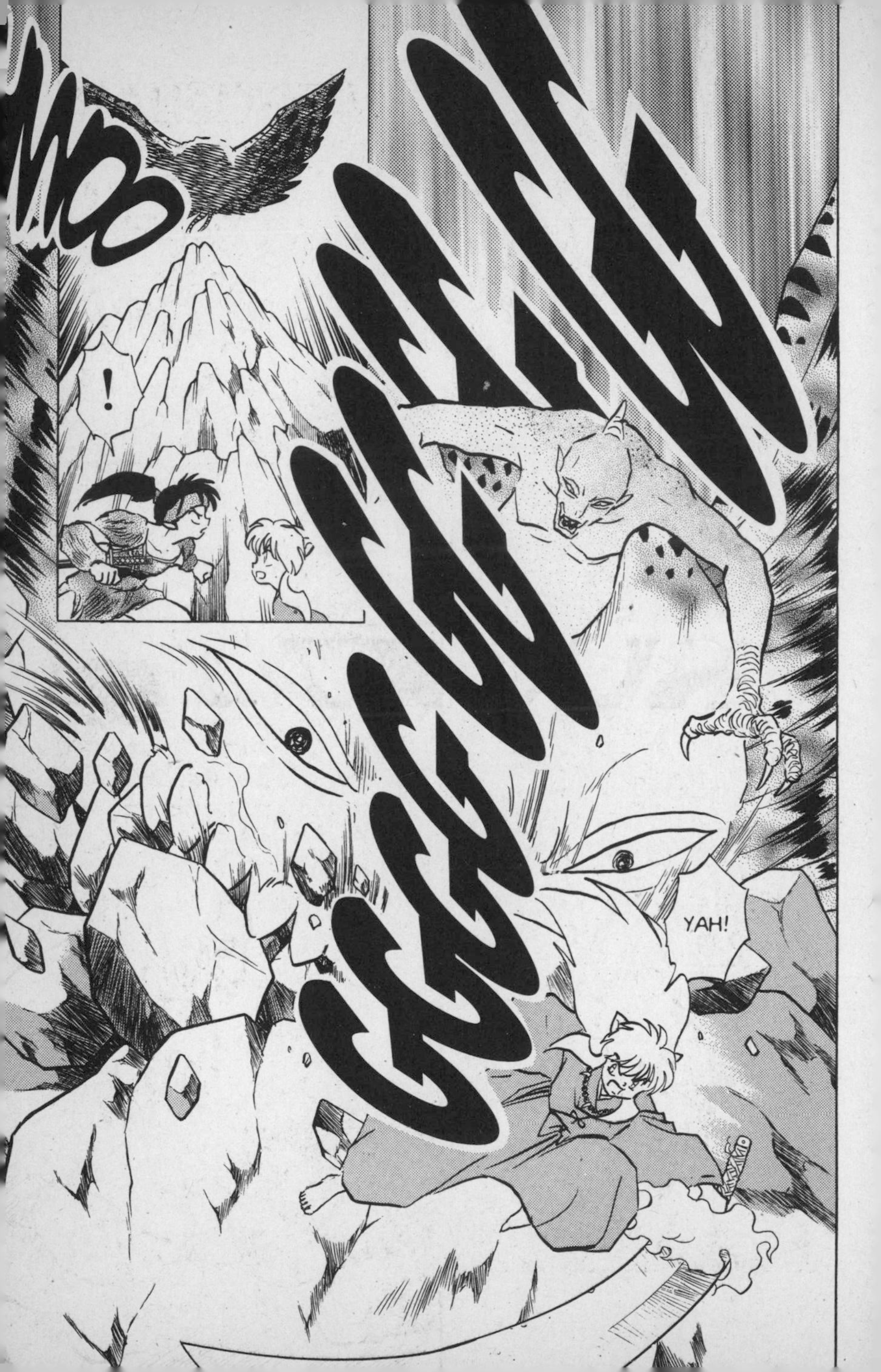
!
YAH!

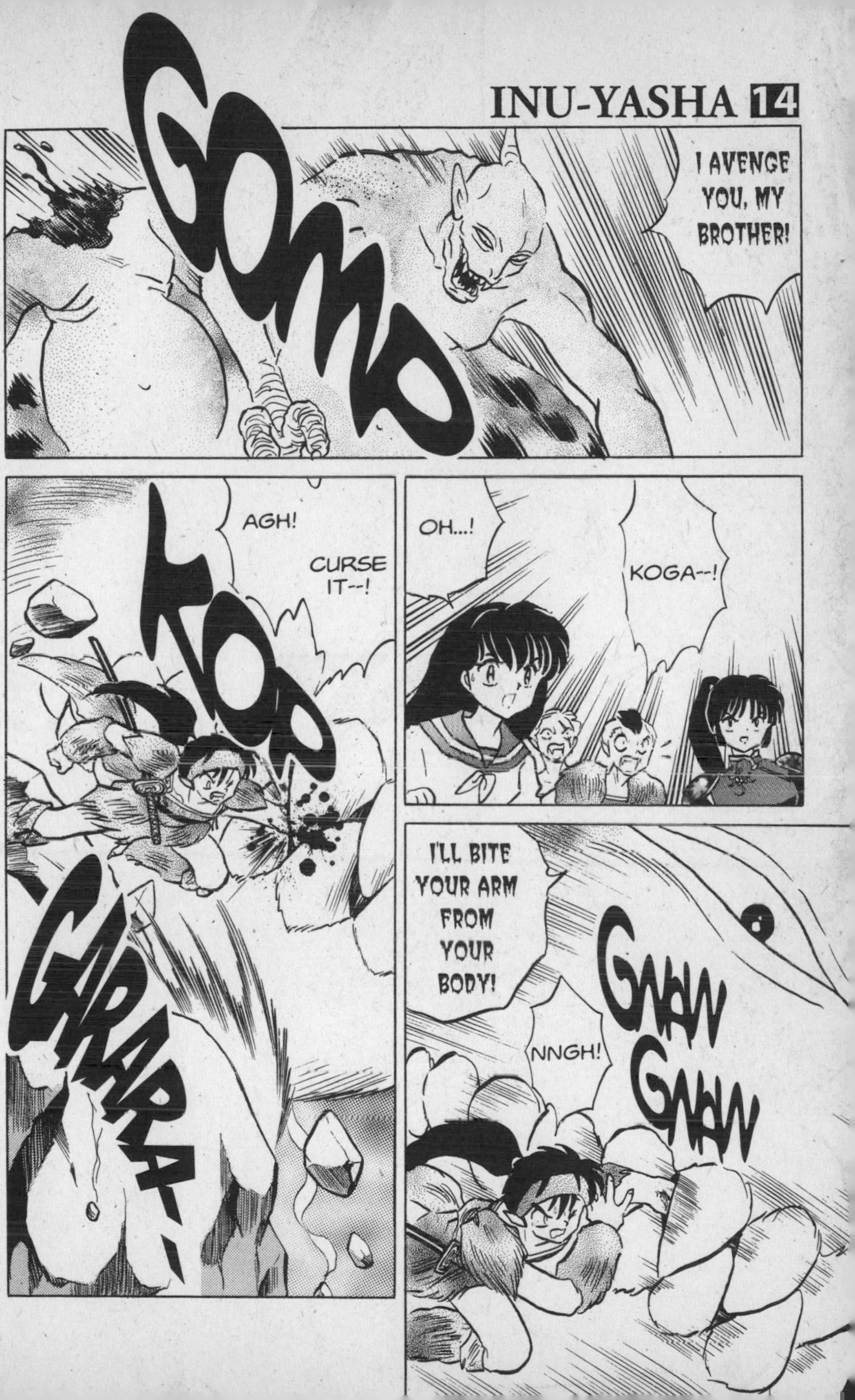
GOMP
I AVENGE YOU, MY BROTHER!
AGH!
CURSE IT--!
GARARA-
OH...!
KOGA--!
I'LL BITE YOUR ARM FROM YOUR BODY!
GNAW GNAW
NNGH!

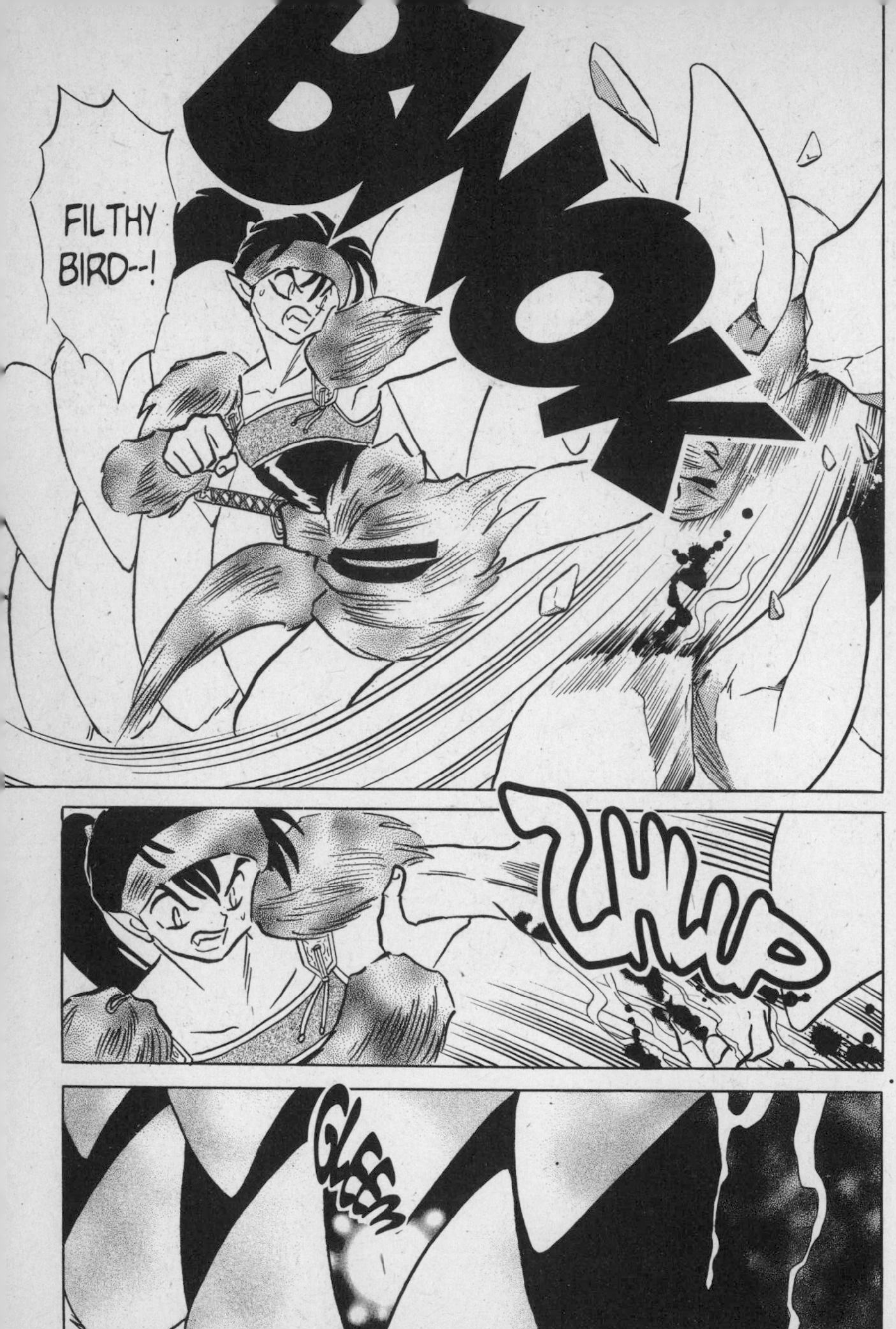
BAMOK
FILTHY BIRD--!
ZHUP
GLEEM

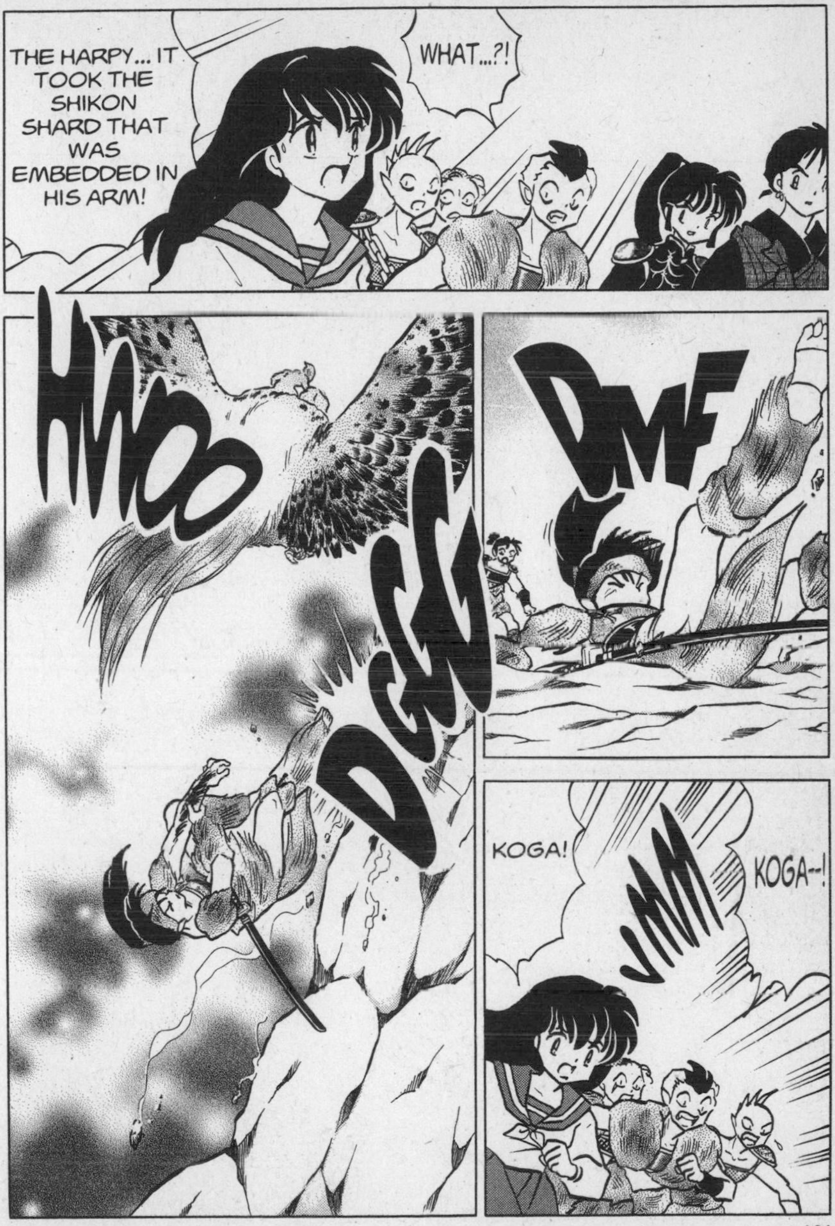
THE HARPY... IT TOOK THE SHIKON SHARD THAT WAS EMBEDDED IN HIS ARM!
WHAT...?!
DMF
KOGA!
KOGA--!

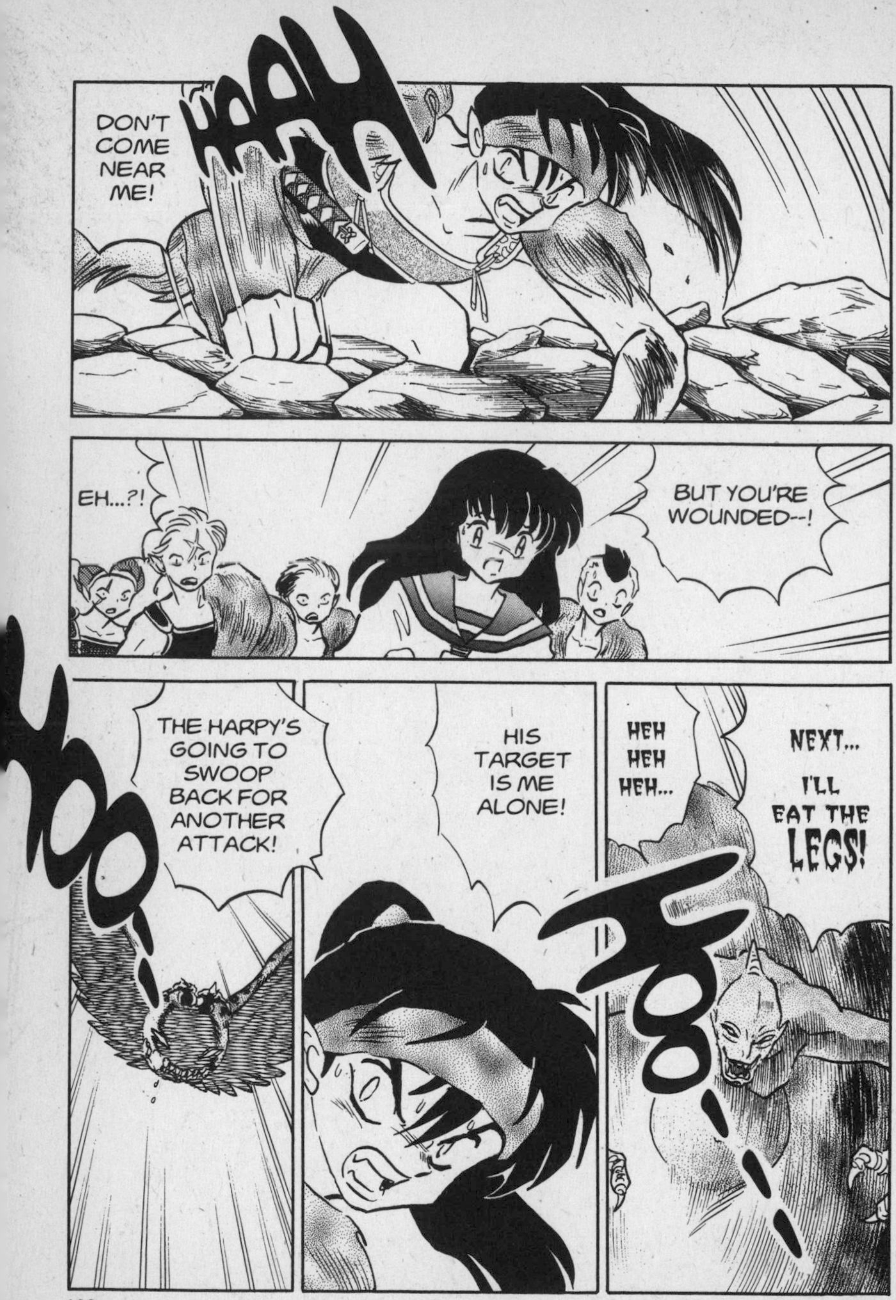
DON'T COME NEAR ME!
EH...?!
BUT YOU'RE WOUNDED--!
THE HARPY'S GOING TO SWOOP BACK FOR ANOTHER ATTACK!
HIS TARGET IS ME ALONE!
HEH HEH HEH...
NEXT... I'LL EAT THE LEGS!

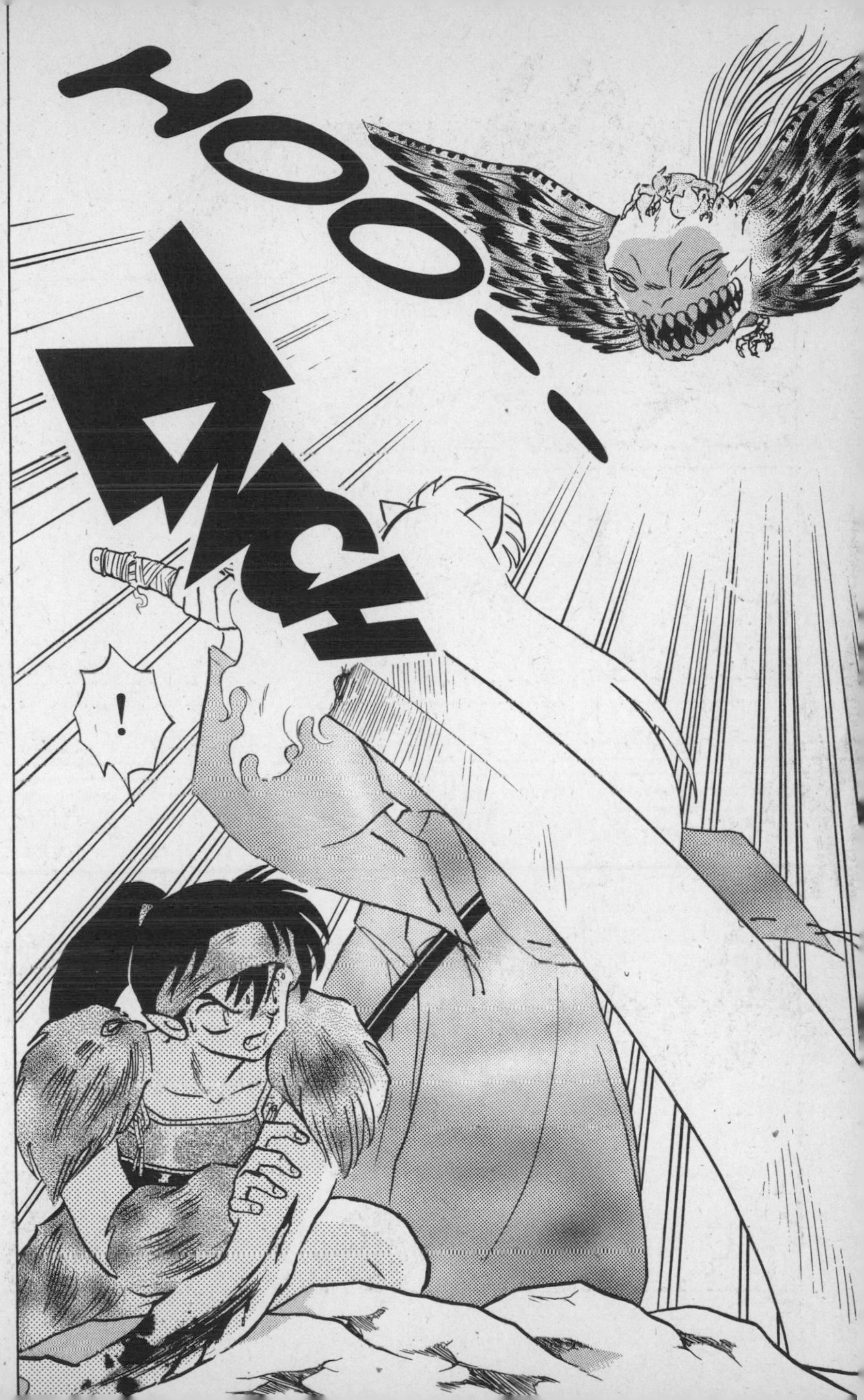
HOO--ZACH
!

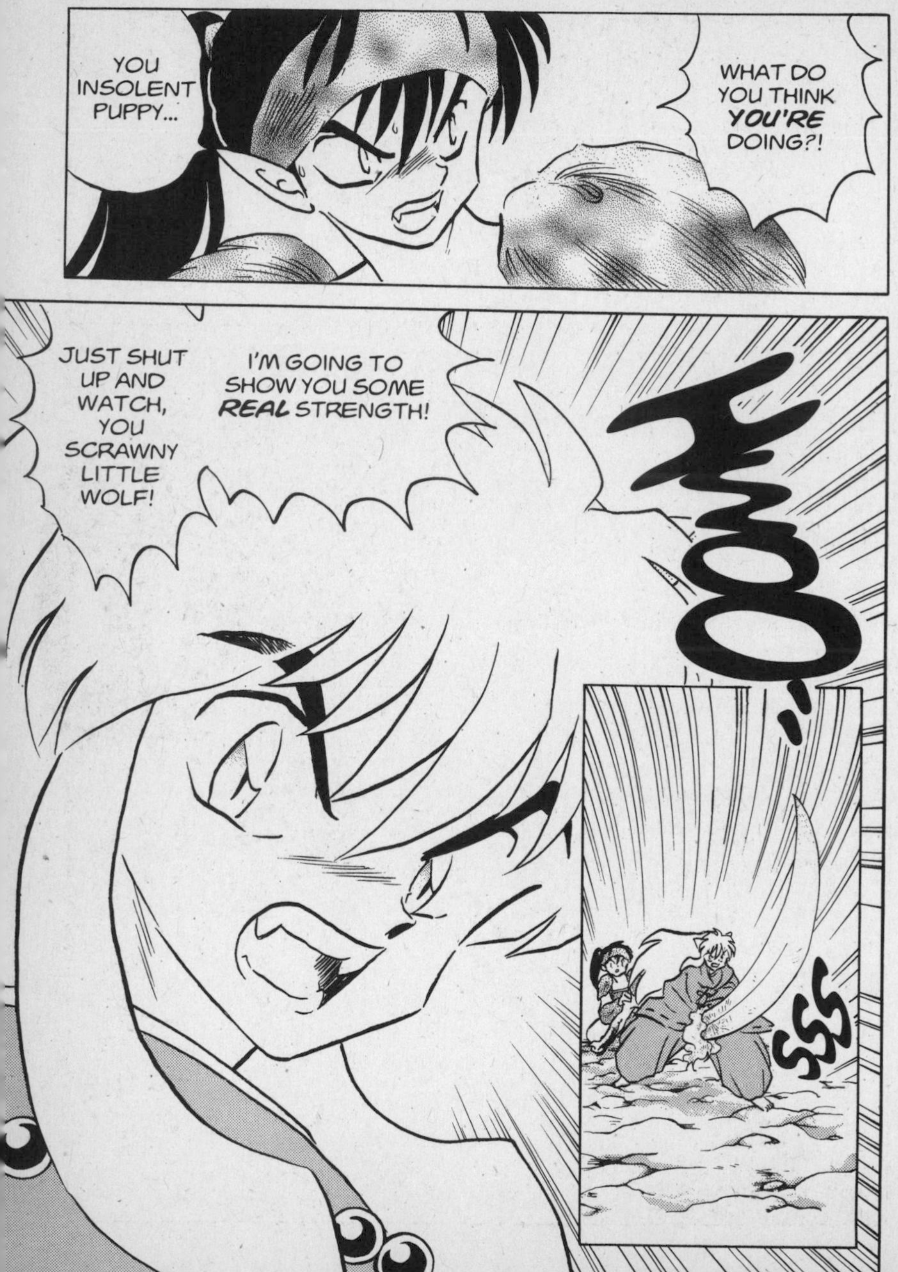
YOU INSOLENT PUPPY...
WHAT DO YOU THINK YOU'RE DOING?!
JUST SHUT UP AND WATCH, YOU SCRAWNY LITTLE WOLF!
I'M GOING TO SHOW YOU SOME REAL STRENGTH!
HMOO
SSS

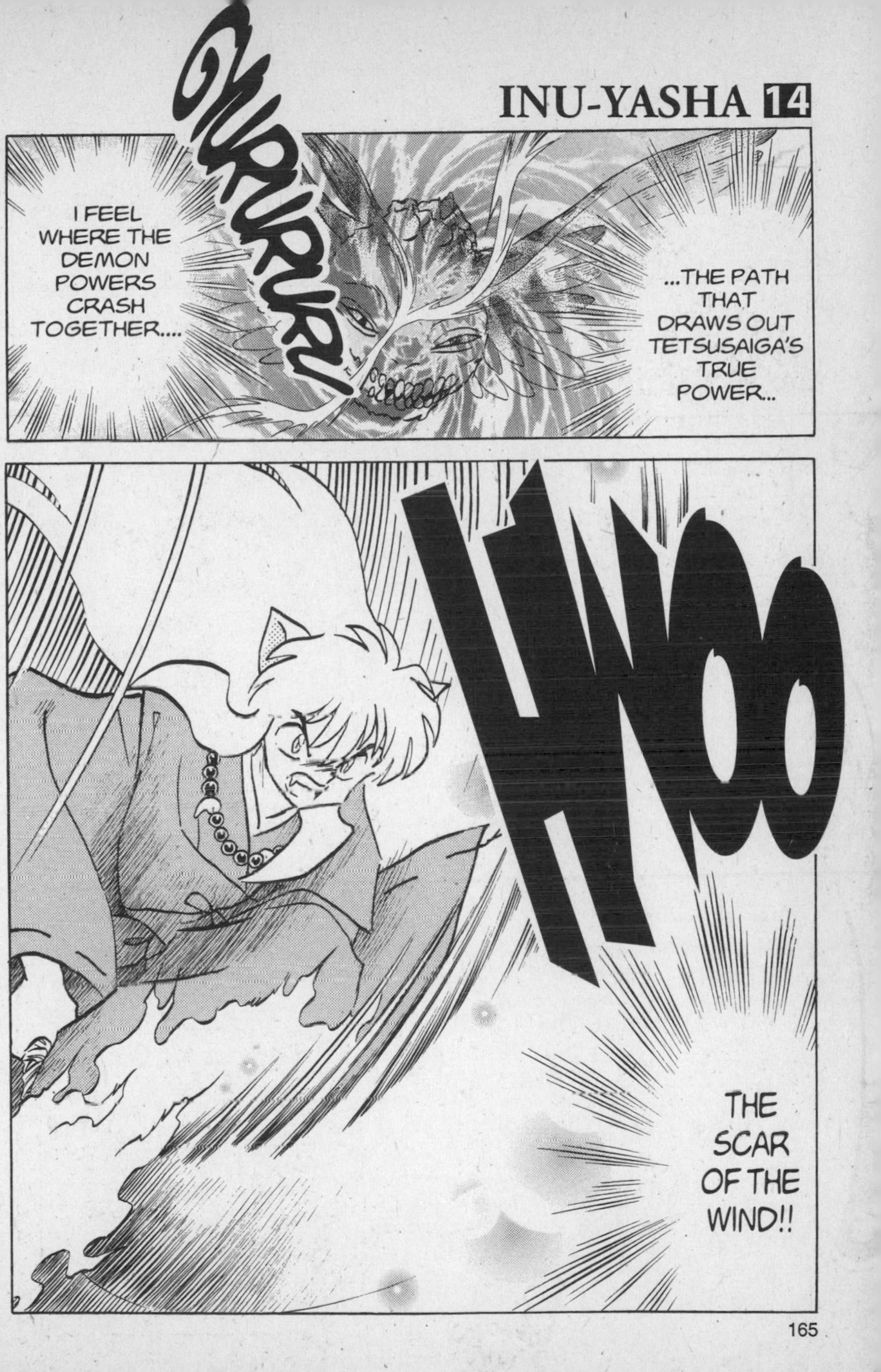
GRURURU!
I FEEL WHERE THE DEMON POWERS CRASH TOGETHER....
...THE PATH THAT DRAWS OUT TETSUSAIGA'S TRUE POWER...
HYOO
THE SCAR OF THE WIND!!

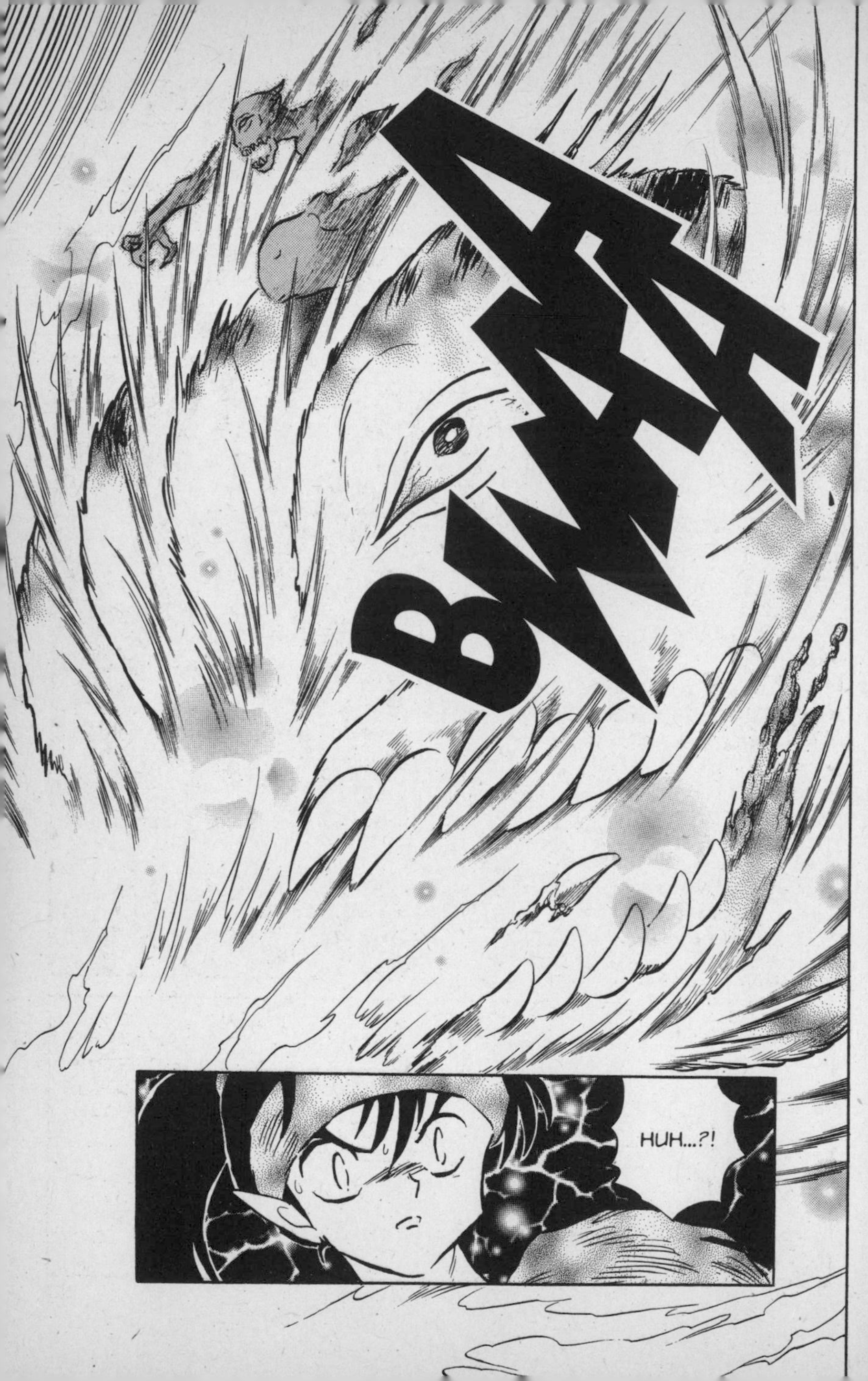
BWAAA
HUH...?!

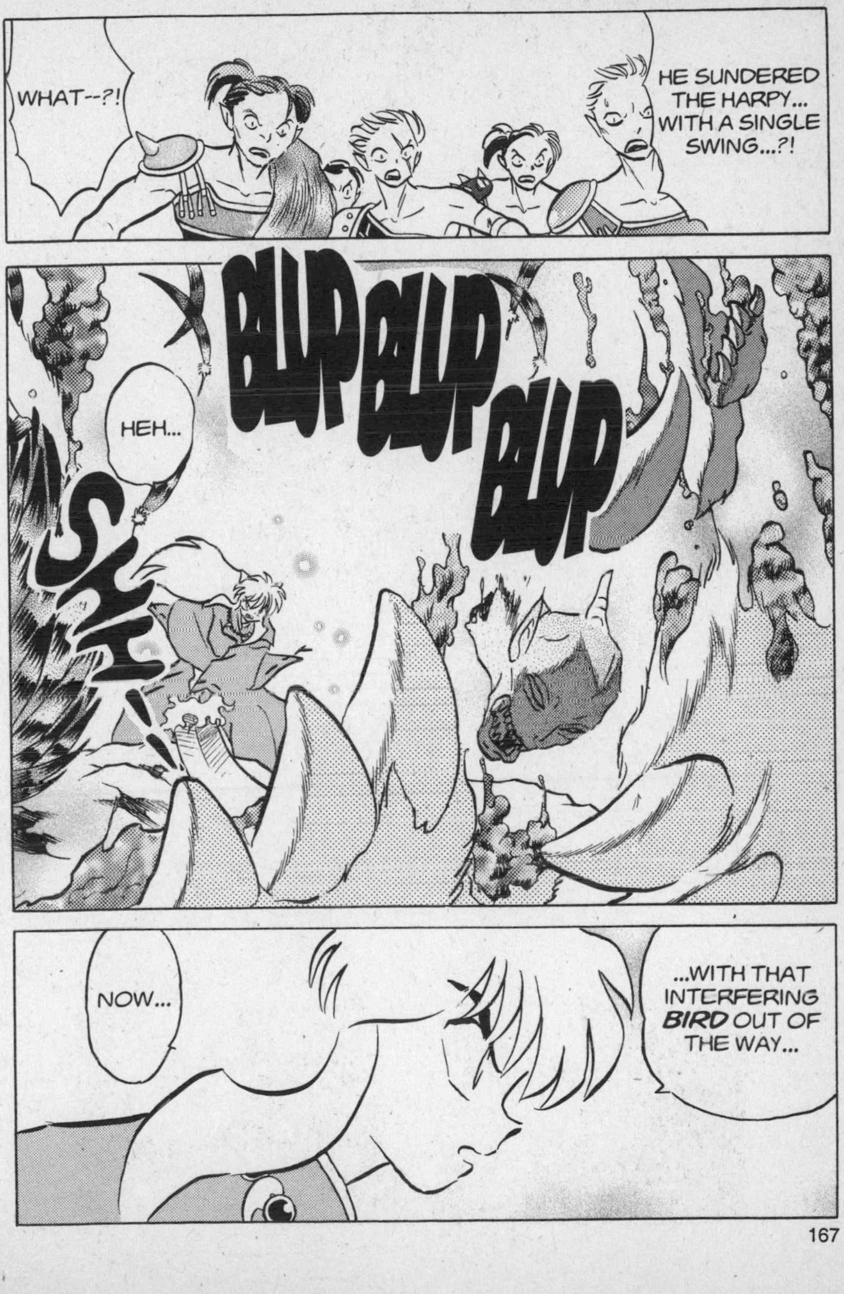
WHAT--?!
HE SUNDERED THE HARPY... WITH A SINGLE SWING...?!
BLUP BLUP BLUP BLUP
HEH...
SHK
NOW...
...WITH THAT INTERFERING ***BIRD*** OUT OF THE WAY...

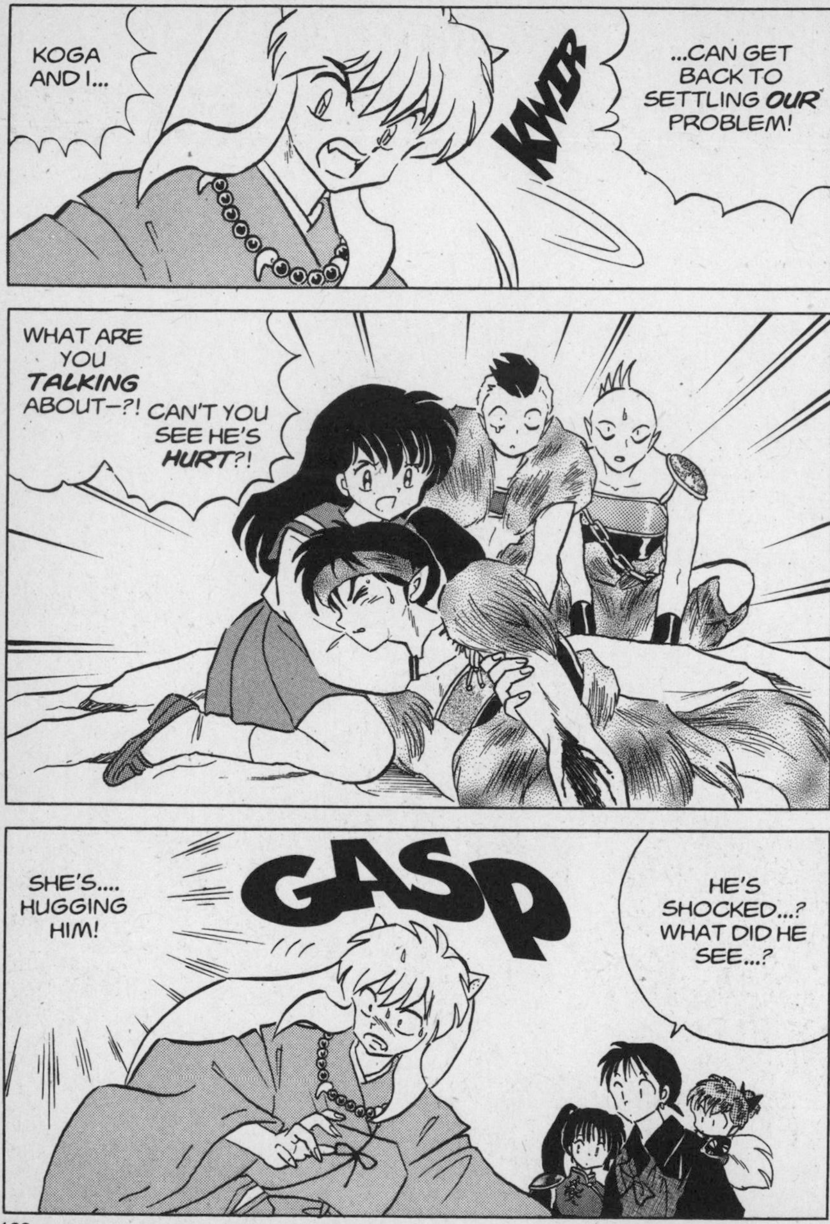
KOGA AND I...
KWIR
...CAN GET BACK TO SETTLING OUR PROBLEM!
WHAT ARE YOU TALKING ABOUT–?!
CAN'T YOU SEE HE'S HURT?!
SHE'S.... HUGGING HIM!
GASP
HE'S SHOCKED...? WHAT DID HE SEE...?

SCROLL TEN

WHY SHE LET HIM GO

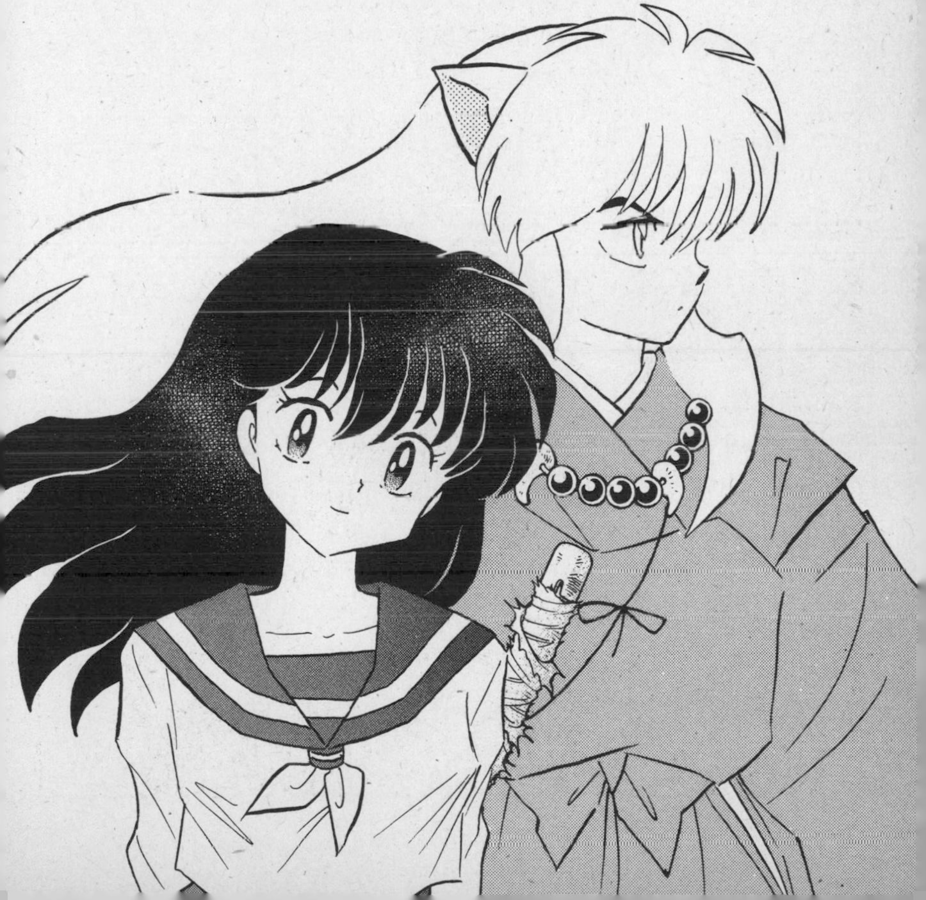

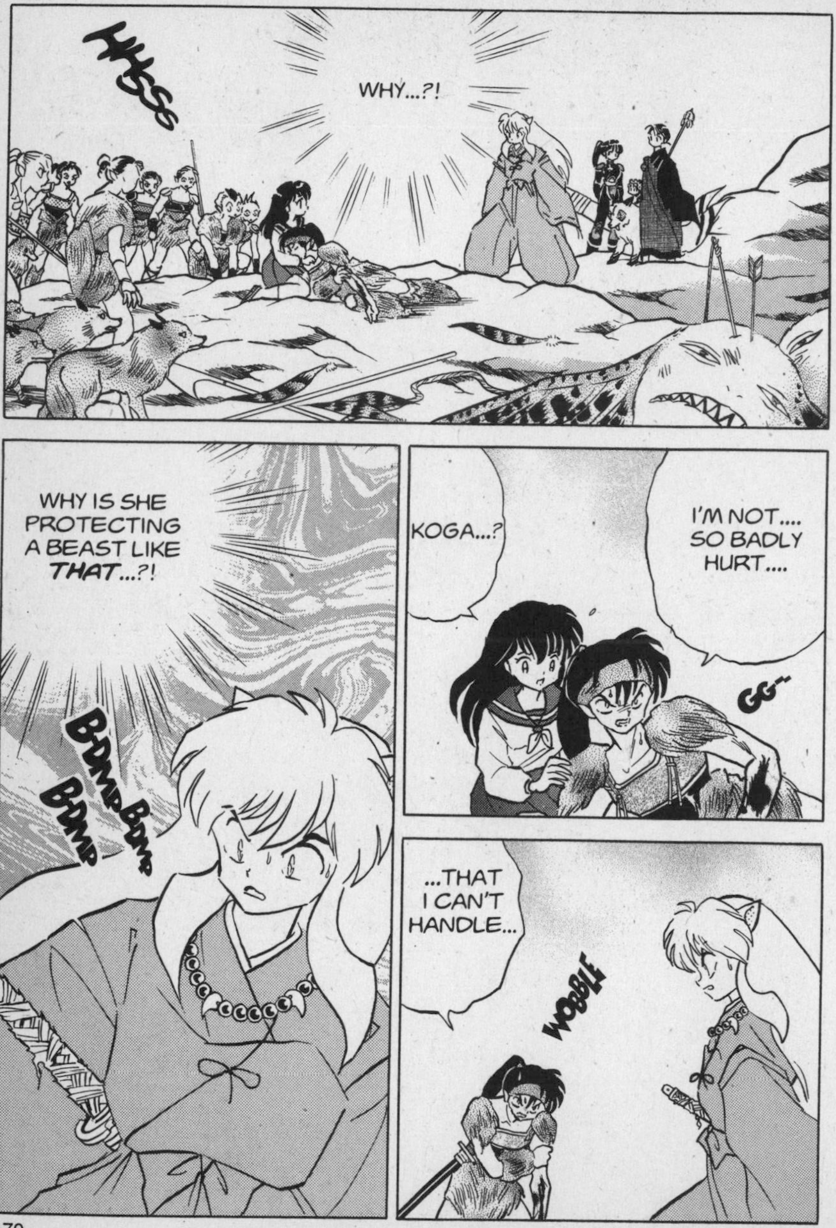
HISSS
WHY...?!
WHY IS SHE PROTECTING A BEAST LIKE *THAT*...?!
B-DMP B-DMP B-DMP
KOGA...?
I'M NOT.... SO BADLY HURT....
GG--
...THAT I CAN'T HANDLE...
WOBBLE

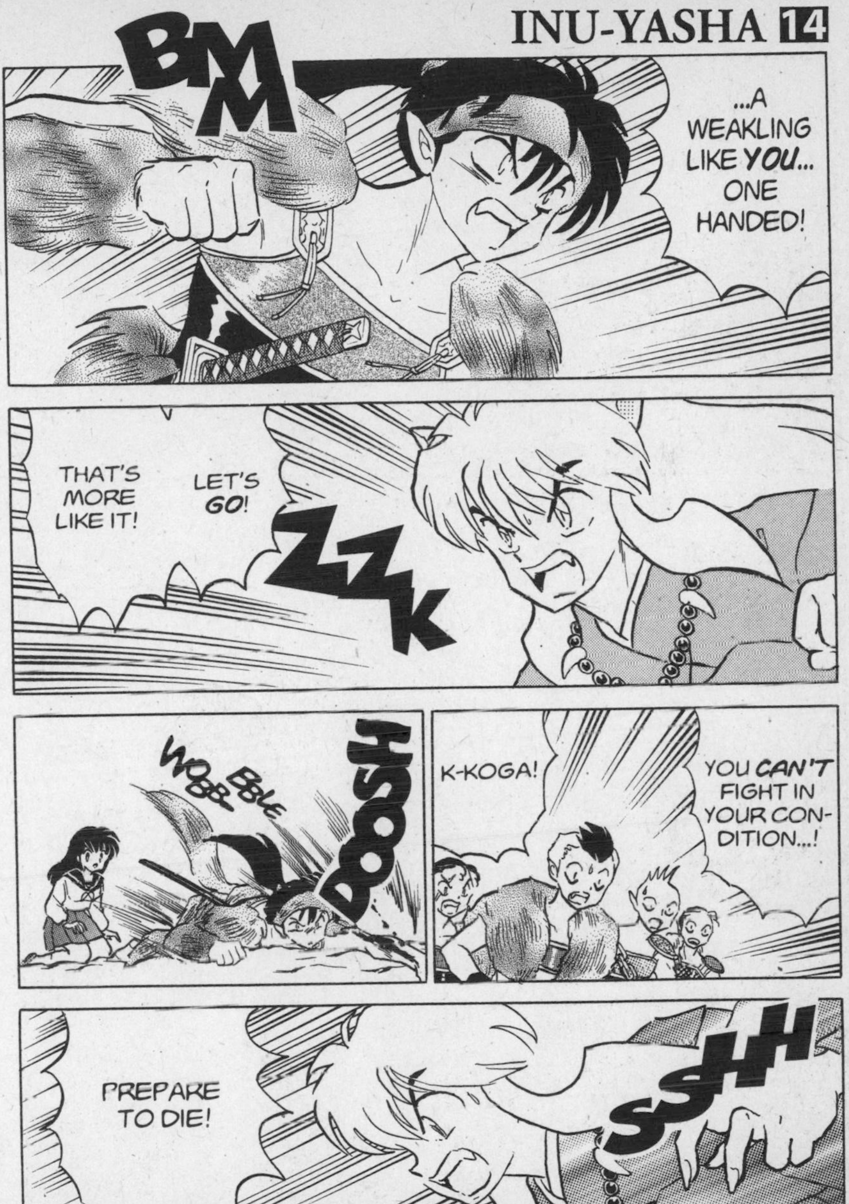
BMM
...A WEAKLING LIKE YOU... ONE HANDED!
THAT'S MORE LIKE IT!
LET'S GO!
ZZAK
WOBB-
BBLE
DOOOSH
K-KOGA!
YOU CAN'T FIGHT IN YOUR CON-DITION...!
PREPARE TO DIE!
SSHH

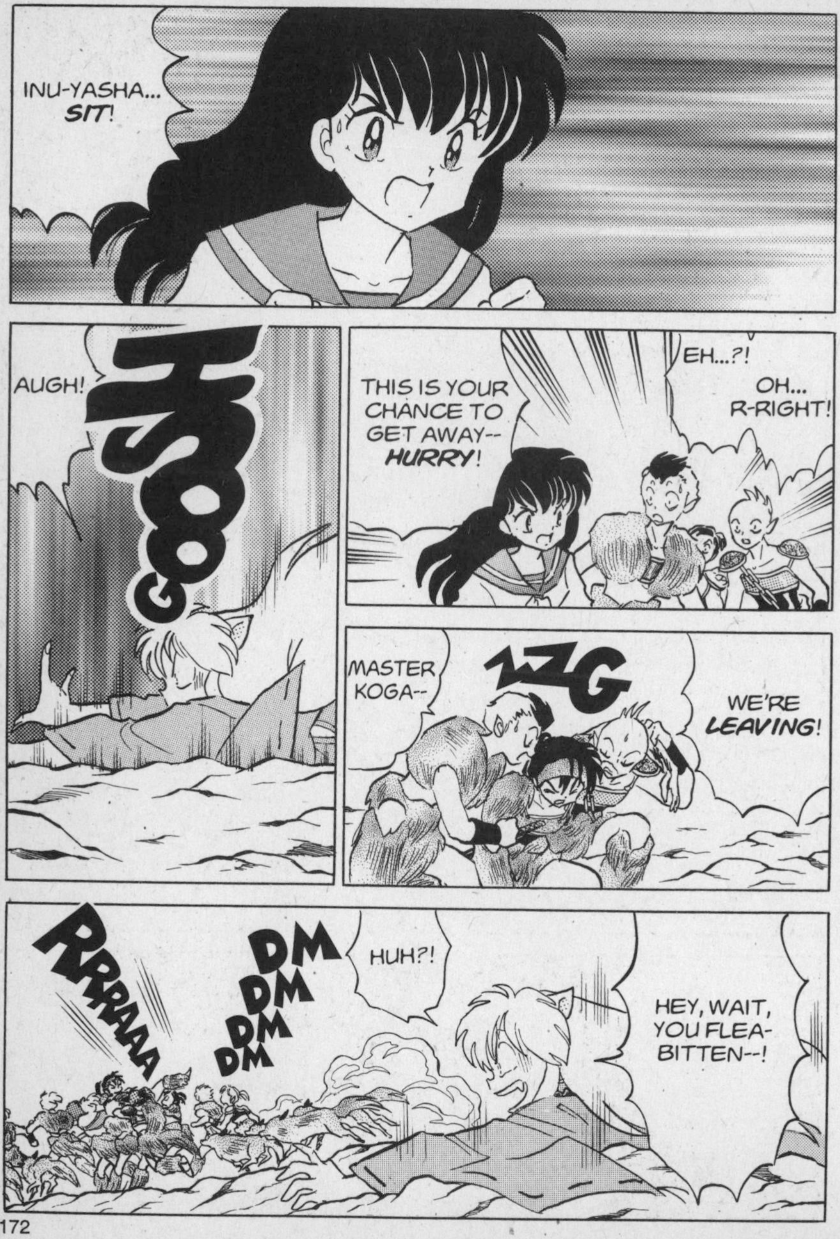
INU-YASHA... SIT!
AUGH!
GOOSH
THIS IS YOUR CHANCE TO GET AWAY-- HURRY!
EH...?!
OH... R-RIGHT!
MASTER KOGA--
ZZG
WE'RE LEAVING!
RRRRAAAA
DM DM DM DM
HUH?!
HEY, WAIT, YOU FLEA-BITTEN--!

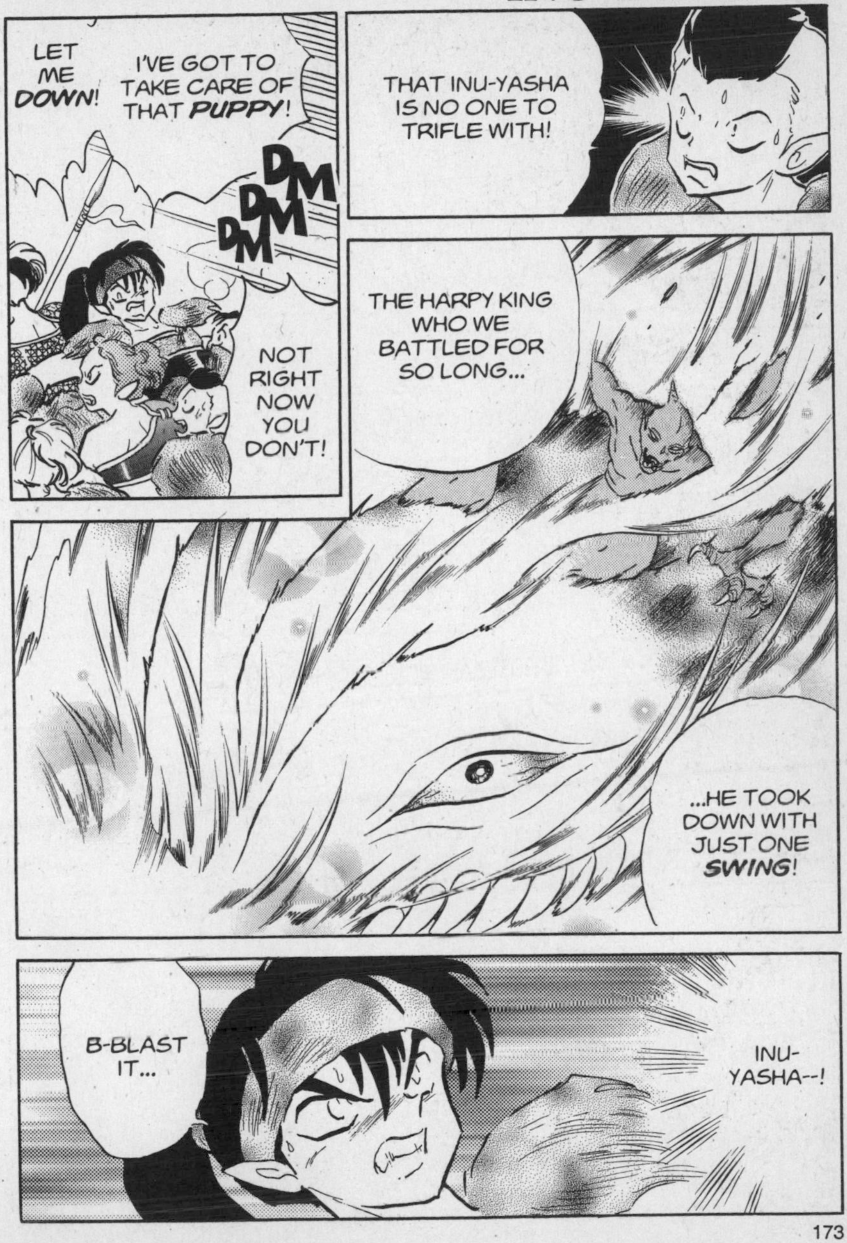
LET ME DOWN!
I'VE GOT TO TAKE CARE OF THAT PUPPY!
DM DM DM
NOT RIGHT NOW YOU DON'T!
THAT INU-YASHA IS NO ONE TO TRIFLE WITH!
THE HARPY KING WHO WE BATTLED FOR SO LONG...
...HE TOOK DOWN WITH JUST ONE SWING!
B-BLAST IT...
INU-YASHA--!

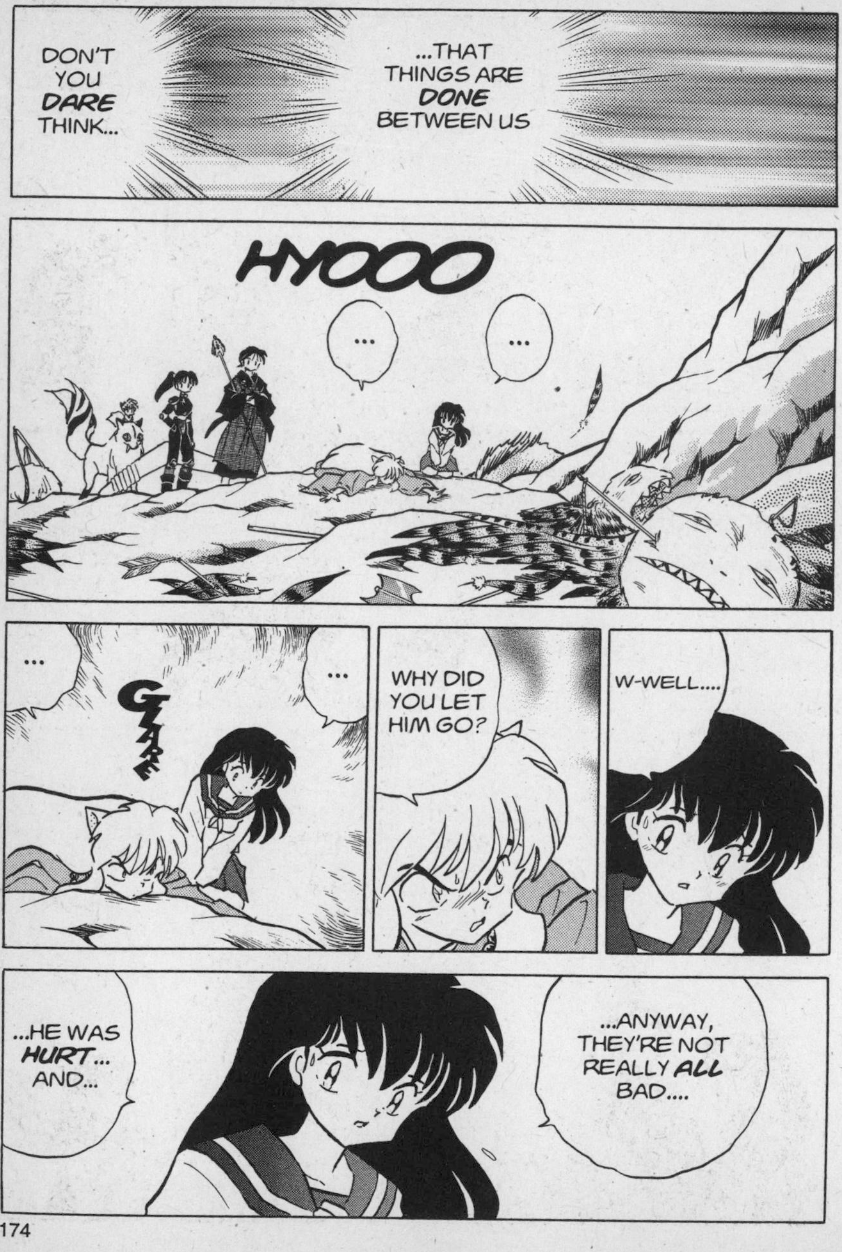
DON'T YOU DARE THINK...
...THAT THINGS ARE DONE BETWEEN US
HYOOO
...
...
...
GLARE
...
WHY DID YOU LET HIM GO?
W-WELL....
...HE WAS HURT... AND...
...ANYWAY, THEY'RE NOT REALLY ALL BAD....

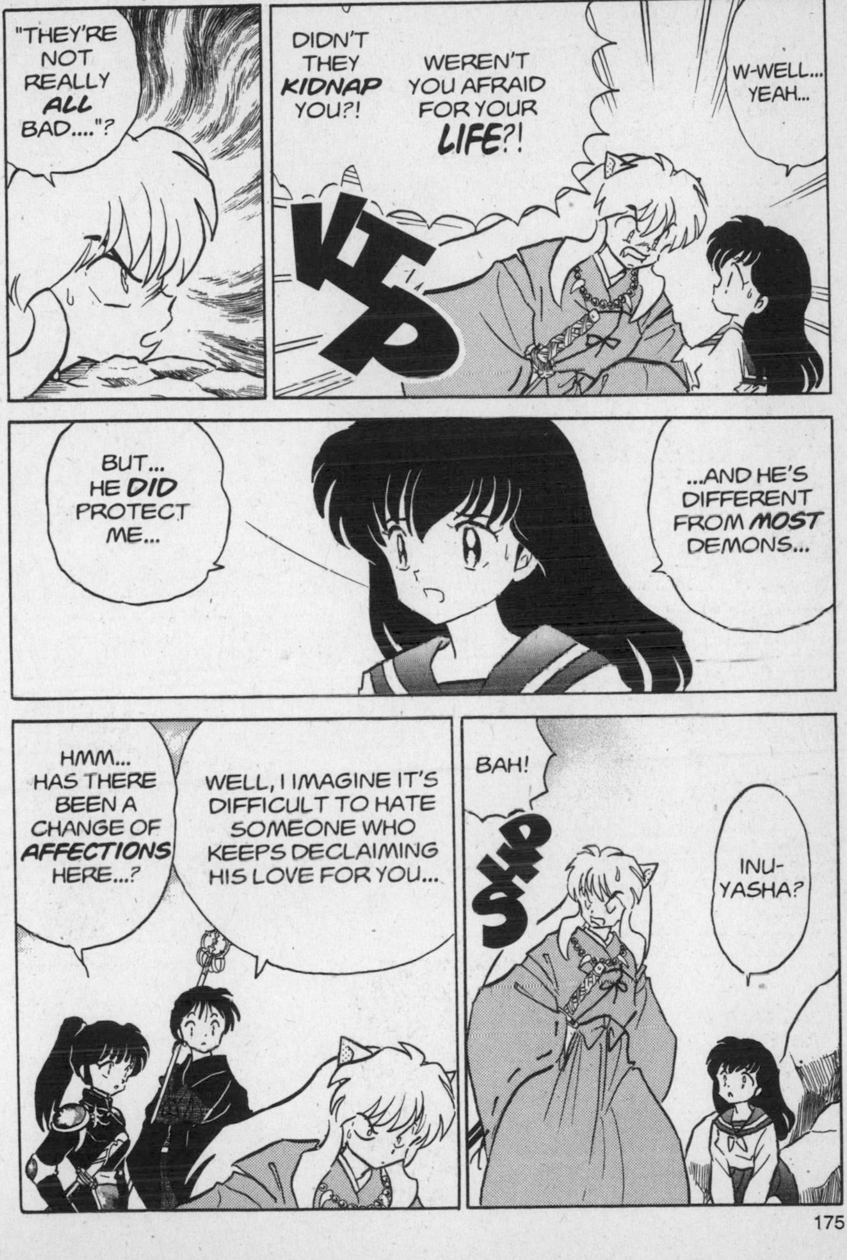
"THEY'RE NOT REALLY ALL BAD...."?
DIDN'T THEY KIDNAP YOU?!
WEREN'T YOU AFRAID FOR YOUR LIFE?!
W-WELL... YEAH...
KTP
BUT... HE DID PROTECT ME...
...AND HE'S DIFFERENT FROM MOST DEMONS...
HMM... HAS THERE BEEN A CHANGE OF AFFECTIONS HERE...?
WELL, I IMAGINE IT'S DIFFICULT TO HATE SOMEONE WHO KEEPS DECLAIMING HIS LOVE FOR YOU...
BAH!
SHP
INU-YASHA?

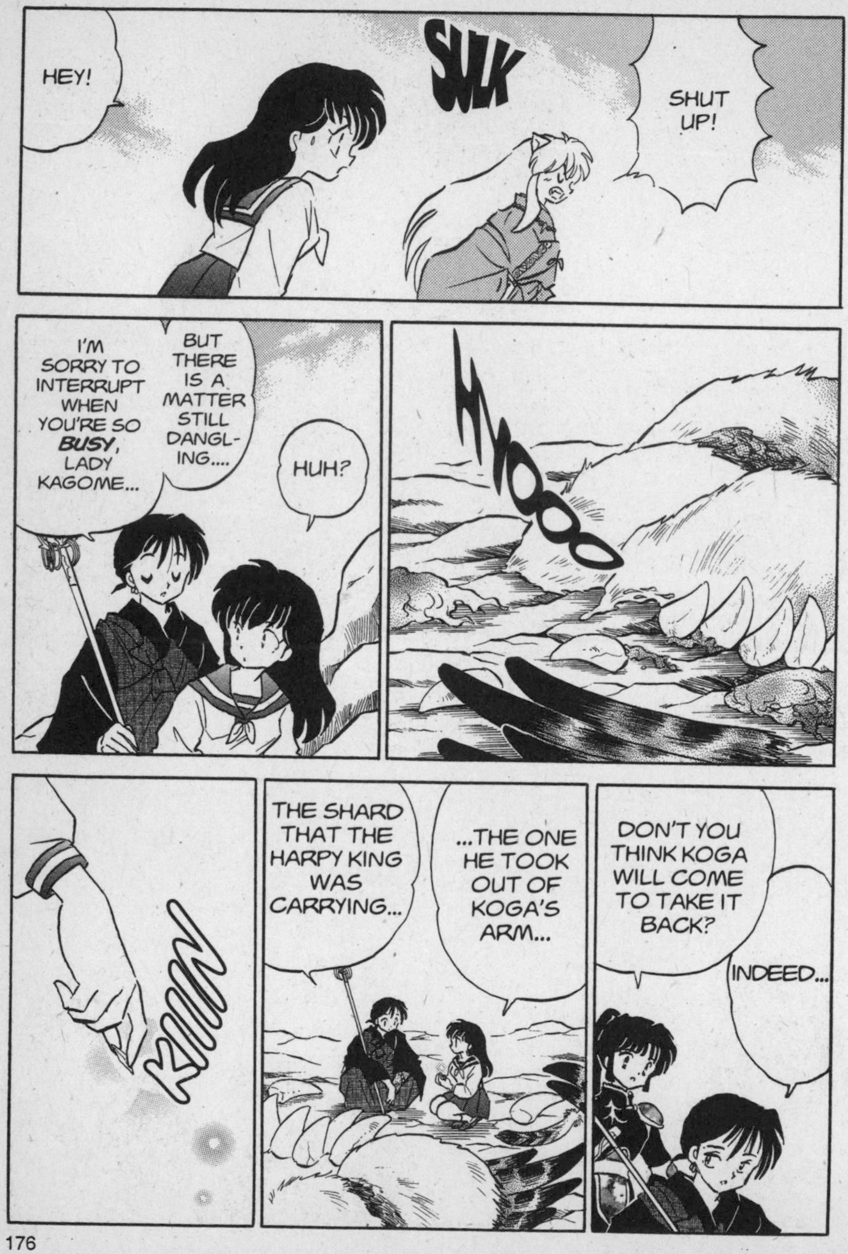
HEY!
SULK
SHUT UP!
I'M SORRY TO INTERRUPT WHEN YOU'RE SO **BUSY**, LADY KAGOME...
BUT THERE IS A MATTER STILL DANGL-ING....
HUH?
THE SHARD THAT THE HARPY KING WAS CARRYING...
...THE ONE HE TOOK OUT OF KOGA'S ARM...
DON'T YOU THINK KOGA WILL COME TO TAKE IT BACK?
INDEED...

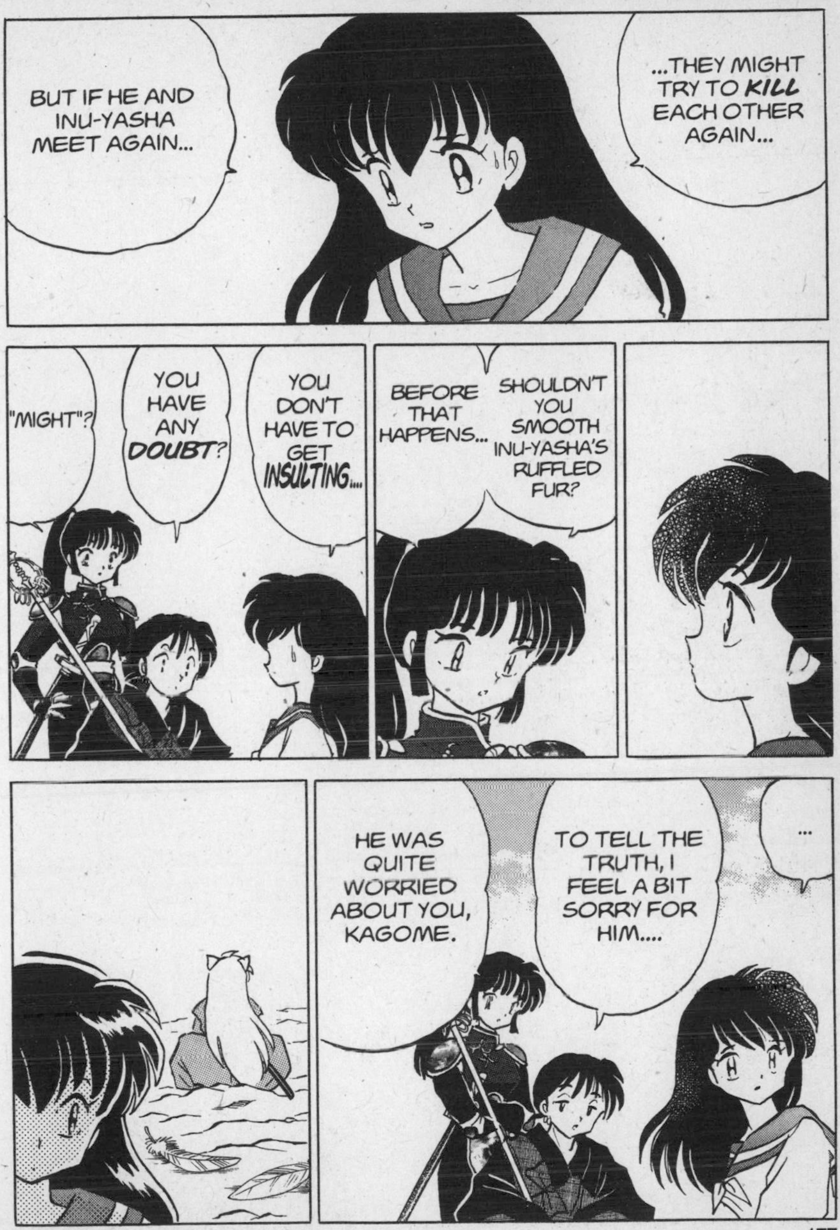
BUT IF HE AND INU-YASHA MEET AGAIN...
...THEY MIGHT TRY TO KILL EACH OTHER AGAIN...
"MIGHT"?
YOU HAVE ANY DOUBT?
YOU DON'T HAVE TO GET INSULTING....
BEFORE THAT HAPPENS...
SHOULDN'T YOU SMOOTH INU-YASHA'S RUFFLED FUR?
HE WAS QUITE WORRIED ABOUT YOU, KAGOME.
TO TELL THE TRUTH, I FEEL A BIT SORRY FOR HIM....
...

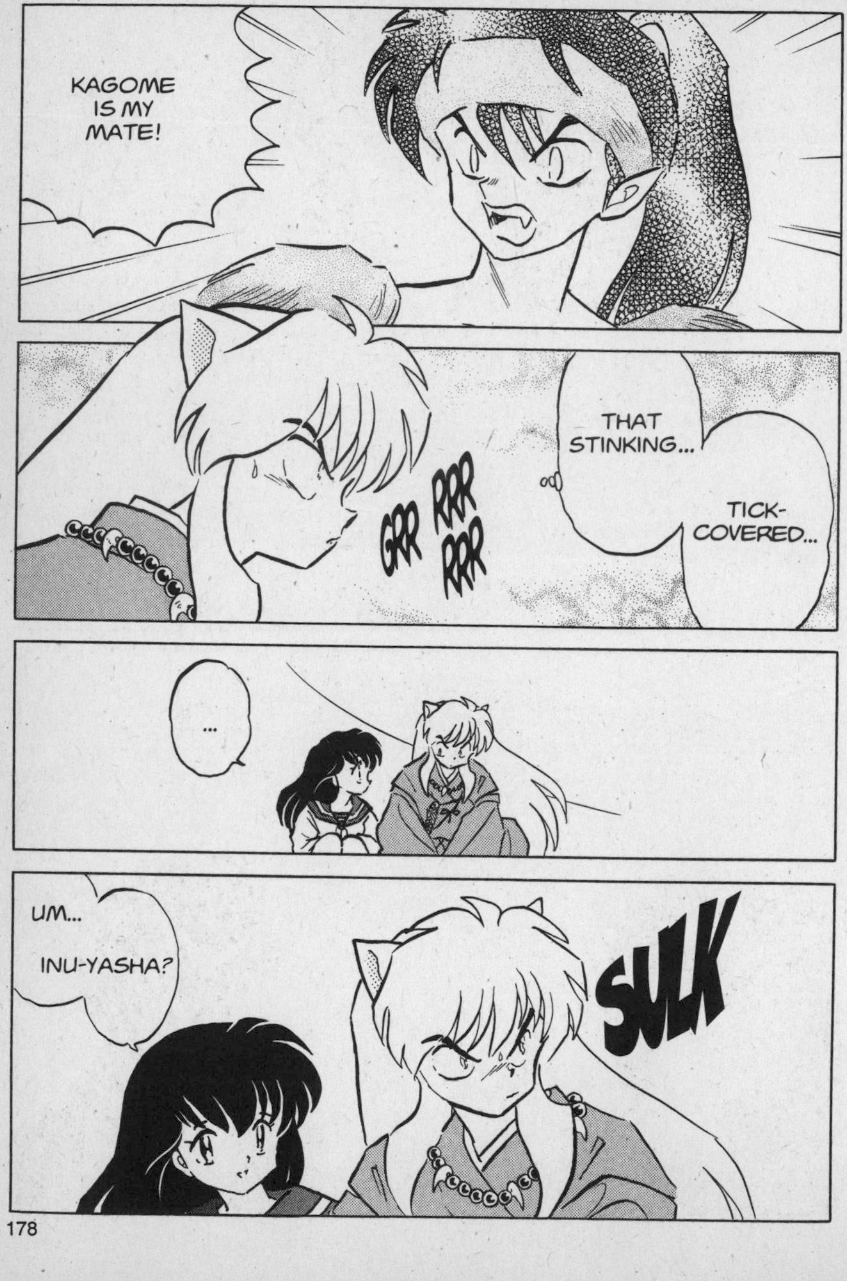
KAGOME IS MY MATE!
THAT STINKING...
TICK-COVERED...
GRR RRR RRR
...
UM...
INU-YASHA?
SULK

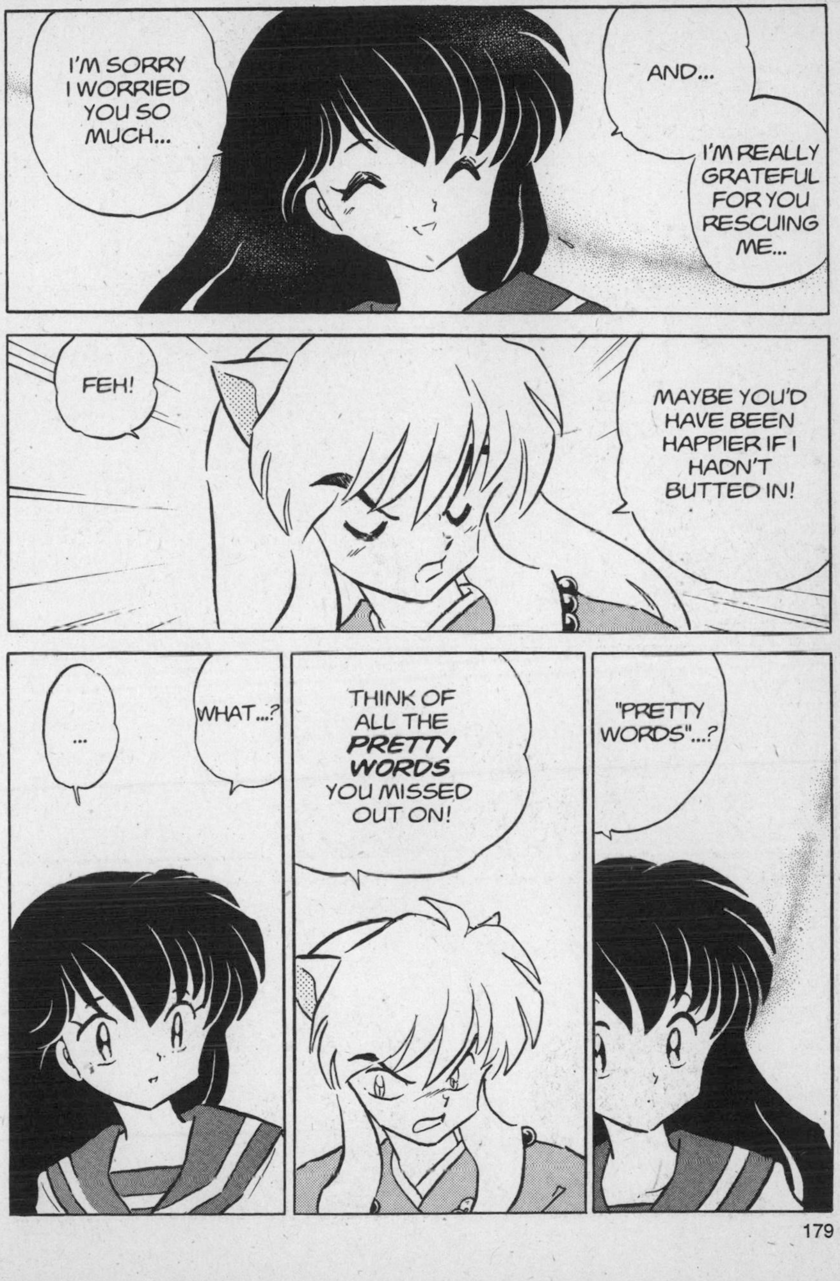
I'M SORRY I WORRIED YOU SO MUCH...
AND...
I'M REALLY GRATEFUL FOR YOU RESCUING ME...
FEH!
MAYBE YOU'D HAVE BEEN HAPPIER IF I HADN'T BUTTED IN!
...
WHAT...?
THINK OF ALL THE PRETTY WORDS YOU MISSED OUT ON!
"PRETTY WORDS"...?

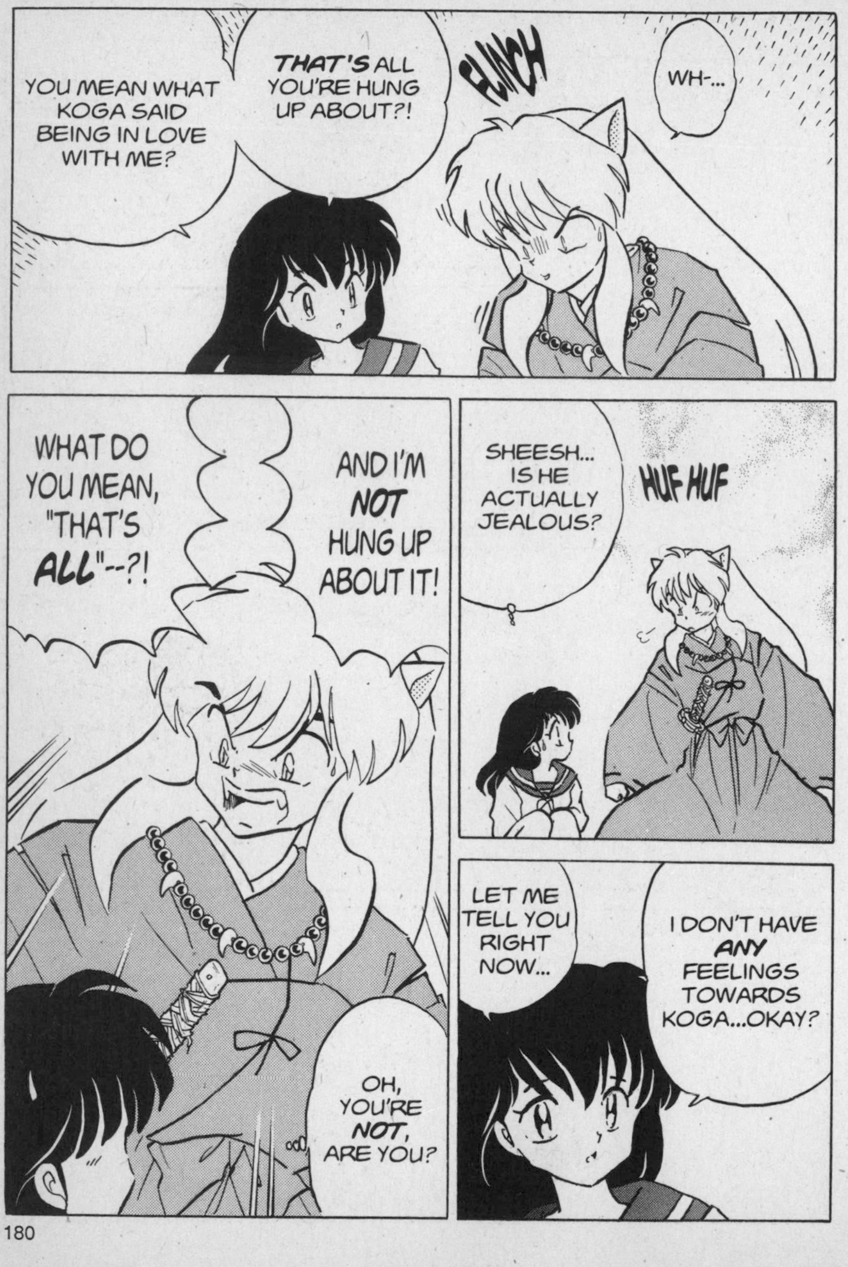
YOU MEAN WHAT KOGA SAID BEING IN LOVE WITH ME?
THAT'S ALL YOU'RE HUNG UP ABOUT?!
FLINCH
WH-...
WHAT DO YOU MEAN, "THAT'S ALL"--?!
AND I'M NOT HUNG UP ABOUT IT!
OH, YOU'RE NOT, ARE YOU?
SHEESH... IS HE ACTUALLY JEALOUS?
HUF HUF
LET ME TELL YOU RIGHT NOW...
I DON'T HAVE ANY FEELINGS TOWARDS KOGA...OKAY?

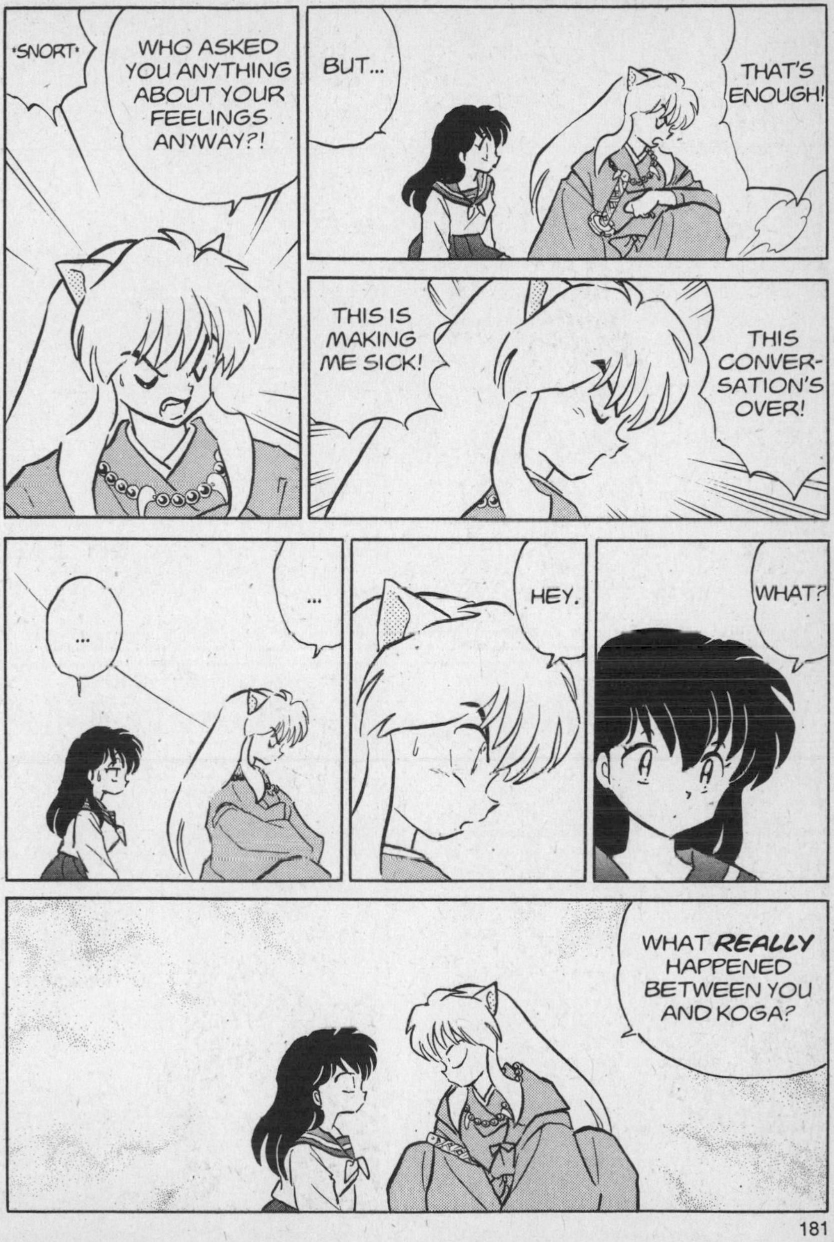
SNORT
WHO ASKED YOU ANYTHING ABOUT YOUR FEELINGS ANYWAY?!
BUT...
THAT'S ENOUGH!
THIS IS MAKING ME SICK!
THIS CONVER-SATION'S OVER!
...
...
HEY.
WHAT?
WHAT *REALLY* HAPPENED BETWEEN YOU AND KOGA?

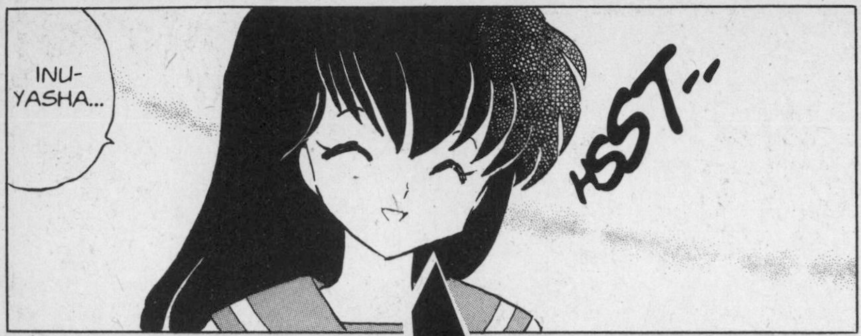
INU-
YASHA...
HSST--

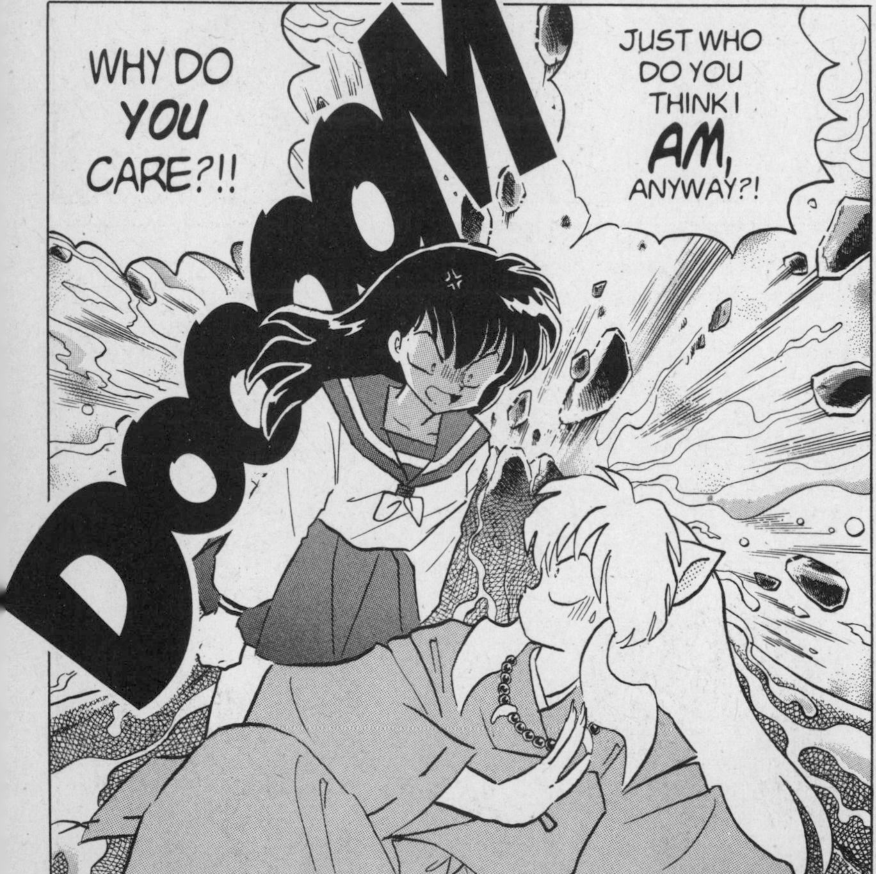
WHY DO YOU CARE?!!
DOOOOM
JUST WHO DO YOU THINK I AM, ANYWAY?!

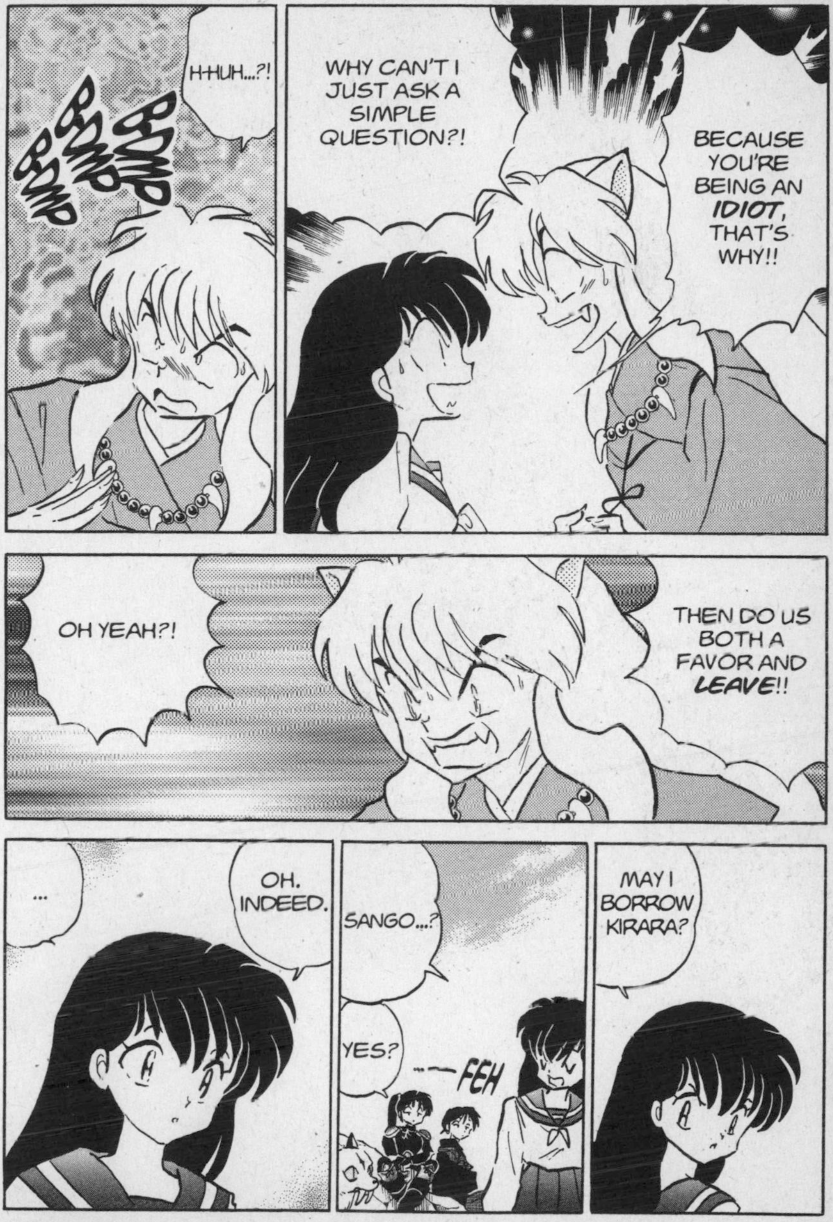
H-HUH...?!
BADMP BADMP BADMP BADMP
WHY CAN'T I JUST ASK A SIMPLE QUESTION?!
BECAUSE YOU'RE BEING AN IDIOT, THAT'S WHY!!
OH YEAH?!
THEN DO US BOTH A FAVOR AND LEAVE!!
...
OH. INDEED.
SANGO...?
YES?
--FEH
MAY I BORROW KIRARA?

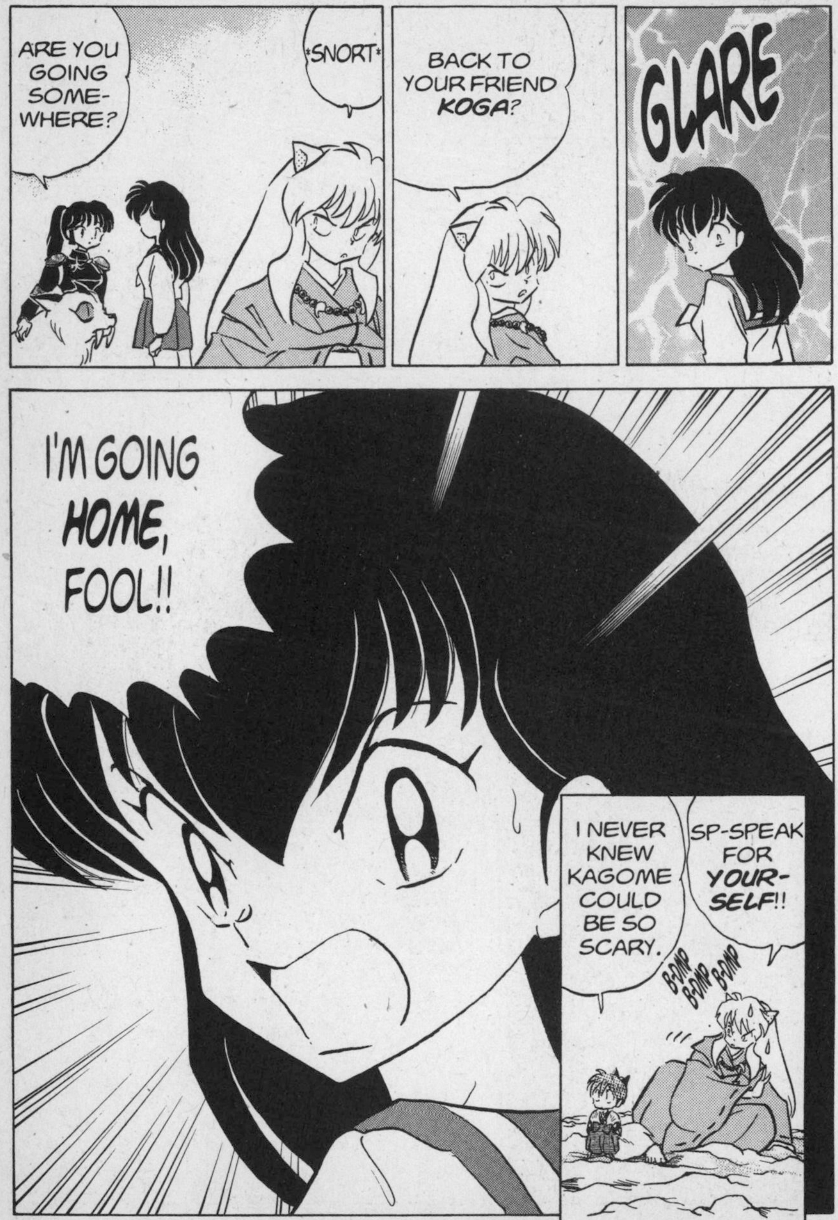

ARE YOU GOING SOME-WHERE?
SNORT
BACK TO YOUR FRIEND **KOGA**?
GLARE
I'M GOING **HOME**, FOOL!!
I NEVER KNEW KAGOME COULD BE SO SCARY.
SP-SPEAK FOR ***YOUR-SELF***!!
B-DMP B-DMP B-DMP

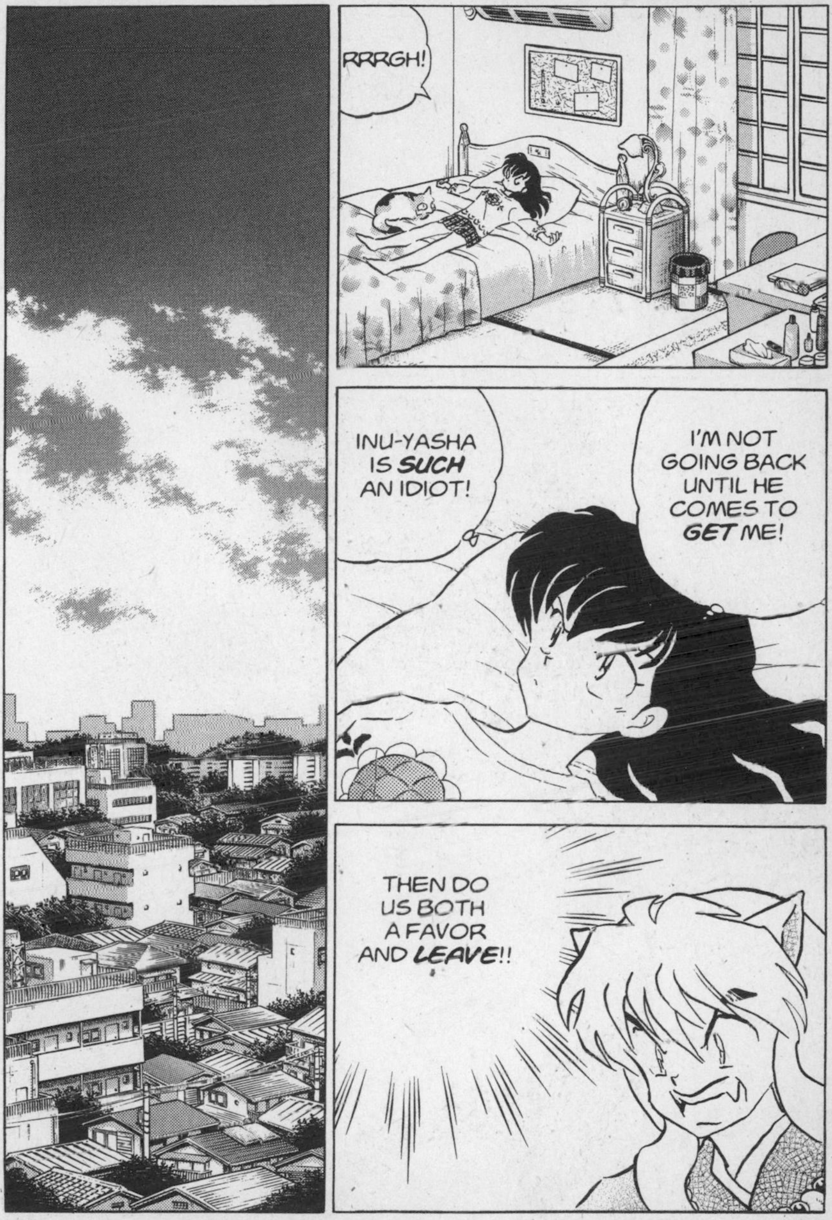
RRRGH!
INU-YASHA IS SUCH AN IDIOT!
I'M NOT GOING BACK UNTIL HE COMES TO GET ME!
THEN DO US BOTH A FAVOR AND LEAVE!!

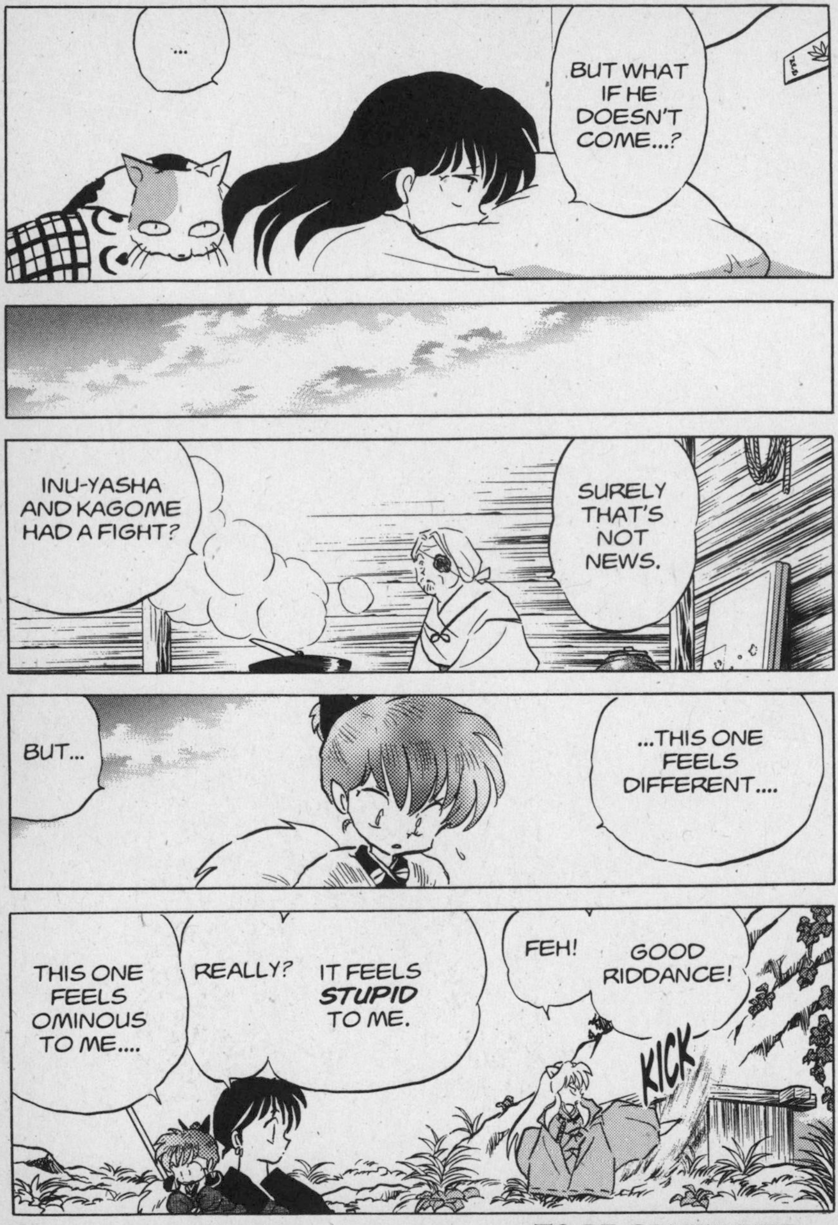
...
BUT WHAT IF HE DOESN'T COME...?
INU-YASHA AND KAGOME HAD A FIGHT?
SURELY THAT'S NOT NEWS.
BUT...
...THIS ONE FEELS DIFFERENT....
THIS ONE FEELS OMINOUS TO ME....
REALLY?
IT FEELS *STUPID* TO ME.
FEH!
GOOD RIDDANCE!
KICK

TO BE CONTINUED...

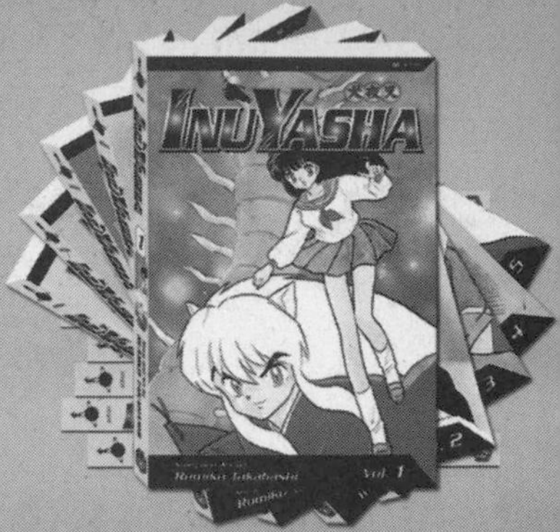

InuYasha
Vol. 1

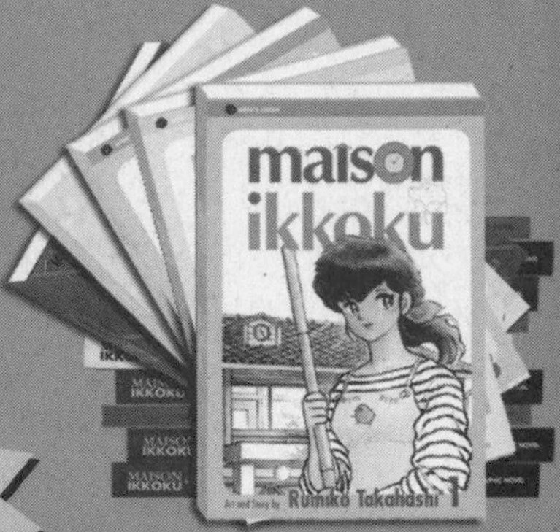

maison ikkoku
Rumiko Takahashi 1

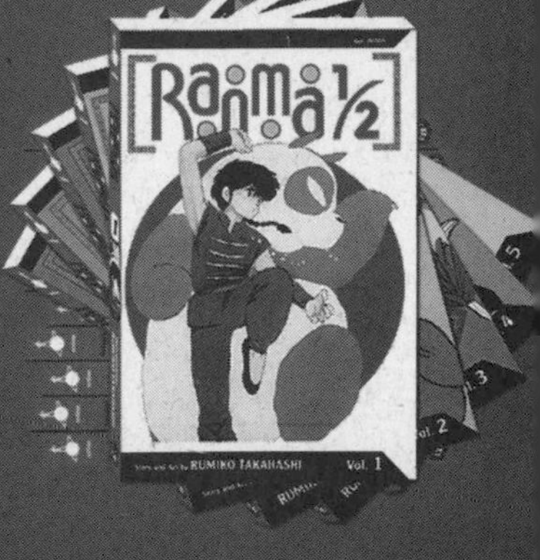

Ranma 1/2
RUMIKO TAKAHASHI
Vol. 1

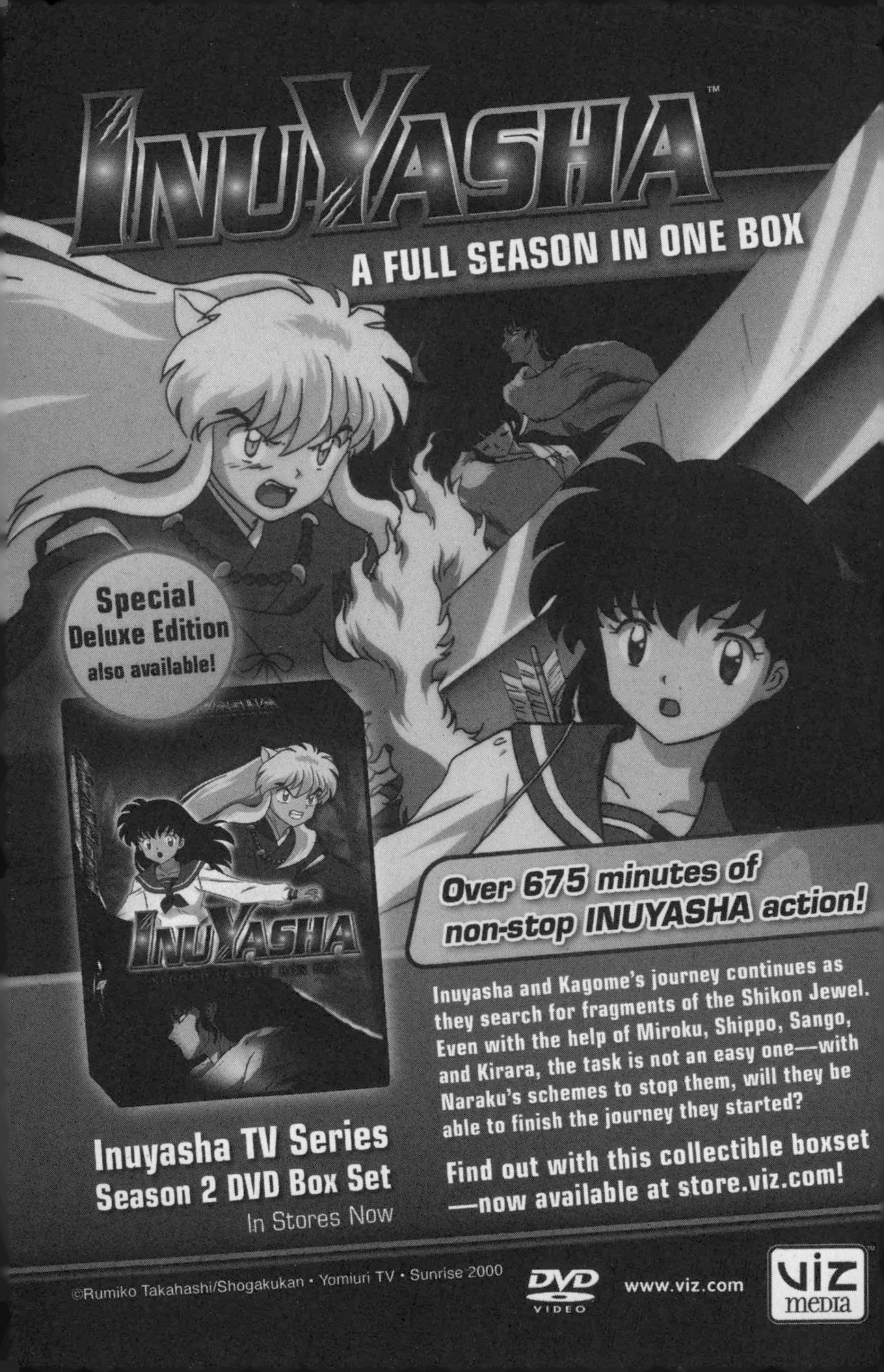
INUYASHA™
A FULL SEASON IN ONE BOX
Special Deluxe Edition also available!
Over 675 minutes of non-stop INUYASHA action!
Inuyasha and Kagome's journey continues as
they search for fragments of the Shikon Jewel.
Even with the help of Miroku, Shippo, Sango,
and Kirara, the task is not an easy one—with
Naraku's schemes to stop them, will they be
able to finish the journey they started?
Find out with this collectible boxset
—now available at store.viz.com!
Inuyasha TV Series
Season 2 DVD Box Set
In Stores Now
©Rumiko Takahashi/Shogakukan • Yomiuri TV • Sunrise 2000
DVD VIDEO
www.viz.com
VIZ MEDIA

LOVE MANGA? LET US KNOW!

☐ Please do NOT send me information about VIZ Media products, news and events, special offers, or other information.

☐ Please do NOT send me information from VIZ Media's trusted business partners.

Name: _____

Address: _____

City: _____ **State:** _____ **Zip:** _____

E-mail: _____

☐ Male ☐ Female **Date of Birth** (mm/dd/yyyy): ___ / ___ / ___ (Under 13? Parental consent required)

What race/ethnicity do you consider yourself? (check all that apply)

☐ White/Caucasian ☐ Black/African American ☐ Hispanic/Latino

☐ Asian/Pacific Islander ☐ Native American/Alaskan Native ☐ Other: _____

What VIZ Media title(s) did you purchase? (indicate title(s) purchased) _____

_____

What other VIZ Media titles do you own? _____

_____

Reason for purchase: (check all that apply)

☐ Special offer ☐ Favorite title / author / artist / genre

☐ Gift ☐ Recommendation ☐ Collection

☐ Read excerpt in VIZ Media manga sampler ☐ Other _____

Where did you make your purchase? (please check one)

☐ Comic store ☐ Bookstore ☐ Grocery Store

☐ Convention ☐ Newsstand ☐ Video Game Store

☐ Online (site:_____) ☐ Other _____

How many manga titles have you purchased in the last year? How many were VIZ Media titles?
(please check one from each column)

MANGA

- ☐ None
- ☐ 1 – 4
- ☐ 5 – 10
- ☐ 11+

VIZ Media

- ☐ None
- ☐ 1 – 4
- ☐ 5 – 10
- ☐ 11+

How much influence do special promotions and gifts-with-purchase have on the titles you buy?
(please circle, with 5 being great influence and 1 being none)

1   2   3   4   5

Do you purchase every volume of your favorite series?

☐ Yes! Gotta have 'em as my own   ☐ No. Please explain: _____

What kind of manga storylines do you most enjoy? (check all that apply)

- ☐ Action / Adventure
- ☐ Comedy
- ☐ Fighting
- ☐ Artistic / Alternative

- ☐ Science Fiction
- ☐ Romance (shojo)
- ☐ Sports
- ☐ Other _____

- ☐ Horror
- ☐ Fantasy (shojo)
- ☐ Historical

If you watch the anime or play a video or TCG game from a series, how likely are you to buy the manga? (please circle, with 5 being very likely and 1 being unlikely)

1   2   3   4   5

If unlikely, please explain: _____

Who are your favorite authors / artists? _____

_____

What titles would like you translated and sold in English? _____

_____

THANK YOU! Please send the completed form to:

NJW Research
42 Catharine Street
Poughkeepsie, NY 12601

Your privacy is very important to us. All information provided will be used for internal purposes only and will not be sold or otherwise divulged.